WOMEN'S STUDIES QUARTERLY
VOLUME 36   NUMBERS 3 & 4   FALL/WINTER 2008

An Educational Project of The Feminist Press at The City University of New York
and the Center for the Study of Women and Society at The Graduate Center,
City University of New York

EXECUTIVE DIRECTOR
Gloria Jacobs, *The Feminist Press at The City University of New York*

EDITORS
Victoria Pitts-Taylor, *Queens College and The Graduate Center, City University of New York*
Talia Schaffer, *Queens College and The Graduate Center, City University of New York*

GUEST EDITORS
Paisley Currah, *Brooklyn College, City University of New York*
Lisa Jean Moore, *Purchase College, State University of New York*
Susan Stryker, *Indiana University*

MANAGING EDITORS
Michael Clark
Anjoli Roy

ADMINISTRATIVE ASSOCIATES
Jess Bier
Stacie McCormick
Zoe Meleo-Erwin

DESIGN & PRODUCTION
Teresa Bonner
Lisa Force

MARKETING ASSISTANT
Amita Manghnani

EDITORS EMERITAE
Diane Hope, *Rochester Institute of Technology 2000–2005*
Janet Zandy, *Rochester Institute of Technology 1995–2000*
Nancy Porter 1982–1992
Florence Howe 1972–1982; 1993–1994

EDITORIAL BOARD

Meena Alexander, *The Graduate Center, City University of New York*
Emily Apter, *New York University*
Rachel M. Brownstein, *Brooklyn College, City University of New York*
Shirley Carrie, *Queens College, City University of New York*
Sarah Chinn, *Hunter College, City University of New York*
Patricia Clough, *The Graduate Center, City University of New York*
Alyson Cole, *Queens College, City University of New York*
Nicole Cooley, *Queens College, City University of New York*
Paisley Currah, *Brooklyn College, City University of New York*
Robin Rogers-Dillon, *Queens College, City University of New York*
Hester Eisenstein, *The Graduate Center, City University of New York*
Shelly Eversley, *Baruch College, City University of New York*
Sujatha Fernandes, *Queens College, City University of New York*
Sharon Marcus, *Columbia University*
Licia Fiol-Matta, *Lehman College, City University of New York*
Elaine Freedgood, *New York University*
Edvige Giunta, *New Jersey City University*
Terri Gordon, *The New School*
Dagmar Herzog, *The Graduate Center, City University of New York*
Anne Humpherys, *The Graduate Center, City University of New York*
Grace Mitchell, *College of Staten Island, City University of New York*
Karmen MacKendrick, *Le Moyne College*
Lisa Jean Moore, *Purchase College, State University of New York*
Cheryl Mwaria, *Hofstra University*
Premilla Nadasen, *Queens College, City University of New York*
Lorie Novak, *New York University*
Jackie Orr, *Syracuse University*
Kathleen Ossip, *The New School, New York*
Rupal Oza, *Hunter College, City University of New York*
Joe Rollins, *Queens College, City University of New York*
Caroline Rupprecht, *Queens College, City University of New York*
Haydee Salmun, *Hunter College, City University of New York*
Mira Schor, *Parsons The New School for Design*
Ida Susser, *The Graduate Center, City University of New York*
Aoibheann Sweeney, *The Graduate Center, City University of New York*
Karen Winkle, *Barnard College*

ADVISORY BOARD

Paola Bacchetta, *University of California, Berkeley*
Jacqueline Bhabha, *Harvard University*
Helene Foley, *Barnard College*
Carol Gilligan, *New York University*
Linda Gordon, *New York University*
Mary Gordon, *Barnard College*
Inderpal Grewal, *University of California, Irvine*
Susan Gubar, *Indiana University*
Danielle Haase-Dubosc, *Columbia University, Paris*
Dolores Hayden, *Yale University*
Dorothy O. Helly, *Hunter College, City University of New York*
Marianne Hirsch, *Columbia University*
Florence Howe, *The Feminist Press at The City University of New York*
Janet Jakobsen, *Barnard College*
Alice A. Jardine, *Harvard University*
E. Ann Kaplan, *State University of New York, Stony Brook*
Anahid Kassabian, *University of Liverpool*
Cindi Katz, *The Graduate Center, City University of New York*
Alice Kessler-Harris, *Columbia University*
Nancy K. Miller, *The Graduate Center, City University of New York*
Afsaneh Najmabadi, *Harvard University*
Linda Nochlin, *Institute of Fine Arts, New York University*
Rhacel Parrenas, *University of California, Davis*
Geraldine Pratt, *University of British Columbia*
Judith Resnik, *Yale University*
Alix Kates Shulman, *New York City*
Sidonie Smith, *University of Michigan*
Valerie Smith, *Princeton University*
Judith Stacey, *New York University*
Domna C. Stanton, *The Graduate Center, City University of New York*
Catharine R. Stimpson, *New York University*
Julia Watson, *Ohio State University*
Elizabeth Weed, *Brown University*

WSQ: Women's Studies Quarterly, a peer-reviewed, theme-based journal, is published in the summer and winter by The Feminist Press at The City University of New York, The Graduate Center, 365 Fifth Avenue, Suite 5406, New York, NY 10016; 212-817-7926.

WEB SITE
http://www.feministpress.org/wsq

EDITORIAL CORRESPONDENCE
WSQ: Women's Studies Quarterly, The Feminist Press at The City University of New York, The Graduate Center, 365 Fifth Avenue, Suite 5406, New York, NY 10016; wsqeditorial@gmail.com.

PRINT SUBSCRIPTIONS
Subscribers in the United States: Individuals—$40.00 for 1 year; $90.00 for 3 years. Students—$28.00 for 1 year. (Student subscribers must provide a photocopy of current student identification.) Institution—$60.00 for 1 year; $144.00 for 3 years. Subscribers outside the United States: Add $15 per year for surface delivery; add $45 per year for airmail delivery. To subscribe or change an address, contact Customer Service, WSQ: Women's Studies Quarterly, The Feminist Press at The City University of New York, The Graduate Center, 365 Fifth Avenue, Suite 5406, New York, NY 10016; 212-817-7920; amanghnani@gc.cuny.edu.

FORTHCOMING ISSUES
Technologies, Karen Throsby, *University of Warwick,* and Sarah Hodges, *University of Warwick*
Mother, Nicole Cooley, *Queens College, City University of New York,* and Pamela Stone, *Hunter College, City University of New York*

RIGHTS & PERMISSIONS
Fred Courtright, The Permissions Company, 570-839-7477; permdude@eclipse.net.

SUBMISSION INFORMATION
For the most up-to-date guidelines, calls for papers, and information concerning forthcoming issues, write to *WSQ: Women's Studies Quarterly* at The Feminist Press at The City University of New York, wsqeditorial@gmail.com or visit our web site, www.feministpress.org/wsq.

ADVERTISING
For information on display-ad sizes, rates, exchanges, and schedules, please write to *WSQ Marketing,* The Feminist Press at The City University of New York, The Graduate Center, 365 Fifth Avenue, Suite 5406, New York, NY 10016; 212-817-7920; amanghnani@gc.cuny.edu.

ELECTRONIC ACCESS AND SUBSCRIPTIONS
Access to electronic databases containing backlist issues of WSQ may be purchased through JSTOR at www.jstor.org. Access to electronic databases containing current issues of WSQ may be purchased through Project MUSE at muse.jhu.edu, muse@muse.jhu.edu; and ProQuest at www.il.proquest.com, info@il.proquest.com. Individual electronic subscriptions for WSQ may also be purchased through Project MUSE.

Printed in the United States of America by Sheridan Press.

Compilation copyright © 2008 by The Feminist Press at The City University of New York. Unless otherwise noted, copyright in the individual essays is held in the name of their authors.

ISSN: 0732-1562   ISBN: 978-1-55861-590-8 $22.00

CONTENTS

9   Editors' Note
    VICTORIA PITTS-TAYLOR AND TALIA SCHAFFER

11 Introduction: Trans-, Trans, or Transgender?
    SUSAN STRYKER, PAISLEY CURRAH, AND LISA JEAN MOORE

PART I—ARTICLES, POETY, AND CREATIVE PROSE

23 Transing and Transpassing Across Sex-Gender Walls in Iran
    AFSANEH NAJMABADI

43 Branded★ Living
    KATE SCHAPIRA

44 Cutting It Off: Bodily Integrity, Identity Disorders, and the Sovereign Stakes of Corporeal Desire in U.S. Law
    ELIZABETH LOEB

64 More Lessons from a Starfish: Prefixial Flesh and Transspeciated Selves
    EVA HAYWARD

86 Riddle Song
    KATE SCHAPIRA

87 Humans, Horses, and Hormones: (Trans) Gendering Cross-Species Relationships
    NATALIE CORINNE HANSEN

106 Which Half Is Mommy?: Tetragametic Chimerism and Trans-Subjectivity
    AARON T. NORTON AND OZZIE ZEHNER

126 How Metaphor Works
    JULIE CARR

127	Transgender Without Organs? Mobilizing a Geo-affective Theory of Gender Modification LUCAS CASSIDY CRAWFORD
144	An FU to the Men in Blue and Midnight Beehive Bike Battle JAMES SHULTIS
146	Perverse Citizenship: Divas, Marginality, and Participation in "Loca-lization" MARCIA OCHOA
170	Electric Brilliancy: Cross-Dressing Law and Freak Show Displays in Nineteenth-Century San Francisco CLARE SEARS
188	Zamboni After Peggy Munson's *Origami Striptease* NOELLE KOCOT
190	Trans/Bolero/Drag/Migration: Music, Cultural Translation, and Diasporic Puerto Rican Theatricalities LAWRENCE LA FOUNTAIN-STOKES
210	Reconstructing the Transgendered Self as a Muslim, Nationalist, Upper-Class Woman: The Case of Bulent Ersoy RUSTEM ERTUG ALTINAY
230	Not Food or Love PATRICIA CARLIN
233	Transgressive and Transformative Gendered Sexual Practices and White Privileges: The Case of the Dyke/Trans BDSM Communities ROBIN BAUER
254	Translating Women and Gender: The Experience of Translating *The Encyclopedia of Women and Islamic Cultures* into Arabic HALA KAMAL

PART II—IMAGES

269   Trans Genital Blueprints
         JOHN NEFF

PART III—PROSE

271   Transparent
         SUSAN DAVID BERNSTEIN

PART IV—A FEMINIST CLASSIC REVISITED

279   Compulsory Gender and Transgender Existence: Adrienne Rich's Queer Possibility
         C. L. COLE AND SHANNON L. C. CATE

PART V—PEDAGOGY

288   TransPedagogies: A Roundtable Dialogue
         VIC MUÑOZ AND EDNIE KAEH GARRISON (Moderators), with Anne Enke, Darcy A. Freedman, Ednie Kaeh Garrison, Jeni Hart, Diana L. Jones, Ambrose Kirby, Jamie Lester, Vic Muñoz, Mia Nakamura, Clark A. Pomerleau, and Sarah E. VanHooser

PART VI—BOOK REVIEWS

309   Donna J. Haraway's *When Species Meet*
         MANUELA ROSSINI

312   Sally Hines's *Transforming Gender: Transgender Practices of Identity, Intimacy, and Care*
         JULIA HORNCASTLE

315   Susannah B. Mintz's *Unruly Bodies: Life Writing by Women with Disabilities*
         ANANYA MUKHERJEA

318   Susan Stryker and Stephen Whittle's *The Transgender Studies Reader*
      BRICE SMITH

321   Lisa Jean Moore's *Sperm Counts: Overcome by Man's Most Precious Fluid*
      ELROI J. WINDSOR

324   David Valentine's *Imagining Transgender: An Ethnography of Category*
      NOMVUYO NOLUTSHUNGU

325   Heather Love's *Feeling Backward: Loss and the Politics of Queer History*
      WAN-CHUAN KAO

PART VII—ALERTS AND PROVOCATIONS

330   Expecting Bodies: The Pregnant Man and Transgender Exclusion from the Employment Non-Discrimination Act
      PAISLEY CURRAH

ERRATA

The March 2007 Columbia University conference, "Objects and Memory: Engendering Private and Public Archives," from which the section on "Object Lessons" in the *WSQ: Witness* issue (36: 1 & 2 [Spring/Summer 2008]) was drawn, was organized by the Columbia Cultural Memory Colloquium: Sarah Cole, Marianne Hirsch, Jennifer James, Joanna Scutts, Kate Stanley, and Sonali Thakkar.

EDITORS' NOTE

Trans-: Transgender, transnational, transspeciation, translation, transformation. Trans- as connection: shared space and time, transatlantic, transhistorical. Trans- as violation: transgression, transsection. Trans- as both assemblage and dissasemblage, as folded into structures of power as well as a movement of *becoming*. Most significantly for us, perhaps, trans- as a way of seeing and thinking.

This issue reaches across disciplinary borders, across spatial and temporal planes, moving as well among public and private, academic and personal, mind and body, and troubling those distinctions. In Paisley Currah, Lisa Jean Moore, and Susan Stryker's moving words, it is "the capillary space of connection and circulation between the macro- and micro-political." It also stretches from writer to reader, a trans-action necessarily invested with hope for language's transformative promise.

Trans-, a prefix with its matching suffix forever suspended, is where we locate ourselves, in the act of reaching, questioning any easy placement of the term. Likewise, Hala Kamals's fascinating account of translating "gender" in Arabic reveals there is no proper match for that word with its heavily coded constellation of meanings. There is also no singularly normative body. Elizabeth Loeb's wonderful study of the oddly arbitrary somatic models underlying gender law, and Aaron Norton and Ozzie Zehner's discussion of the bodies that violate medicalized definitions of motherhood, reveal that the medico-juridical norm is as arbitrarily constructed, internally fissured, and profoundly contradictory, as any of the paradigms that challenge it. There is no ideal space, nor one that is easily bounded. From the urban-sprawl wastelands of James Shultis's prose-poems, to the uncomfortably small towns of Lucas Crawford's memories, trans-bodies traverse regions and nations: Turkey, Venezuela, Iran, Germany, New York City, generating affiliations that complicate nation and citizenship as well as other categories of identification.

We called this reading experience a trans-action, to emphasize the extent to which this issue is a call to action, yet the model of a transaction perhaps suggests too much finality, as if you read the articles and then you're done. Perhaps the trans- we need is "transference," the name for the mistake that makes psychoanalysis possible, but in addition the name for a relationship that is also a gift, as in transferring something among us: the readers, writers, and editors.

This issue, *Trans-*, also represents a transition for this journal. This is our first issue as general editors. Our new team also includes an expanded editorial board, including some exciting younger scholars, our wonderful new administrative associates, Jess Bier, Stacie McCormick, and Zoe Meleo-Erwin, and our new fiction/nonfiction editor, Susan Daitch, who joins our poetry editor, Kathy Ossip. At the Feminist Press, we have relied upon the expertise of Anjoli Roy, our managing editor, and we thank her as we also, sadly, say goodbye, as this is her last issue. We are delighted to be entrusted with this dynamic, exciting, experimental journal, and we look forward to developing upon the work the previous editors, Nancy K. Miller and Cindi Katz, accomplished with such flair. Look for more issues about interdisciplinary, gender and culture, an expanded web presence, a presence in databases like JSTOR and Project MUSE, and a new set of issues on topics like technologies and mothering.

We are proud to inaugurate our editorship with this issue, which we believe represents what Eva Hayward, in her article in this volume "More Lessons from a Starfish: Prefixial Flesh and Transspeciated Selves," calls a "critical enmeshment." For Hayward, critical enmeshment is "always a verb just as it is also situated and historical." As in her work, in this issue critical enmeshment "enfolds" language, bodies, art, music, and thought as "lively . . . relatings of others to each other." The enfoldings throughout this volume, we hope, also offer "prefixial lessons" worth deep consideration.

>Victoria Pitts-Taylor
>Professor of Sociology
>Queens College and The Graduate Center,
>City University of New York

>Talia Schaffer
>Professor of English
>Queens College and The Graduate Center,
>City University of New York

INTRODUCTION: TRANS-, TRANS, OR TRANSGENDER?

SUSAN STRYKER, PAISLEY CURRAH, AND LISA JEAN MOORE

The title that appears on the cover of this journal is *Trans-*, not Trans, and not Transgender. A little hyphen is perhaps too flimsy a thing to carry as much conceptual freight as we intend for it bear, but we think the hyphen matters a great deal, precisely because it marks the difference between the implied nominalism of "trans" and the explicit relationality of "trans-," which remains open-ended and resists premature foreclosure by attachment to any single suffix.

Our call for papers read: "Trans: -gender, -national, -racial, -generational, -genic, -species. The list could (and does) go on. This special issue of *WSQ* invites feminist work that explores categorical crossings, leakages, and slips of all sorts, around and through the concept 'trans-'." While gender certainly—perhaps inevitably—remains a primary analytical category for the work we sought to publish in this feminist scholarly journal, our aim in curating this special issue specifically was not to identify, consolidate, or stabilize a category or class of people, things, or phenomena that could be denominated "trans," as if certain concrete somethings could be characterized as "crossers," while everything else could be characterized by boundedness and fixity. It seemed especially important to insist upon this point when addressing transgender phenomena.

Since the early 1990s, a burgeoning body of scholarly work in the new field of transgender studies has linked insights and analyses drawn from the experience or study of phenomena that disrupt or unsettle the conventional boundaries of gender with the central disciplinary concerns of contemporary humanities and social science research. In seeking to promote cutting-edge feminist work that builds on existing transgender-oriented scholarship to articulate new generational and analytical perspectives, we didn't want to perpetuate a minoritizing or ghettoizing use of "transgender" to delimit and contain the relationship of "trans-" conceptual operations to "-gender" statuses and practices in a way that rendered them the exclusive property of a tiny class of marginalized individuals.

Precisely because we believe some vital and more generally relevant critical/political questions are compacted within the theoretical articulations and lived social realities of "transgender" embodiments, subjectivities, and communities, we felt that the time was ripe for bursting "transgender" wide open, and linking the questions of space and movement that that term implies to other critical crossings of categorical territories.

This issue of *WSQ* centrally address the challenges presented to traditional feminist scholarship by the transgender sociopolitical movement of the past two decades, but it aims to resist applications of "trans" as a gender category that is necessarily distinct from more established categories such as "woman" or "man." Rather than seeing genders as classes or categories that by definition contain only one kind of thing (which raises unavoidable questions about the masked rules and normativities that constitute qualifications for categorical membership), we understand genders as potentially porous and permeable spatial territories (arguable numbering more than two), each capable of supporting rich and rapidly proliferating ecologies of embodied difference.

Our goal is to take feminist scholarship in expansive new directions by articulating the interrelatedness and mutual inextricability of various "trans-" phenomena. Any gender-defined space is not only populated with diverse forms of gendered embodiment, but striated and crosshatched by the boundaries of significant forms of difference other than gender, within all of which gender is necessarily implicated. To suggest a few examples: do transgender phenomena not show us that "woman" can function as social space that can be populated, without loss of definitional coherence, not only by people born with a typical female anatomy and reared as girls who identify as women, but also by people reared as girls who identify as women but who have physical intersex conditions, or by people who were born with a typical male anatomy but who self-identify as women and take all possible steps to live their lives that way, or by people born female who express conventionally masculine social behaviors but who don't think of themselves as or want to be men? Do transgender phenomena not show us that some who unproblematically occupy the space of social manhood have vaginas rather than penises, or that some men can choose to wear dresses without surrendering their social identities as men? Likewise, does not a working-class woman who makes her living through manual labor cross boundaries of middle-class feminine respectability because of the dirt under her nails? Hasn't Hillary

Clinton been called mannish because she is politically powerful? Didn't white men denying black men the vote through Jim Crow legislation in the years before female suffrage assign black men the same citizenship status as that given to white women? In all of these examples, "transgendered" bodies occupy the same gender-spaces as nontransgendered ones, and transgender characteristics can be attributed, as a form of disciplining, to bodies that might not subjectively identify as being transgendered.

A fundamental aspect of our editorial vision for this special issue of *WSQ* is that neither "-gender" nor any of the other suffixes of "trans-" can be understood in isolation—that the lines implied by the very concept of "trans-" are moving targets, simultaneously composed of multiple determinants. "Transing," in short, is a practice that takes place within, as well as across or between, gendered spaces. It is a practice that assembles gender into contingent structures of association with other attributes of bodily being, and that allows for their reassembly. Transing can function as a disciplinary tool when the stigma associated with the lack or loss of gender status threatens social unintelligibility, coercive normalization, or even bodily extermination. It can also function as an escape vector, line of flight, or pathway toward liberation. A fundamental question we would like to pose is: What kinds of intellectual labor can we begin to perform through the critical deployment of "trans-" operations and movements? Those of us schooled in the humanities and social sciences have become familiar, over the past twenty years or so, with queering things; how might we likewise begin to critically trans- our world?

In her recent *Queer Phenomenology*, Sarah Ahmed asks her readers to pay attention to the spatial dimensions of the term "orientation," reminding them that orientation fundamentally pertains to the relationship between bodies and space, and that many terms related to sexuality—straight, bent, deviate, perverse, and so on—describe patterns of bodily movements through, and occupations of, space. In a similar spirit, we invite our readers to recognize that "trans-" likewise names the body's orientation in space and time; we ask them to reorient themselves toward transgender phenomena, and to begin imagining these phenomena according to different spatio-temporal metaphors. It's common, for example, to think of the "trans-" in "transgender" as moving horizontally between two established gendered spaces, "man" and "woman," or as a spectrum, or archipeligo, that occupies the space between the two. (We ourselves began this introduction with precisely these spatial metaphors.) But what if we think instead of "trans-" along a vertical axis, one that moves between the concrete biomateriality of individual living bodies and the biopolitical realm of aggregate populations that serve as resource for sovereign power? What if we conceptualize gender not as an established territory but rather as a set of practices through which a potential biopower is cultivated, harnessed, and transformed, or by means of which a certain kind of labor or utility extracted? "Trans-" thus becomes the capillary space of connection and circulation between the macro- and micro-political registers through which the lives of bodies become enmeshed in the lives of nations, states, and capital-formations, while "-gender" becomes one of several set of variable techniques or temporal practices (such as race or class) through which bodies are made to live.

What counterdominant work might we accomplish by putting "trans-" in the place that Foucault assigned to sexuality in the "The Right of Death and Power Over Life" at the end of volume 1 of *The History of Sexuality*, making it our name for the space of passing between the "anatamo-political" corporal techniques of subjective individualization and the bio-political management and regulation of populations? What might be gained, in other words, by regarding "trans-," rather than gender, as the stable location where current forms of capital and sovereign power seek to reproduce themselves through our bodies, and where we—if we can or if we must—might begin to enact and materialize new social ontologies? How might we begin transing these two perspectives on transgender, dancing back and forth between the temporality of "trans-" and the spatiality of "-gender," and the spatiality of "trans-" and the temporality of "-gender"? How might we move between the necessary places of identity where we plant our feet and the simultaneous imperative to resist those ways in which identities become the vectors through which we are taken up by projects not of our own making? How might we begin to link "trans-" to other suffixes that target bodily zones or functions other than those addressed by "-gender", and thus begin to articulate what might be called a general "somatechics," or analytics of embodied difference?

The movement between territorializing and deterritorializing "trans-" and its suffixes, we want to suggest, as well as the movements between temporalizing and spatializing them, is an improvisational, creative, and essentially poetic practice through which radically new possibilities for being in the world can start to emerge. As part of the making-real of the trans-movements we envision, we have assembled in this special issue of *WSQ* work we consider to be "doubly trans-" in some important sense—work that situates "trans-" in relation to transgender yet moves beyond the narrow politics of gender identity.

Afsaneh Najmabadi opens this issue with an original, empirically grounded analysis of transsexuality within the Islamic Republic of Iran. She pays particular attention to the ways in which Eurocentric medical discourses and identity categories mean differently in Iranian contexts, and she offers a sophisticated reading of the ways in which state sanction of sex-reassignment surgeries not only provides material benefits for many transsexuals, but can also create safer social spaces for nontransgendered homosexual men and women. Her careful scholarship on this point is a welcome corrective to the increasingly frequent and rhetorically powerful deployment in the West of the figure of "the Iranian transsexual" to demonstrate the "backwardness" of Islam in relation to Eurocentric narratives of political progress and personal liberation. At an historical moment when the United States seems poised for war with Iran, the vital transnational and cross-cultural perspective on Iranian transgender sociocultural formations found in Najmabadi's work helps counter the veiled Islamophobia which can be found even in "progressive" Euro-American queer and feminist discourses.

If the case of transsexuality in Iran demonstrates that seemingly identical practices of bodily transformation can perform quite different kinds of work in different national contexts, Elizabeth Loeb's article on bodily integrity, identity disorders, and the sovereign stakes of corporeal desire within U.S. law helps show how seemingly dissimilar practices can in fact function as different instantiations of the same enabling logic of power. Loeb grapples with the relationship between bodily integrity and sovereign power from the perspective of "Wannabes," a term self-applied by some individuals who seek to amputate "healthy" limbs. Loeb notes how Wannabes increasingly frame their arguments for redefining their own sense of corporeal integrity by making reference to transsexual practice, essentially asserting that if it's acceptable for transsexuals to cut off some body parts, it should be acceptable for them to cut off other parts. She demonstrates how "Gender Identity Disorder," the disciplinary metric that legitimates gender reassignment surgeries, has been deployed to justify the creation of "Body Identity Integrity Disorder," a new pathologizing designation through which Wannabes hope to decriminalize and legitimate the medical practice of self-demand limb amputation. In investigating the current criminalization of this consensual surgery, performed in circumstances no different from those of elective cosmetic surgeries, Loeb not only documents the legal construction of Wannabe amputee desire or practice as an incursion on state sovereignty, but also argues that "identity disorder" is itself a pervasively deployed strategy of biopolitical management within neoliberal organizations of sovereign power.

In her meditations on the Antony and the Johnsons's song "The Cripple and the Starfish," in which the singer equates the act of loving with the act of cutting off a finger that can "grow back like a starfish," Eva Hayward addresses, from an strikingly different angle of approach, the question of amputation raised by Loeb. Hayward, who uses her own transsexuality autoethnographically in the articulation of her argument, disavows the assumption of loss and lack implied by the concept off "cutting off." She refuses to be haunted by a nostalgia for an imagined wholeness that has been surgically diminished and, rather, understands that her surface been refolded and differently spatialized. Hayward suggests productive links and lines of thinking between transgender discourses and disability studies in an effort to show how multiple forms of bodily difference or atypicality can be nonhierarchically related to one another. She also brings a critical science studies perspective on nonhuman animal embodiment to the same question, asking what transspecies lessons could be learned from the regenerative potential of starfish limbs.

Natalie Corinne Hansen similarly takes up the question of transgender and transspecies relationality in her excellent close reading of a short first-person narrative by Ken in Dean Kotula's transgender anthology, *The Phallus Palace*. Hansen directs her attention to the reliance of Ken's narrative, which works to authenticate his hormonal transition from female to man, on the concept of gender's biological determination, as well as on a belief in the human dominance over other animals. Hansen argues that Ken's transition-narrative depends on assigning limited agency to animals, while reinforcing binary systems of gender oppression. But her analysis of Ken's stake in his story, and her critique of reductionist views of human-animal relationships, are not the sole contributions of this essay. Hansen also asks how one might construct gendered identities across species boundaries without falling into the trap of biological determinism.

In yet another account of biology that confounds the presumed dichotomy of sex difference, Aaron Norton and Ozzie Zehner discuss "tetragametic chimerism," the creation of organisms with intermingled cell lines. Noting that "chimeras" are also mythical monsters described in Western literature as long ago as the eighth century B.C.E. Norton and Zehner refract this cultural construct through the lens of trans-genomic science to interrogate the multiple narratives that converge in the lives of two mothers, both tetragametic chimeras, in order to explore the role of genetic technologies in the cultural production of motherhood. In so doing the authors show how sciences of life are also cultural practice. Their analysis of chimerism is in dialogue with an eclectic range of critical concepts, including Haraway's cyborg, Butler's gender performativity, and Strathern's notions of kinship. Norton and Zehner argue that chimerism is a trans-phenomena that has the potential to radically alter our beliefs about embodiment, kinship, and motherhood.

Lucas Crawford's essay on "transgender without organs" offers an explicitly Deleuzian approach to "trans-" questions of many sorts. At the level of concrete description, the essay uses Crawford's experiences growing up in small-town Nova Scotia to critique the urban biases of transgender theorizing and to demonstrate the geographical specificity of various techniques and modalities of gender transitioning. At a higher level of theorization, however, Crawford launches a brilliant account of the interrelationship between embodiment, geographical location, spatial movement, and affective experience. Drawing the same distinction between "affect" (that which moves us) and "feeling" (that which holds us in place) that Deleuze and Guattari make in *A Thousand Plateaus*, Crawford critically interrogates the most familiar trope of transgender experience, "feeling trapped in the wrong body." In doing so, he links the practice of materializing a transgender embodiment with critical practices of deterritorialization that always point toward the horizon of new possibilities, rather than with the sentimentality of "going home."

Like Crawford, Marcia Ochoa examines the relationship between transgendering and specificity of place, in ways that resonate with the state- and sovereignty-oriented analytical frameworks of both Najmabadi and Loeb. Through her punning neologism "loca-lization," Ochoa explores the complex processes in Venezuela through which transformistas (individuals assigned male at birth who "present themselves in their everyday lives as women") are produced as marginal to citizenship and excluded from the political imaginary. Her essay examines the concepts of citizenship and civil society not by analyzing the political theory of participatory democracy, or by collecting empirical data on NGOs, but rather by foregrounding the exclusion of certain citizens she calls locas. The loca makes sense only within the complex, mutually constitutive "processes of modernity, nation and globalization" that assemble uniquely at any given geospatial location. Her ethnographic research in Venezuela recounts how locas/transformistas pervert and rearticulate the "modern project of disciplining nature" via their micropolitical bodily practices. In doing so, their interventions (re)create the affective, aesthetic, and structural projects of citizenship.

The excluded bodies of the locas described by Ochoa find their counterpart in Clare Sear's concept of the "problem body," which Sears develops as a more generalized form of Jennifer Terry and Jacqueline Urla's notion of the "deviant body." By juxtaposing freak show displays of gender nonconformists in nineteenth-century San Francisco with the regulation and production of normatively gendered bodies in public space, Sears launches a broader discussion of how certain kinds of bodies (such as the bodies of racialized others, of the "maimed" or "crippled," as well as non-normatively gendered bodies) become targets of certain state-sanctioned operations—including, but not limited to, the operation of exclusion from civic life. And as was the case with Ochoa's locas, Sears's problem bodies can likewise become the site of contestatory practices that challenge the state's organization and control of the territory it occupies.

Lawrence La Fountain-Stokes takes the notion of the loca in yet another direction. In his hands, transloca becomes an "enabling vernacular critical term that accounts for the intersection of space (geography) and sexuality in the work and lived experience of queer diasporic artists who engage in male-to-female drag." The centerpiece of La Fountain-Stokes's article is a reading (performative in itself) of Jorge Merced's performance of Ramos Otero's story "Loca de la locura," in El Bolero, as that of a transloca. For La Fountain-Stokes, "trans-" mediates and conjoins the translocal and the transgender. In this sense, he contends, "trans-" does not necessary connote "unstable, or in between, or in the middle of things, but rather…the core of transformation—change, the power or ability to mold, reorganize, reconstruct, construct—and of longitude: the transcontinental, transatlantic, but also transversal."

Shifting the national and political focus of the volume back toward Western Asia, Rustem Ertug Altinay offers a critical biography of Bulent

Ersoy, a popular performer of Ottoman classical music in present-day Turkey, who happens to be transsexual. Altinay shows how multiple cultural and social institutions construct an identity for Bulent Ersoy that is suitable for public consumption, weaving between knowledge of her life prior to transitioning as well as her current life. Ersoy's public persona engages with contemporary meanings of being Muslim, and being upper-class, as well as being transsexual. Altinay recounts how, in the process of her transition, Ersoy's persona progressively challenged codes of masculinity through the medium of music. He then contrasts this deployment/contestation of masculinity with the exaggeratedly Muslim, and exaggeratedly upper-class and feminine, presentation of self that has enabled Ersoy to survive and thrive under highly disciplinary codes of gendered behavior and appearance.

Robin Bauer writes of his sociological participation/observation in BDSM communities in Western Europe and the United States, and interviews with fifty other members of these communities. Bauer defines BDSM as a broad range of embodied practices that may or may not include bondage, discipline, and sadomasochism. Treating these informants as experts on their own phenomenologically experienced, socially situated, and materially embodied lives, Bauer interrogates their expertise to establish BDSM as a venue in which individuals transgress social taboos, including gender strictures, often with erotic effects. He argues that these communities have a highly attenuated and deeply embodied understanding of nonheteronormative gender identities that enable productive transformation within the context of safe erotic playgrounds. Such BDSM experiences have the potential to transform human relationships and social power in the social worlds beyond the safe spaces of BDSM play.

Hala Kamal's contribution, "Translating Women and Gender: The Experience of Translating The Encyclopedia of Women and Islamic Cultures into Arabic," positions "trans-" as a problem of translation. In this piece, Kamal examines the politics and processes of translating the word "gender" from English to Arabic. "Trans-gender" in this contribution's iteration is not about individual gender transitivity, but rather about the attempt to migrate the concept of "gender" across linguistic and cultural barriers. Kamal, a member of the Women and Memory Forum, the group that translated the encyclopedia, was charged with the task of translating "gender." The impossibility of the attempt to make "gender" legible in Arabic, with all the English specificities and connotations valued by the translator—socially constructed and feminist, among others—and finding or creating a term that would work with Arabic language grammatical rules was revealed by the author's ultimate choice: a transliteration, al-jender.

Most issues of *WSQ* have a section that revisits a "feminist classic," whether it be poetry or prose, fiction or visual pieces. For the *Trans-* issue, we present C. L. Cole and Shannon L. C. Cate's meditations on Adrienne Rich's landmark 1980 essay "Compulsory Heterosexuality and Lesbian Existence." Although Rich's crucial intervention has faded into the distance in many feminist and queer studies landscapes, Cole and Cate remind us of the importance of its theoretical operations, such as denaturalizing heterosexuality and viewing the lesbian continuum as "a strategic mechanism for generating politically viable identities and alliances." They suggest that Rich's thought should not be seen as occupying only one end of several related binaries: essentialist not constructionist, second wave rather than next wave, feminist in opposition to queer. Instead, in their incisive commentary, they show how Rich's critical frameworks can be transposed to imagine a "transgender continuum on which so-called male-born men and female-born women can find themselves building political connections with those whose gender is more obviously outside society's narrow 'frame' of the normal."

The call for papers for the *Trans-* issue garnered a number of responses from individuals interested in questions of pedagogy. Rather than selecting just one author to write a full-length article, we chose a format that would spark dialogue and debate among a number of individuals, writing from a range of perspectives. Vic Muñoz and Ednie Kaeh Garrison agreed to curate a "textual conversation" on "TransPedagogies." The questions participants wrangled with are too numerous to completely inventory here, but to provide some sense of the range and depth, a few of them are: How does the concept of "gender identity" fail to describe the dialogical processes through which gender is constituted? How does trans-disciplinarity in the academy contest the boundaries between researchers and participants, and how might it be analogized to trans-gendering? How does the presence of "trans-" students in the classroom change how gender is taught? What should women's colleges do when they admit female students who subsequently come out as "trans-"?

WSQ regularly includes a section called "Alerts and Provocations," whose purpose is to focus readers' attention on matters of topical interest or timely political significance. In this issue, Paisley Currah's contribution, "Expecting Bodies: The Pregnant Man and Transgender Exclusion from the Employment Non-Discrimination Act," highlights the issue of trans/sexed bodies in public policy contexts. He uses the media sensation of the "pregnant man" as a tease for readers, and then situates that incident in a larger analysis of legal constructions of "unexpectedly sexed" bodies. He shows how the particular gender logics framing the public response to the pregnant man also governed the decision by the Democratic leadership in the U.S. House of Representatives to cut "gender identity" from a bill that would ban workplace discrimination based on sexual orientation.

Finally, the content we have described above is interspersed with images, poetry, creative prose, and book reviews, all selected because of their potential thematic connections to "trans-." We won't attempt to render those interjections into the thumbnail sketches that define the particular academic form known as the "introduction to the special issue," but we do invite readers to approach those selections both as stand-alone pieces with their own (in-transitive) integrity, and as fragments whose migrations into this special issue bring new, unanticipated meanings to "trans-."

ACKNOWLEDGMENTS

We would like to thank WSQ's outgoing general editors, Cindi Katz and Nancy Miller, for the original invitation to curate this special issue; WSQ's new general editors, Victoria Pitts-Taylor and Talia Schaffer, for their work shepherding the project to completion; WSQ editorial associates Jess Bier and Stacie McCormick, for their conscientious labor on this issue; fiction/visual images editor Susan Daitch and poetry editor Kathy Ossip, for their thoughtfulness in selecting material appropriate to the issue's theme; the anonymous reviewers, for their helpful comments on the articles; and Rayden Sorock, a student at Purchase College, State University of New York, for his help in coordinating the book reviews, readers' reports, and other details for the journal.

SUSAN STRYKER is an associate professor of gender studies at Indiana University. She is the author or editor of several books, most recently the introductory text *Transgender History* (Seal Press. 2008), as well as the Emmy

Award-winning public television documentary *Screaming Queens: The Riot at Compton's Cafeteria* (ITVS/Frameline, 2005).

PAISLEY CURRAH teaches political science at Brooklyn College of The City University of New York. He is a coeditor, with Richard M. Juang and Shannon Price Minter, of *Transgender Rights* (Minnesota University Press, 2006). He is a founding board member of the Transgender Law and Policy Institute. His next book, *The United States of Gender: Regulating Transgender Identities*, is forthcoming from New York University Press.

LISA JEAN MOORE is a professor of sociology and gender studies at Purchase College. She teaches courses in feminist theory; the sociology of birth and death; science, technology, and queer theory; and the sociology of men. Her previous book, *Sperm Counts: Overcome by Man's Most Precious Fluid*, is published by NYU Press. She has just completed the book *Missing Bodies: The Politics of Visibility* (NYU Press) with Monica Casper.

TRANSING AND TRANSPASSING ACROSS SEX-GENDER WALLS IN IRAN

AFSANEH NAJMABADI

Something happened in 2003–4: transsexuals and transsexuality in Iran suddenly became a hot media topic, both in Iran and internationally.

The medical practice of sex change by means of surgery and hormones dates to at least the early 1970s in Iran; for nearly three decades the topic had received occasional coverage in the Iranian press, including a series of reports (presumably based on real lives) published in a popular magazine, *Rah-i zindigi* (Path of Life), beginning in 1999.[1] Iranian press coverage of "trans-" phenomena increased sharply in early 2003, however, and it has continued intensely ever since—sometimes the reports directly address transsexuals and transsexuality, and sometimes they pertain to them in the context of other people marked as "vulnerable to social harm," such as prostitutes (both male and female) and runaway girls, who reportedly live trans-dressed lives. It was these last two topics that drew the attention of documentary filmmaker Mitra Farahani to the subject of transsexuals in Iran. Her documentary *Just a Woman* won international acclaim at the 2002 Berlin Gay and Lesbian Film Festival and elsewhere and seems to have ignited broader international attention to the issue of transsexuality in Iran. A flurry of articles appeared in the world press in 2004–5. *The Guardian*, for example, wrote on July 27, 2005, that "today, the Islamic Republic of Iran occupies the unlikely role of global leader for sex change," adding, "Iran has even become a magnet for patients from eastern European and Arab countries seeking to change their genders." A number of television documentaries in France, Sweden, Holland, and the United Kingdom followed, as well as several independent documentary film productions (Abdo 2000; Eqbali 2004; Fathi 2004; McDowall and Khan 2004; Harrison 2005; Stack 2005; Tait 2005).

The celebratory tone of many of these reports—welcoming recognition of transsexuality and the permissibility of sex change operations—is sometimes mixed with an element of surprise: How could this be happening in an Islamic state? In other accounts, the sanctioning of transsexuality is tightly framed by comparisons with punishments for sodomy and the presumed illegality of homosexuality—echoing, as we shall see, some of the official thinking in Iran.[2]

While transsexual surgeries are not new in Iran, over the past decade such operations seem to have increased not only in publicity, but also in actual frequency. At the first national symposium on transsexuality, "Studying Gender Identity Disorder," held in the northeastern provincial capital of Mashhad in May 2005, Dr. Aliriza Kahani, from the National Legal Medical Board, reported that in the fifteen years between 1987 and 2001, 200 males and 70 females had submitted sex change petitions to the board, and 214 had been approved. Over the following four years, between 2001 and 2004, another 200 petitions had been received (*Shakh-is*, May 24, 2005).[3] Anecdotal statistics from a private sex change clinic in Tehran point to similar increases—for the period 1985–95, 125 of 153 clients went through partial or full sex change operations; in the decade that followed, the numbers increased to 200 surgeries in a client population of 210.

The increasing frequency of sex change petitions and operations is not an unproblematically positive development, empowering though this trend has been for transsexuals. Many political challenges are posed by framing transsexuality within a dominant mapping of sexuality that explicitly renders as diseased, abnormal, deviant, and at times criminal any sexual or gender nonconformity (including transsexuality itself, as well as same-sex desires and practices). For legal and medical authorities, sex change surgeries are explicitly framed as the cure for a diseased abnormality, and on occasion they are proposed as a religio-legally sanctioned option for heteronormalizing people with same-sex desires or practices. Even though this possible option has not become state policy (because official discourse is also invested in making an essential distinction between transsexuals and homosexuals), recent international media coverage of transsexuality in Iran increasingly emphasizes the possibility that sex-reassignment surgery (SRS) is being performed coercively on Iranian homosexuals by a fundamentalist Islamic government (Ireland 2007). This narrative framing (along with similar ones concerning the suppression of women's rights and other political and labor struggles) circulates within larger reductive and totalizing Euro-American discourses on Iran and

Islam that equate them both with the most conservative factions of the Iranian government and with the views of the most fundamentalist Islamists. Conservative forces in both Iran and the West have a common stake in ignoring the lively reform discourse and history of progressive activism within contemporary Iran that offers alternative notions of rights within an Islamic society and of alternative modes of living a Muslim life.

While the pressures on gays and lesbians in Iran to transition from one gender to another are very real, these pressures are not produced primarily by fear of criminality.[4] On the contrary: the religio-legal framework of transsexuality has been productive of paradoxical, and certainly unintended, effects that at times benefit homosexuals. Simply put, the religio-legal prohibition of same-sex practices does contribute to pressures on gays and lesbians to consider transsexuality as a religiously sanctioned legal alternative (which is particularly important for religiously observant persons), but instead of eliminating same-sex desires and practices, it has actually provided more room for *relatively* safer semipublic gay and lesbian social space and for less conflicted self-perceptions among people with same-sex desires and practices. As one pre-op FtM (female-to-male transsexual) succinctly put it: "Once I was diagnosed as TS (transsexual), I started having sex with my girlfriend without feeling guilty."

A BRIEF HISTORY OF TRANSSEXUALITY IN IRAN

Some of the earliest discussions in Iran of transgenderism and transsexuality appeared in the 1940s, within a body of popular marital and parental advice literature translated into Persian (largely from American popular-psychology authors, such as David Rubin and George Hearth), in which discussions of love, desire, sex, and marriage supplied occasions to write about gender disidentification, homosexuality, intersex conditions, and sex change. (Some of the earliest discussions of transgenderism and transsexuality in Europe and the United States appeared in these very same sources.)[5] Surgeries to alter congenital intersex conditions were reported in the Iranian press as early as 1930 (*Ittila'at*, October 27, 1930), and the intensification of reporting on these surgeries in the 1940s and 1950s forms an important backdrop to the subsequent history of transsexuality in Iran. By the late 1960s, notions of "gender disorder" and hormonal or genetic "sex and gender determination" began to enter Iranian medical discourse via translated behavioral psychology books and medical texts.

The earliest nonintersex sex change surgery reported in the Iranian press (that I have found so far) dates to February 1973 (*Kayhan*, February 17, 1973), and by the early 1970s, at least one hospital in Tehran and one in Shiraz were carrying out SRS. A 1976 report by Dr. Kariminizhad of Jahanshah Saleh Women's Hospital stated that over the previous three years, some fifty persons with transsexual tendencies had been seen at the hospital and that twenty of them had gone through SRS (*Kayhan*, October 11, 1976). Around the same time, the Medical Association of Iran (MAI), a professional state-affiliated organization of physicians, began discussing the medical ethics of surgical sex change. In a 1976 decision, the MAI declared that sex change operations, except in intersex cases, were ethically unacceptable—a ruling that was not reversed for more than a decade.

As early as 1967, Ayatollah Khomeini had published a fatwa sanctioning sex change, but this ruling, issued by a dissident Khomeini then still living in exile in Iraq, did not influence the policies of legal or medical institutions in Iran (Khomeini 1967, vol. 2, 753–55). There is no unanimity of opinion among leading clerics in Iran on the issue of transsexuality. Numerically speaking, the majority of opinion-issuing clerics consider only intersex surgeries to be acceptable unequivocally. The opinion that ultimately matters, however, is that of the cleric(s) in *political* power, regardless of relative religious authority. The historically specific relationship between jurisprudential and political authority that has characterized Iran since the early 1980s translates clerical opinion, sanctioned through a complex legal process, into law. With Ayatollah Khomeini as a politically unchallenged supreme authority after the 1979 revolution until his death in 1989, the reissuance in 1985 of his 1967 fatwa on SRS, in Persian this time rather than Arabic, set in motion the process that culminated in new state-sanctioned medicolegal procedures regarding transsexuality.[6]

From the earliest pronouncement to present-day opinions, reflections on transsexual surgery in Iran seem to have been informed in part by linking these bodily changes to similar questions posed about intersex bodies. Classical Islamic discourse categorized every human body as either male or female, yet accepted the possibility that in the case of hermaphrodites it was difficult and at times impossible to determine the body's "true genus" (*kind* or *type*).[7] Jurisprudents then elaborated rules of behavior to deal with the possible threat of gender transgressions that such impossibility of knowing would produce (Sanders 1991). In its modern reconfiguration, jurisprudents argued that new medical sciences could help unravel the puzzle of proper genus in difficult cases of hermaphroditism and that medical technology could correct the manifestation of that genus.

Importantly, by the 1960s, the approval of medicalized means for manifesting the proper genus of the hermaphroditic body converged with, and eventually (in the post-1979 period) acted as, religious sanction for the emerging medico-psycho-behavioral discourse on gender and sexual dimorphism. Not only did the true sex become knowable in spite of ambiguous genitalia, a determinate relation between gender identification, gender role behavior, sexual desire, and subjective gender identity was envisioned for each and every body. The convergence of these discourses consolidated a powerful religio-legal-psycho-medical notion of "unnatural and deviant" sexualities that now circulates in the Iranian national press, in religious texts, in biomedical and psychological writings, and in marital and parental advice literature. With the establishment and consolidation of the Islamic Republic in the 1980s, this discourse gained state support, finance, and force of law, providing the conditions of possibility for transsexuality in Iran on a new scale, while setting the contours within which transsexuals fight their battles and live their lives, often with imaginative successes, and at other times with frustration and terrible loss.

The "trans-friendly" jurisprudential discourse on transsexuality that began as an elaboration on intersex discourse now approves of transsexuality on the discretionary grounds that it has not been specifically forbidden in the Qur'an. Invoking a distinction between the physical body and the soul, this discourse argues that in most people there is harmony between the two, but that in a small number of people a disharmony produces transsexuality; since we cannot change a person's soul, but medical advances have made it possible to change a person's body, transsexual surgery is a permissible solution to this disharmony between soul and body. As a discretionary matter, SRS is not required—or even recommended—for a person diagnosed as transsexual, unless a religiously observant transsexual fears falling into sinful deeds.[8] Some of the more accepting people among the friends and kin of transsexuals have come to terms with transsexuality through understanding it as a "wonder of creation," or sign of God's power. Some trans-friendly and gay-friendly psychotherapists use the same language in working with families. While this may sound to many of us terribly "essentialist," I have come to hear it as an alternatively enabling script, especially as compared with the more dominant (and no less essentialist) psychomedical discourse.

Public knowledge of transsexuality has been shaped not only by jurisprudential and biomedical discourses, but also by intensive coverage in the Iranian press (and to some extent by satellite television broadcasts). In addition to the previously mentioned reports in *Rah-i zindigi*, the topic of transsexuality has been covered in a number of magazines, such as *Zanan* and *Chilchiraq,* and important dailies, such as *I'timad-i melli, I'timad, Hamshahri,* and *Sharq,* where long articles and interviews have appeared in medical and science sections. The "yellow press" also covers transsexuality, and for a brief period in 2004–5 gave the topic frequent full-page coverage, sometimes featuring translated articles that had appeared in the international press. This sustained coverage, despite the lean quality of the content—sometimes the same story is repeated in various issues of the same journal—has made transsexuality one of the stock attention-grabbing stories for the scandal sheets, along with stories about film stars' lives and various sexual and social scandals. The combination of kinds of coverage—with the dailies and science journals making transsexuality a respectable topic of social conversation and the sensational press bringing it into popular knowledge—has made transsexuality a widely recognized topic, though by no means one that is generally approved of. It is possible that the increased frequency of SRS in the past decade has been enabled by this expansion of public discourse. Many transsexuals I listened to, especially those coming to Tehran from provincial towns, said they had found out about SRS clinics through the press coverage (including satellite broadcast of documentaries).

What kind of subjectivity is afforded to transsexuals through their public recognition as strange creations or scandalously diseased bodies, and how do transsexuals themselves respond to these representations? Some of the intimate details of transsexuals' lives that are reported in the tabloids would be unimaginable if the subjects were recognized as "normal heterosexuals." It is only as transsexuals that their sexual lives become printable stories. What effects does this possibility of scandalous or "strange" public intimacy generate for conceptions of gender and sexuality more generally—especially given that the scandal sheets, like the rest of the press, have to be wary of violating the restrictions of the Ministry of Islamic Guidance? As Dupret (2001) and Ferrié (1995) have asked of Egypt and Morocco, respectively, what happens when claims for certain intimate lives become possible largely through "publicizing the private," their regulation justified through their potential criminality? When the cover of the tabloid visually frames the headlines about transsexuals with headlines about murder, urban crimes, and cannibalism, what kind of empathy can even a sympathetic transsexual story generate, bordered as it is by stories designed to provoke urban panic and moral revulsion?[9]

VENTURING INTO ETHNOGRAPHY

It was with these uneasy thoughts that I began my research in Iran in May 2006. Two questions informed my initial thinking: First, in a cultural-legal context where same-sex desire is considered shameful and same-sex practices are illegal, but within which transsexuality, even if overwhelmingly understood as shameful, is nevertheless legal and state subsidized, how does this configuration shape sexual and gender subjectivities? Second, how do insistent state regulations and religio-cultural codes and rituals concerning proper gender conduct shape sexual desires and gender subjectivities? How does this context map the terrain on which individuals come to identify as TS and decide how far to go in their transitions?

For instance, the protocols of sex change often involve a prolonged period of supervised transition, during which the person lives socially as the other gender. In Iran, I had imagined, this procedure would face difficulties because of a whole series of state regulations on gender segregation. How do people in transition, I wondered, navigate gender regulations? Religious and state regulations aim to produce a sense of bodily appropriateness through daily observations of gendered homosocializing practices, whether at home (for religiously observant families), in streets and parks, or in offices and universities. What is the legally sanctified gender of a transdressed in-transition person, given that the public dress code is so insistently gender regulated? What might the "impossibility of living as the other gender" mean for the concepts and practices of sex change? Despite my initial forebodings, my ethnographic research (the results of which are summarized in what follows) soon made it clear to me that some highly paradoxical effects have been produced by the explicit framing of transsexuality as linked with, and yet distinct from, homosexuality and other sexualities that are rendered deviant and sometimes criminal.

The typical autobiographical narrative, as well as the diagnostic psychological symptomization and the supervised process of legal certification of transsexuality, have all keyed themselves to the distinction established between transsexuality and homosexuality. A typical autobiographical narrative begins with the familiar recounting of a childhood in which the subject did not wish to dress and play gender appropriately. Popular parental advice psychology literature now routinely warns parents about such early symptoms. Parents are advised to not encourage such childhood tendencies by thinking of cross-gender behavior as cute; they are told to consult child psychologists to get help in dealing with this "problem" as early as possible, to prevent the "full-blown stage" of adult transsexuality.

In the dominant narrative of the transsexual life-course, a cross-gendered childhood usually leads to a troubled adolescence in which same-sex desires torment the subject, especially given that all schools in Iran are gender segregated. The strong relationship between childhood "transgender symptoms" and adolescent "sexual symptoms" signals the many ways in which gender and sex are not taken to be distinct categories in all registers in Iran. Indeed, in some registers, lives are made possible through that very indistinction—as in the case of certified non-operated transsexuals who would become illegal subjects should "transgender" (that is, nonmedicalized cross-gender living) become widely accepted as distinct from transsexual.

Transsexuals who profess religious beliefs usually emphasize that they had not engaged in any same-sex acts despite persistent desires. Others hint at same-sex activities as a further corroboration of their transsexuality. Both groups tend to recite a series of school troubles, leading to parents being informed that their child has "problems," referrals to psychologists, possibly dropping out of school, or being expelled if suspected of improper sexual activities. These troubled years begin the long process toward eventual gender transition.

Often this is the beginning of long family battles. Parents resort to sometimes horrifying measures to dissuade their adolescent teenagers from their contrarian sexual/gender desires. Some transsexuals succeed in hiding their sexual/gender desires from parents and improvise their own livable patterns. Even post-op, some live complicated multiple lives to be able to stay connected to their families. They leave home dressed as one gender, then change to the other. This strategy is easier for FtMs, who can just take off their outer covers, than for MtFs, who must not only adjust clothes, but also apply makeup under bridges, in garages, in public toilets in parks, and at other available public spaces—all of which are potentially dangerous for them, with regular reports of MtF transsexuals being attacked and occasionally murdered in such locations.

Adolescents sent by school authorities or concerned parents for help from therapists and physicians are sometimes diagnosed as "afflicted by GID (gender identity disorder)" and often find themselves thrown into a combative situation with therapists who decide to cure them of these wrong gender/sexual desires. Such practitioners include both mainstream psychologists as well as a vocal group of psychotherapists who advocate and practice Islam therapy (sometimes called spiritual therapy). Adolescence is the period in which many transsexuals, especially MtFs, find family life unbearable and either leave, at least temporarily, or are thrown out by families. Family severance is a very serious social issue, as so much of one's life is defined and made possible (or impossible) through one's location within an intricate network of extended family members, family friends, and acquaintances. Thus, severance from family often means not only emotional hardship and homelessness for prospective transsexuals, but also a loss of education and job opportunities. While transsexuals tend to find each other and form alternative kin worlds of their own, they often face enormous problems in the immediate period of being thrown out into a hostile world. MtFs are much more likely to face this predicament than are FtMs. Correspondingly, family reconciliation is often easier for FtMs than for MtFs. Several close relatives of (pre-/non-/post-op) FtMs explicitly said their acceptance of their daughter/sister becoming a son/brother would have been unimaginable if it had been the other way around.

The reason for this disparity is not simply gender bias, though it is that too—namely, the preference for a male offspring. More important, the disparity arises from the repugnance and shame that the culture associates with "passive" male same-sex practices. MtFs seem, sadly and ironically, to live forever under the sign of being *kuni*s (literally meaning "anal," but in Persian connoting persons who are receptive of anal penetration), even though that is precisely what in many cases they are trying to disavow and move away from through sex change.[10] In their autobiographical narratives, many reiterate that they have never allowed themselves to be anally penetrated even with their longtime boyfriends, and that they have been patiently going through the legal and medical changes in order to acquire a vagina before they get married. Yet their physiological changes and insistent self-narrativizations notwithstanding, they continue to carry the burden of that stigmatization with them even postoperatively. For their families, they remain a lifelong source of shame among their kin and neighborhood networks. Even families that have *not* reconciled with their offspring "lost" to sex change sometimes move to a new neighborhood or town in order to live again without shame. The insistence of many transsexuals to distinguish themselves individually and as a group from homosexuals is thus not simply because of the religio-legal status of transsexuality and their need to protect themselves from charges of homosexuality; this attempted disarticulation nevertheless carries with it, and participates in regenerating, a sign of stigmatization. It is a delineating move that in fact reinforces a burden they cannot shed.

FILTERING

The legal process of gender transition is firmly framed by the pivotal distinction between homosexuality and transsexuality. Colloquially referred to as "filtering," legal gender transitioning involves a four- to six-month course of psychotherapy, accompanied by hormonal and chromosomal tests. It aims to distinguish and segregate "true transsexuals" (for whom any same-sex desire and even hints of same-sex practices are considered symptomatic of their transsexuality) from misguided or opportunist homosexuals (whose same-sex desires and practices are viewed as signs of moral deviancy) seeking to avoid anti-homosexual censure.[11] In the worst cases, filtering establishes a very hostile and at times terrifying relationship between the therapist and the client. This is particularly the case with those therapists who practice Islam therapy. Several transsexuals recounted contemplating or attempting suicide during the filtering process. Other therapists, however, actually have used filtering to support their gay and lesbian clients, and to form separate individual and group sessions for them, thereby providing important social venues.

As I have already hinted, the very process of psychological filtering and jurisprudential wall-building between gender and sexual categories, far from eliminating gays and lesbians (if that is indeed what the authorities hope for), paradoxically has created new social spaces. Instead of constructing an impassable border, the process has generated a porously marked, nebulous, and spacious domain populated by a variety of "not-normal" people. In order to persuade some gays and lesbians ("symptomatic homosexuals") to consider transing bodily, and to filter out the true ("morally deviant") homosexuals, this process needs to offer a safe passage between categories. As the filtering and sorting processes depend above all on individual self-narratives, the potential uses of this "nebula" are limited only by each involved person's creativity—a decidedly abundant resource.

As a wise friend urged me back in 2005, before I began my field research, "Don't worry, people are very creative and make their own uses." And this is what I have in fact learned: not to underestimate the real problems and challenges, and at times dangers, that transsexuals, gays, and lesbians face in Iran, but also to see the productivity (in a Foucauldian sense) of the power of legal-medical-religious regulations, as well as the creativity with which transsexuals, gays, and lesbians use the spaces such regulative power provides and the ways in which their active participation and struggles change things.

Here is where refusing a distinction between sex and gender has been very productive. One can live what we may name a transgendered life (that is, non-operated yet sex/gender discordant) as a certified transsexual. This is perfectly legal and religiously permissible. As one trans-friendly cleric, Hujjat al-Islam Kariminia, agreed in the course of our many conversations and written communications, physiological transitioning is something that is allowed but not required. This means that a certified transsexual can, but does not have to, take hormones or go for surgery. S/he can legally live as the other gender. While legal and religious officials do not like this, they cannot do much about it. They are not being lenient and tolerant; rather, the very mechanisms of their project to filter and sort homosexuals from transsexuals depends on turning a blind eye to the "space of passing" across the very walls they have tried to erect.

Indeed, one doesn't even have to engage with the filtering process to be able to speak, at least in some spaces, as openly gay. In official circumstances, homosexually oriented persons, with or sometimes without certification as transsexual, refer to themselves in various ways. For example, one man who, in a safer space, self-identified as gay, would say in a weekly TS group session held at the Social Emergency Unit of Welfare Organization, "I am not sure what I am, maybe I am gay, maybe I am TS, I am here to find out." In the 2005 Mashhad seminar on gender identity disorder, an MtF-looking person from the audience asked Hujjat al-Islam

Kariminia about rules for certain religious observances for "those of us who are *bilataklif* [undecided, ambivalent, in a conundrum]. Do we enter the Imam Riza Shrine through the men's entrance or the women's?" Hujjat al-Islam Kariminia's response was very telling: "You should go through the entrance that is appropriate for how you are dressed." This would, of course, not resolve their actual dilemma, in contrast to their hypothetical jurisprudential one; for upon entering the apparently gender-appropriate entrance, one is subjected to bodily security searches that would result in serious trouble for a TS. Yet Kariminia's answer itself was what astonished me, because in a conversation in his office in Qum, in response to my suggestion that transsexuals should be allowed to live as transgender and not necessarily be pushed to hormonal and surgical treatment, he had insisted that the anatomical body defined maleness or females in Islam. In a later conversation, however, he agreed that certified transsexuals could trans-dress, and in a written communication he confirmed that they could even live as the other gender in all ways except for having sex with someone of their own bodily sex. Clearly, the context of asking made for different responses, as anyone familiar with the tradition of Islamic (or Jewish) responsa literature would immediately recognize.

The legal and religious authorities, in short, have a stake in keeping open the nebulous domains of passing, even as they try to clear them of any "opportunistic squatters" and keep their population under surveillance.[12] The passageways that cross the porous boundaries between homosexuals and transsexuals at times fuels the hostility of some MtFs (especially those who are post-op) toward gay men. In keeping with general social attitudes, the former consider gay men to be shamefully anally receptive and suspect them of being actual or potential sex workers and HIV carriers; "They give us all a bad name" was an oft-repeated phrase. Despite all these challenges, however, these passages ought to remain open.

ALTERNATIVE ALLIANCES

Recently, an alternative alliance has emerged between some MtF transsexuals and gay men.[13] They argue that they have much in common as people who differ from social norms and expectations and that the state-regulated filtering process should not become a hostile division between them. In 2006, one transsexual group began to welcome gays and lesbians to its weekly meetings.[14] These emerging openings and alliances have begun to create conditions for rethinking and reappropriating dominant cultural concepts. In the TS meeting held at the Welfare Organization, a gay man argued before a government-appointed social worker that since the culture named them all as deviants, those who were thus labeled therefore possessed the power to redefine what that label might mean. Think metaphorically of driving, he argued, maintaining that most people take the straight highway to get where they want to go, but gays, lesbians, and transsexuals deviate from the straight path and take some side roads—a much more interesting way to travel than the boring straight highway. Even within such relatively open and hospitable spaces, however, the overall social stigmatization of gay men and transsexual women produces enormous pressure on them to police each other's lives. The public appearance of MtFs, many of whom often display their femininity by "excessive" styles of clothes and makeup, in a social context in which female public visibility is heavily scrutinized, is a continuous subject of approbation by others. MtFs who are even rumored to engage in sex work are a continuous target of harsh criticism.

I do not wish to deny the enormous pressures on gays and lesbians to physically transition, which some gays and lesbians do consider in order to make their lives more livable. Their decision to transition derives not merely from religious sanctions or as a result of laws being enforced against same-sex practices. It cannot be dismissed simply as a "false recognition" achieved under therapeutic duress, or incited by the media (as in the formula "I read an article or saw a TV program and now realize I am TS"). Nor does it represent a "lack of imagination," as one diasporic self-identified queer Iranian once put it to me. Such moments of medicopsychological diagnosis or self-recognition are occasioned by larger social and cultural patterns of gender and sexual life, in particular the pressure to marry and form families. They are informed by all the simple pleasures of daily life from which same-sex partners are excluded; as one such woman said, "We can't be together at Nawruz [Persian New Year]; each of us has to be with her family. We start every new year in separation."

The social expectation for every adult to get married, later if not sooner, affects sexual and gender relations in important ways. While there has been a great deal more open premarital sexual experimentation (including same-sex activities) among adolescents and young adults in recent years, these remain just that: *pre*marital. Male-male and female-female couples live under, and compete with, the severe threat of the marriage demand. At times, "passive" males overact their femininity in a desperate attempt to avert the threat of a "real" woman and the loss of their male partner to marriage. The same is true of female-female couples: there are abundant sad narratives of long-term lesbian relationships breaking apart because the "femme" partner finally opted for marrying a "real" man (or finally gave in to familial and social expectations to do so), in spite of the heroic butch performance of her former lover. This same pressure for marriage informs the dominant culture's deep investment in the performance of masculinity and femininity, and it partially accounts for heavily gender-coded roles within same-sex partnerships. This, perhaps even more than the illegality of same-sex practices and the legality of transsexuality, pushes some people who may otherwise define themselves as butch lesbians and effeminate gays toward transing. They expect transing to make marriage available to them and, in a few instances, to salvage a threatened same-sex relation. Nevertheless, relationships involving transsexuals still always exist under the threat of inauthenticity. Post-op transsexuals, even though they have aspired to be bodily like the other sex, are often dismissed as "plastic replicas," and social pressures sometimes lead the partners to contemplate leaving a "fake" man or woman for a "real" one—as many post-op breakup stories reiterate. Despite the circulation of such sad stories, the larger social pressures for marriage continue to push some people in the transsexual direction.

CONCLUSION

Having provisionally mapped some configurations of sexuality and gender in contemporary Iran, I will conclude with a few questions that may be of interest for transnational comparison. What does it mean that concepts of gender, sex, and sexuality—along with their (in)distinction from, and relations to, one another—have been formed in a context that has not been shaped to any substantial degree by the identity politics of gender and sexuality, or by queer activism and queer critical theory? Some of the distinctions between these categories within Euro-American contexts, including the distinction sometimes made between transgender/transsexual (based on the body that has been surgically modified), have been shaped over the past couple of decades by a particular set of political struggles and debates. How do seemingly similar assignations mean differently (or not) within a different politics of sex, sexuality, and gender? While identity struggles have raged within transnational diasporic Iranian communities, many gays, lesbians, and transsexuals in Iran wish to keep national and international politics out of their daily lives. Indeed, some have become quite wary of international coverage of transsexuality in Iran, feeling that the effects of such coverage, within this volatile scene of meaning making, is beyond their control. Despite their aversion to the international politics of human and civil rights for sexual and gender identities, some of these global discussions have nevertheless reached Iran through Web logs, satellite TV broadcasts, and other transnational media. Loan words and expressions, such as "straight," "gay," "lesbian," "transsexual," "homosexual," "top," "bottom," and "versatile," among many others, pronounced in Persian just as they are in English, are freely used in these discussions. How do these enunciations mean differently, and do a different cultural work, in Tehran compared with New York? Perhaps one of the problems with the current heated debates between proponents of "global gay" and opponents of "gay international" resides in the presumption, common to both groups, that "I am gay," or "I am transsexual" means the same thing anywhere it is pronounced. [15]

ACKNOWLEDGMENTS

This essay has been enabled through numerous conversations with transsexuals, gays, and lesbians in several cities in Iran during 2006–7. It has also taken shape through discussions after its presentation at several campuses: Tehran University, Barnard College, Harvard School of Public Health, University of Connecticut, Princeton University, University of Washington, University of Illinois, several campuses affiliated with the Greater Philadelphia Women's Studies Consortium, University of Pittsburgh, Yale University, University of Delaware, Stanford University, University of California (Berkeley), Harvard University (Center for Middle Eastern Studies), Simon Fraser University, Dalhousie University, Wellesley College, and Williams College. I am deeply indebted and grateful to all the people involved, but as at present I cannot thank the first group by name, I opted for skipping all names, except that of Susan Stryker, whose critical feedback and skillful editing transformed a very raw essay into a more readable text.

AFSANEH NAJMABADI teaches history and women, gender, and sexuality studies at Harvard University. Her last book, *Women with Mustaches and Men without Beards: Gender and Sexual Anxieties of Iranian Modernity* (University of California Press, 2005), received the 2005 Joan Kelly Memorial Prize from the American Historical Association. She is currently working on the two-volume *Sex in Change: Configurations of Sexuality and Gender in Contemporary Iran (vol. 1: Transing and Transpassing: Trespassing Sex-Gender Walls in Iran; vol. 2: Genus of Sex: Configurations of Sexuality and Gender in Twentieth-Century Iran)*.

NOTES

1. These reports ran from February 4, 1999, to January 5, 2000. The same journal ran another series of autobiographical essays from November 22, 2003 to November 22, 2005. This body of writing constitutes the most extensive published transsexual narratives we have.

2. I say "presumed illegality of homosexuality" because what is a punishable offense is sexual acts between members of the same sex, with anal penetration of one man by another (*liwat*) [sodomy] being a capital offense. In international coverage, *liwat* is almost always translated as "homosexuality." The problem with this translation is that such reports find their way back into Persian, and in their Persian effects they converge with the medical and psychological discourses in which the dominant concepts are sexual orientation and typologies of desire, centered on the naturalness of heterosexuality. In that domain, instead of the legal-jurisprudential category of sodomy, it is homosexuality (rendered in Persian as *hamjisgara'i*, meaning "being inclined to a person of one's own sex") that is discussed as a sexual deviation along with a whole gamut of other deviations. While most theologically trained persons use *liwat*, more often than not, professionals (social workers, surgeons, and therapists) use *hamjisgara'i*. It is this slippage between the two concepts in different registers that are increasingly crossing paths—especially within various state institutions that deal with transsexuals-transgenders and with some individuals who do name themselves gay or lesbian—that makes me cautious about a simple usage of this term. I am concerned about keeping this distinction because in conversations in Iran it became quite clear that this is a productive distinction for many Iranian gays and lesbians, who find a degree of safety in insisting that homosexuality is not illegal, providing them with a sense of possibility of testing public spaces where some indication of their sexual desires (keeping it clear of what sex they do) may be a worthy risk. When I quote from English documentary sources, I have no way of knowing which term had been used in Persian, except in case of documentaries that have a Persian soundtrack.

3. More recently, the Welfare Organization reported that it received three new TS applications a day. Other reports estimate the total number of transsexuals in Iran at anywhere between three thousand to five thousand, and sometimes as high as twenty-five thousand. My use of "TS" in this article is occasioned by its usage as a self-identification category among Iranian transsexuals. It is used in Persian, pronounced "ti-es."

4. I realize that this is a controversial claim, since much of the current coverage of transsexuality in Iran claims otherwise. My conclusions in this essay are based on

fieldwork in Iran in 2006–7 that is impossible to present at any length within the scope of an essay. While transsexuals, gays, and lesbians whom I listened to over that period expressed many anxieties, fears, desires, and dreams, none were related to anything that was linked with fear of criminality. The issue of criminality is, of course, not trivial: criminality, and in particular capital punishment for sodomy, dynamizes many other legal restrictions and social fears.

5. Some very well known transsexuals include Christian Jorgensen, Elizabeth Call, Vince Jones, Juliet (formerly Julius, no last name given in report), Robert Allen, Edwin Emerton, Roberta Cowell, Rollando Cassioti, April Ashley (formerly George Jameson), Gino Malti, Jeanette Jiousselot, and Phoebe Simple.

6. Commentators favorable toward Iran often contrast that nation with other Muslim countries; the legality of certain medical technologies (not only SRS, but also a wide array of reproductive technologies) in the former and their illegality in some of the latter countries is narrated as if somehow linked with an ahistorical Shi'i-Sunni divide. This perpetuates such historically unsound arguments as the claim that the gate of *ijtihad* (issuing jurisprudential opinion) was closed in the Sunni world, thus making Shi'ism more open to change. While this argument may seem almost commonsensical (especially to many Shi'is), it misses the key issue of the historically specific relationship between jurisprudential and political authority that has characterized Iran since the early 1980s, which translates clerical opinion into the state's legal code.

7. I use the word "genus" for *jins* in this context to highlight the distinction between what today is commonly referred to as "sex" (*jins*) and the earlier connotations of the same term in classical Islamic writings on this topic—an issue further elaborated in Najmabadi 2008.

8. Despite my own earlier foreboding (Najmabadi 2005; see also my critical self-reflections on this piece in an H-Net discussion, Subject: Re: Reportage: Iran: Change Sex or Die, posted May 19, 2007, H-Histsex@H-Net.msu.edu), I know of no case in which a homosexual has been forced to change sex. Nor have I seen such evidence offered by commentators who claim punitive use of SRS for gays in Iran.

9. Some of my thinking here has been deeply influenced by conversations with Judith Surkis on her current research project, "Scandalous Subjects: Indecency and Public Order in France and French Algeria."

10. The entry into Persian and wide circulation of the words "gay" (pronounced as in English) and, less frequently, "lezbish" (lesbian butch) may indicate (contrary to the presumption of imitation of or imposition by the "gay international" on unsuspecting naive Iranians) in part an attempt to move away from the burden of the stigma that the term *kuni* (and, to a lesser extent, *baruni*, used for the "active" partner in a lesbian relationship) carries with it. In other words, to the extent that the adoption of the terms gay and lesbian into Persian nomenclature can be viewed as some sort of mimicry, it is a strategic move to shed the cultural stigma of *kuni* (and *baruni*). Other Englishisms serve similar cultural effects, as the wide use of "bi-ef" (BF) and "gi-ef" (GF) for "boyfriend" and "girlfriend." Whether these language moves work or fail is not determined because of the presumed shortcoming of "mimicry," or because of the cultural power of domination by a presumed "gay international" that is exporting

its identity categories in imperial fashion. Its potential source of trouble is the tight gender grid within which same-sex relationships in contemporary Iran are configured. This configuration is in turn an effect of the marriage imperative (see below) that shapes particular notions of masculine and feminine performance (within heterosexual relationships as well). Same-sex partners, however, are prone to "overperformance" because of dominant pressures and hazards of marginalized lives. In the context of South Asia, the adoption of such English words is sometimes seen as "a class-specific rejection of indigenous categories." See the thread "Homosexual/gay/queer" in June and July 2007 on H-Net Histsex. I am not convinced that such straightforward class delineations can be made.

11. The process includes a series of written tests for which translations of MMPI (Minnesota Multiphasic Personality Index) and SCL-90-R (Symptom Checklist-90-R) are used to make sure the TS is not suffering from other mental disorders and, if so, to be treated first for these problems to make sure the presumed line of causality runs from TS to other symptoms rather than the other way around. TSs prepare for these tests and coach each other for oral interviews, much as graduating high school students in Iran prepare for the national entrance exam to universities. Oral interviews cover questions about details of life stories, but there are also totally idio(syncra)tic questions and gestures, such as checking what kind of watch the person is wearing, if they have shaved legs, color preferences, how they squeeze a toothpaste tube (from bottom up or from the middle), and so on. When TSs were recounting these questions, their laugher expressed better than anything else the performativity of this procedure—something of which officials and others, including therapists I interviewed, are fully aware.

12. The legal and social scene is highly fluid as I write these lines. Some authorities try to tighten what they see as unfortunate loopholes; others in different ministries and state organizations have formed supportive working relations with TS activists and help them to neutralize or go around restrictions and get legal, medical, housing, and other material benefits. One of the challenges of my project, practically and analytically, is that more than twenty-nine years after the revolution, the Iranian state remains highly fractured, internally changing, and volatile. While a lot has been written on the fractured nature of the Iranian political system since the revolution of 1979, early in my research it became clear that thinking of the state even as a fractured mosaic of competing and at times conflicting mini pieces would not do; perhaps a better visual imaginary would be pieces that are continuously shifting *and* changing colors, *with no well-defined edges* of any sort. How such a structure does not burst at the mobile junctions of these shifting pieces, how it does its stately work, so to speak, is a question I put aside for now. This situation allows transsexuals (and other activists) to cultivate their own horizontal and vertical networks in and out of various governmental bodies that do not fit neat categorizations as "governmental" and "nongovernmental." While permitting a vast degree of creativity, it also makes their work highly susceptible to the ebbs and flows of rapid political changes that mark the country. Several trans-rights activists have emerged from the transsexual community over the past four or five years, and the current changes are above all their achievements.

Their efforts to challenge and change the medical, legal, and police abuses that transsexuals and gay men (and to a much lesser extent lesbians, for a complicated set of reasons) face are very impressive. They go to various government bodies almost daily and lobby for their rights and the benefits they expect the government to provide for them. There are often setbacks. The legal hoops that they are often made to go through are mind-boggling, and it is a testament to their fighting spirit and their sense of citizenship that they continue their work. One major issue is the understandable desire of many post-op transsexuals to become "invisible" and live "normal lives." This has meant a huge turnover of activists and the loss of continuity and organizational experience. The legal process, and the existence of some social welfare support for transsexuals, does not, of course, mean that transsexuals are not targets of threats, harassment, and arrest by police and paramilitary forces—but these attacks do not have a uniform pattern. There are highs and lows. In this, the transsexual community's situation is not different from those of others who cross various "red lines" in Iran. Whether the attacks on gays and transsexuals are more severe than they are on other groups, or on other moral or political grounds, I don't know. I don't know of any study that has actually brought together all the rape, adultery, and sexuality-charged trials and figured out if there is a pattern. I don't know of anyone who has systematically studied the attacks on workers and students rights activists, women's rights activists, journalists, and political dissidents, and those more ordinary daily attacks, such as arrests of women on charges of incorrect veiling and assaults on parties, as compared with arrests of gays and assaults on gay parties, to know if there is a difference.

13. Lesbians are largely absent from this scene. There seems to be a pattern in which female sexual and affective relationships and socializing networks take shape largely in spaces that are not publicly visible.

14. This was opposed by other MtFs and became a subject of much debate. The group subsequently had to stop its meetings because the magazine in whose office the they were held was closed down. The magazine itself had been charged with crossing "red lines" in its coverage of explicitly sexual topics in the language of psychology.

15. Altman 2001 as well as Massad 2007 and 2002 are perhaps the most polarized points of this debate. Publication of these writings has generated a much larger conversation, especially among scholars and activists concerned with issues of sexuality in non-Euro-American cultures. See, for example, Rofel 2007.

WORKS CITED

Abdo, Geneive. 2000. "Sex-Change Iranian Hates Life as Woman." *Guardian,* June 20, World News sec.

Altman, Dennis. 2001. *Global Sex*. Chicago: University of Chicago Press.

Dupret, B. 2001. "Sexual Morality at the Egyptian Bar: Female Circumcision, Sex Change Operations, and Motives for Suing." *Islamic Law and Society* 9(1):42–69.

Eqbali, Aresu. 2004. "Iran's Transsexuals Get Islamic Approval, But!" *Middle East Online*, September 30, http://www.middle-east-online.com/english/?id=11423.

Fathi, Nazila. 2004. "As Repression Eases, More Iranians Change their Sex." *New York Times,* August 2, World sec.
Ferrié, J. N. 1995. "Lieux intérieurs et culture publique au Maroc." *Politix* 31:187–202.
Harrison, Frances. 2005. "Iran's Sex-Change Operation." *BBC Newsnight,* January, http://news.bbc.co.uk/1/hi/programmes/newsnight/4115535.stm.
Ireland, Doug. 2007. "Change Sex or Die." http://direland.typepad.com/direland/2007/05/change_sex_or_d.html.
Khomeini, Ruhallah. 1967 [or 1968 (1387ah)]. *Tahrir al-wasila.* Najaf, Iraq: Matbaʻat al-Adab.
Massad, Joseph. 2002. "Re-Orienting Desire: The Gay International and the Arab World." *Public Culture* 14(2):361–85.
———. 2007. *Desiring Arabs.* Chicago: University of Chicago Press.
McDowall, Angus, and Stephen Khan. 2004. "The Ayatollah and the Transsexual." *Independent*, November 25, World sec.
Najmabadi, Afsaneh. 2005. "Truth of Sex." *Iranian.com,* January 12, http://www.iranian.com/Najmabadi/2005/January/Sex/index.html.
———. 2008. "Genus of Sex: Configurations of Sexuality and Gender in Twentieth-Century Iran."
Rofel, Lisa. 2007. *Desiring China: Experiments in Neoliberalism, Sexuality, and Public Culture.* Durham: Duke University Press.
Sanders, Paula. 1991. "Gendering the Ungendered Body: Hermaphrodites in Medieval Islamic Law." In *Women in Middle Eastern History: Shifting Boundaries in Sex and Gender*, ed. Beth Baron and Nikki Keddie. New Haven: Yale University Press.
Stack, Megan K. 2005. "Changing Their Sexes in Iran." *Los Angeles Times*, January 25.
Tait, Robert. 2005. "A Fatwa for Freedom." *Guardian*, July 27, World News sec.

BRANDED* LIVING

KATE SCHAPIRA

*The reek of burned hair and singed flesh, the squeals, the loosened bowels, the fellowship of suffering, something, together, what makes us members is the smell, the share, our share of suffering, the corral, the state of it.

Freak is printing an assembly of body parts that all fit together so nicely. All nest, finger muscles sheathing pads that lock squeegee and bone, a stretched tympanic membrane. The final color like a long wet whistle spatters over two Freakish hands. Layers over layers of dirty music, inefficient music, to Freak as birdsong, true sound of what surrounds them. All motions produce beauty and protest, motions practice what motions preach, the gender of the future's unsurprisingly hollow bones. The final layer will emulate the empty window but in the red of promise, not the red of demolition. What demolition leaves as its ghost, no chemical depression, approaches flight as music, as pinions.

KATE SCHAPIRA is the author of three chapbooks, *Phoenix Memory* (horse less press), *Case Fbdy.* (Rope-A-Dope Press), and *The Saint's Notebook* (CAB/NET Chapbook Series). She is proud of recent acceptances to/appearances in *Aufgabe, Practice, Ecopoetics, Word for/Word,* and *Denver Quarterly*. She lives, writes, teaches, and coordinates the Publicly Complex Reading Series in Providence, Rhode Island.

CUTTING IT OFF: BODILY INTEGRITY, IDENTITY DISORDERS, AND THE SOVEREIGN STAKES OF CORPOREAL DESIRE IN U.S. LAW

ELIZABETH LOEB

DESCARTES THE WANNABE: AMPUTATION AND LIBERAL PHILOSOPHY

In the *Discourse on Method and Meditations Concerning First Philosophy*, Descartes prefaces his much-famed *cogito* with a curious series of physical acts. Before announcing that he thinks, and therefore he is, Descartes first dismembers himself, asking what of his "I" would remain were he to amputate his ears, his arms, his eyes (Dayan 1995). Descartes concludes: "Although the whole mind seems to be united to the whole body, I recognize that if a foot or arm or any other part of the body is cut off, nothing has thereby been taken away from the mind" (Descartes 1986, 59). Even as Descartes degrades, discards, and dismisses physical experience in relation to human subjectivity, his "discovery" of a first principle of that humanity nonetheless depends on his traversement and modification of a corporeality that he calls his own. Invoking a prior "whole" body that properly belongs to or lies under the domain of his "I," Descartes arrives at his enlightenment through a fantasy of his ability to discorporate, take apart that supposed prior whole. His sovereignty of self follows from a sovereignty of corpus. Or, if a regime of sovereignty might bleed into a regime of property, his self becomes his own (Best 2004).

In considering the political and inherited stakes of what makes a body one's own or sovereign, of what makes a body count as whole, and of the privileges that counting as whole might bring, I am writing this essay squarely on the backs of many infinite others. I do so in the hope of building an intellectual practice that responds to the exploitative, violent connections between the juridical sovereignty of the U.S. state and the enforcement of corporeal "wholeness" or "integrity." For example, Nikki Sullivan and Susan Stryker have an important forthcoming article on this very subject. Focusing on self-demand amputation and transsexual surgery, Sullivan and Stryker trace the concept of bodily integrity through histories of the sovereign in order to show how urgently we have been missing a critique of "integrity" as an enabling fiction that works to legitimize all-too-material distributions of capital, property, and freedom in a contemporary sphere.

In the end, Descartes, stripped of his limbs and eyes and ears at his own volition, triumphantly proclaims that he has become what he has always truly been, "a thinking thing" (Descartes 1986). The "thinking" aspect aside, I am struck by the ease with which Descartes elides into reification, into a thing rather than subject "I" with which he began. For Descartes, the assertion and imagining of agency that allows him to become an individuated subject also allows him to throw it all away, to become not a subject but a thing. In this sense, his self-amputation, his musculation into thing-ness marks the apotheosis and exemplary state of his newly minted subjecthood.

How to read this moment, then, knowing full well that in the United States, the making of people-as-things was the juridical prerogative of hundreds of years of African chattel slavery, of laws that guaranteed that wives would function as the property of husbands and girls as the property of fathers (Best 2004; Farley 2004; Johnson 2003; Pateman 1988)? It seems easy to say that the problem here might be a notion of liberal consent, or agency—that what matters is whether "you" or "I" make me into a thing (Johnson 2003). Rather than attempt to scale the philosophical peak of Mount Agency directly, however, in this essay I will attempt to make a series of small cuts and observations into the sexed and gendered politics of bodily integrity in contemporary U.S. law. In doing so, I am leaving aside much work on the particularly raced character of U.S. state sovereignty, and on how the connections between bodily integrity and U.S. state sovereignty continue to organize around white supremacy. Here I am mindful of Timothy Mitchell's writing on the process by which writers fetishize, reify, and unify state effects and processes through the repetition of "the state" as a literary and substantive conceit. Urging scholars to replace "the state" with the more dynamic "state-effects," Mitchell's poststructural analysis serves as an effective reminder that "the body" should also not be taken for granted as a static or reified set of closed boundaries, but as a contested and shifting landscape within physical and psychic experience (Mitchell 1999).

FOR EXAMPLE: THE UNBEARABLE QUEERNESS OF CUTTING

Feminist scholarship, disability studies, queer theory, critical race theory, and so many other areas of research have shown that U.S. law regulates bodily practice in a raced and sexed fashion and that the "whole" of which Aquinas and Descartes write arrives as neither a prior nor an uncontested state of being (Hyde 1997; Cheah, Fraser, and Grbich 1996; Bornstein 1995). For example, in the contemporary United States, I may legally consent to participate in a boxing match, despite the certainty of grievous physical harm, without any risk that my opponent could be prosecuted successfully for assault (Hanna 2001). Yet my consent will not serve as an effective defense in the criminal prosecution of my sexual partner for assault should I ask him or her to whip me (Pa 2001). Getting into a boxing ring makes me more of a man, makes my body more whole even as it's beaten. Asking to be whipped makes me a queer, less of a proper subject, a violated deviant in need of help.

Not surprisingly, scholars have repeatedly shown that (1) some practices are regulated differently from others and (2) some categories of persons are regulated differently with regard to their practices (Spade 2003). Not surprisingly, by "some" categories and practices, I mean to say that legal regulations of corporeal practices in the United States organize around axes of race, class, and sex and that these practices work to reproduce white supremacy, patriarchy, and capitalist exploitation, even when doing so means regulating corporeal practice in uneven, arbitrary, and incoherent ways that are often unsupported by the logic of liberal, rationalized legitimacy (Minow 1987; Hartman 1997; Butler 2004).

My birth certificate states that I am "female." As researchers such as Anne Fausto-Sterling have shown, human infants are born with a wide array of genitals, chromosomes, and sexual characteristics. Although the majority of infants conform, within a certain range, to the set of traits known as "male" and "female," many do not, and even those that do exhibit a broad spectrum of variety and difference (Madeira 2002; Fausto-Sterling 2000; Kessler 1990). As such, the medical and legal assignation of sex according only to the binary options of "male" and "female" constitutes something of an accident for each of us, an assignation of status that belies and homogenizes our unique physicalities into enforced norms.

These norms shape our social lives and determine our legal identities. They also help to create the very sexed bodies that they purport to describe. For example, along with a sexual status, I also currently enjoy the civilian status of one who is neither incarcerated nor enlisted in the U.S. military. As a result, given access to a sufficient amount of money, I may walk into the office of any licensed surgeon and pay to have my mammary tissue cut, excavated, and filled with saline for no reason other than my own desire to have it be so (Bridy 2004; Spade 2003). To legally obtain the exact same surgery should my birth certificate happen to read "male," I would have to receive a psychiatric diagnosis of "gender identity disorder" and would have to follow a strict, externally mandated regime of hormones and behavior for a lengthy amount of time before being "prescribed" a surgical remedy by a psychiatrist (Bridy 2004; Spade 2003).

Were I not to follow this protocol, both my doctor and I could be prosecuted or held liable under an avalanche of state and federal charges, including assault, attempted murder, malingering, conspiracy to commit mayhem, and the unauthorized practice of medicine. Courts would hold us as liable under these laws no matter how clear or informed my consent had been (Furlong 2003; Furth and Smith 2002; Pa 2001; Harrison 1993; Rubin 1975).

As TV shows such as *Extreme Makeover* have repeatedly shown, plenty of folks are telling stories about uncovering a "true self" by undergoing as many invasive surgeries as they so choose without a trace of juridical approbation or punishment (Kuczynki 2004; Warren 1999). The catch is that such legal and cultural permission holds steady only so long as my choices map onto the landscape of normative and normativizing physical norms of race, sex, and gender (Gilman 1999; Matsunaga 1985). Taking out a rib so that I can model for a Gucci show? Yes! Cutting off my penis to more fully express my felt gender? No!

Such contradictions might or might not be familiar to my readers, but I am rehearsing them here because for the past few years I've been talking with a group of folks, many of whom self-identity as "Wannabes," who desperately want to amputate limbs categorized as otherwise healthy ones by the medical establishment (J. 2006; *Whole* 2003; Elliot 2003, 2000). Many Wannabes talk about being "born in the wrong body" and about the desire for a limbic amputation as an irrefutable fact of their life, as the expression of their "true self." Many Wannabes who obtain an amputation describe intense and long-lasting feelings of contentment and elation (Smith 2007; Furth and Smith 2002).

As an increasingly visible community, self-identified Wannabes often draw explicit parallels to transsexual experience (Smith 2007; Elliot 2003; Furth and Smith 2002; Elliot 2000). In my reading, research, and interviews, I've found that Wannabes compare themselves to people of transsexual experience most often as a way of making a rights claim or of claiming an essentialized validity. That is, I've often been told that "if they can cut off their penis, then I have the right to cut off my arm," and "I was just born into the wrong body" (Amputee Wannabe Info 2000).

In an attempt to obtain legal surgeries, many Wannabes refer to the concept of "gender identity disorder" as a positive model, arguing that they should be given the increasingly popular diagnosis of "body identity integrity disorder," or "BIID," and that amputative surgery should be prescribed by licensed doctors as a cure for that disorder (Society for Body Integrity Identity Disorder 2007). Absent such availability, many people have obtained "off-market" amputations or have gone outside the United States (*People v. Brown* 2001; Furth and Smith 2002). Others have attempted to self-amputate, or have purposefully injured themselves in ways that might cause a physician to perform a medically recognized amputation (Smith 2007; Elliot 2003; *Whole* 2003).

Why do Wannabes and their doctors face criminal and civil prosecution as a result of a consensual surgery when performed in compliance with established safety guidelines for elective and aesthetic surgery? Why do U.S. courts describe Wannabes as simply suffering disturbance in the usual course of identity formation while simultaneously punishing their attempts at amputation as an assault on the sovereign (*People v. Brown*, 2001)? So many bodies are everyday resorting to painful, dangerous, and sometimes fatal methods of corporeal modification because the legal practices of the United States, and doctors who submit to the authority of those practices, refuse to provide professional assistance for people whose bodily desires appear unauthorized or abnormal (*Whole* 2003; Smith 2007; Wilchins 1997). How might this be changed? What historical knowledge of law must be excavated to persuade the dominant order to adjudicate otherwise?

FROM TREASON TO DISORDER: THE SOVEREIGN POLITICS OF CORPOREAL IDENTITY

According to the theoretical-historical mappings of Foucault, Agamben, and Derrida, among many others, bodies have long been marshaled to the call of a political sovereign. Whether it be through "the power over life and death" (Foucault 2007; Agamben 1995), or through the placement of a death row prisoner on suicide watch, whether it be through military conscription, incarceration, institutionalized chattel slavery, forced institutionalization, or designation as an enemy combatant, political sovereignty has functioned in U.S. law as justification for forcibly injuring bodies and, simultaneously, for physically preventing those same subjects from themselves engaging in corporeal modification (Foucault 2007).

The demand that bodies remain available to discorporation *solely* at the prerogative of the sovereign has deep roots in Anglo law (Foucault 1975; Scarry 1985). Elaine Scarry has argued that political theorists such as Locke, Rousseau, and Mill developed visions of radical resistance in direct response to this sovereign prerogative over the body. According to Scarry, Locke and company imagined that the hold of the sovereign over the body must be dissolved to effect political transformation and potentially, a state of liberation for subjects. Scarry describes all three theorists as attempting the same radical move—the redistribution of sovereignty from the body politic of the king and into the body corpus of every individual subject (Scarry 1990). Under the law of sovereignty in England, the mutilation of one's self or another, regardless of circumstance or consent, constituted a crime against the person of the king, and later a crime of treason against the national sovereign, insofar as the mutilation or corporeal modification diminished the subject's fitness for and availability for military service or labor (Clark 1995; Mendelson 1996).

Since the inception of the United States, court cases and statues have established that under the power of the sovereign, persons taken into incarceration or enrolled in military service function as "government property" and that the unauthorized self-modification (or consensual but unauthorized assisted modification) of their bodies constitutes a property crime (Halley 1999; Olguin 1997). Slaves who self-mutilated or malingered (often in a attempt to evade the more severe violence of their forced labor, or the overseer, or a sale), and slaves who tattooed or pierced were forced to pay for the "cost" of such acts as a diminution in value of the master's property (Rose 1970). Slaves were made liable for the financial loss to the master that the modification in their body supposedly incurred (*State v. Hale* 1823; *George v. State* 1859; Rose 1970).

In the contemporary United States, the large number of prison inmates who engage in elective amputation or self-mutilation as a strategy for resisting, or at least interrupting, the forced extraction of labor from their bodies within prison are also criminally prosecuted for their actions. Similarly, tattoos, piercings, and other forms of body art are prohibited in U.S. prisons under the same laws (Olguin 1997). In the military, the many soldiers who self-amputate or engage in what would otherwise be construed as self-mutilation in order to end their duty are charged with treason and with the crime of destroying government property (Useem 1973; Commerce Clearing House 1940; Serlin 2003; Fletcher 2007).

While slavery, the military, and prisons offer clear institutional lines along which bodies are submitted to the totality of a political sovereign, explicit submission does not mark the only way in which corporeal practice intertwines with legal concepts of sovereignty and state power. In the early modern and Victorian periods, there were large numbers of documented self-amputations and maimings by the poor in England. These amputators were in most cases attempting to do one of two things: to escape the forced labor extractions of the prison or the poorhouse in which they'd been put for the crime of vagrancy, or to capitalize on the rise of sentimental interiority that lead more well-off citizens to offer far greater sums to the street beggar with only one foot as opposed to the beggar whom the donor regarded as "able bodied" and thus able to "work for one's self" (Mendelson 1996). In both instances, the courts punished these elective amputations under the "law of maims" or the crime of mayhem—a crime that exists as good and active law in all fifty of the United States today (Mendelson 1996; Champlin and Winslow 1965; Corpus Juris 2006; Dietz et al. 2006).

During the mid-nineteenth-century, courts in the United States became increasingly vocal on the entitlement of white men to the "right of bodily integrity" (Clark 1995). Articulated in contemporary doctrine as a right against invasion by the state or medical regime into one's "own" body (Dietz et al. 2006; *Roe v. Wade* 1973; *Washington v. Glucksberg* 1997; Clark 1995), my readings of "bodily integrity" find fantasizing a fully agentive, masculated, triumphant subject that acts out onto the world, inviolable and unviolated by feminized or queered forms of penetration (*Canterbury v. Spence* 1972; *Schloendorff v. Society of New York Hospital* 1914; McRuer 2002).

Although sovereignty and rights of integrity offer two possible models for understandings for why and how U.S. law regulates consensual corporeal practice, and for why and how "mutilation," "injury," and "wholeness" figure so prominently in legal discourses of consensual corporeal practice, I am increasingly drawn by a third model. Beginning in the early 1950s with the arrival of Freud, Valium, and postwar trauma in U.S. fashion (Yates 1961; Evans and Koelsch 1985), courts began to understand corporeal practices as evidence of deviance or psychological disorder (*Bowers v. Hardwick* 1986; *Williams v. Attorney General of Alabama* 2004; *Holmes v. Mississippi Shipping Company* 1962; *U.S. v. 491* 1966; *Ramos v. Lamb* 1980). At the same time, psychiatrists and doctors began mapping an assortment of perversions and identity disorders. By the 1990s, practices of self-modification previously described as "mutilation," "treason," "property damage," "unnatural acts," or "dieting" (Roman 2006) were firmly established within law, medicine, and psychiatry as evidence of "gender identity disorder" or "body dysmorphic disorder" or "body integrity identity disorder" (American Psychological Association 1994; Spade 2003).

While courts continue to embrace the "long cherished right of bodily integrity" for straight, white, male-designated property owners (*Vacco v. Quill* 1997), subjects within contemporary jurisprudence who resist gender/sex-normative or work-normative "able bodied" corporeality are granted no such right—their desires are marked by the contemporary convergence of psychiatry, medicine, and law as "identity disorders"—as the sickness and deviance of a partial subject who has not yet earned the corporeal rights of the properly "integrated" bodily subject (*People v. Brown* 2001).

These notions of "identity disorder" legally arbitrate which categories of person are and aren't allowed to engage in technologically similar acts. As I have already once rehearsed in the opening of this essay, some of us can go to a surgeon and have our breasts technologically removed without legal or medical approval, and some of us can't. If I have "male" on my birth certificate and am troubled by fatty tissue atop my pectorals, not only will a licensed professional gladly perform the procedure without legal concern or additional medical cause, but in many instances, my health insurance will foot the bill (Spade 2003). If, however, my birth certificate states "female," I must be diagnosed by a licensed psychiatrist with gender identity disorder and spend two years proving that I "really have" this condition in order to obtain the exact same surgery, and even then, no insurance provider will cover the costs (Spade 2003). Should a doctor or friend perform the procedure without the diagnosis, that person is criminally liable for assault under the state's police power, regardless of my consent (*People v. Brown* 2001). Should I try to do it myself, I am legally subject to forced institutionalization for a mental disorder, and most states retain the right to transfer my children to foster care while I "recover" (Whole 2003).

If I am in prison or the military, even if I have legally obtained surgery or hormone treatments through a "GID" diagnosis, the U.S. state, through the exercise of its sovereign power over my body as its property, has full discretion over whether I can continue to take the hormones or complete the surgical procedure (*Phillips v. Michigan Dept. of Corrections* 1990; *Smith v. Rasmussem* 1999).

These discrepancies have further implications for persons designated intersex at birth. Bodies that do not conform at birth to the medical invention of binary sex are vulnerable to nonconsensual invasion by medical practitioners—an invasion that often causes medically unnecessary, long-term physical and psychic harm (Fausto-Sterling 2000; Greenberg 1999). Under current state and federal laws, my legal parent cannot consent to the performance of a nonmedically necessary rhinoplasty on my infant nose, but she can consent to the removal of my infant clitoris for purely cosmetic purposes should the doctor deem the clitoris so large as to constitute "ambiguous genitalia" (Hanisco 2000; Greenberg 1999).

Finally, the explicitly and simultaneously raced and sexed project of the incoherence I am attempting to chart can be seen in the U.S. statute prohibiting and criminalizing the practice of what the statute terms "female genital alteration" or "female genital mutilation" (18 U.S.C. § 116; Maguigan 1995). The inconsistency that irks me here is the one drawn by U.S. law between the practices named under the "female genital mutilation" statute, and the common practice of nonconsensual infant male circumcision. Male circumcision is a practice associated with Caucasian religious cultures (Povenmire 1999). The practices of "female genital mutilation" so named in the statute are explicitly conceived by legislators and courts as practices associated with varied Muslim and African cultures (18 U.S.C. § 116; Maguigan 1995). U.S. law goes to great lengths to ensure the open availability of nonconsensual circumcision for male-designated infants. At the same time, the federal "female genital mutilation" statute prohibits any form of female genital alteration for female-designated bodies under the age of eighteen, *even in an instance of full consent* (18 U.S.C. § 116; Davis 2001). Of course, given that patriarchy continues to dominate the context in which decisions about genital alteration are made, "full consent" invokes and erects its own troubling fantasy, one that threatens to deny the pervasive coercion at play in these situations.

The statute has an explicit, textual exception, however, for surgeries "necessary to the health of the person on whom it is performed" (18 U.S.C. § 116). While this exception allows for the genital mutilation of intersex infants by doctors who find it medically necessary to make the infants' genitals look "normally" and hence "healthily" sexed despite the loss of sexual function and the medical risks that comes from such surgery (Greenberg 1999), the statute clearly states that in applying the health exception, "no account shall be taken of the effect on the person on whom the operation is to be performed or any belief on the part of that person, or any other person, that the operation is required as a matter of custom or ritual" (18 U.S.C. § 116).

Courts have categorized 18 U.S.C. § 116 as an act of sovereign foreign policy because of its impact on refugee law (Hanisco 2000). By erasing the possibility or material import of any "outside" consent or belief, this sovereign statute erases persons seen by the court as brown or black girls from legal subjectivity and from the autonomous consent that liberal traditions place at the foundation of personhood (Best 2004). The structural impossibility of their consent to a bodily practice constitutes the visibility of their social and legal subjecthood (Butler 1997; Brown 1995).

Returning to identity disorders and Wannabes, despite my dainty sense of liberal umbrage at the arbitrary cuts that law makes into our bodies, most Wannabes would gladly go through a process of psychiatric diagnosis and monitoring in a manner like that faced by people of transsexual experience if their doctors would in the end " prescribe" a safe, surgical amputation as the treatment for the "disorder," even if, like many people of transsexual experience, Wannabes do not understand themselves as suffering from psychic or medical problem. The problem, rather, lies in the legal obstacles between them and safe surgical amputations (Furth and Smith 2002).

MY BODY, MY SELF: NEOLIBERALISM, RESPONSIBILIZATION, AND STRUCTURAL POWER

So far in this essay I have studiously avoided what has now become an unavoidable question. Is my concrete goal a redistribution of rights? Am

I simply working for a more expansive neo/liberal juridical regime, one in which the structures remain but queered and raced bodies are recognized as having rights and agency and integrity so as to allow those bodies the sorts of practices already allowed more normative subjects? Perhaps. My goals are practical and this essay is short. Because I feel that I cannot possibly answer the question of the Master's Tools with any justice here, I will impermissibly bracket the question, opting instead for an exploration of the logic that, in part, frames the choice itself.

Jean and John Comaroff offer something of a map for this in their beautiful essay, *Millennial Capitalism and the Culture of Neoliberalism*. Explaining how the contemporary formation of neoliberalism goes through and beyond that maxim of "personal as political," the Comaroffs write:

> As neoliberal conditions render ever more obscure the rooting of inequality in structures of production, as work gives way to the mechanical solidarities of "identity" in constructing selfhood and social being…politics is treated as a matter of individual or group entitlement…social wrongs are transposed into an issue of "rights"…diffuse concerns about cultural integrity and communal survival are vested in "private" anxieties about sexuality, procreation, or family values. (Comaroff and Comaroff 2000, 306)

To address this observation, I must first note that the legal regulation of consensual corporeal practice rarely poses a problem for the wealthy. If equipped with sufficient funds and resources, almost anyone can find a safe, trained professional surgeon outside U.S. borders who is able and willing to legally assist with any desired form of corporeal modification. Should state services attempt to place your children in foster care as punishment for your "deviant" consensual practices (such as BDSM or unusual body modifications), sufficient funds and resources will allow you to leave U.S. jurisdiction (though the legal consequences of such a move depends on the particular state and form of investigation) or to hire the attorneys and expert witnesses that are often the only method of successfully combating a understaffed and underfunded family services office. In a similar way, the paucity of doctors able to take on the insurance costs or social costs of performing abortions in many states most intensely affects pregnant persons, most of whom identify as women, without the resources to travel across state lines or seek out private doctors in other areas who are not within their insurance plan (Roberts 1998).

Why then, the persistence of legal regulation? Why don't these oh-so-very-neoliberal United States leave bodily practices entirely to the whims of the market? The Comaroffs commit themselves to the premise that institutions assign and enforce raced and sexed deviance to protect capitalist distributions of power and wealth (especially insofar as capitalism might be described as global socialism for the wealthiest 5 percent) (Roediger 1999; Harris 1993; Balbus 1982). In *The Twilight of Equality?* Lisa Duggan defines neoliberalism as a complex cultural and economic system with a foundational characteristic of upward redistribution of resources matched to a social/political/legal strategy of nonredistributive "equality." Duggan shows that in order to maintain this upward distribution in the United States, large numbers of people have to act and vote against their own economic interests. How to guarantee such an occurrence? By cultivating a fear of blacks and browns and queers, and by then justifying economically disadvantageous policies as a necessary measure in the fight against these deviant subjects. As Alisa Solomon of the *Village Voice* once wrote, "When there's scant support for your campaign to downsize public institutions, seek out the sex—especially when it's female or gay" (qtd. in Duggan 2003, 31).

We cannot separate our lived ideas of what constitutes a "whole" body or a "normal" man from our lived experience of patriarchy, white supremacy, violent colonialism, and capitalist exploitation. This is not to say that we're all wandering around duped into false consciousness, and it is not meant to question certain desires as a pathology of oppression. Rather, even as I honor and advocate for a promiscuous access to bodily practice and desire, I am also glossing desires, and the judgments they elicit, as irreducibly political formations (Munoz 1999).

As to what the politics of those formations might be, I offer the following: (1) the prominence of "identity disorders" serves to bolster a neoliberal distribution of power and resources, and (2) the frame "identity disorders" individualizes fault, shaping subjects and consciousness in ways that defines the problem as your desire, rather than the structure of oppression in which your desire finds only punishment or frustration. The prominence of identity and disorder as frames for understanding resistive behavior can also be found in cases of criminalized self-mutilation in institutional settings of clear state sovereignty such as the military

(*Danese v. Asman* 1987; *High Tech Gays v. Defense Industrial Security Clearance Officer* 1990).

The political use of individuated fault comes from a formidable literature that maps the concepts, histories, and processes of "responsibilization" (Foucault 2007). As scholars such as Nikolas Rose and Mariana Valverde have shown, this process of responsibilization mobilizes the deviant construction of desire as a technology through which dominant actors, consolidations, and networks obscure and thus reproduce the structural workings of power and resources distribution as legitimate despite the widespread oppressions at play (O'Malley 1998, Valverde 2003; Rose 1989). To use a prominent example from the field of disability studies, the issue isn't who's abled and disabled, it's that all bodies are in some way less than perfectly able, and the problem is that we live in a built environment that privileges and accommodates certain bodies over others (McRuer 2002).

CONCLUSION: INALIENABLE DESIRES

In conclusion, I have written this essay not as a complete gesture, but as a beginning, a first installment for further writing and research. In future work, I hope to take these first musings on sovereignty and bring them toward a deeper consideration of "inalienability" as a concept in U.S. law (Best 2004). In its classical, eighteenth-century form, does then inalienability of rights against the sovereign assert that the subject's juridical right to consensual corporeal practice should not be a contingent one? If we live in a juridical world that works through a language of rights, then am I attempting to argue back to that language by animating an already respected legal tradition in which rights to bodily practice cannot be brokered or exchanged through a filter of cultural approval or social policy?

In a world where discourses of poststructuralism may be gorgeous and convincing to some but illegible in a court of law, I wonder whether we might argue to judicial decision makers that the constitutionally recognized right to bodily integrity cannot be limited by the diagnosis of the court, or by the will of the political sovereign. It would not be enough for me to play at Cassandra or Portia, pointing toward law only to say, "Hey, that's not fair." How, as a trained lawyer, might I create legal practices that respect the desires and experience of Wannabes, and of all of us who experience bodies outside gendered and sexed normativization? Perhaps, in this way, what I'm really writing about is abortion.

Following *Planned Parenthood v. Casey* (1992) and *Gonzales v. Carhart* (2007), the right to legally obtain an abortion procedure, and hence the female-designated "right to bodily integrity" trumpeted in *Roe v. Wade* (1973), does not stand as an actual right. Rather, *Casey* and *Carhart* frame abortion and the rights of female-designated body as a negotiable permission of the state, as a balance of interests, subject entirely to the court's medical and cultural determinations.[1] At the same time, in the ruling in *Carhart*, the Supreme Court case that upheld state bans on medical practices known as "partial birth abortions," the justices obsess over the details of fetal dismemberment, writing for pages about arms and legs and skulls that may or may not become detached from the fetuses in the process of extraction. According to the Court, should a fetus be extracted whole, it is an abomination, an act that takes the form and shape of murder. Yet should the fetus be extracted in parts, it is a monstrosity, an unbearable mutilation of what should have been. Curiously, these physical details have little to do with the juridical reasoning of the Court's decision, which as mentioned above, rests on both the state's sovereign ability to determine what constitutes an "undue burden" on a constitutional right, and on the state's "regulatory interest" in fetal life (*Gonzales v. Carhart* 2007). Nonetheless, the justices continually justify their decision not in legal terms, but in physical ones, asserting again and again their ability to determine the terms of corporeal life.

In her article "Dismembered Selves and Wandering Wombs," Drucilla Cornell (2002) takes on the juridical and theoretical landscape of abortion and the right of bodily integrity. Writing as a deeply committed feminist within the language of poststructuralist analysis, Cornell argues that reproductive capacity marks "women" as violable, and thus as less than persons under the law. That is, the supplement to the female-designated body that is an actual or potential fetus makes that body always and inherently less than whole, less than fully integrated, and thus less than able to articulate rights of corporeal agency within law.

While recognizing and tracing the theoretical complexity of these relationships, Cornell nonetheless concludes that "women" must have the option of becoming legible as whole, coherent, individuated, and integrated juridical bodies in order to become full and equal juridical persons. Although she understands this mode of personhood as a projection, a fantasy, and a cipher, she also understands that it is a status made material by the force of law, the imagination of which manifests as all too actual, and thus, she does aspire to a place within law for women to have full rights of bodily integrity, concluding that such a place would also mean the arrival of women into the supposed fullness of juridical personhood in the classic liberal mode.

I think that Cornell does feminism a great service by recognizing both the theoretical complexity and the material exigency at play in abortion law. And yet what of the structure of power whereby courts and lawmakers have the right to negotiate the terms of our physical acts, to weigh their interests and meanings against our own—most articulations of self and desire? Even if one could articulate female-designated bodies as deserving the full rights of bodily integrity under the law, such rights are not themselves inviolable—they remain subject to alienation, to trade, and to barter. Moreover, even should some bodies, or certain classes of bodies, win the integrity lottery in new ways, courts retain the power to determine which bodies count, which bodies are properly so. The distribution of disenfranchisement may shift, but the structure of power remains, and we are all of us vulnerable to its whims.

In this article, I have tried to unsettle the primacy of integrity as a model by which bodies are judged. As a legal strategy, however, we may need more than such an unsettling. Even were we to replace the construction of integrity with some other mode of imagining, what we may really need is the right to tell the court what our bodies mean to us, rather than the other way round. My suggestion is that U.S. legal practice must be forced to recognize the probative value of subjective experience. Courts must be made to respect a sovereignty of meaning, and we must find ways to do this with and alongside strategies such as Cornell's, which have a greater chance of resulting in much-needed wins, however incomplete or short term (Scott 1992; Deloria 1969).

Litigation and legislation are indeed tools of the master. I nonetheless believe that they are also practices through which we might forge spaces of legal access to the bodies we desire by asserting that our rights are not up for exchange, that this is not a give and take, that radically our bodies are our own. I know that this essay lays grand plans without actually showing how they might be done, but I do hope that in its own small way, my research might make the articulation of such demands a bit more possible.

ACKNOWLEDGMENTS

Many thanks to Susan Stryker, whose comments and encouragement were invaluable. Thank you as well to Lexi Adams, Paulette Caldwell, Lisa Duggan, Peter Fitzpatrick, Katherine Franke, Christine Harrington, Sally Merry, Walter Johnson, Crystal Parikh, Paul Passavant, and Avital Ronnel, all of whom generously offered their time and advice in bringing this work into fruition. Thank you to Paisley Currah, whose editorial suggestions and kindness as a colleague made the publication process a joy. This work is truly based on the gifts of many friends and communities, and I am so very lucky to be writing in such circumstances.

ELIZABETH LOEB is an attorney, activist, and PhD candidate. She has worked with Housing Works, the Center for Constitutional Rights, and various community-based LGBTQ organizations in New York City. Elizabeth is currently completing her dissertation in the Law and Society Program at New York University. In the fall of 2009, she will join the American Civil Liberties Union as a litigation fellow with the Drug Law Reform Project.

NOTE

1. At the time of *Casey* (*Planned Parenthood v. Casey* 1992) and *Carhart* (*Gonzales v. Carhart* 2007), jurists had not considered that persons of trans experience who are legally or medically or socially male might also become pregnant by way of the ostensibly "female" reproductive organs with which they were born. In fact, all abortion and pregnancy decisions thus far in the courts assume that all pregnant persons are clearly female by medical, legal, and social standards. Despite the fact that this assumption may be inaccurate, the force and repetition of it makes the question of abortion in some sense an unavoidable referendum on the legal status of the female-designated body.

WORKS CITED

Agamben, Georgio. 1995. *Homo Sacer: Sovereign Power and Bare Life*. Trans. D. Heller-Roazen. Stanford: Stanford University Press.
American Psychological Association. 1994. *Diagnostic and Statistical Manual*. 4th ed. New York: American Psychiatric.
Amputee Wannabe Info. 2000. http://www.geocities.com/starstranger_2000/.
Balbus, Isaac D. 1982. *Marxism and Domination*. Princeton: Princeton.
Best, Stephen M. 2004. *The Fugitive's Properties: Law and the Poetics of Possession*. University of Chicago Press.
Bornstein, Kate. 1995. *Gender Outlaw: On Men, Women, and the Rest of Us*. New York: Vintage Books.

Bowers v. Hardwick. 1986. 478 U.S. 186 (1986).
Bridy, Annemarie. 2004. "Confounding Extremities: Surgery at the Ethical Limits of Self Modification." *Journal of Law, Medicine and Ethics* 32:148.
Brown, Wendy. 1995. *States of Injury: Power and Freedom in Late Modernity.* Princeton: Princeton University Press.
Butler, Judith. 1997. *The Psychic Life of Power.* New York: Routledge.
———. 2004. *Precarious Life: the Powers of Mourning and Violence.* New York: Routledge.
Canterbury v. Spence. 1972. 464 F.2d 772 (1972).
Champlin, Linda K. and Mark E. Winslow. 1965. "Elective Sterilization." *University of Pennsylvania Law Review* 113:415.
Cheah, Pheng, David Fraser, and Judith Grbich. 1996. *Thinking the Body Through Law.* New York: New York University Press.
Clark, Elizabeth B. 1995. "The Sacred Rights of the Weak: Pain, Sympathy, and the Culture of Individual Rights in Antebellum America." *Journal of American History* 82(2):463.
Comaroff, Jean, and John L. Comaroff. 2000. "Millennial Capitalism: First Thoughts on a Second Coming." *Public Culture* 12(2):291–325.
Commerce Clearing House. 1940. *Conscription, Law, and Regulation.* Chicago: Commerce Clearinghouse.
Cornell, Drucilla. 2002. "Dismembered Selves and Wandering Wombs." In *Left Legalism, Left Critique,* ed. W. Brown and J. Halley. Durham: Duke University Press.
Corpus Juris Secundum. 2006. S.v. "Mayhem," 56:2.
Danese v. Asman. 1987. 670 F.Supp. 729 (E.D. Michigan 1987).
Davis, Dena S. 2001. "Male and Female Genital Alteration: A Collision Course with the Law?" *Health Matrix* 11:487.
Dayan, Joan. 1995. "Codes of Law and Bodies of Color." *New Literary History* 26(2):283–308.
Deloria, Vine, Jr., 1969. *Custer Died for Your Sins: An Indian Manifesto.* Norman: University of Oklahoma Press.
Descartes, René. 1986. "Second Meditation." In *Meditations on First Philosophy.* Trans. J. Cottingham. Cambridge: Cambridge University Press.
Dietz, Lauren, Alan Jacobs, Lucas Martin, Anne Payne, JDs, et al. 2006. *American Jurisprudence,* 2nd ed., s.v. "Death," 22a:443.
Duggan, Lisa. 2003. *The Twilight of Equality: Neoliberalism, Cultural Politics, and the Attack on Democracy.* Boston: Beacon Press.
Elliot, Carl. 2000. "A New Way to Be Mad." *Atlantic Monthly.* (December). www.theatlantic.com/issues/2000/12/in dex.htm.
———. 2003. "Costing an Arm and A Leg," *Slate Online Magazine.* www.slate.com/id/2085402/.
Evans, R. S., and W. A. Koelsch. 1985. "Psychoanalysis Arrives in America: The 1909 Psychology Conference at Clark University." *American Psychologist* 40:942–48.

Farley, Anthony Paul. 2004. "Perfecting Slavery." *Loyola Law Journal* 36:225.
Fausto-Sterling, Anne. 2000. *Sexing the Body: Gender Politics and the Construction of Sexuality*. New York: Basic Books.
Fletcher, Roger 2007. Interview by the author.
Foucault, Michel. 1975. *Discipline and Punish and The Birth of The Prison*. Trans. A. Sheridan. New York: Vintage.
———. 2007. *Society Must Be Defended*. Trans. G. Burchell. New York: Picador Press.
Furlong, Ray. 2003. "Frenzy Builds For German 'Cannibal' Trial." BBC News, World ed. December 2, 2003. news.bbc.co.uk/2/hi/europe/3258226.stm.
Furth, Gregg M., and Robert Smith. 2002. *Amputee Identity Disorder: Information, Questions, Answers, and Recommendations About Self-Demand Amputation*. New York: First Books.
George v. State. 1859. 37 Miss. 316 (1859).
Gilman, Sander L. 1999. *Making the Body Beautiful: A Cultural History of Aesthetic Surgery*. Princeton: Princeton University Press.
Gonzales v. Carhart. 2007. 530 U.S. 914 (2007).
Greenberg, Julie. 1999. "Defining Male and Female: Intersexuality and the Collision Between Law and Biology." *Arizona Law Review* 41:265.
Halley, Janet E. 1999. *Don't: A Reader's Guide to the Military's Anti-gay Policy*. Durham: Duke University Press.
Hanisco, Christina M. 2000. "Acknowledging the Hypocrisy: Granting Minors the Right to Choose Their Medical Treatment." *New York Law School Journal of Human Rights* 16:899.
Hanna, Cheryl. 2001. "Sex Is Not a Sport: Consent and Violence in Criminal Law." *Boston College Law Review* 42:239.
Harris, Cheryl I. 1993. "Whiteness as Property." *Harvard Law Review* 106:1709.
Harrison, Keith M. 1993. "Law, Order, and the Consent Defense." *St. Louis University Public Law Review* 12:477–503.
Hartman, Saidiya. 1997. *Scenes of Subjection: Terror, Slavery, and Self-Making in Nineteenth Century America*. Oxford: Oxford University Press.
High Tech Gays v. Defense Industrial Security Clearance Officer. 1990. 895 U.S. 563 (9th Cir. 1990).
Holmes v. Mississippi Shipping Company. 1962. 301 F.2d 474 (5th Cir. 1962).
Hyde, Alan. 1997. *Bodies of Law*. Princeton: Princeton University Press.
J. 2006. "Denise Anne: An Interview With the Ultimate Wannabe." Overground. http://www.overground.be/article.php?code=36andlan=en.
Johnson, Walter. 2003. "On Agency." *Journal of Social History* 37(1):113–24.
Kessler, S. J. 1990. "The Medical Construction of Gender: Case Management of Intersexed Infants." *Signs: Journal of Women in Culture and Society* 15: 3–26.
Kuczynki, Alex. 2004. "The World—On Order: Brad Pitt's Nose; A Lovelier You, with Off-the-Shelf Parts." *New York Times*, May 2.
Madeira, Jody Lynee. 2002. "Law and a Reflection of Her/His-story: Current Institutional Perceptions of, and Possibilities for, Protecting Transsexuals' Interests

in Legal Determinations of Sex." *University of Pennsylvania Journal of Constitutional Law* 128=128–84.

Maguigan, Holly. 1995. "Cultural Evidence and Male Violence: Are Feminist and Multiculturalist Reformers on a Collision Course in Criminal Courts?" *New York University Law Review* 70: 36-99.

Matsunaga, Ronald S. 1985. "Westernization of the Asian Eyelid." *Archives of Otolaryngology Head and Neck Surgery* 3(111):149–53.

McRuer, Robert. 2002. "Compulsory Able-Bodiedness and Queer/Disabled Existence." In *Disability Studies: Enabling the Humanities*, ed. S. Snyder. New York: Modern Language Association.

Mendelson, Danuta. 1996. "Historical Evolution and Modern Implications of Concepts of Consent to, and Refusal of, Medical Treatment in the Law of Trespass." *Journal of Law and Medicine* 17:1.

Minow, Martha. 1987. "Justice Engendered." *Harvard Law Review* 101:10.

Mitchell, Timothy. 1999. "Society, Economy, and the State Effect." In *State/Culture*, ed. G. Steinmetz. Ithaca: Cornell University Press.

Munoz, Jose Esteban. 1999. *Disidentifications: Queers of Color and the Performance of Politics*. Minneapolis: University of Minnesota Press.

Olguin, B. V. 1997. "Tattoos, Abjection, and the Politics Unconscious: Toward a Semiotics of the Pinto Visual Vernacular." *Cultural Critique* 37:159.

O'Malley, Pat. 1998. *Crime and the Rise of Society*. Oxford: Ashgate .

Pa, Monica. 2001. "Beyond the Pleasure Principle: The Criminalization of Consensual Sadomasochistic Sex." *Texas Journal of Women and the Law* 11:51.

Pateman, Carol. 1988. *The Sexual Contract*. Stanford: Stanford University Press.

People v. Brown. 2001. 109 Cal. Rptr.2d 879 (Cal, App. 4th 2001).

Phillips v. Michigan Dept. of Corrections. 1990. 731 F.Supp.792 (W.D.Mich. 1990).

Planned Parenthood v. Casey. 1992. 505 U.S. 833 (1992).

Povenmire, Ross. 1999. "Do Parents Have the Legal Authority to Consent to the Surgical Amputation of Normal, Healthy Tissue from Their Infant Children? The Practice of Circumcision in the United States." *American University Journal of Gender and Social Policy* 7:87.

Ramos v. Lamm. 1980. 639 F.2d 559 (10th Cir. 1980).

Roberts, Dorothy. 1998. *Killing the Black Body: Race Reproduction and the Meaning of Liberty*. New York: Knopf.

Roe v. Wade. 1973. 410 U.S. 113 (1973).

Roediger, David. 1999. *The Wages of Whiteness*. New York: Verso.

Roman, David. 2006. *Acts of Intervention: Unnatural Acts*. Bloomington: University of Indiana Press.

Rose, Nikolas. 1989. *Governing The Soul: The Shaping of the Private Self*. New York: Free Association Books.

Rose, Peter I. 1970. *Old Memories, New Moods*. New York: Atherton.

Rubin, Gayle. 1975. "The Traffic of Women: Notes on the Political Economy of Sex." In *Toward an Anthropology of Women*, ed. R. R. Reiter New York: Monthly Review Press.

Scarry, Elaine. 1985. *The Body in Pain: The Making and Unmaking of the World*. New York: Oxford.

———. 1990. "Consent and the Body: Injury, Departure, and Desire." *New Literary History* 21:867.

Schloendorff v. Society of New York Hospital. 1914. 211 N.Y. 125, 128 (1914).

Scott, Joan. 1992. "Experience." In *Feminists Theorize the Political*, ed. J. Butler and J. Scott. New York: Routledge.

Serlin, David. 2003. "Crippling Masculinity: Queerness and Disability in the U.S. Military Culture, 1800–1945." *GLQ: A Journal of Lesbian and Gay Studies* 9:1–2.

Smith, Susan. 2007. "I Won't Be Happy Until I Lose my Legs." *Guardian*, January 28.

Smith v. Rasmussem. 1999. 57 F.Supp.2d 736. (N.D. Iowa, 1999).

Society for Body Integrity Identity Disorder. 2007. http://www.biid.org/.

Spade, Dean. 2003. "Resisting Medicine, Re/Modeling Gender." *Berkeley Women's Law Journal* 18:15.

State v. Hale. 1823. 2 Hawks 582 (1823).

Sullivan, Nikki and Susan Stryker. Forthcoming. "'King's Member, Queen's Body: Transsexual Surgery, Self-Demand Amputation, and Sovereign Power.'" In *Somatechnics: Queering the Technologisation of Bodies*, ed. S. Murray and N. Sullivan London: Ashgate.

Useem, Michael. 1973. *Conscription Protest and Social Conflict: The Life and Death of a Draft Resistance Movement*. New York: Wiley.

Vacco v. Quill. 1997. 521 U.S. 793 (1997).

Valverde, Marianne. 2003. *Law's Dream of a Common Knowledge*. Princeton: Princeton University Press.

Warren, Peter M. 1999. "A Cap and Gown-and New Breasts." *L.A. Times*, May 21.

Washington v. Glucksberg. 1997. 521 U.S. 702 (1997).

Whole. 2003. Melody Gilbert, dir. Los Angeles: L.A. Film Festival.

Wilchins, Riki Anne. 1997. *Read My Lips: Sexual Subversion and the End of Gender*. New York: Firebrand Press.

Williams v. Attorney General of Alabama. 2004. 378 F.3d 1232 (11th Cir. 2004).

Yates, Richard. 1961. *Revolutionary Road*. New York: Vintage.

MORE LESSONS FROM A STARFISH: PREFIXIAL FLESH AND TRANSSPECIATED SELVES

EVA HAYWARD

Mr. Muscle forcing bursting
Stingy thingy into little me, me, me
But just "ripple" said the cripple
As my jaw dropped to the ground
Smile smile

It's true I always wanted love to be
Hurtful
And it's true I always wanted love to be
Filled with pain
And bruises

Yes, so Cripple-Pig was happy
Screamed "I just completely love you!
And there's no rhyme or reason
I'm changing like the seasons
Watch! I'll even cut off my finger
It will grow back like a Starfish!
It will grow back like a Starfish!
It will grow back like a Starfish!"
Mr. Muscle, gazing boredly
And he checking time did punch me
And I sighed and bleeded like a windfall
Happy bleedy, happy bruisy

I am very happy
So please hit me
I am very happy
So please hurt me

I am very happy
So please hit me
I am very very happy
So come on hurt me

I'll grow back like a Starfish
I'll grow back like a Starfish
I'll grow back like a Starfish
I'll grow back like a Starfish

I'll grow back like a Starfish
I'll grow back like a Starfish
I'll grow back like a Starfish
I'll grow back like a Starfish
Like a Starfish . . .

(Antony and the Johnsons 2000)

I call this piece a critical enmeshment rather than a personal account. For I want this to be a doing and a knowing that I get knotted into—a kind of phenomenological telling that grapples with the mundane and sublime. I am not only describing and articulating, not merely charting the geography, but am pulled into the fleshy gerunds of what I write out. That is to say, I am not telling my story; rather I'm simply entangling myself within the stitches of ongoing processes. I am here not to confess, but to confect.

As such, the following sections or interludes are not some teleological account of transsexual/trans-species becoming, or a disclosure of my stakes. Instead, it is in the encountering of my body with Antony's song, in the interacting of the text/sound and myself, in the changing patterns of lifeways that this essay is sense making. "Critical enmeshment" is always a verb just as it is also always situated and historical. And for this essay, critical enmeshment is a phenomenological compounding or enfolding in which language, music, and matter are lively (even bumptious) relatings of what Donna Haraway calls, "others to each other" (2003).

A MOMENT OF SPECIES AND SEXES

I listen to the "The Cripple and the Starfish"; I find the layered tones of Antony's voice haunting and the lyrics startling: "I'll even cut off my finger"; "I'll grow back like a Starfish"; "Happy bleedy, happy bruisy." My iTunes player calls the song "alternative," that ambiguous, overpopulated term. The music "ripples" through styles and textures. Antony's voice vibrates (vibrato), fluctuating and undulating with emotional expressiveness: sometimes soft and tender and ripe with satiety and fulfillment ("I am very happy/So please hit me") then shifting in cadence to declarative, even triumphant ("I'll grow back like a Starfish"). Following the rise and fall of the song, Antony's voice shifts between low and high, deep and bright. His/her voice creates a waving space, a singing sea—the pace and rhythm of his/her phrasing expresses frenetic and calm movements, the periodicity or the punctuated changes of things and events, as with something gone adrift in its passage through material-discursive space, as a bloom of jellyfish carried by riptides and doldrums may be rinsed out to sea or washed up onto sand or rocks. Could it be that Antony sings the tones of whales calling, the syncopation of pods, the transfiguring surf? This is to ask, nearby Gaston Bachelard's (1983) own wonderings about the literal matter of meaning, how do the tone and the wording of "The Cripple and the Starfish" put us in touch with specific senses, things, places, and relations that it mentions or hints at?

And I wonder, thinking about the transsexual *trans*-formations and the starfish *re*-generations that are suggested in the song, what is the transformative and re-lational power of prefixes like "trans-" or "re-"? I want to understand how "re-" (as in "re-turn" or "re-new") and "trans-" (as in "elsewhere") are differently embodied. Beyond my own identity as a transsexual woman, or the political formation of transgender/transsexual, I am not certain about the ontological processes of bodily transformation (my own or others').[1] How does *re*-assignment define transitioning for some trans-subjects? Moreover, I wonder if "starfish"—"I'll grow back like a Starfish"—or more properly "sea stars," might provide me (and maybe others) some prefixial lessons or guides through language, metaphor, and other tropological terrains. Do not some starfish regenerate themselves from injury? Is not the "cripple" of the song repairing him/

herself through the act of cutting? Is transsexual transformation also regenerative? Am I not in part a transsexual through the re-working and re-folding of my own body, my tissue, and my skin? In becoming transsexual, am I not also becoming "like a starfish" as the song suggests? When do metaphor and metonymy "ripple" into one another? Is the analogical device of "like-ness" ("like a starfish" or like a woman) too clumsy a rhetorical device for the kind of poetic and material enactments of trans-sexing/speciating?

These personal and scholarly questions are not maps for already chartered territories. In principle, this essay remains a work in progress. Tentatively and curiously, I am suggesting here that in some ways language, music, starfish, and myself encounter one another and share in the mutuality of our different materializations. By attending to the material nature of semiotic and embodied encounters, I hope to engage materialism at its most radical and come to recognize as precious the boundedness *of my flesh as part of the world*. This is to say, "we" (as in you and me) are ourselves specific parts of the world's ongoing refiguring; "we" are part of the world in its (and our) dynamic structuration, its (and our) differential becoming. It is my hope that this essay plays some small part in making explicit the embodied premises that we live in a process of constant enfolding and that it encourages a deeper and more expansive regard for ways that life comes together.

SOME NOTES FROM AN ARTIST

During an interview with *Velle Magazine*, Antony, the founder of Antony and the Johnsons, discusses the emergence of the band:

> The Johnsons' name is a reference to a hero of mine named Marsha P. Johnson, who was a street activist from the mid 60's all the way through to her death in the early 90's. Marsha P. Johnson was a street prostitute and a very visible figure on Christopher Street through the 70's and 80's, very renowned for her kindness. You know, her nickname was Saint Marsha. She was a very gregarious sort of outsider street presence and she was rumored to have thrown the first bottle in the Stonewall Riot—I mean whether that was true or not was a bone of contention among several different queens (Uchill 2007, 49).

Marsha Johnson, or Saint Marsha, and Sylvia Rivera, an important figure in the nascent transgender civil rights movement, started a group in 1970 called STAR, Street Transvestite Action Revolutionaries.[2] In Antony's own words, a transgender legacy is written into the music group; she, an outsider, a queen of color, who threw the first bottle, who was murdered in 1992, structures the creative and political intent of the band. Johnson is Antony's hero, perhaps, and I say this only speculatively, an ego ideal.

About her/his creative process, Antony is clear to emphasize the collage quality of her/his music and sound.

> I think my creative process has always been what I've described as accumulative. I collect a lot of different shards and pieces, and I create something that feels meaningful to me by finding relationships between them and putting them into a kind of a collage. . . . You know, for me, I'm really drawn to singers that are full of feeling and are seeking transformation. I like transformative singing, you know, singing that starts one place and ends in another place (Uchill 2007, 50).

Classification is evaded for something more "transformative," something "that starts one place and ends in another place." "Trans-," a prefix weighted with across, beyond, through (into another state or place—*elsewhere*), does the now familiar work of suggesting the unclassifiable. To be *trans-* is to be transcending or surpassing particular impositions, whether empirical, rhetorical, or aesthetic. Antony speaks of the affective force of his/her transformation in songs and in singing. Transformations—not unlike transgenders—are produced through emotive forces. Shards and pieces (again, of something broken) are reworked into meaningful integrities, but not wholes.

In another interview, with the *Guardian* (Peschek 2007), Antony discusses her/his album *I Am a Bird Now*, which was included as an installation piece in the 2004 Whitney Biennial.[3] The record is described by Antony as "A record of transformations and survival. Its characters move between states—life and death, male and female, human and animal—searching for sanctuary and fulfillment" (Peschek 2005). Antony proposes transformation as a trope for reworking the relationality of male and female, of human and animal. Perhaps I am the only one hearing it, but in the texture of Antony's voice, in the instrumental variations, and in the lyrics themselves, boundaries of sexual and species differences, artificial and authentic orderings, and nature and culture are affectively and literally *trans*-ed in "The Cripple and the Starfish."

"Trans-," as articulated by Antony, is meant to disturb purification practices; the well defined is confounded at multiple material and semiotic levels. Psychical and corporeal experiences are blended. For example, gender and the embodiment of gender are contingencies that may hold for a moment then fall away into another set of relationships. Species exist in taxonomic differences (*Homo sapiens sapiens* is not the same as *Octopus vulgaris*), but species are also *always already* constitutive of each other through the spaces and places we cohabit—this of course includes language and other semiotic registers (Haraway 2003). Indeed, species are relationships between species—relationality is worldhood. We are not human alone—we are human with many. Matter is not immutable, suggests Antony, it is discursive, allowing sexes and species to practice transmaterialization. The meat and meaning for humans and starfish have no structuring lack, no primordial division, but are sensuously intertwined.

BECOMING WITH STARFISH

After listening to the song, I am plunged into the trans-species implications of primate digits = starfish rays. Starfish (as material/discursive objects) work as interesting figures to theorize re-embodiment with (but they are not only here to think with; they "are fleshy material-semiotic presences") (Haraway 2003, 5). A few reminders: starfish (though not fish) are marine invertebrates that belong to kingdom *Animalia* and phylum *Echinodermata*, class *Asteroideae*. Starfish are capable of sexual and asexual reproduction. For sexually reproducing species, fertilization takes place externally with males and females releasing their gametes into the environment—broadcast spawning. The fertilized embryos form part of the zooplankton—the animal part of the pelagic. Some species of starfish also reproduce asexually by fission, often with part of a ray becoming detached and eventually developing into another individual. Fissioning has led to some notoriety.[4] Most species must have the central part of the body intact to be able to regenerate, but a few can grow an entire starfish from a single ray.

Although many echinoderms do not have many well-defined sensory inputs, they are sensitive to touch, light, temperature, orientation, and the status of water around them. The tube feet, spines, and pedicellaria found on starfish are sensitive to touch, while eyespots on the ends of the rays are light sensitive. In this way, Antony's starfish rays may not just be stand-ins for penis = finger, but interventions in phallus = vision. Indeed, if becoming transsexual is becoming with starfish then some of that work is done with *fingery-eyes*.[5] No eyes, but their rays are full of luminous touch, of sensing, or rather of being literally *tact*, being touch; their rays respond to the surface effects, caressing. Their pedicellaria tremble and deform in the movements; gropes, manipulations, and reaches succeed one another. That is all to say, it is not that their sensing system is visually haptically embodied; rather their very *being* is a visual-haptic-sensory apparatus. The song might produce some notion of lack (some kind of castration), but more interestingly it also refigures the ocular-centrism needed for the recognizing self from other by becoming *with* starfish. Consequently, self and other are not easily ordered (as in speciation)— again, species of all sorts are constituted through encounters. Vision/touch/penis/phallus are at stake not simply through lack/castration, but also through speciation, through fingery-eyes. This kind of enfolding of gender/animality serves as shared zoontology (Wolfe 2003).

TRANS-ABLING

In "The Cripple and the Starfish," transformation is indeed a fusing of organisms, energies, and sexes. I am intrigued by the phrase "cut off my finger, it'll grow back like a starfish." Let us start with the cut—the "cripple" wants "Mr. Muscle" to "please hurt me," and "cripple" will "even cut off my finger." From what has been suggested by the song and Antony him/herself, I presume that "cripple" wants to transform through cutting (amputation or castration); the "cripple" can be heard as a transsexual/transgender MtF seeking transformation. At first, the cut finger leads me, and perhaps other listeners/readers, to think that the cut is an act of castration—the finger works as a substitute for the penis. "Cripple" wants to become a woman through the cutting off of her penis. Certainly, some transsexual women "cut off" their penises in order to have solidarity with females or become female themselves to name only some transsex formations.[6]

Perhaps some readers will worry that my reading the "Cripple" as a trans-subject will iterate the pathologization of trans-folks. For some transsexual/transgender subjects, originary gender assignments can feel disabling, even wounding. I'm speaking about this kind of traumatic experience, not about transgressive exceptionalism (Halberstam 2005) in which gender/sex changes prompt revolutionary potential. I am simply returning to my own bodily knowledge—carnal logics—of pain and possibility, my own experience of becoming transsexual as a welcomed cut. And yet, I am concerned with how my own calculus of gender dis-phoria as dis-ability = yearned-for transformation codifies a naive understanding of disability (or dis-phoria) as intolerable. This troubles me. So, following Robert McRuer's (2006) vibrant work on queerness and disability, I want to suggest that disability theory has long refused, even relexified, the prefixial logics of "dis-." Indeed, McRuer recasts dis-ability as kinds of queer embodiments, initiating a resignification of cutting and amputation as forms of becoming that are not located in morbidity, fetishism, or wholeness. While I am not here by any means suggesting that on a foundational or formative level "trans" must always (or even frequently) embody disability, the song almost demands it. So although I might find my born-sex dis-abling, I also see my trans-sex as a cut-sex that "cripples" an imagined wholeness even while I find that position to be livable even desirable position rather than annexed or repudiated. This is to say, for me, I invite the cut that leaves sex-scars and other unfulfilled wishes so that I might live differently my gender dys-phoria, my dis-comforting born-sex. The "cripple" might yearn for transformation, to "diss" dysphoria, but the corporeal act and affect of transformation (as in a cut, for example) does not cure but trans-figures embodiment. Risking an unsetting union, I propose that *trans-abling* allows cut-sex (or even other kinds of transitions) to be something other than curative.[7]

CUTTING PREFIXES

Does "cut" *have* an onomatopoetic quality? Do we acoustically/haptically experience the sharp-edged tool slice, sever, nick, slash? When I read Susan Stryker's (1994) "The Surgeon Haunts My Dreams"—"As He falls upon me I see the knife glinting in His hand, and I know this water will soon be turning red. When I lift my hips to meet Him as He enters me, He will surely see that nothing other than my desire brings Him here"— the words cause my own "cut-sex" to ache.

I am not interested in how the cut in the song is an absence (as in castration) but rather in how cutting is a generative enactment of "grow[ing] back" or healing. The cut enacts trans-embodiment—to cut is not necessarily about castration, but an attempt to recast the self through the cut body. The whole (body) and the part (cut) are metonymically bound in an attempt to trans-form in toto. However successful or not, however uncomfortable for listeners/readers, however seemingly masochistic, "cut off my finger" and "please hit me" can be understood as wished-for metamorphosis by the "cripple." To cut off the penis/finger is not to be an amputee, but to produce the conditions of physical and psychical regrowth. *The cut is possibility.* For some transsexual women, the cut is not so much an opening of the body, but a generative effort to *pull the body back through itself* in order to feel mending, to feel the growth of new margins. The cut is not just an action; the cut is part of the ongoing materialization by which a transsexual tentatively and mutably becomes. The cut cuts the meat (not primarily a visual operation for the embodied subject, but rather a proprioceptive one), and a space of psychical possibility is thereby created. From the first, a transsexual woman embodiment does not necessarily foreground a wish to look like or look more like a woman (namely, passing)—though for some transwomen this may indeed be a wish (fulfilled or not). The point of view of the looker (those who might read her) is not the most important feature of trans-subjectivity—the trans-woman wishes to be *of* her body, to speak from her body.

When I pay my surgeon to cut my penis into a neovagina, I am moving toward myself through myself. As the surgeon inserts the scalpel and cuts through the thickness of my tissue, my flesh immediately empurples. For weeks afterward, my groin remains discolored and swollen. Between the surgeon's efforts and my body's biomechanics, my cut spills blood and affect. My cut enacts a regeneration of my bodily boundaries—boundaries redrawn. Through my cut, I brush up against invocations and revelations; my cut is not passive—its very substance (materially and affectively) is generative and plays a significant role in my ongoing materialization. My cut is *of* my body, not the absence of parts of my body. The regenerative effort of my cut is discursive; my transfiguring cut is a material-discursive practice through which I am *of* my body and of my trans-self. My cut penis entails being and doing, materiality and affect, substance and form. My cut is generative within material limits but not with affective fixity; my tissues are mutable insofar as they are made of me and propel me to imagine an embodied elsewhere.

Not surprisingly, scholars, activists, students, and artists have questioned the meaning and significance of transsexual/transgender embodiment. Rather simplistically, it has been suggested that the pre-operative transsexual feels constrained by the wrong body and desires a healed body, which is articulated as a male or a female form. According to this account, transsexual selfhood is entangled with images of bodily wholeness—what's more, there is an idea of inside and outside the body that are at odds (Prosser 1998). The body is a container—a body bag of nouns to keep the proper ones in order. The transsexual aspires to make the so-called defective body intact in order that it may be me. As Jay Prosser has suggested, it is undeniable that such agonizing experiences of disembodiment are true for some transsexuals; nor is it difficult to believe that transsexual alterations are not simply chosen, but rather are *the transformation of an unlivable, fragmented body into a livable whole* (Prosser 1998).

What I find troublesome about this articulation of transsexualism is not the trouble of containment; it is the limiting of the body to containment alone. To be comfortable in one's own body is not *only* to be restricted, limited, contained, or constrained as whole or complete. It is to be able to embody the body's multiplicities, its vicissitudes, its (our) ongoing process of materialization. The body (trans or not) is not a pure, coherent, and positive integrity. The important distinction is not the binary one between wrong body and right body, or between fragmentation and wholeness; it is instead a question of experiencing multiple and continually varying interactions between what can be defined indifferently as coherent transformation, decentered certainty, or limited possibility. Transsexuals do not transcend gender and sex. We create embodiment by not jumping *out* of our bodies, but by taking up a fold in our bodies, by folding (or cutting) ourselves, and creating a transformative scar of ourselves. There is no absolute division, but continuity between the physiological and affective responses of my different historical bodies. Again, I am *of* my body in order that I might experience a subjective, energetic transformation.

A transsexual (myself, for example) is never discontinuous from different states of embodiment, or at least I am only generally distinguished from different historical states of my own beingness.[8] If my subjective embodiment has always been transgender, then my material transformation is an attempt to congeal my differently trans-embodied experiences of body and mind. What I am suggesting when I say that embodiment is coherence is that I am always *of* my tissue even in its ongoing transformation. Whatever the transsexual grants to vision, subjective embodiment is always only partially visible.

Changeability is intrinsic to the transsexual body, at once its subject, its substance, and its limit. Our bodies are scarred, marked, and reworked into a livable gender trouble, sex trouble, or uneven epidermis. Transsexuals survive not because we become whole, but because we embody the reach and possibility of our layered experience—we have no choice. This is all to say, the transsexual body, my body, is a body created out of necessity, ingenuity, and survival—to carry the heft of my various social identities. I, like many transsexuals, may desire some mythic wholeness, but what is truly intact for me, what I live, what I must be part of, is a body pliant to a point, flexible within limits, constrained by language, articulation, flesh, history, and bone.

RE-FORMING METAPHOR

What are the differences between refraction and reflection as contemplative activities? How might a refracted relationship to a text function differently from a reflected one? "Refractory" defines behaviors and materials that are obstinate, unresponsive, and resistant. Evoking these terms simultaneously refocuses matter's stubborn, even blunt, capacity for demarcating externality and internality. In a cruder sense, "refraction" and "refractory" also share origins with "refractory period"—the period that follows effective stimulation, during which excitable tissue fails to respond to a stimulus of threshold intensity (Hayward 2005). Associated with sexual pleasure or "love life," the refractory period as expiration suggests the inertia of the entropic and the return toward the inanimate. Stillness that falls after excitation carries the residue of sensate experience. Sense is carnal; senses are refractory.

"I'll grow back like a starfish." From the start, I notice two things: first, my finger has been substituted for "I"; second, we have moved from the metonymy of the cut to the metaphor of trans-speciation. The starfish seemingly appears as a stand-in for transsexual transformation—the animal appears only as a tool for thinking about beingness. Let us not forget, the metaphor is a displacement: a nominative term is displaced from its everyday context and placed elsewhere so as to illuminate some other context through its reconfiguration. Thus, the relationship is based on the relationship of ideas rather than objects—metaphor does not owe any allegiance to the literal object. The "cut," in contrast, is structured by a metonymy of embodied correspondences and correlations. Metonymy is a tropological enactment quite different from metaphor. Metonymy brings together two objects, each of which constitutes a separate whole; "metonymy" refers to conditions of correspondence: cause to effect, instrument to purpose, container to content, "cut" to trans-body.

I wonder if the starfish is more than metaphor (not that metaphor isn't enough). Playing on the side of zoomorphism, I wonder if being starfish shares in the ontological imaginary of becoming trans-sexed. I don't want to propose that transsexualism is the *same as* trans-speciation, but rather that both share in the materialization of the trans-figure described in "The Cripple and the Starfish." Both the starfish and the transsexual "grow back," differently but with similar phenomenological goals of bodily integrity and healing. Is it possible, and here I take a leap, that while the "cut" has a metonymic force in trans-embodiment, could not "like a starfish" also suggest a metonymy of trans-speciation? For example, literal animals are always part of figural animals; animals cannot be displaced by words; rather, words carry the nervous circuitries, the rhythms, the tempos of the literal. Animals are always constitutively formed in language—human and not, animal and not. Animals (though not necessarily animals alone—but that is for another series of essays) are bound in language such that language cuts into flesh but does not completely devour the body. The literal cut bleeds around the word "cut," which is where the conditions of subjective transformation emerge. Likewise, the starfish, an echinoderm, a regenerating body, an invertebrate that can in some species reproduce new individuals through bodily divisions, exceeds the metaphoricity of likeness because starfish is only ever partially digested, defined, explained, used by language.

How might the "cripple" yearn for *re*generation in order to *trans*-form? "I'll even cut off my finger. It will grow back like a starfish." To me, this is a literal instantiation of sea star biodynamic—s/he will *re*-grow her/his finger, but not necessarily *trans*-form her/his finger. In broader terms, s/he is also *re*-sexed body just as she/he also becomes subjectively trans-sexed. Although subtle, the work might be in how prefixes shape and reshape the prepositions of the discourse; *re*- is *of* the body, not *in* the body (as trans embodiment is often articulated—for example, "trapped in the wrong body"). "Re-" makes all enactments constitutive of the form-er (even if the form-er is an ongoing process of materialization). "Re-" might offer a more "rippling" approach to the limit and containment of the flesh. Regenerativity is a process that is enacted through and by containment (the body). In this way, regeneration is a re/iterative enactment of not only growing *new* boundaries (rebodying), but also of imperiling static boundaries (subjective transformation). Regeneration can attend to desire, pathos, and trauma, but also to modes of corporeal intimacy, fleshy possibility, and most important, reembodiment.

Regeneration is something that both transsexuals and starfish do. Transsexuals and starfish do other kinds of prefixial relationships between inside/outside, subject/object, or predator/prey, but in "re-" they share a phenomenological experience of reshaping and reworking bodily boundaries. How might prefixes help us understand the ways that we (starfish, transsexuals, and others) autonomize and generate embodiment? Re-grow, re-differentiate, re-pattern, re-member, re-nucleate: our bodily structures, our biodynamics, are materially enacted through ongoing relationships with the world, as part of that world. Transsexuals and starfish challenge disembodied metaphors (such as like, resemblance, or simile), and propose how we are metonymically stitched to carnal substrates. *In other words, I'm not like a starfish; I am of a starfish. I am not trapped in my body; I am of my body.*

MEAT OF MEANING

I'm worried about how real starfish that roam clam beds literally matter here in my prose, in my enmeshmest of the many actors and presences whose doings resemble a coralline reef. Generations of spineless marine organisms, with their light-sensitive spots and neural webs, release their eggs into open waters, followed by larval feeding, will settle, eat each other and passers-by, and generate their own hungry drifters. When I say "Starfish," or describe their lifeways, how do these words retain the presences, properties, and behaviors of invertebrates undergoing metamorphosis? Perhaps it is a frivolous desire on my part, even ridiculous, to want to understand how words focus our attention, leading us to see/hear/feel interactions, requiring us to attend to a perpetual, worldly motion.

Here, thinking about Antony's "Starfish," I turn to mentors. Looking, listening, and living attentively in concert with "critters," Donna Haraway teaches us, might just give humans new forms of relationship practice to use productively both among themselves and with a menagerie of emergent others. The kind of relating she calls for has prepositional import: *worlds are of relationships*. The ontology of interrelationality, according to Haraway, is ongoing, constitutive, metamorphosing, living, and material. She articulates her verb-heavy practice of ontogenesis with the biologically flavored word "metaplasm," meaning "a change in a word by adding, omitting, inverting, or transposing its letters, syllables, and sounds" (Haraway 2003, 20–21). The term is from the Greek *metaplasmos*, meaning remodeling or remolding. Metaplasm is a generic term for almost any kind of alteration in a word, intentional or unintentional. . . . Compare and contrast protoplasm, cytoplasm, neoplasm, and germplasm. There is a biological taste to metaplasm—just what I like in words about words. Flesh and signifier, bodies and words, stories and worlds: these are joined in naturecultures. Metaplasm can signify a mistake, a stumbling, a troping that makes a fleshly difference. For example, a substitution in a string of bases in a nucleic acid can be a metaplasm, changing the meaning of a gene and altering the course of life.

Added to her fourth semiotic category of diffraction, set forth in *Modest Witness*, "metaplasm," according to Haraway, means, "the remodeling of dog and human flesh, remodeling the codes of life, in the history of companion species" (Haraway 2003, 20). Metaplasm: not as lofty or as graphic as diffraction, can cause the transformation of one type of differentiated tissue into another, such as granular inclusions within cytoplasm. Metaplasm entails the constitutive enactment of ontology and epistemology, materiality and intelligibility, substance and form, fungibility and sustainability. Metaplasm: sensual materiality enacted. Metaplasm is the intertwining and enmeshing of noumena and phenomena; that is, metaplasm is about materially activated—moving matter—ways of being, doing, and knowing. Metaplasm, says Haraway, gets its start from the interrelationship of human animals and nonhuman animals. Unlike diffraction, metaplasm begins in the sensual and carnal intercourse between and among species, constantly changing and reworking boundaries between subject and object, us and them, there and here, me and it. Intervening in the optic-driven epistemology engines of science studies and cultural theory, metaplasm gives Haraway's diffraction a whiff of fecundity, a meaty taste, intimacy, pleasure, pain, and hunger.

It would be wrong to read metaplasm as utopian. Haraway is precise when she talks about the life-and-death stakes of getting it wrong. Metaplasm is an approach to ethics that does not hold out an end story, a teleological end point. Rather, metaplasm attends to the ways that enactors (enfolded actors: constitutive of each other while differentiated: doing and knowing while being) constitute themselves through assemblages composed from biological and phenomenological entanglements. Metaplasm is ripe with relational shit, yolks, and cancerous metaplastic pyloric glands. Metaplasms are ossifications, transformations, and keratinizations of raw sensation—hearing, seeing, smelling, tasting, and touching become fibrous, heteromorphic, and unruly. Metaplasm is a kind of enactment with relationship as part of the relationship, a practice of enfolding relationships in their ongoing materializations. However, the risks are high; the sticks and stones of relational *mattering* can disease the intestine with carcinoma and fill the bone with anemia and haematopoiesis. Metaplasm is a kind of trope that takes biology and semiotics very seriously—differences are material and discurive. It is ardent with consequence. Metaplasm is an enactment (as in enfolded action: diacritically invested and active in making sense and meaning *in and of the world*). It is this kind of iterative ontogenetic and epistemological entangling that Haraway calls for in "significant otherness," a thickly mediated/mediating way of being HumanAnimal in the contemporary moment.[9]

In concert with Haraway's call for fleshy difference and material semiotics, I turn to Akira Mizuta Lippit's important discussion of "animetaphor" (a play on "antimetaphor" and "animal metaphor," that is, animals exceed metaphoricity). Lippit writes, "The animetaphor is . . . never absorbed, sublimated, or introjected into the world but rather incorporated as a limit . . . . The animetaphoric figure is consumed literally rather than figuratively" (1998, 1115). The animetaphor (that which tries to speak for/about specific animals) is metonymic, foregrounding the ways that the lived being always already inhabits language, grammar, syntax, and metaphor. The animetaphor is about how animals *exist within* practices of signification—nonhuman animals are not merely subjected to primate language; nonhuman animals are always already reworking language. The real animal is constantly present in Adam's Genesis. Animals, in their own ways, inhabit language. Language emerges from an ontology that is ecological, *anima*, the animal den, the wave, and the invertebrate.

Lippit suggests that the animetaphor foregrounds the complex ways that animal representations are always haunted, vexed, reworked, and enfolded by real animals. Animals expose the limits of representation. Lippit shows how animality, animal spirits, and organisms themselves reside as real within representations. He writes:

> On the verge of words, the animal emits instead a stream of cries, affects, spirits, and magnetic fluids. What flows from the animal touches language without entering it, dissolving memory, like the

unconscious, into a timeless present. The animal is magnetic because it draws the world-building subject toward an impossible convergence with the limits of world, toward a metaphysics of metaphor. The magnetic animal erases the limits of the metaphor, affecting an economy of the figure that is metamorphic rather than metaphoric. It forces a transformation of the figure (1120).

Lippit posits that metaphors and representations create spaces where non-human animals can be pointed to without naming, subsumed without securing. That is to say, the animetaphor, the living metaphor, is always pointing to a space (even if it is always already in language) outside language, exposing the limits of language.[10]

Working with the "antimetaphor" figure of Nicholas Abraham and Maria Torok (Abraham and Torok 1994), Lippit is suggesting here that animals in language are always transforming figure into flesh, always *disfiguring* representation. Animals are always troubling the language that attempts to name animals. In this way, nonhuman animals seem to put an oral void into language. Animals cannot be named without invoking the limits of the process of naming. This is not a tautology. Animals are *in and of* language and representation, but their lived bodies are always restoring words to beings. Lippit writes, "When the metaphoricity of the metaphor collapses, the concept becomes a metonymic thing that can be eaten" (1998, 1122). Because animality is often the measure by which humanity measures itself as such, animals in language rest at the edges of the mouth, my mouth; I taste the failure of language to describe animals and savor the presence of real animals flanking my sentences, my words. My language cannot digest the tissue and meat of nonhuman animals—a meal that cannot be digested.

Taking Lippit's "animetaphor" and applying it to "The Cripple and the Starfish," "starfish" points to the limits of representation, where "like a starfish" has corporeal meaning. The starfish referent is constantly touching me and devouring its representation. Antony's starfish is fiercely present as a regenerating body in the song about it. Eating and hearing are collapsed as phenomenological modes of encounter within this starfish song. Antony's starfish consumes me through the excess of its referentiality. The listening subject (myself, for example) is wholly or partially touched by the soma of the named starfish. The referent itself establishes itself as *that-which-is-reembodying-this*. As I listen to Antony's song, rather than anthropomorphizing the starfish through identification, I am simultaneously chewing on and being chewed on by an economy of excess, carnality, and materiality.

The word "starfish" puts me in contact with starfish themselves—a kind of material imagination in which the word stems directly from matter. As Antony sings "starfish," the literal starfish resounds in his/her voice. The word maps out the dense tissue of starfish lifeways. For me, Antony intensifies the encounter, the meeting, between the bodies of species. "Like a starfish" enacts an artistry on the starfish and the subject of the animetaphor. That "I will grow back like a starfish" solicits both "I" and the starfish to inhabit those words; with those words we move into life. "I" is a word that finds roots in oneself; "starfish" transposes a literal element into a figural one. Out of the murmuring sensations of "The Cripple and the Starfish" come words and the babble of others that are uttered into oneself, into one's bone marrow, one's anatomy, and one's circadian rhythms. This *intra*-corporeality of starfish (material) and "starfish" (semiotic), of "I" and me, is a kind of loving, a kind of nearness that invokes a voluptuary of trans-speciation and imagines a co/passionate kind of presence. Language and music, then, enact a caressing, a sensuous immersing in the ardent materiality of worldhood.

RIPPLE

"Ripple":

1. A slight cut, scratch, or mark. Verb: to scratch slightly; to graze or ruffle.
2. A piece of shallow water in a river where rocks or sand-bars cause an obstruction; a shoal.
3. A light ruffling of the surface of water, such as is caused by a slight breeze; a wavelet.
4. A wave on the surface of a fluid the restoring force for which is provided by surface tension rather than by gravity, and which consequently has a wavelength shorter than that corresponding to the minimum speed of propagation.
5. A sound as of rippling water.
6. To mark with or as with ripples; to cause to undulate slightly. (Oxford English Dictionary)

"Ripple" creates the ruffling within the subject that allows "Happy bleedy, happy bruisy" to become the conditions for bodily regeneration, psychical transformation, and trans-speciation. "Ripple" tears and fiddles with the idea that language/representation is a cut between the phenomenal world and the knowing subject. "Ripple" with the "The Cripple and the Starfish" creates the carnal foundations for prefixial enactments that take meat and meaning seriously. The "cripple" and "like a starfish" provide an extreme collapse between the figural and the real. In other words, prefixes ("trans-" and "*re-*") are kinds of relationships that ripple and rupture the field of representation. The starfish and the transsexual point beyond the limits of language, allowing both figures to exceed any kind of palliative function (like a woman or "like a starfish").

The transsexual—again I speak of this experience not to the side of my body, but because of my body—energetically ripples the body, marks the meat, with *re-*form, *re-*grow, re-shape so that subjective transformation may occur: transition, transsex, *trans-*be; this is prefixial rippling. The prefix re- must take up the body in order that trans- might become. The starfish, depending on species, can *re-*grow a damaged ray. The lost ray, again in some species, may become another individual, rippling into another state of being. This is to say, the starfish changes its biogeometry in relationship to its environment—it is entangled and reshaped and transfigured through encounters. Moreover, the metonymic qualities of embodiment always links semiotics to matter. "Starfish" is a representation with tube feet; transsexual is an identity that bleeds and is cut.

"Ripple" reminds me of starfish locomotion. Starfish have hydraulic water vascular systems that facilitate movement. Ocean water comes into the system via the madreporite (a small opening in the aboral surfaces of starfish). Salt water is then circulated from the stone canal to the ring canal and into the radial canals. The radial canals carry water to the ampullae and provide suction to the tube feet. The tube feet latch on to surfaces and move in a wave, with one body section attaching to the surfaces as another releases. "Ripple" defines the biomechanics of tube feet.

"Ripple," on a somatic level, reminds me of my own physical vulnerability—my animate transsex flesh. Might I share this same somatic sensitivity with the starfish in the most basic sense of redressing harm: regeneration as an act of healing. Transsexing is an act of healing. This is some kind of mutuality—some kinds of shared ontology. Trans-morphic as zoomorphic—if we can understand the cut as an act of love, then can we not imagine that "like a starfish" is an enactment of trans-speciating? We, transsexuals and starfish, are animate bodies; our bodies are experienced and come to be known through encounters with other animate bodies. These epistemological moves describe a shared phenomenological ontology. This is sensate intertwining-intercorporeal zones between these bodies in language and in experience. Starfish and transsexuals share worldhood both semiotic (as metonymic kinds) and phenomenological enactments—is this not some form of *inter*corporeality?

"It's true I always wanted love to be hurtful," says Antony in "The Cripple and the Starfish." If, as I hope I've illustrated here, the literal and the figural—the *matter that means* and the *meaning that means*—emerge as interlocking and dynamic. "Hurt" is not a masochistic enactment (or, at least, not this alone), but signals a breach in language, and a tear in the traditional subject/object formation. The material, the literal matter, of being, surfaces and resurfaces as a constitutive force that cannot be digested in the acid fluids of anthropic concerns. Animetaphor and metonymy apply a figurative sense as a literal one, while yet retaining the look or feel of figurality. A phenomenology of the rippling subject having and making sense of the song reveals to us the intercorporeal function of lived bodies—as both carnal and conscious, sensible and sentient—and how it is we can apprehend the sense of the song both figurally and literally.

Correlatively, a phenomenology of the experience of this lived intercorporeality and differentiation in the song exposes to us—in the metonymic articulations of language—the reversible and oscillating structure of the lived body's experience of language. To put it simply: in the act of making sense of the song, metonymy is to language as rippling is to lived bodies. Metonymy not only points to the gap between the figures of language and literal lived-bodies' experiences but also intercorporeally, rippling, bridges and intertwines a sensate ontology. Thus, "The Cripple and the Starfish" mobilizes, differentiates, and yet entangles lived bodies and language and foregrounds the intercorporeality of sensible matter and sensual meaning. As zoomorphic, *re*-morphic, and *trans*-morphic subjects, then, we possess an embodied knowledge that opens us beyond our discrete capacity for listening to a song, opens the song far beyond its containment in iTunes's "alternative," and opens language to a metonymic and biodynamic knowledge of specific origins and limits.

This is what my being transsexual knows about being a starfish.

EVA HAYWARD is an assistant professor in the Department of Cinematic Arts and the Interdisciplinary Film and Digital Media Program at the University of New Mexico. She has published and lectured widely on animal and visual studies.

ACKNOWLEDGMENTS

I need to say a few things. First, I want to thank Susan Stryker for calling my attention to this song and suggesting that I write about it. Her guidance and editorial eye have been invaluable. Second, portions of this essay have appeared in a slightly different form in Noreen Giffney and Myra J. Hird, ed., *Queering the Non/Human* (Aldershot, U.K.: Ashgate, 2008) under the tile "Lessons from a Starfish." This current essay, "More Lessons from a Starfish," attempts to evolve some of the nascent ideas that I put forward in the first essay. In particular, I hope new readers will welcome my discussions of disability (as "cripple" is uncompromisingly named in the song), trans-species somaticity (how through metaphor and metonym flesh and signifier are joined), and a continued effort in the animate approximation of my own prose style.

NOTES

1. I use "transgender" and "transsexual" interchangeably in this essay. I do so not to elide the significant differences between these identities, but to foreground the shared concerns and desires for embodiment. This is to say, being transgender does not exclude bodily change, nor does being transsexual mean you will have sex reassignment surgery.

2. Here are several links that offer biographical material on the late Marsha P. Johnson: http://en.wikipedia.org/wiki/Marsha_P._Johnson; an obituary, http://gender.org/remember/people/marshajohnson.html; a poem by Qwo-Li Driskill, http://www.lodestarquarterly.com/work/248/.

For a bio on Sylvia Rivera, which sadly is also an obituary, go to http://www.workers.org/ww/2002/sylvia0307.php.

My suggestion that STAR was a "transgender" political organization is a bit ahistorical, considering that "transgender" as a social identity was still only emerging during these years. However, too often gender-variant communities, and their contributions to social change, get lost in more traditional gay/lesbian historiographies. So, I risk playing the part of a "bad historian" in the hopes of encouraging more inclusive historical projects.

3. Antony and the Johnsons collaborated with filmmaker Charles Atlas and thirteen transwomen from New York City on a concert/live video installation staged in

London, Rome, and Paris. During "turning," Antony and the Johnsons present a concert while Charles Atlas creates live video portraits of each model. "turning" was first presented as a part of the 2004 Whitney Biennial in New York City.

4. A story of misunderstanding: starfish can be pests to fishers who make their living on the capture of mollusks, as starfish prey on these. The fishers would presumably kill starfish by chopping them up and disposing of them at sea, ultimately leading to their increased numbers. For more information, see Vicki Pearse, *Living Invertebrates* (Pacific Grove, CA.: Boxwood Press, 1987).

5. Elsewhere I have described "fingery-eyes" as making seeing analogous to touching; fingery-eyes, optical groping, or tactful eyes haptically and visually orient the sensual body across mediums. This kind of seeing through/across/with interfaces requires a perception that navigates by constantly referencing the medium of the environment. Fingery-eyes are about closeness, near proximities—visual distance is not an option here.

6. I use "solidarity" to suggest something other than identification. I'm not suggesting that transsexual women do not become female (some certainly do), but I want to hold out the possibility that the transsexual woman can also become a kind of woman *made of* her various ontologies. I want to value the experience of becoming transsexual as something particular to transsexuals, even as that experience is constitutive of other sexes and their constitutiveness—together all the way down. This line of reasoning is explored in Sandy Stone's (1993) formative essay "The Empire Strikes Back."

7. So much more needs to be said about the relationship between transgender/transsexual subjectivities and disability (and its subtending theories of). I hope the reader recognizes my brief reflections as an attempt to tenderly unpack this potentially volatile issue. I am currently working on an essay on "Trans-abling" in which I further explicate the "noncurative, but wished-for aims" of transitioning.

8. I am not suggesting that "male privilege" is carried into female embodiment—I am not making a sociocultural argument about authenticity. The debate that many MtFs continue to express a perspective on the world that derives from socialization as members of a privileged sex class remains molten. I encourage readers interested in this theme to consult Stryker and Whittle's (2006) excellent anthology *The Transgender Reader*.

9. I do not know if this term, or collapse of terms, has been coined elsewhere (surely it has). I deploy this neologism (in the spirit of "technoscience" or "natureculture") to foreground the constitutive nature of these terms as well as the different histories and institutions that form and reform their meanings. Moreover, I use the compound term to suggest that in an encounter between human and animal, both entities become enyolked in one another, become "fleshed out" (as Merleau-Ponty might say), become literally *of* one another.

10. Lippit is working from Jacques Derrida's (2000, 1991) work on the limits of subjectivity.

WORKS CITED

Abraham, Nicholas, and Maria Torok. 1994. "Mourning or Melancholia: Introjection Versus Incorporation." In *The Shell and the Kernel*, ed. Nicholas Rand. Chicago: University of Chicago Press.

Antony and the Johnsons. 2000. "The Cripple and the Starfish." Rebis Music (SC104). Originally released May 1, 2000.

Bachelard, Gaston. 1983. *Water and Dreams: An Essay On the Imagination of Matter*. Trans. Edith Farrell. Dallas: Pegasus Foundation.

Derrida, Jacques, and Anne Dufourmantelle. 2000. *Of Hospitality*. Stanford: Stanford University Press.

Derrida, Jacques, and Peggy Kamuf. 1991. *A Derrida Reader: Between the Blinds*. New York: Columbia University Press.

Halbertsam, Judith. 2005. *In a Queer Time and Place: Transgender Bodies, Subcultural Lives*. New York: New York University Press.

Haraway, Donna. 2003. *The Companion Species Manifesto: Dogs, People, and Significant Otherness*. Chicago: Prickly Paradigm Press.

Hayward, Eva. 2005. "Enfolded Vision: Refracting the Love Life of the Octopus." *Octopus: A Visual Studies Journal* 1 (Fall). 29-44.

———. 2007. "Coralogical." In *Encyclopedia of Human-Animal Relationships*, ed. Mark Bekoff. Westport, CT: Greenwood Press.

Lippit, Akira Mizuta. 1998. "'Magnetic Animal: Derrida, Wildlife, and Animetaphor.'" *MLN* 113(5):1111–25.

McRuer, Robert. 2006. *Crip Theory: Cultural Signs of Queerness and Disability*. New York: New York University Press.

Pearse, Vicki. (1987). *Living Invertebrates*. Pacific Grove, CA: Boxwood Press.

Peschek, David. 2005. "Boy George Wants Me!" *Guardian*, March 16. http://arts.guardian.co.uk/features/story/0,,1438695,00.html#article-continue.

Prosser, Jay. 1998. *Second Skins: The Body Narratives of Transsexuality*. New York: Columbia University Press.

Stone, Sandy. 1993. "The Empire Strikes Back: A Posttranssexual Manifesto." In *Body Guards: Cultural Politics of Gender Ambiguity*, ed. Julia Epstein and Kristina Straub. New York: Routledge Press.

Stryker, Susan Stryker. 1994. "The Surgeon Haunts My Dreams" *Transsexual Women's Resources*. http://www.annelawrence.com/twr/surgeonhaunts.html.

Stryker, Susan, and Stephen Whittle. 2006. *The Transgender Reader*. New York: Routledge Press.

Uchill, Rebecca K. 2007. "Interview with Antony." *Velle Magazine*, January 18. 48–53.

Wolfe, Cary. 2003. *Zoontologies : The Question of the Animal*. Minneapolis: University of Minnesota Press.

RIDDLE SONG

KATE SCHAPIRA

(Who)'s walking toward you across
the staked lands. The width of the country's
called for, the bottles marshaled, walkers
reach for their blindfolds, the bottles removed for sleek
high-stepping feet and laughter. (Who) in
the meantime crosses where there are mountains,
cars and people, where people gather at the TV campfire
turning their hands. Kudzu, ailanthus,
sagebrush and smoky darkness. Usual reasons
shake (who) into their past like taillights
rocketing into line. Who's crossing a width
that inclines toward hedges and metal verges.
At the water's edge, every word turns
into a fish. Between you. (Who)'ll cross on their backs.

KATE SCHAPIRA is the author of three chapbooks, *Phoenix Memory* (horse less press), *Case Fbdy.* (Rope-A-Dope Press), and *The Saint's Notebook* (CAB/NET Chapbook Series). She is proud of recent acceptances to/appearances in *Aufgabe, Practice, Ecopoetics, Word for/Word,* and *Denver Quarterly*. She lives, writes, teaches, and coordinates the Publicly Complex Reading Series in Providence, Rhode Island.

HUMANS, HORSES, AND HORMONES: (TRANS) GENDERING CROSS-SPECIES RELATIONSHIPS

NATALIE CORINNE HANSEN

In this essay I discuss a brief autobiographical text from Dean Kotula's *The Phallus Palace*, a collection of narratives on aspects of female-to-male transsexual transition (Ken 2002).[1] This essay is part of a larger project that engages animal studies to examine how species difference is deployed in demarcating boundaries between humans and other animals and in understanding species difference in the context of long histories of human dominion over, and perhaps longer histories of human intimacy with, animals. The project is equally invested in feminist and queer critiques of normative gender relations and in conventional psychoanalytic narratives of female development, with particular attention paid to cross-species and cross-gender identifications. Animal studies and feminist and queer analyses partner productively in thinking about material and semiotic relations across differences and about related questions of embodiment, subjectivity, and agency.

In "Ken," the narrative that I analyze here, the author, Ken, tells a story of how his relationship with his horse was transformed during and by the former's hormonal transition. Ken's story speaks of the experience of transsexual embodiment and also of the experience of cross-species identification and relationality. The narrative combines an exploration of human-equine social relations with the experience of gender crossing, as relayed through Ken's experience of transition and its personal and social ramifications.

Ken's reading of his horse's understanding of him as a sexed body locates the horse as representing instinctual and transparent responses. In Ken's reading, his horse, unnamed and decontextualized, acknowledges Ken as a natural being, a man, as marked by Ken's smell, over and above the technological mediation of the transition itself. In his story of transition, Ken is saying that nature, read as biology, determines culture (how bodies are socially gendered), while acknowledging the use of technology to alter nature/biology to make his body legible to both self and society. Through a cross-species relationship, Ken enlists his horse as a participant in the confirmation, and therefore maintenance, of hegemonic economies of difference, in a humanist employment of animality to confirm humanity, and in the phallocentric employment of woman to define man. How to make sense of this complicated tangle of reasoning?

To begin, I identify key points in Ken's narrative of his relationship with his horse and how they relate to his experience of hormonal transition. Ken's horse proves instrumental in helping Ken to understand the embodied changes of transition and how these changes are perceived and received by human and nonhuman animals. The narrative plots questions of species difference by applying cross-species biological essentialism as a way of foregrounding the imperative of transsexual transition. The writing is framed by Ken's own trans-species and transsexual experiences, and, while functioning to affirm the personal and social validity of Ken's transition, it reduces the intersectional histories and materialities that engender this particular cross-species relationship and simplifies the questions of ethical responsibility that necessarily arise within the relationship. I then go on to suggest other ways in which the cross-species relationship might be translated to better account for the agential participation of both man and horse. The emphasis is on how narratives of relationality, with the self and others, can translate into lived relations and the concrete material consequences of these relations as they validate the subjective and agential participation of both human and nonhuman interactants. In asking how bodies become articulate within and across species difference through mutually transformative processes of domestication, I consider how nonhuman agency and subjectivity can be represented to more fully honor the diversity and specificity of bodies, identities, and beings that constitute the various worlds we inhabit as social, political, and cultural actors.

TRANSMAN AND HORSE

Ken's story foregrounds his becoming a man by employing the familiar juxtaposition of man, the male human endowed with masculine traits, and animal, representing nature. The narrative reiterates cultural mythologies of man's dominion over animals, which are, moreover, reflected in material realities of how humans and other animals live together. Ken's relationship with his horse, who remains unnamed throughout the narrative, predates the beginning of Ken's hormonal transition. Ken describes their pre-transition relationship as marked by certain moments of conflict:

> My horse had known me for over a year as female. It had been a difficult relationship. Gelded late in life, he had retained a "studdy" attitude and considered himself dominant over every other horse in the stable. Although he was pleasant and friendly when I wasn't asking him to work, he had trouble accepting my authority. In retrospect, I think he was confused by someone that [sic] smelled like a "mare" acting like a male. The conflicting signals made him uncomfortable (Ken 2002, 59–60).

Ken identifies his horse as decidedly masculine in his behavior, as "studdy," meaning the horse acts like a stallion, an uncastrated male, which, Ken suggests, is reflected in his behavior as "dominant" in relations with other horses. The fact that his horse was "gelded late in life" implies that there may be residual hormonal causation for his aggressive behavior (namely, he has continued high or higher levels of testosterone) or that the behaviors he displayed as a stallion (read here as social dominance) were unaffected by his castration.[2] The horse's resistance to Ken's request for "work" may mark Ken's own resistance to conceptualizing their cross-species partnership as collaborative. Ken understands his horse's resistance to "authority" to be a result of Ken's hormonal signature, which, pre-transition, marked him as female, as a "mare," from whom the horse had difficulty receiving orders but with whom he was otherwise "pleasant and friendly."

Ken reads his own body and that of his horse, as well as communications between these bodies, as hormonally determined. The male horse displays dominant behavior as the result of testosterone, while Ken's pre-transition body is marked as female, nondominant, through its absence of that hormone. Ken's reading of his horse as accepting his authority only when he smells male conflates authority and dominance, identifying both as masculine traits associated with male bodies. The narrative implies that Ken's horse requires a dominant—read here as an adult male—actor in order to accept authority, which in turn relies on readable masculinity, as determined by a certain threshold level of testosterone.

Ken's equation of authority with biological masculinity contrasts with the way that contemporary equine scientists interpret relations of authority within groups of horses. Contemporary ethological descriptions of equine relationality characterize mares, and typically established older mares, as the leaders within mixed-sex groups (Crowell-Davis 2007; Keiper and Sambraus 1986; Linklater et al. 1999; S. M. McDonnell 2003, 2000; Mills and Nankervis 1999; Zeitler-Feicht 2004), whereas stallions appear to demonstrate conflictual relationships with each other (Linklater and Cameron 2000). So, although Ken's reading of himself as a "mare" is interesting in its suggestion of cross-species gender identification, the relationship of authority he describes remains figuratively coherent only when naturalized ideas of male dominance among humans is imposed on horses, resulting in a reading of equine relations that posits a dominant stallion with a harem of subordinate mares.[3]

According to Ken, the dissonance in their relationship is resolved after he begins taking testosterone:

> About two weeks after I started on "T," the horse noticed that something had changed. He sniffed me intently, with the same abstracted look that horses have when inspecting a stranger's dung pile.... After a few days the intense scrutiny stopped, but I sensed a gradual change in his attitude. He seemed to relax. Over time, he came to view me as a "buddy" that [sic] was one small rung above him on the social ladder. For such a dominant animal, this was saying something (Ken 2002, 60).

Ken suggests here that his horse smells the testosterone that is newly circulating in Ken's body and that this smell translates for the horse into a new consideration of Ken as a "buddy," but a buddy who is socially dominant and whose authority the horse defers to. Ken suggests that the resolution of the hormone-behavior incoherence—as the horse is able to identify Ken as male by matching Ken's dominant behavior (his demands for work) with his masculine smell—enables the horse to accept Ken's position of authority within their relationship. The buddy relationship is a type of friendship, an enactment of male homosociality (Sedgwick 1985, 1) (in this case, male species sociality), which includes mutual understanding and bonding; however, Ken locates this buddy relationship within a system of hierarchical species relations wherein the male human is dominant over and authoritative with nonhuman beings.

Ken's reading of his horse's behavior relies on the assumption that the horse both smells the testosterone in Ken's system and interprets this smell as signifying Ken's authority. Both these assumptions, that the horse smells Ken's T and interprets T as signifying authority, are projections of Ken's own ideas about sex/gender relations onto his relationship with his horse. He equates the horse's olfactory inquiry of his body with the way horses gather identifying information by smelling manure piles. Horses' olfactory capacities are understood to be greater than ours (Budiansky 1997; Crowell-Davis and Houpt 1986; Waring 1983; Zeitler-Feicht 2004), but it remains conjectural whether horses smell human hormones in the way they seem to smell equine olfactory signals.[4] It seems likely that the smell (or taste) of Ken's skin secretions contain testosterone by-products that smell (or taste) different from the secretions he produced while female bodied. Because horses use the vomeronasal organ (VNO) to sense pheromones, it is hard to say if the horse is actually smelling Ken's hormonal difference; sensing it with the VNO; tasting it on Ken's skin; or perceiving it some other way, such as through the effect that increased testosterone levels may have on Ken's body language.[5] Ken does not consider the effect of behavioral cues, which might be influenced either by the T itself or by his own culturally or hormonally mediated belief that he commands more authority as a man.

In focusing uniquely on his horse's sense of smell as it validates his experience of hormonal transition, Ken negates the social and material histories that both he and his horse bring to the relationship. Working with horses involves complex exchanges of body language, nonverbal communications signaling intentions that are translated by both horse and human to, ideally, engender mutual understanding. Ethological observations and the testimonies of horse trainers reveal how social relations are established and communicated significantly through body language. For example, the positioning of the axis of the body or of legs, neck, ears, or tail or small changes in facial expressions are used to negotiate personal space and obtain access to food, water, and companionship. It is possible that testosterone may have affected Ken's sense of embodiment and his enactment of authority through body language, which could then shift the terms of his relationship with his horse. It is also possible that the horse connects the smell of T with a previous authoritative male handler. In any case, Ken's narrative leaves out the possibility that this particular human–equine relationship reflects an ongoing process of negotiating communications based at least as much on the social history as on the present species and gender identity of each partner (Despret 2004; Haraway 2003, 2008; Hausberger and Muller 2002; Hearne 1986; Waiblinger et al. 2006).

Part of the work of locating dominance in smell in Ken's narrative is the association of smell (both the sensory acuity of smelling and the smell of bodies) with animals of the nonhuman variety. On the one hand, as a nonhuman animal, Ken's horse represents the authority of scent recognition (or other nonvisual sense), confirming Ken's biological maleness in a way that humans do not or cannot, given our preference for visual cues to demarcate sex and gender. On the other hand, smell, as a sense associated with animals and their smells, also works to reinforce species difference.[6] The animal that Ken both is (by his smell) and is not (by his also being man), works to camouflage the technical mediations of his transition. By naturalizing the effects of transition, lending them the authority and authenticity of biological fact, the constructedness of both his relationship to his own body and his relationships with other bodies is erased:

> Humans, whether they be heterosexual or homosexual, instinctively respond to "male" and "female" bodies and odors differently—just as other mammals do. I believe those who argue that gender is merely a social construct, and that in a more enlightened society people would not care what sex their partners were, are ignoring biological reality. And those who attempt to discourage transsexuals from hormones and surgery do us a terrible disservice. Transsexuals cannot reasonably expect others to accept us as male or female simply because that's what we say we are (Ken 2002, 60).

This radical division between biological essentialism and social constructivism that Ken articulates here reflects an ideological separation between nature and culture that Ken himself, in his transsexual transition from female bodied to male bodied, negates.

Ken articulates his understanding of transsexual difference as a type of technologically mediated naturalization:

> Taking hormones didn't just change my body to match my internal self-image—a feat miraculous enough in itself. It has made me able

> to interact with other creatures—both human and nonhuman—far more harmoniously than I ever had in my life. Though the solution I chose may seem bizarre and technological to some, it came out of the realization that humans too are guided by instinct. We are unique, but not separate from the rest of animal creation (Ken 2002, 61).

Ken uses his experience with his horse to counter accusations that transsexuality and the medical aspects of transition are not "natural," accusations that they are, as he puts it "bizarre and technological," artificial—terms that devalue the authenticity of transsexual experiences and embodiments. Ken generalizes from his experience with his horse to those with humans, who, as he sees it, react "instinctively"—automatically, unconsciously—in reading bodies as sexed:

> Nature has devised a relatively simple set of cues by which humans distinguish male and female, and a simple mechanism by which those distinguishing traits develop from the same basic pattern. By introducing one simple chemical into my body, I developed all the traits necessary for humans—and other animals—to see me as male (specifically, a deeper voice, facial hair, and a distinctively male aroma). Without hormone injections, and without enough natural testosterone to induce these crucial traits, my efforts to be perceived as male were doomed to failure (Ken 2002, 60).

Ken's experience with his horse convinces him that the way humans, like horses, react to biologically sexed bodies is biologically determined. By naturalizing his own transition, Ken accords himself a clear identity as male, a location within culture as a natural man, unambiguously recognizable as such through his biological composition. This part of his experience is important to Ken in terms of his history, as he describes being unable to pass when he was pre-transition: "The world saw me as female, no matter how I dressed or acted" (58). Ken doesn't interpret his being read as a woman, pre-transition, as caused by "malice or institutionalized sexism"; instead, he concludes that "people are animals like any other, and they respond instinctively to certain visual, auditory, and olfactory cues" (58). He suggests that there is a fundamentally biological way that animals (including humans) respond to sexed bodies, regardless of heterosexual or homosexual orientation, which, in terms of the ambiguity of transsexual embodiment, is what the technology of transition resolves. However, I also think Ken's statement about resistance to accepting transsexual embodiment without the biological alterations of hormonal or surgical transition points to the importance of cultural context in interpretations of sex and gender. We can only be accepted as "what we say we are" if our presentation corresponds with our culture's coding of gendered difference.[7]

Reducing difference to an effect of either biological essentialism or cultural construction negates the varieties of sexes and gender expressions that emerge from the interplay of biological and social factors, in the same way that nature and culture are not separate entities but co-constitutive (Haraway 1994, 2003, 2008). I would argue that for transsexual identities and embodiments, as well, no materiality preexists meaning, that meaning and material come into existence intra-actively (Barad 2001, 232), which is exactly why, in the context of current U.S. practice, transsexuality (Gender Identity Disorder) requires *DSM* (DSM-IV-TR 2000) diagnostics and the mediation of medical professionals. Judith Butler underscores the intersectionality that is at work in bringing objects and subjects into being:

> It must be possible to concede and affirm an array of "materialities" that pertain to the body, that which is signified by the domains of biology, anatomy, physiology, hormonal and chemical composition, illness, age, weight, metabolism, life and death....But the undeniability of these "materialities" in no way implies what it means to affirm them, indeed, what interpretive matrices condition, enable and limit that necessary affirmation (Butler 1993, 66–67).

It is not only the multiplicity of materialities that matter here but also how we "affirm them," the "interpretive matrices" within which they find individual, social, and cultural meanings. Ken's narrative fails to account for the varieties of "situated knowledges" (Haraway 1991, 183) that he and his horse are engaged in together, considerations that bring feminist and animal studies together in developing "articulated, differentiated, accountable, located, and consequential theories of embodiment, where nature is no longer imagined and enacted as resource to culture or sex to gender" (Haraway 1991, 148). In what follows, I will ask how embodied relationships to the human self and to animal others might be otherwise framed to better account for individual and collective material relations.

EMBODIED CO-DOMESTICATIONS

Ken's figuring of self—like all our figurings of selves—shapes the possibilities of his relationships with others, human and nonhuman. His (psychic and material) embodiment as male is his means of translating experiences of relationality, and insofar as he succeeds in attaining a coherent body ego, he has realized the way that "the body is not a static phenomenon, but a mode of intentionality, a directional force and mode of desire" (Butler 1986, 38). The ambivalence and contradictions in Ken's narrative reflect tensions between the way the narrative disrupts sex and species category boundaries and how it also works to enforce them and reflect the various stakes involved in both rupture and enforcement. Taking the narrative as a whole, Ken collapses biological and social factors in a way that rebiologizes sexual difference and analogizes human and horse behavior so that cultural influences are reduced to natural phenomena. Ken's story fails to account for the fact that "bodies can only be understood, only become legible, through their historically contingent specificity" (Salamon 2006, 583). What is at stake for Ken is a feeling of closure, but at stake both for Ken and for us are relations of power and powerlessness. While Ken resorts to biological essentialism to attain his closure, I think the problem lies in resistance to visibility and acknowledgment of the diverse possibilities of sex and gender variations.

The experience of being a body is already implicated in culturally reinforced systems of difference. Judith Butler suggests that the psychical and physical are connected through a differentiation and asks, "What is excluded from the body for the body's boundary to form?" (1993, 65). The answer depends on what kind of body is being formed. Western conceptions of the human exclude the animal, as the construct of man excludes woman.[8] Difference works within these categorizations to demarcate power and powerlessness. The differentiation Ken relies on in his narrative involves a loss of female hormonal signification and a gain of male hormonal signification, which translates, for him, into an embodied transition from femaleness to maleness, from powerlessness to empowerment. Butler's articulation of the relation between psychic and material suggests that it is the interface between these two that works to constitute bodies: "Psychic projection confers boundaries and, hence, unity on the body, so that the very contours of the body are sites that vacillate between the psychic and the material. Bodily contours and morphology are not merely implicated in an irreducible tension between the psychic and the material but are that tension" (66).

Butler is saying here that the body, the material, does not preexist the psychic, the idea of, or the subjective experience of, the body. Rather, the body emerges from tensions between the material and the psychic, from their intersections and disjunctions. How does this map onto Ken's experience with his horse? The horse provides a defining other for Ken, affirming both his masculinity and his human dominion (which then become the same): "The ego's identifications with others…secure for it the illusion of a corporeal coherence that its own lived experience belies. Through its fantasized identity with others, it is able to take up the body as *its* body, to produce a separating space between it and others, between it and objects" (Grosz 1995, 85). For Ken, bodily integrity is materialized with the incorporation of testosterone as a marker of maleness, and given humans' lack of olfactory sensitivity or awareness, it is important that Ken finds confirmation of his altered status through his horse, who shows respect for Ken's newly male body and the authority that comes with it.

The narrative of Ken's relationship with his horse works to validate his experience of transition and to authenticate his post-transition embodiment. The narrative is empowering for him and figures the horse as an active participant in this horse-human interaction through the horse's resistance, his interest, and his cooperation. How could these positive aspects of the relationship be rearticulated by using language that is more inclusive of the various materialities at work in Ken's relationship with his horse and that works more self-consciously to account for equine subjectivity and agency? What other models might be useful in understanding embodied relationality, and how might they be applied to the evolving relationships that Ken describes, in terms of both the development of his relationship to his own changing body and the development of his relationships to other bodies? Euro-American representational practices typically construct nonhuman animals as "passive surfaces on to which human groups inscribe imaginings and orderings of all kinds" (Fudge 2002, 5). What I and other animal studies scholars argue for is "to give credence to the practices that are folded into the making of representations, and—at the core of the matter—to ask how animals themselves may figure in these practices" (Fudge 2002, 5). A fundamental challenge for animal studies is how to represent these cooperative partnerships using language that automatically privileges the human subject.

Applying Bruno Latour's concept of "articulation" (2004, 209), the process whereby a body learns to be affected by an other, to the story Ken tells about himself and about his horse foregrounds the question of what it means to be in relationships across difference:

> An inarticulate subject is someone who whatever the other says or acts always feels, acts and says the same thing.... In contrast, an articulate subject is someone who learns to be affected by others—*not by itself*.... A subject only becomes interesting, deep, profound, worthwhile when it resonates with others, is affected, moved, put into motion by new entities whose differences are registered in new and unexpected ways. Articulation thus does not mean the ability to talk with authority...but being affected by differences (Latour 2004, 210).

How do Ken and his horse become "articulate" to each other? Ken acknowledges both his horse's resistance and the change that comes about in his horse's attitude to him post-T. The horse recognizes the shift in Ken's embodied self and articulates the change through his compliance with Ken's demands. Together, posthormonal transition, they form a different combination from the one they had configured previously. Both become different bodies by learning to be affected differently within the specificity of this relation.

To understand how what they become together is different from what they were, and why this requires different embodied relations, I turn to Vinciane Despret's suggestion that the interactions between two beings produce "a practice of *domestication*," which is a creating of new experiences, new practices, for both parties and, as such, is transformative of both. Despret is specifically interested in cross-species relationships and describes domestication as "an 'anthropo-zoo-genetic practice,' a practice that constructs animal and human" (2004, 122). Despret emphasizes, in contrast to conventional understandings of domestication as adaptation to human needs through selective breeding, that anthropo-zoo-genetic practice is transformative for both human and animal, changing both human and animal bodies to more closely account for their interactive needs. To effect such change, domestication (as anthropo-zoo-genetic practice) must include "resistance" to the questions being asked, to the demands made, as opposed to being conceived of as "docility" (123) or compliance. Within a reciprocal relationship, through resistance, the questions, along with the questioner, have the potential to be transformed. Can we imagine that the questions that Ken asked pre-T to his horse did not make sense until after the start of the former's hormonal transition or the answers provided by the horse's resistance were not comprehensible to Ken until after transition began?

The mutual transformation that happens within domestication as anthropo-zoo-genetic practice is what Despret calls a relationship of "being-with" (130–31). "Being-with" involves co-creating, a broadening that maintains discreteness as opposed to a merging or simple identification. Difference is maintained within this relationship and offers the grounds for new learning for both parties. Despret suggests that in the negotiating of differences the body can become a "domesticating device" as it is used "as a tool for knowing, as a tool for asking questions, as a means to create a relation that provides new knowledge" (129).

The knowledge that is being produced in the relationship between Ken and his horse is suggested in the photograph that accompanies Ken's narrative. It shows Ken, dressed in jeans, white T-shirt, and unbuttoned dress shirt, standing next to his horse, one hand loosely holding a lead rope with a stud chain attached to the horse's halter and one hand reaching toward the horse. (A stud chain is a narrow metal chain that goes over the horse's nose to provide the human handler more control. It is commonly used with stallions and works through applying intensified pressure or pain on the bridge of the horse's nose.) In spite of the barely visible threat of the chain, both Ken and his horse are smiling in what appears to be mutual communication and enjoyment. Ken is smiling in the way we normally recognize humans as smiling, looking directly at the camera/viewer; his horse's head is tilted toward the camera/viewer with his lips apart just enough so that we can see his teeth, representing what a human might interpret as a horsy "smile." The horse is likely responding with pleasure to Ken's scratching his neck or withers, which is something horses do with their equine friends during mutual grooming sessions. The visual text underscores the meaningfulness of Ken's relationship with his horse and the importance of the horse's mediation of Ken's experience of transition. The becoming man of Ken's narrative is affirmed by his horse's acceptance of Ken's authority, an aspect of their relationship that has evolved through the technology of hormonal transition but that remains under negotiation, as implied by the unspoken presence of the chain over the horse's nose. The differences Ken negotiates, both in his narrative and in the photo with his horse, remain within hierarchical frameworks of both species and sex/gender difference.

CONCLUSION

As work in animal studies explores how nonhuman animals assert their subjectivity and agency within relations with humans, there are calls within trans-studies for transsexual subjects to articulate their own experiences apart from definitions allotted by the medical establishment, with its central role in actualizing transsexual transition.[9] How do we articulate the experience of nonhuman subjects within language, with its categories, definitions, and grammars, which resist the apparent contradiction of a "nonhuman" subject? Another way to ask this question is to ask how the language we use to tell our stories, steeped as it is in historically entrenched binaries of male and female, human and animal, nature and culture, can account for differences in terms of multiplicity? How do we tell different stories? As Donna Haraway argues, there are material implications to how we tell our stories: "Figures are not representations or didactic illustrations, but rather material-semiotic nodes or knots in which diverse bodies and meanings coshape one another. For me, figures have always been where the biological and literary or artistic come together with all the force of lived reality. My body itself is just such a figure, literally" (2008, 4). All bodies are stories of creation and stories in creation.

Stories of gender transition require similar attention to unresolvable multiplicity. Transsexual transition marks a period of flux, of change, of border crossing: "An intermediate nonzone, transition represents the movement in between that threatens to dislocate our ties to identity places we conceive of as essentially (in every sense) secure" (Prosser 1998, 3). But what of the security of these "identity places" and the generalizing, categorizing, and simplifying of multiple and overlapping identities that they require? What is the relation of transsexual becoming to the feminist/queer understanding that "a concept of coherent inner self, achieved (cultural) or innate (biological), is a regulatory fiction that is unnecessary—indeed inhibitory—for feminist projects of producing and affirming complex agency and responsibility" (Haraway 1991, 135)?

As the problems in Ken's narrative suggest we must, how can we productively ask similar questions about what makes us identifiable as *human*? Is there a "trans"-itive location in being human? What kind of uncertainty would have to exist for us to feel "uncertain of how to read" (Prosser 1998, 2) our human identity?[10] The narrative falls short in accounting for the multiple "interpretive matrices" in which sex, gender, and species are couched, as each of these categories has "a history and a historicity" involving "boundary lines" and "relations of discourse and power" that they cannot be separated from. Ken's narrative of transsexual transition and his story of cross-species recognition show how the histories, boundaries, and plays of power are troublesome in their interconnectivities, how they are at once "persistent and contested regions" of experience that reflect the material possibilities of embodiment in terms of sex, gender, and species.

I hope to have shown how complex this one human-horse relationship is, how much is invested in it, and how significant the payoffs are for both parties in the relationship. I also insist that other horse-human relationships require similar attention. Ken, regardless of my feminist critique, gains an empowering self-identity; his horse gains a better working relationship. The narrative provides an unacknowledged agency to the horse as he is an active shaper of the horse-human interaction through his resistance, his interest, and his cooperation. The narrative also validates transsexual experience in allowing Ken a means by which to authenticate his post-transition embodiment and demarcates the significance of human-animal relationships in the work of developing a coherent sense of self. However, I suggest that there is more work for humans and horses to do together, specifically in working toward improved relations of power and powerlessness between humans and nonhumans, as well as between humans. In the ongoing work of illuminating systems of power and powerlessness, regardless of whether they are expressed in terms of race, sex, species, ethnicity, class, age, abilities, or other frameworks, the fact remains that collusions at the level of individuals and bodies remains our challenge. If the idea of domestication is conceived of here in terms of mutual questioning, resistance, and accommodation, the idea of both horse and human bodies as mutually domesticating devices suggests new ways to conceptualize and enact not only cross-species relationalities but also relationalities between humans.

ACKNOWLEDGMENTS

Thanks to Carla Freccero, Carra Stratton, Robin Tremblay-McGaw, and Kris Weller for reading early drafts of this essay.

NATALIE CORINNE HANSEN is completing her dissertation in literature with a special notation in feminist studies at the University of California, Santa Cruz. Before beginning doctoral studies, she worked with horses professionally and continues to enjoy equine companionship. Natalie welcomes feedback at nchansen@ucsc.edu.

NOTES

1. In the section of Kotula's book containing Ken's short narrative, the men who authored their stories are identified by only their first names, which are used also as titles. The writer whose narrative I discuss here also has an essay, "We Were There: Female-To-Male Transsexuals in the Civil War" (Morris 2002) included in Kotula's collection; see note 8, below.

2. Castrating male horses is very common because it makes them easier for humans to handle and to house. Male horses are typically castrated between the ages of four months and two years; however, Ken's horse happened to have been castrated as an adult, "late in life."

3. Changes in narratives concerning equine social relations are also reflected in contemporary accounts of "natural horsemanship" as practiced by horse trainers (Dorrance 2001; Lyons 1991; Rashid 2000; Roberts 1997), some of whom suggest that the best approach to developing working relationships with horses is by simulating the authority of the "dominant" or "lead" mare, an approach they contrast with other (and popularly outmoded) techniques that use force to subdue horses, to "break" them, rendering them compliant to human authority. See also Keaveney 2007.

4. But see Sacks 1987, describing the case of Stephen D., who after dreaming one night that he was a dog "in a world unimaginably rich and significant in smells" (156), woke up being able to smell like that very dog he dreamed he was: "He found he could distinguish all his friends—and patients—by smell: 'I went into the clinic, I sniffed like a dog, and in that sniff recognized, before seeing them, the twenty patients who were there. Each had his own olfactory physiognomy, a smell-face, far more vivid and evocative, more redolent, than any sight-face.' He could smell their emotions—fear, contentment, sexuality—like a dog" (157). See also Keller 2006, in which Helen Keller describes "person-odor" as allowing her to distinguish between individuals, to know what kind of work they do, to trace their movements in space, explaining: "Human odors are as varied and capable of recognition as hands and faces" (182).

5. There is disagreement about the role of pheromones in mammals (see Wyatt 2003). Herz (2006) states that pheromones "are not odors" and require other means of detection. Temple Grandin (2005) discusses research suggesting that Old World

primates, humans included, lost pheromone signaling in exchange for three-color vision (62).

6. Discussions of "animality," in the form of smell, as associated with racially or ethnically "othered" human populations can be found in Drobnick 2006. Also see Mbembe 2001 for discussion of the dehumanization/animalization of native/indigenous populations that accompanies colonization.

7. Interestingly, Ken narrates the power of nonbiologically mediated trans experience in Morris 2002. Here, he discusses a number of specific instances of women who served as male soldiers (without being recognized as women) for long periods (he also mentions the few early female-to-male transsexuals who managed to procure hormones or breast removal surgery). His purpose is not just to identify that there were women fighting as men in the Civil War; he reads some of the letters and writings collected from these soldiers to argue for a difference between transmen, lesbians, and women and to argue that transsexuality existed prior to the medical procedures of the 1930s (Morris 150–51). In both his personal transition narrative (Ken 2002) and the Civil War piece (Morris 2002), Ken is working toward defining a specific identity for transmen. In his view, female-to-male transsexuals are humans, born as women, who experience themselves, their bodies, their behaviors, their interests and tendencies, as male, with a sense of male masculinity that is different from butch lesbian masculinity or "female masculinity" (Halberstam 1998). This underscores the importance of biological essentialism in Ken's argument.

8. See, for example, Luce Irigaray's (1985) critique of the figure of woman in phallocentric language and practices. An analogy between the "othering" of animals and the "othering" of women (or members of radicalized or other marginalized groups) may be interesting in a figurative sense; however, the different situations, embodiments, and conditions of living for each population involves critical and untransposable differences. See Anderson 2002 and Halley 2000.

9. Jay Prosser (1998) "attempts to recreate the 'living space' of transsexuals in cultural theory by reading the transsexual as authorial subject" in order to counteract the reductionist work of "mediocodiscursive texts" and "to reexamine the whole problematic of the subject's construction in postmodern theory" (9). For transsexual subjects, Prosser suggests honoring narratives that come into being apart from the medical context of biological transition: "The transsexual's capacity to narrativize the embodiment of his/her condition, to tell a coherent story of transsexual experience, is required by the doctors before their authorization of the subject's transition. As they remain invested in the therapeutic/analytic origins of the transsexual story, published transsexual autobiographies underline the continuing importance of narrative for transsexual subjectivity: where transsexuality would heal the gendered split of transsexuality, the form of autobiography would heal the rupture in gendered plots. Narrative is not only the bridge to embodiment but a way of making sense of transition, the link between locations: the transition itself" (9).

Prosser's idea here, that transsexual narratives have the potential to bring together lived contradictions both in bodily experience and in the stories that describe particular bodies, is reflected in Ken's story about his experience with his horse, a narrative about coming into being as a man and of being recognized as such by his equine companion.

10. These questions are being asked by animal studies scholars; see Adams 1991; Anderson 2002; Derrida 1992; 2003; Despret 2004; Haraway 2003; 2008; Wolfe 2003.

WORKS CITED

Adams, Carol. 1991. *The Sexual Politics of Meat: A Feminist-Vegetarian Critical Theory*. New York: Continuum.

Anderson, Kay. 2002. "The Racialization of Difference: Enlarging the Story Field." *Professional Geographer* 54.1:24–30.

Barad, Karen. 2001. "Scientific Literacy - Agential Literacy = (Learning + Doing) Science Responsibly." In *Feminist Science Studies: A New Generation*, ed. Maraless Mayberry, Banu Subramaniam, and Lisa H. Weasel. New York: Routledge.

Budiansky, Stephen. 1997. *The Nature of Horses: Exploring Equine Evolution, Intelligence, and Behavior*. New York: Free Press.

Butler, Judith. 1986. "Sex and Gender in Simone De Beauvoir's *Second Sex*." *Yale French Studies* Volume #72. Simone de Beauvoir: Witness to a Century. 35–49.

———. 1993. *Bodies That Matter: On the Discursive Limits of "Sex."* New York: Routledge.

Crowell-Davis, Sharon. 2007. "Sexual Behavior of Mares." *Hormones and Behavior* 52(1):12–17.

Crowell-Davis, Sharon, and Katherine A. Houpt, eds. 1986. *Behavior*. Philadelphia W. B. Saunders.

Derrida, Jacques. 1992. "'Il faut bien manger' ou Le calcul du sujet." In *Points de suspension: Entretiens; Choisis et présentés par Elisabeth Weber*. Paris: Galilée.

———. 2003. "And Say the Animal Responded." In *Zoontologies*, ed. Cary Wolfe. Minneapolis: University of Minnesota Press.

Despret, Vinciane. 2004. "The Body We Care For: Figures of Anthropo-Zoo-Genesis." *Body and Society* 10(2–3):11–134.

Diagnostic and Statistical Manual of Mental Disorders. "Gender Identity Disorder." Fourth Edition, Text Revision (DSM-IV-TR). American Psychiatric Association. Washington, DC. 2000. 576-582.

Dorrance, Tom.. 2001. *True Horsemanship Through Feel*. With Leslie Diamond. Guilford, Conn.: Lyons Press.

Drobnick, Jim, ed. 2006. *The Smell Culture Reader*. New York: Berg.

Fudge, Erica. 2002. "A Left-Handed Blow: Writing the History of Animals." In *Representing Animals,* ed. Nigel Rothfels. Indiana: Indiana University Press.

Grandin, Temple. 2005. *Animals in Translation: Using the Mysteries of Autism to Decode Animal Behavior*. New York: Scribner.

Grosz, Elizabeth. 1995. *Space, Time, and Perversion: Essays on the Politics of Bodies*. New York: Routledge.

Halberstam, Judith. 1998. *Female Masculinity*. Durham and London: Duke University Press.

Halley, Janet. 2000. "'Like Race' Arguments." In *What's Left of Theory*, ed. John Guillory Judith Butler, and Kendal Thomas. New York: Routledge.

Haraway, Donna. 1991. *Simians, Cyborgs, and Women: The Reinvention of Nature*. New York: Routledge.

———. 1994. "A Game of Cat's Cradle: Science Studies, Feminist Theory, Cultural Studies." *Configurations* 2(1):59–71.

———. 2003. *The Companion Species Manifesto: Dogs, People, and Significant Otherness*. Chicago: Prickly Paradigm Press.

———. 2008. *When Species Meet*. Ed. Cary Wolfe. Minneapolis and London: University of Minnesota Press.

Hausberger, Martine, and Christine Muller. 2002. "A Brief Note on Some Possible Factors Involved in the Reactions of Horses to Humans." *Applied Animal Behaviour Science* 76:339–44.

Hearne, Vickie. 1986. *Adam's Task: Calling Animals by Name*. New York: Vintage.

Herz, Rachel S. 2006. "I Know What I Like: Understanding Odor Preferences." In *The Smell Culture Reader*, ed. Jim Drobnick. New York: Berg.

Irigaray, Luce. 1985. *This Sex Which Is Not One*. Ithaca, New York: Cornell University Press.

Keaveney, Susan M. 2008. "Equines and Their Human Companions." *Journal of Business Research* 61(5). 444-454.

Keiper, Ronald R., and Hans H. Sambraus. 1986. "The Stability of Equine Dominance Hierarchies and the Effects of Kinship, Proximity, and Foaling Status on Hierarchy Rank." *Applied Animal Behaviour Science* 16(2):121–20.

Keller, Helen. "Sense and Sensibility." In *The Smell Culture Reader*, ed. Jim Drobnick. New York: Berg.

Ken. 2002. "Ken." In *The Phallus Palace: Female to Male Transsexuals*, ed. Dean Kotula. Los Angeles: Alyson.

Latour, Bruno. 2004. "How to Talk About the Body? The Normative Dimension of Science Studies." *Body and Society* 10(2–3):205–29.

Linklater, Wayne L., and Elissa Z. Cameron. 2000. "Tests for Cooperative Behaviour Between Stallions." *Animal Behaviour* 60:731–43.

Linklater, Wayne L., Elissa Z. Cameron, Edward O. Minot, and Kevin J. Stafford. 1999. "Stallion Harassment and the Mating System of Horses." *Animal Behaviour* 58:295–306.

Lyons, John. 1991. *Lyons on Horses*. With Sinclair Browning. New York: Doubleday.

Mbembe, Achille. 2001. *On the Postcolony*. Berkeley and Los Angeles: University of California Press.

McDonnell, Sue. M. 2003. *A Practical Field Guide to Horse Behavior: The Equid Ethogram*. Lexington, Ky.: Eclipse Press/ Blood-Horse.

McDonnell, Sue M. 2000. "Reproductive Behavior of Stallions and Mares: Comparison of Free-Running and Domestic in-Hand Breeding." *Animal Reproduction Science* 60–61:211–19.

Mills, Daniel S., and Katheryn J. Nankervis. 1999. *Equine Behaviour: Principles and Practice.* Malden, Mass.: Blackwell Science.

Morris, Ken. 2002. "We Were There: Female-to-Male Transsexuals in the Civil War." In *The Phallus Palace: Female to Male Transsexuals,* ed. Dean Kotula. Los Angeles: Alyson Publications.

Prosser, Jay. 1998. *Second Skins: The Body Narratives of Transsexuality.* New York: Columbia University Press.

Rashid, Mark. 2000. *Horses Never Lie: The Heart of Passive Leadership.* Boulder, Colo.: Johnson Books.

Roberts, Monty. 1997. *The Man Who Listens to Horses.* New York: Random House.

Sacks, Oliver. 1987. "The Dog Beneath the Skin." In *The Man Who Mistook His Wife for a Hat and Other Clinical Tales.* New York: Harper and Row.

Salamon, Gayle. 2006. "Boys of the Lex: Transgenderism and Rhetorics of Materiality." *GLQ* 12(4):575–97.

Sedgwick, Eve Kosofsky. 1985. *Between Men: English Literature and Male Homosocial Desire.* New York: Columbia University Press.

Waiblinger, Susanne, Xavier Boivin, Vivi Perdersen, Maria-Vittoria Tosi, Andrew M. Janczak, E. Kathalijne Visser, and Robert Bryan Jones. 2006. "Assessing the Human-Animal Relationship in Farmed Species: A Critical Review." *Applied Animal Behaviour Science* 101:185–242.

Waring, George H. 1983. *Horse Behavior: The Behavioral Traits and Adaptations of Domestic and Wild Horses, Including Ponies.* Park Ridge, N.J.: Noyes.

Wolfe, Cary. 2003. *Animal Rites: American Culture, the Discourse of Species, and Posthumanist Theory.* Chicago: University of Chicago Press.

Wyatt, Tristram D. 2003. *Pheromones and Animal Behaviour: Communication by Smell and Taste.* Cambridge: Cambridge University Press.

Zeitler-Feicht, Margit H. 2004. *Horse Behaviour Explained: Origins, Treatment, and Prevention of Problems.* Trans. Katharina Lohmann. Consultant, Katherine A. Houpt. London: Manson.

WHICH HALF IS MOMMY? TETRAGAMETIC CHIMERISM AND TRANS-SUBJECTIVITY

AARON T. NORTON AND OZZIE ZEHNER

Imagine being told by a doctor that a twin, one you never knew you had, exists inside you. It is well known that fraternal twins arise from two fertilized eggs that develop into nonidentical siblings. Less well known is that these two zygotes sometimes overlap and fuse so completely as to develop into one body with two distinct sets of DNA, a phenomenon called tetragametic chimerism (Tippett 1983). We explore how this rare occurrence exposes complex links between understandings of DNA, human subjectivity, and definitions of motherhood. We focus on cases in the United States of two chimeric women, Lydia and Karen, who were subjected to genetic tests for parentage and subsequently deemed by medical authorities not to be the mothers of their children. The stories of these two women offer opportunities to investigate how definitions of motherhood are constructed, legitimized, and contested by and through science.

According to Marilyn Strathern (1992), nature does not offer us an adequate basis on which to develop a culturally relevant model for kinship. Nevertheless, Western perceptions of kinship increasingly refer to genetic categorizations of bodies as means for defining legitimate mothers and fathers. Aryn Martin (2007a) suggests that there is something of the self that has "become bound up in cells, in response to a cultural rhetoric of genetic reductionism…facilitated by a broader political shift toward privatization and individual responsibility in the late twentieth century in America and in other advanced liberal states" (222). We outline the foundations that enabled this shift toward valuing genetic makeup as a component of modern citizenship. Specifically, we argue that the process of genetic testing works to publicly legitimate the effectiveness of the test itself while acting to stabilize a narrow and powerful definition of motherhood based on testable biological attributes. We then compare the performative aspects of the chimeric mother with notions of "passing" and offer a consideration of human chimerism as posthuman drag. Finally, we argue that the political implications of the established means used to define legitimate mothers extend beyond the trans-genomic quality of chimeric mothers to inform inquiry into reductionist arguments confronted by transgender parents and their children.

For our analysis, we largely focus on the experiences of Lydia and Karen as they are presented in the *New England Journal of Medicine*, a National Public Radio interview, and a Discovery program with the title *I Am My Own Twin*. We conduct a genealogy of the conditions that have led to the momentary unintelligibility of chimeric mothers within a genetic reductionist framework and extend this to other trans phenomena. Throughout the analysis, we apply Foucault's concept of biopower, whereby the chimeric individual undergoes a process of objectification and subjectification within a framework of technoscientific expertise and intervention.

INTRODUCING THE MYSTERY

The Discovery (2005) documentary first introduces Lydia, a Caucasian single mother with two young children and pregnant with a third, applying to receive welfare aid for her family. Through standard procedure, she and the African American father of her children took requisite blood tests to verify parentage. The lab results reported that the father was a match, but that Lydia could not possibly be the mother of her children. She and her family were subjected to multiple tests, emotional anguish, and accusations that she had obtained her children through illicit means. Even Lydia's father suspected she was not being honest about her conception and pregnancy. Eventually she was accused of welfare fraud and taken to court so that the state could determine parentage and reassign custody of the children accordingly. A tearful Lydia describes dropping her children off to day care with the concern it might be the last day she would see them. Unable to procure a lawyer because of the strength of the DNA evidence against her, she appeared in court alone. Seeing that Lydia was pregnant with her third child, the judge appointed a witness to observe Lydia's birth and run DNA tests on both her and the infant. The results came back negative, suggesting she was telling the truth, though to Lydia's chagrin the new results only fostered accusations that she had been a surrogate.

The second case in the documentary involves Karen, a financially secure Caucasian mother of three grown children. During the histocompatibility process for a kidney replacement, Karen's doctors insisted that only one of her sons was related to her; the other two were not. Karen claims that she believed the hospital had made a severe mistake. Nevertheless, she started to look at her children differently. Was there something about her third son that made him more like her? Would her other sons accept her as their mother? Could she treat them the same way as before? Karen relates to the viewer her fear that the other two sons might "somehow think of her as less their mother and that was very saddening…that somehow it was more like an adoption or it was just not the same as being their mom" (Discovery 2005). Unlike Lydia, who was threatened with losing custody of her children, Karen attracted the attention of a physician at the National Institutes of Health (NIH). Believing that she was an "upstanding citizen," researchers asked her to take part in an NIH-funded study to find a scientific explanation for this conundrum.

After extensive testing involving genetic identifications of several parts of her body, the researchers determined that Karen was a tetragametic chimera. Instead of the standard twenty-three pairs of chromosomes, she had forty-six. As a result, some of her tissues and organs were genetically mapped to a first set of chromosomes and others to a second. Karen's case was outlined in an article published in the *New England Journal of Medicine* (Yu et al. 2002), which fortuitously caught the attention of a state attorney involved in Lydia's case. After being introduced to the theoretical possibility that Lydia *could* be a chimera and following the established precedent of Karen's case, the judge eventually granted Lydia official motherhood of her children. After the court's determination, Lydia continued to cooperate with scientists, she too having become interested in her origins. During extensive examinations of her tissues, two sets of chromosomes were identified in her cervical smear results.

The identification of Lydia and Karen as "chimeras" follows a long etymology of the term, which we briefly summarize here. A chimera in Greek mythology (dating back to Homer, circa eighth century BCE) refers to a monstrous creature made of the parts of several different animals, typically the head of a lion, the body of a goat, and a snake for a tail (Lesky 1966). Beginning in the early twentieth century, the term has been applied metaphorically within scientific discourse to describe various phenomena, from grafted plants containing cells derived from different sources, to viruses that have appropriated genetic material from another organism, to nonhuman animals incorporating genetic material from an outside source. However, it was not until 1953 that the term "chimera" was first applied to a human being (Martin 2007b). In that year, geneticists identified the presence of two blood groups, A and O, in a woman referred to in the literature as Mrs. McK. Though the term "chimera" was being used in the 1950s to refer to an organism whose cells were derived from two distinct zygotes, this was never definitively demonstrated in Mrs. McK's case. Martin (2007b) suggests that researchers' expansion of the term to include Mrs. McK reflects the "politics and contingencies of scientific nomenclature" (102). In a more recent application, Donna Haraway (1991) uses the word when discussing cyborgs, referring, in part, to technohuman hybrids, or humans bodily incorporating varying degrees of technology.

Few definitive cases of tetragametic chimerism have been recorded since the 1950s. Until Lydia and Karen, most chimeras had presented with particular phenotypic characteristics, such as nonstandard genitalia or patchy skin and eye pigmentation (Yu et al. 2002), which prompted further inquiry and diagnosis. Karen and Lydia presented no such outward signs; the discordance between their DNA and that of their children most likely would have gone undetected had they and their children not been subjected to genetic testing.[1]

Given the experiences of these women, we might ask whether genetic testing is an effective way of establishing motherhood. But such a question presupposes that the concept of motherhood is durable or even an attribute that can be tested for in the first place. The event of human chimerism in childbearing women does not challenge genetic testing as much as it problematizes Western definitions and regulations encompassing maternity. An effect of genetic testing is that it in part structures our concept of what motherhood is. These tests can only be effective arbiters of motherhood to the extent that they are seen as legitimate and given power to reinforce particular notions of what being a mother means. Karen shares DNA with her sons but only approximately half her cells contain that DNA. Genetically speaking, she is both their mother and their aunt. Which organs are related to the children and which are not? Is she only a fraction of a mother?

SITUATING THE CHIMERIC MOTHER

Anthropologists have long dealt with complexities involved in defining kin and the centrality of resulting definitions in social interactions. The Western concept of biologically determined structures within the technos of kinship is only one of many explanations for "blood relations" between kin.[2] For example, some Australian aboriginal relations involve totem systems and concepts of reincarnation, which do not rely exclusively on knowledge about physiological procreation or notions of individual paternal consanguinity (Malinowski 1913). While contemporary Western definitions of kinship are strongly associated with cipherable biological links, in some cultures this link is neither as clear nor as durable. These biological associations have not always been so salient in Western traditions of kinship.

Through what conceptual mechanisms have genetic codes come to occupy a privileged position in Western definitions of motherhood? In the sections that follow, we argue that explanations can be found in the historical development of modern medicine's treatment of the human body, the rise of medical and scientific authority, and undercurrents of determinism in Western culture. We extend this familiar account to include the legitimating cycles of bio-identity performances, both social and institutional.

OBJECTIFICATION

Contemporaneous with the rise of public hospitals, clinics, and laboratories during the eighteenth and nineteenth centuries was a shift in the way doctors developed understandings about patients, their bodies, and their diseases. Before this shift, doctors were in an inferior social position to that of their mostly wealthy patients and relied primarily on patient descriptions of feelings and symptoms. Afterward, doctors became actively involved in the exploration of patients' bodies through visual inspection, palpation, percussion, taste, and auscultation (Bynum 1994).

In French schools, surgery and medicine were treated as two branches of the same science. Resultantly, corpses were provided to medical students, who were taught to see disease the way a surgeon would, in terms of anatomic structures (Bynum 1994; Risse 1984). With few therapies available for suffering patients, nineteenth-century diagnosticians concentrated their efforts on nosology. This biologically based mode of categorization has been characterized as a shift toward the objectification of bodies (Rosenburg 1981; Waldby 2000). Through such an understanding, bodies are envisioned as things to be studied, as a corpse would be. During the process of objectification, the human is silenced and investigated as a mechanism. A decoupling is achieved, one that separates the physical body that people *have* from the person that they *are*.

Lydia and Karen's trans-genomic status presents an opportunity to expose these strains of objectification involved in the sorting out of their status as mothers. Before the process of testing had begun, both women entered the phlebotomist's station as whole selves. Inside, they were fractured by a needle, which sucked away a part of their bodies to be interrogated. Their slightly damaged selves left the room, while a small part of their bodies stayed behind to be stored, shaken, mixed, dropped, inspected, recorded, verified, and eventually thrown away. Wrapped in a barcoded and numbered label, this part of their bodies represented them completely. Their selves became silent as this part of their body alone spoke for their experiences, capabilities, honesty, and other attributes, including their status as mothers. Importantly, these test outcomes eventually entered into Lydia and Karen's consciousness, informing their own subjectivity as mothers. This process is a variation of what Foucault views as a technology of confession, whereby expanding methods of science coerce bodies and their internal mechanisms to speak for people. The mother is rendered an object of knowledge whose internal structures tell the truth about her and become the basis of self-scrutiny—a simultaneity of objectification and subjectification (Dreyfus and Rabinow 1983).

SCIENTISM AND APPEALS TO METHOD

Through what historical and contemporary conceptualizations have these scientific confessions achieved their legitimacy? By the mid-nineteenth century, both the United States and Britain had established medical educational facilities, licensing, professional societies, periodicals, and laws regulating medical practice. Doctors understood that a privileged scientism could combat calls for lay control of medical practice. Shortt (1983) argues that inhabitants of the nineteenth century "internalized first the authenticity and then the utility of science" (167–168). Furthermore, scientific inquiries became increasingly shaped around the techniques and restrictions encountered in a laboratory setting as well as by opportunities enabled through chemistry, measurement instruments, and laboratory materials. Olga Amsterdamska (1993) explains that "sometimes the technical opportunities begin to serve not only as means to an independently specified goal, but as an end in themselves" (38). This importance of method as a constituent of science is further supported by John Moore (1993), who claims that "science is both knowledge of the natural world expressed in naturalistic terms and the procedures for obtaining that knowledge" (502).

From an eighteenth-century perspective, the thought that a vial of blood could speak for emotions, sexual experience, pregnancy, childbearing, and love would seem perfectly ludicrous. Even if the technological capacity for such a performance were available two centuries ago, it would not have been esteemed but more likely considered a criminal act. In contemporary Western society, however, the vial of blood calls upon established expertise and claims on method. These performances are involved in a process heavily influenced by a scientism whereby contents of a statement can become less significant than the established expertise of the person doing the stating.

DETERMINISM

In the early twentieth century, biological determinism surfaced as a way of bringing findings of medical research to bear on social issues. In its extreme form, social problems were seen as the result of genetic flaws that could be tracked and eliminated through eugenics. For example, William March's (1954) book and subsequent film, both titled *The Bad Seed*, follow the realization of a mother that her adolescent daughter, despite her ideal upbringing, has "inherited" a murderous instinct from her grandmother. Determinist explanations presume biological attributes as foundations for social interactions and identities. For instance, if a woman is a biological mother, she is presumed to be capable and interested in fulfilling society's ideal standards of motherhood (Rogus 2003).

Today's predominantly biogenetic model for defining kin, often assumed as self-evident and impartial, has been criticized for being recent, modernist, ethnocentric, and heteronormative (Franklin 1997; Hird 2004). David Schneider (1980) argues that this model of kinship should be understood as a specific symbolic system, one that is markedly Eurocentric. In the "American cultural conception," he notes, "kinship is defined as biogenetic. This definition says that kinship is whatever the biogenetic relationship is. If science discovers new facts about biogenetic relationship, then that is what kinship is and was all along" (1980, 23).

The experiences of Lydia and Karen also expose a degree of determinism present in contemporary scientific definitions of motherhood. For example, why did Lydia's court case revolve around DNA testing and not statements by her children indicating who their mother was? Even medical records showing that Lydia had given birth to her children were apparently trumped by an epistemological framework that privileges genetic evidence. Why were interrogations aimed at blood samples and not her family, her community, or members of her church? A court might argue that none of these people could speak authoritatively on whether she was a surrogate or perhaps adopted or even stole her children. The "legitimate" mother in this case is not the adopting mother, the caregiver mother, the family mother, or perhaps even two gay male "mothers," but the person who can display that her DNA forms a match with her children's. The result is a specific type of motherhood that is defined through seemingly fixed and lawlike biological attributes (Franklin 1995). So if Lydia's going to claim to be a mother, she'd better have the chromosomes to prove it.

PERFORMANCE, LEGITIMACY, AND POWER OF KINSHIP MODELS

According to Dorothy Nelkin and Susan Lindee (2004), media representations largely influence public conceptions of genetic relatedness. Television programs increasingly highlight individuals searching for their "roots" through locating their biological parents. Other shows bring families on stage to genetically sort them out into "real" parents and others—as if factors involving child rearing and care were less important if not accompanied by a complementary set of genetic material. Cultural weightings in the technos of kinship, largely derived through interactions with family and relations, are dialectically engaged with concepts of biological commonality.

In the same way that performativity of gender becomes part of the power associated with gender (Butler 1997; 1999), so DNA testing achieves credibility not exclusively through its functional value of defining related kind but through its very performance as such an indicator. The biological tests are *doing* kinship. And through the doing of kinship, biological testing enters into the flow of power surrounding the identification and definition of shared kind. A key aspect to performativity is repetition (Butler 1997). Every television show, magazine article, or interpersonal conversation that relates the story of a genetic test for parentage builds the power of the test as a valid means of identification. In addition, legitimacy develops by proxy through various other public discourses featuring essentialist claims, from genetic factors in depression to the search for a "gay gene."

Additionally, the repetition of performance acts to position biological surveillance as a *meaningful pursuit*. Private or public institutional support for genetic testing that is spoken, written, enacted, or implicitly embodied through policy bolsters the validity of the entire project of genetic testing and lends legitimacy to bio-experts as justified actors pursuing legitimate activity (Yanow 1996). The result is a self-reinforcing system whereby subsequent calls for political attention start from a higher level of legitimacy. For mothers, these repetitive performances act to buttress a narrowing toward biogenetic policing of their status as parents.

Performances and the resulting power flows involved in the legitimation of this model, however, should not be characterized purely as an autonomous technoscientific process. Undoubtedly, actors are involved in every step. For example, we might expect mothers themselves to invest less in biologically determined definitions of motherhood. After all, they have their own experiences as mothers to draw upon. Wouldn't a genetic test be insignificant in the face of such experience? In the case of Lydia and Karen, the answer is clearly *no*. After Karen's transplant and Lydia's court case, both women volunteered to cooperate with further genetic testing of their tissues. Their actions serve to patch the cracks formed in the genetic foundation of kinship and to restore the related science to a now stronger position as the legitimate arbiter of motherhood. It seems their experiences are in part structured through genetic understandings of kinship and cannot be so easily separated from these biological associations.

The salience of biologically bound definitions of motherhood becomes evident as we witness Karen questioning the nature of her own motherhood after having conceived, carried to term, given birth to, and raised her children. She reflects, "I felt that part of me hadn't passed on to them. I thought, 'Oh, I wonder if they'll really feel I am not quite their real mother'" (NPR 2003). One of her sons had DNA that formed a match with her own, prompting Karen to speculate, "Are there certain physical characteristics that make this third son look more, act more, is his personality more in tune with what my group of genes is producing?" (Discovery 2005). As Karen begins to call into question her own relationship to her children, we see the Foucauldian notion of subjectification at work—the process whereby subjects come to work on themselves within a disciplinary technology of the self (Foucault 1990)—redefining their own sense of subjectivity and their identities as mothers in biogenetic terms. Karen and her husband called a family meeting to tell their children that the doctors were saying they were not related to their mom. Her legitimacy as a mother came into question as the biological link between her and her children was contested. Perhaps this is why she agreed to subject her body to a series of highly invasive tests in order to determine her "origins" and to harmonize her biologically bound status as a mother with her otherwise understood standing as one.

POSTHUMAN DRAG

In Jenny Livingston's (1991) documentary film *Paris Is Burning,* a light-skinned Latina preoperative transsexual named Venus Xtravaganza effectively appropriates "realness norms" as a white woman in drag pageantries and as a sex worker on the streets; ultimately, however, she fails to pass on one occasion when she is killed by a client, presumably for violating gender norms. Judith Butler (1993) points to both what she calls drag's simultaneous denaturalization and reidealization of gender norms in moments of passing and to the exposure of extreme regulatory forces at work when Venus fails to pass and is murdered.

We propose the possibility that human chimeras could be envisioned as a form of drag that readily passes as that which it seeks to imitate—like Venus Xtravaganza, who passes, yet doesn't pass, in a "repetition which works at once to legitimate and delegitimate the realness norms by which it is produced" (Butler 1993, 131). The human chimera passes when her bodily manifestation of dual genetic material appears indistinguishable from a body that arose from one set and fails to pass only in moments of kinship marking. Furthermore, considering that reproductive technologies such as in vitro fertilization and implantation of multiple embryos result in an estimated thirty-three-fold increase in the chances of human chimerism (Strain, et al. 1998), the chimera could be viewed as a kind of posthuman subject, in line with Haraway's concept of a cyborg—an integration of human and technology. In such instances, the chimera can be read as "human" and is revealed to be passing only via a set of genetic technologies, which, ironically, are related to those that allowed for her creation.

Marjorie Garber (1992) ponders the dualism of "passing" and "not passing" and what it reveals about the performativity of gender and its problematic linear trace back to biological sex by asking: If females cross-dressing as males are "taken for males throughout their lives, to what gender *do* they belong?" (47). We might pose a comparable question of chimerism: If chimeras pass as humans with a single set of DNA, to which side of the emerging dividing practice of chimera/nonchimera do such people belong? Must a person be conscious of her status as "other" to be said to pass, and what happens when this "other" is not yet available within consciousness as an alternative? To address these questions we turn briefly to Garber's reference to Ellen Craft, a light-skinned slave who escaped from slavery by passing as a white man, described in William and Ellen Craft's *Running a Thousand Miles for Freedom*. The family that owned the Crafts became annoyed when Ellen was mistaken for a white child in the family. Garber argues that "Ellen Craft's 'crime,' in the eyes of the white family, is to look as if she belongs—a kind of 'passing' which is not deliberate but inadvertent, based upon similarity and contiguity: passing as metonymy" (1992, 282). Chimerism is just this sort of unintentional passing, which is revealed as such only in the moment that it no longer passes. In other words, "not passing" here requires exposure of both an admission of the possibility *to* pass and the admission of a successful passing prior to the moment at which one is said *no longer to* pass.

Anne Fausto-Sterling (2000) offers a more recent example of this unintentional passing, which begins to expose the role of scientific authority in both the identification and resolution of norm violations. Maria Patiño, a hurdler on Spain's 1988 Olympic team, was summoned, per regulations, for chromosomal sex testing before her event. To her surprise, Maria failed the test: "She may have looked like a woman, had a woman's strength, and never had reason to suspect that she wasn't a woman, but the examination revealed that Patiño's cells sported a Y chromosome, and that her labia hid testes within" (1). Consequently, Maria was barred from the Olympics as well as future events, stripped of past titles, and publicly outed by the press, which led to a number of upheavals in her personal life, including the loss of a boyfriend and a scholarship, as well as difficulty securing a job. Like our chimeric mother Lydia, Maria also became dependent on the intervention of scientific experts in her defense. After being diagnosed with an intersex condition called androgen insensitivity syndrome, Maria underwent a number of extensive examinations in order to argue that her cells' "inability to respond to testosterone" (2) had left her body "feminine enough to compete," according to her doctor (Vines 1992, 41). In 1992, following the intervention of medical authorities, Maria was reinstated by the International Olympic Committee.

Notably, chimeras with both XX and XY genetic makeup can be phenotypically male, female, or intersex, as a result of presumably differential proportions of cell lines in the gonads (Simon-Bouy, et al. 2003; Tippett 1983). Those with phenotypically standard genitalia might be said to be "passing" within a narrowly conceived biomedical framework that often insists upon concordance between gender identity and sexual anatomy, including chromosomes, as evident in Maria Patiño's case.

Lydia's "crime" appears to be similar to that of Ellen Craft and Maria Patiño, but in her case, she was passing as a mother. It seems clear that the court held the relationship between genes and motherhood to be self-evident. Motherhood was defined solely on evidence establishing a genetic link between mother and child. Had Lydia been the surrogate mother of these children, we might imagine none of this to have ever occurred. Her only crime was claiming to be a "real" mother, when, viewed within a scientifico-legal framework, she was merely a pseudomother. At the end of the trial, Lydia provided no more evidence that she was not a surrogate than at the beginning. The legitimacy of the claim that Lydia *could* be a chimera appears to have motivated the court to grant her official motherhood status.

Karen, unlike Lydia, enters into this discourse with science "on her side," but the overall process is one of the regulation of knowledge and bodies. What can we say, then, about passing in Karen's case? Can she be said to pass as something she was not aware she was *not* in the first place (a human with the standard twenty-three pairs of chromosomes)? While "chimera" is not yet a household term for another kind of being, the inexplicable genetic status of both Karen and Lydia was, in fact, used as a dividing practice within medical and juridical discourse and one that had profound effects on their own identity and subjectification. Like Lydia, the moment at which Karen can be said to pass comes when it is revealed that the DNA of her children does not match her own. Despite her normal appearance, she is revealed to be a chimera who had managed to evade the regulatory radar. In the moment at which Karen is diagnosed as chimeric, a moment in which science is said to have found the answer, the chimera simultaneously reidealizes the regulatory norm of science as purveyor of truth, reidealizes the status of the "normal" human being, and denaturalizes the entire framework by exposing the process at work.

THE ROLE OF EXPERTISE IN TECHNOLOGICAL CONFESSION

Donna Haraway (1997) defines kinship as "a technology for producing the material and semiotic effect of natural relationship, of shared kind" (53). The technology of kinship was once understood and practiced on a level immediately accessible to the actors and clans of actors involved in its regulatory application. Because of their human scale and accessibility, Aboriginal as well as early Western kinship models allowed citizens to be equals in comprehension of their placement in social structures. The shift toward a more exclusive view of a biological determinant of kinship is a movement away from accessible technologies that deliver the self to the social world and toward inaccessible technologies that direct inquiry inward.

Contemporary Western understandings of kinship are informed by complex genetic tests, which are neither fully understood nor simple enough to be administered by individuals. In contrast to social movements, such as that involving HIV/AIDS activists whose lay expertise transformed related clinical research and treatment (Epstein 1996), the chimera is isolated and can travel only to a certain point before being required to proceed on faith. Such a system carries democratic implications as it erodes informed choice and bypasses the feedback mechanism upon which democratic engagement relies.

If, for example, Lydia had a more comprehensive knowledge of the genetic means through which she was being judged, or at least a representative with such an understanding, she might have been better able to protect her motherhood status by challenging the specificity of the genetic test from the beginning. In Karen's case, having a class advantage over Lydia, one recognizes variability in the regulatory process of power. Karen was offered medical representation from the NIH, which helped her navigate the complexities involved in dealing with a motherhood model grounded in highly technical definitions of kinship. Conversely, Lydia initially ended up alone in a courtroom, unable to afford legal or alternate medical representation to defend her family.

From the experiences of Lydia and Karen, we can see that defense against accusations of false motherhood requires either highly specialized expertise or an intermediary technician. These technical resources, whether learned through education or provided through a representative, are not distributed evenly in American society. Lydia, coming from a lower socioeconomic position, did not have the resources that were available to Karen for her legal defense. Nor was a simple mode of engagement sufficient to adequately secure her status as a legitimate mother. Lydia never made claims that her DNA matched her children's. She entered the court claiming simply that she was the natural mother of her children and had the birth certificates to prove it. Yet these were the wrong tools to counter accusations framed in a court recognizing only genetically based relations between women and their offspring.

We note here the similarity between Lydia's situation and the challenges transgender parents face in a juridical system that silences the individual while privileging the medical knowledge and expertise that confesses on their behalf. Taylor Flynn (2006) thoroughly chronicles legal precedents involving transgender adults whose parental relationships were nullified by the courts. In case after case, trans parents who *are* genetically related to their children have had their parental relationships erased because they do not conform to societal standards of parenthood that insist on concordance between sex assigned at birth and gender expression or identity. Trans parents who are not biologically related to adoptive children by marriage may also find this legal relationship voided if their marriages are deemed fraudulent on the grounds that they are in same-sex relationships as indicated by their sex assigned at birth. Even in relatively rare cases when courts have sided with transgender people, appeals are made to scientific expertise, particularly the argument that internal biological attributes such as brain sex are causally related to the stability of gender identity (Flynn 2006). Confessions of trans people are expunged in favor of assertions by intermediary technicians who speak on their behalf, often after invasive and humiliating examination.

Like other trans people, human chimeras must undergo extensive examinations to establish their intelligibility as persons within a system where "scientific norms…seem almost sacred" (Dreyfus and Rabinow 1983, 174). However, unlike the phenotypically standard chimera who does not necessarily present a gender identity discordant with the sex assigned at birth, other trans individuals face additional moral obstacles associated with gender and sexuality; Flynn references a court that forbade visitation between a trans mother and her children because of "the need to protect the children's 'moral development'" (Flynn 2006, 42).

THEORETICAL, LEGAL, AND POLITICAL IMPLICATIONS

Paul Rabinow (1999) addresses the influence of biological attributes on social structures with the term "biosociality," a play on the word "sociobiology." The concept of biosociality stresses the prominence of biological means as culture is naturalized through constitutive metaphors of nature. Definitions of motherhood are constantly defined and redefined within these increasingly biologically informed technos through the actions and tacit understandings of the participants involved. We have argued that an effect of genetic testing is its increased predominance in the construction of kinship conceptualizations.

Strathern (1992) proposes that shifts in conceptualization have cultural consequences. Strains of objectification, scientism, and determinism in modern medicine allow for the deployment of technocratic means to categorize not only kin relations but bodies more broadly. Through the process of objectification, the physical body that a mother occupies is decoupled from the person that she is. This physical element is interrogated alone but allowed to speak for the entire mother as if she had not been fractured at all. Appeals to scientific expertise lend credibility to the means by which this process is performed. Furthermore, tacit and determinist understandings, outlining what mothers are and should be, come to be inscribed onto physical body elements. In effect, a new mother is formed through this inscription. Each performance of this fracture and fusion further legitimates the process until the underlying practice is eventually understood as natural truth, which is unquestioned and obvious. The event of chimerism in childbearing mothers offers a site of resistance, wherein the physical elements do not so neatly match with the determinist and idealized inscription being applied.

Scientific authorities create technological confessions for these mothers through a privileged objectification of their biological attributes. The women can challenge this confession but cannot challenge the process of confession itself. Through widespread and repetitive performances, the technological confession is articulated as it gravitates toward stabilization, which, in effect, sanctifies it. Both transgender and transgenomic parents are restricted to working within the scientific frame to refute confessions that have been made for them.

When the widely accepted and unquestioned technos of kinship is revealed to be a means of regulatory control, the foundations of a collective human subjectivity are fractured and the process begins again, but never entirely from scratch. The pieces of scientific knowledge are recycled, erected in novel ways, rather than fully discarded, and thus, subjectivity becomes inseparable from the technological processes that are used to construct those individual units of knowledge. Authorization and allocation of power is distributed throughout the process, resulting in a delocalized power network (Foucault 1990). Members of the scientific community may not consciously aim to control Karen and Lydia, but they are working within the means-based rationality of an established system of truth, which eventually does control the women's status as mothers.

Mechanisms of control are not limited to the scientific and legal communities; Karen and Lydia come to work on themselves, redefining their own identity as mothers. The control is so powerful that it changes the way Karen conceptualizes her relation with her sons. The mothers are forced to wait in a fractured state until a scientific explanation can sweep up the pieces, reassemble them in a novel way, and ultimately reaffirm the utility of science as a purveyor of truth.

In the face of new reproductive technologies and a multiplicity of family structures, agencies of the state struggle to hold on to rules of kinship based on traditional sex-differentiated notions of family. The expected increase in diagnosis of both existing chimeras and chimeras resulting from new reproductive technologies threatens to further disrupt these markers of kinship (Strain et al. 1998). By officially decreeing Lydia as the mother of her children with the emerging possibility that she could be a chimera, the state reinforces its power to determine lineage, reaffirms scientific practice as an integral part of juridical discourse (the introduction of the concept of chimerism into the discourse having affected the outcome), and exposes itself to contestation by revealing the instability of biogenetic definitions of motherhood. This completes the Foucauldian framework of power that flows reciprocally between bodies and the scientific framework in which they are inscribed to a legal system that socially enacts the resultant technologies to maintain and manage that framework.

In contrast to chimeric mothers, who can ultimately demonstrate a genetic link to their children, many biological transgender parents find this is not enough to secure their legal rights. The insistence that anatomy at birth determines one's gender as well as one's ability to be an appropriate mother or father appears to trump shared genes in this case. For Lydia, as well as biological and nonbiological transgender parents, there is a common reductionist tendency to privilege anatomical information over other possible criteria in defining one's ability to be an effective parent.

Like other trans phenomena, human chimerism positions itself as one among many possible sites of contestation revealing the science of life as cultural practice. Earlier, we claimed that chimerism does not challenge genetic testing as much as it challenges Western definitions and regulations surrounding kinship. The phenomenon of human chimerism will expand the already growing diversity of families, comprising both trans and nontrans individuals, for whom genetically referenced categorizations of kinship will hold less practical significance. A challenge to professionals and lay individuals is (and will continue to be) to imagine alternative legal and medical frameworks that open more space to valuing lived experience over genetic codes. Legal precedents such as functional parenthood, which can extend custodial or child visitation rights to genetically unrelated adults, are likely only the beginning of a larger trend in this direction. These legal precedents will not only directly challenge deterministic genetic assumptions but will also become reflexively involved with our evolving conceptualizations of bodies and their interrelations.

AARON NORTON worked as a research fellow in a molecular genetics lab at the National Institutes of Health. He holds an MA in psychology from the University of California, Davis, where he studied attitudes toward transgender people. He is currently enrolled in the doctoral program in sociology and science studies at the University of California, San Diego.

OZZIE ZEHNER'S primary research focuses on the sociology and politics of energy use. He is currently writing a public science book, *The Alternative Energy Fetish: Better Alternatives to Alternative Energy*. He is an architect and holds an MS in science and technology studies from the University of Amsterdam.

NOTES

1. We are not aware of any paternity disputes involving chimeric fathers and therefore do not examine this possibility, though we imagine there are cases that have gone undetected.

2. We borrow this terminology from Haraway (1996), who speaks in terms of a kinship "technos" when discussing genetics and genetic patenting. We use "technos" here to highlight that concepts of kinship are constructed technical systems, not mirrors of natural fact.

WORKS CITED

Amsterdamska, Olga. 1993. "From Pneumonia to DNA: The Research Career of Oswald T. Avery." *Historical Studies in the Physical and Biological Sciences* 24:1-40.

Butler, Judith P. 1993. *Bodies That Matter*. New York: Routledge.

——— . 1997. *Excitable Speech: A Politics of the Performative*. New York: Routledge.

——— . 1999. *Gender Trouble: Feminism and the Subversion of Identity*. New York: Routledge.

Bynum, William F. 1994. "Medicine in the Hospital." Pp. 25-54 in *Science and the Practice of Medicine in the Nineteenth Century*. Cambridge: Cambridge University Press.

Discovery. 2005. "I am My Own Twin." in Discovery Health. USA: Discovery Channel.

Dreyfus, Hubert L. and Paul Rabinow. 1983. *Michel Foucault: Beyond Structuralism and Hermeneutics*. Chicago: University Of Chicago Press.

Epstein, Steven. 1996. *Impure Science: AIDS, Activism, and the Politics of Knowledge*. Berkeley: University of California Press.

Fausto-Sterling, Anne. 2000. *Sexing the Body: Gender Politics and the Construction of Sexuality*. New York: Basic Books.

Flynn, Taylor. 2006. "The Ties That [Don't] Bind: Transgender Family Law and the Unmaking of Families." Pp. 32-50 in *Transgender Rights* edited by P. Currah, R. M. Juang, and S. P. Minter. Minneapolis: University of Minnesota Press.

Foucault, Michel. 1990. *The History of Sexuality*. Translated by R. Hurley. New York: Vintage.

Franklin, Sarah. 1995. "Science as Culture, Cultures of Science." *Annual Review of Anthropology* 24:163-184.

——— . 1997. *Embodied Progress: A Cultural Account of Assisted Conception*. London: Routledge.

Garber, Marjorie. 1992. *Vested Interest: Cross-dressing and Cultural Anxiety*. New York: Routledge.

Haraway, Donna J. 1991. *Simians, Cyborgs, and Women: The Re-invention of Nature*. London: Free Association.

Haraway, Donna J. 1996. "Universal Donors in a Vampire Culture: It's All in the Family: Biological Kinship Categories in the Twentieth-Century United States." In *Uncommon Ground: Rethinking the Human Place in Nature,* ed. W. Cronon, 321-78. Boston: Norton.

Haraway, Donna J. 1997. Modest-Witness@ second-Millennium. *Femaleman-Meets-Oncomouse: Feminism and Technoscience*. New York: Routledge.

Hird, Myra J. 2004. "Chimerism, Mosaicism and the Cultural Construction of Kinship." Sexualities 7:217-232.

Lesky, Albin 1966. *A History of Greek Literature*. Translated by J. Willis and C. d. Heer. London: Methuen.

Livingston, Jennifer. 1991. "Paris is Burning." Prestige/ Off White Productions.

Paris Is Burning [video recording]; produced and directed by Jennifer Livingston. 71 min; color; USA; English.

Malinowski, Bronislaw. 1913. *The Family Among the Australian Aborigines*. London: University of London Press.

March, William. 1954. *The Bad Seed*. New York: William Morrow.

Martin, Aryn. 2007a. "The Chimera of Liberal Individualism: How Cells Became Selves in Human Clinical Genetics." OSIRIS 22:205-222.

——— . 2007b. "'Incongruous Juxtapositions': The Chimaera and Mrs Mck." *Endeavour* 31(3):99–103.

Moore, John A. 1993. *Science as a Way of Knowing*. Cambridge: Harvard University Press.

Nelkin, Dorothy and Susan Lindee. 2004. *The DNA Mystique: The Gene as a Cultural Icon*. Ann Arbor, MI: University of Michigan Press.

NPR. 2003. "Sophisticated DNA Testing Turning Up More Cases of Chimeras, People with Two Sets of DNA." in *Morning Edition,* August 11. Washington, DC.

Rabinow, Paul. 1999. "Artificiality and Enlightenment: From Sociobiology to Biosociality " Pp. 407-416 in *The Science Studies Reader*, edited by M. Biagioli. New York and London: Routledge.

Risse, Günther B. 1984. "A Shift in Medical Epistemology: Clinical Diagnosis, 1770-1828." in *History of Diagnostics: Proceedings of the 9th International Symposium on the Comparative History of Medicine- East and West*, edited by Y. Kawakita Osaka: Taniguchi Foundation: Division of Medical History.

Rogus, Caroline. 2003. "Conflating Women's Biological and Sociological Roles: The Ideal of Motherhood, Equal Protection, and the Implications of the Nguyen v. INS Opinion." *Journal of Constitutional Law* 5:4.

Rosenburg, Charles. 1981. "Inward Vision and Outward Glance: The Shaping of the American Hospital, 1880-1914." Pp. 19-55 in *Social History and Social Policy*, edited by D. J. Rothman and S. Wheeler. New York: Academic Press.

Schneider, David M. 1980. *American Kinship: A Cultural Account*. Chicago: University of Chicago Press.

Shortt, Samuel E. D. 1983. "Physicians, Science, and Status: Issues in the Professionalization of Anglo-American Medicine in the Nineteenth Century." *Medical History* 27:235-268.

Simon-Bouy, Brigitte, Michelle Plachot, Ali Mokdad, Nicole Lavaud, Christine Muti, Alain Bazin, François. Vialard, and Joëlle. Belaisch-Allart. 2003. "Possible Human Chimera Detected Prenatally After In Vitro Fertilization: A Case Report." *Prenatal Diagnosis* 23:935-7.

Strain, Lisa, John Dean, Mark Hamilton, and David Bonthron. 1998. "A True Hermaphrodite Chimera Resulting From Embryo Amalgamation After In Vitro Fertilization." *The New England Journal of Medicine* (338):166–69..

Strathern, Marilyn. 1992. *Reproducing the Future: Essays on Anthropology, Kinship and the New Reproductive Technologies*. Manchester: Manchester University Press.

Tippett, Patricia 1983. "Blood Group Chimeras: A Review." *Vox Sang* 44:333-59.

Vines, Gail. 1992. "Last Olympics for the Sex Test?" *New Scientist* 135:39-42.
Waldby, Catherine. 2000. *The Visible Human Project: Informatic Bodies and Posthuman Medicine* London: Routledge.
Yanow, Dvora. 1996. *How Does a Policy Mean?: Interpreting Policy and Organizational Actions*. Washington: Georgetown University Press.
Yu, Neng, Margot S. Kruskall, Juan J. Yunis, Joan H. M. Knoll, Lynne Uhl, Sharon Alosco, Marina Ohashi, Olga Clavijo, Zahid Husain, and Emilio J. Yunis, Jorge J. Junis and Edmund J. Yunis. 2002. "Disputed Maternity Leading to Identification of Tetragametic Chimerism." *The New England Journal of Medicine* 346:1545.

HOW METAPHOR WORKS

JULIE CARR

Bits of food on the floor represent abundance and decay
The removal of a lens cap is history and memory loss
Weedy lawn means rain's exuberance and the absence of love
Sexual desire is an uncapped marker and an overturned bucket
The tear in her skin means sugar
The tear in her skin means the Industrial Revolution
Is a page of the Koran and a bit of food on the floor
A sleepless night is a hard commute and a broken zipper
News of a bombing and a locked museum
Are blood in an infant's veins
Excess is a streaming ribbon or a streaming ribbon a song
A distant cloud is the perfection of the present and a mark of
    inattention
The end of the honey is one's mother's death and one's mother

The plagiarist is a dish of cherry seeds

A boy's curved shoulder, a twelve-foot crater
Where once was a town center
A bottle of water is order in the capital
    and the ambitions of an art student
Ink is my face and is a sleepless night
A streaming ribbon is the end of the honey
A distant cloud a lens cap removed

A torn bucket is a bit of food on the floor of her thought

JULIE CARR'S books are *Mead: An Epithalamion* and *Equivocal*, out from Alice James Books this year. Recent work appears in *Verse, New American Writing, Parthenon West, Colorado Review,* and *Denver Quarterly* and in the anthologies *Not for Mothers Only* (Fence Books) and *Best American Poetry 2007*. With Tim Roberts she is the coeditor of Counterpath Press. She teaches poetry and literature at the University of Colorado, Boulder, and lives in Denver.

TRANSGENDER WITHOUT ORGANS? MOBILIZING A GEO-AFFECTIVE THEORY OF GENDER MODIFICATION

LUCAS CASSIDY CRAWFORD

1977, Halifax, Nova Scotia. My parents will work in their hometown, Halifax, until they save enough money to move to the country: not the neopastoral country of idyllic retirement, leisure, or quaintness, but rather a place of quietude, crops, and the moral high ground that (at least reportedly) makes the country such a good place to raise kids. But just now, my mother works in the emergency room of the Halifax Infirmary, has recently married my father, and remembers having had a crush on Billy Conway in high school. Billy comes by Outpatients almost biweekly, and receives a day of psychiatric treatment when he asks the sympathetic but distant doctor for a sex change. One day, Billy arrives with his severed penis wrapped in a Kleenex, is made to dwell slightly longer in the psych ward before once again being released; he then promptly hangs himself in his boarding room in the city's North End. Soon after, when Billy's former doctor plans to marry an ex-nun (dyke?) he knows, a man who claims to be the doctor's lover arrives in the emergency room after his own suicide attempt. The doctor comes out as gay, but dies a year later of a then unfathomable virus. The infirmary closed in 1998 and was demolished in 2005, after Ron Russell, the minister of transportation and public works, condemned the building as "unsafe and unusable."

When the ruggedly boyish character Moira debuted in season three of Showtime's (in)famous program *The L Word,* many of us working-class, rural, or butch dykes finally undid the collective knot in our boxers. Moira's impromptu move from Skokie to Los Angeles coincided with hir transsexual awakening, however, and s/he transitions to become "Max" in subsequent episodes. Relocating from Illinois to California puts Moira not only literally but also figuratively in different states: of mind, of identity, and of desire. The queer pilgrimage to the city is a far from innovative motif, and even in theories that are attuned to the role of place in queer life, the role of the rural is presumed to be inconsequential. For instance, Jay Prosser (1998) claims that narratives of pre- and post-operative transsexuality belie their authors' nostalgia for bodily homes that never existed, a style of feeling that not only shores up the power we attribute to hominess but also traces on our bodies a one-way journey home. As this model configures gender modification as a safe return rather than a risky exploit or experiment in embodied selfhood, Prosser finds relief in the "transgender ambivalence" (177) he finds in the narratives of non-operative gender-variant writers. Their ambivalence towards place, he argues, reflects and generates their nonteleological orientation to practices of gender modification. For both varieties of trans life, styles of affect are constitutive technologies of embodiment; how one is moved emotionally informs and illustrates the mobility of one's gender and one's home.

Even in the transgender texts Prosser analyzes, however, the reader encounters linear and one-way trips from the country to the city—supplemented, at best, with a short trip or two back to the protagonist's hometown. As an (albeit far more interesting) forerunner to *The L Word's* Max, Leslie Feinberg's character Jess in *Stone Butch Blues* moves from "the desert" (15) to Buffalo and eventually to New York City, while the protagonist of her other novel, *Drag King Dreams*, lives out her days in this same urban center. The many representations of Brandon Teena's life (especially in *Boys Don't Cry*) work in tandem with such representations of urban queer freedom, attributing Brandon's murder to regressive, purportedly rural, attitudes that are seldom imagined as characteristics of urban communities.

Philosophical and political accounts of queerness all too often corroborate these valorizations of the urban; Kath Weston describes and decries the "Great Gay Migration" to the city (1995, 253), while Douglas Victor Janoff suggests in *Pink Blood: Homophobic Violence in Canada* that "smaller communities...would benefit from [the] strategy of reaching out to isolated citizens and connecting them with support and services in larger centres" (2005, 243). The link between the city and the queer seems ineluctable in both instances; in the former, smart queers will eventually come to the city, while in the latter, the city eventually comes to all queers. As a small-town trans person whose life is becoming urban and mobile (in various senses), this link certainly feels experientially true for me, as my cities get bigger and my old dot on the map looks smaller.

Given the filmic and literary examples cited above, an attraction to the urban undoubtedly rings true for many other transgender or transsexual people who crave the emotional and medical resources seemingly unavailable in rural spaces. In this ubiquitous city of queer imaginings, such people might join a movement like Queer Nation; change their gender "citizenship," as Susan Stryker recently described transition at a lecture at the University of Alberta; and read Janice G. Raymond's renowned polemic *The Transsexual Empire* or Sandy Stone's famous reply, "The Empire Strikes Back: A Posttranssexual Manifesto." Curiously, the experience of gender modification seemingly demands metaphors of sovereign territoriality as well as literal movement from place to place by those who practice it. This coincidence of various kinds of mobility with various kinds of space motivates some preliminary questions: How do geographical or nationist metaphors of transgender community—empire, citizenship, nation, home—both reflect and reify the apparent need for a transgender person's geographical (urban) relocation? Might something more nuanced than access to medical resources, anonymity, and communities based on identity politics or rooted in urban subcultural practices lie behind the geographical relocation of transgender people? If we can imagine that trans people may remain (or wish to remain) in the country by choice and not by accident or unfortunate circumstances, we could see instead that holding our ground says something about our styles of affect: that each bodily transition (from gender to gender or place to place) may be a matter of spatial ethics as much as sexual ones, of orientation to place as much as to the body, of being moved in certain ways as much as moving.

This essay is animated, then, by the question of how our styles of affect and movement may become "trans" in ways that cast doubt upon our current valorization of cities in representations of queer space. How might we trouble our certainty that small towns need to be escaped, that less populous cities can never quite do the trick or ever offer us enough tricks, that migrating to big cities is an uproblematically happy experience untainted by culture shock, or that one's desire to be there is unsullied by contributory conditions such as class or economic need? My motivation for raising such questions is neither to archive nor to justify existent modes of living gender rurally, but rather to point toward new creative potentials. Drawing on Deleuze and Guattari, my aim is to unsettle—their word, significantly, is "deterritorialize" (1987, 156)—the model of the transgender or transsexual subject, if only because this increasingly coherent model of the subject entails practices that demand medical, subcultural, and financial resources often unavailable to (or undesired by) some rural gender-fuckers—and probably many urban ones as well.[1] Prying open the terms "transgender" and "transsexual" in a way that might allow more people to belong to them or to desire them is an important project; however, the vignettes and theoretical interventions that constitute this essay also revel in the deterritorializing potential of *not* being recognized, *not* being counted, of being ignored by urban trans theories and cultures, and of finding or crafting ceaseless mobility in seemingly static and conservative locales in ways that may never move trans-urbanites.

HOW TRANS MOVES US

1996, Kingston, Nova Scotia (population twenty-five hundred). Women in this village wear ties daily—they work at the military base. After I am issued my air cadet uniform, I even wear my tie to school sometimes. I excel at being an air cadet, perhaps because the first year of training could be called "How to Be a (Versatile) Butch Bottom" and summarized thus: 1. No long hair. 2. No insubordination within our playful little roles. 3. No makeup. 4. No fancy jewelry. 5. No problem! Air cadet camp is the sleepaway summer program for twelve-year-old proto-butch kids itching for queer kitsch, for boot-campy kids who wax nostalgic for the drag days of summer drill team when August oranges into rural-school September, and for everyone else who wants to black boots and train their bodies for years to earn the privilege of being called Sir or (like me) Ma'am. In ostensibly impersonal militaristic interactions, more than a few queer kids (who always seem to take the top ranks) thrive on feeling very much in the right body and never quite at home with it in the barracks, parade square, or semiformal dances. We, like the other cadets, cry, but with more grit than melancholy, perhaps because we want a witness to our imperceptible gender-fucking. Perhaps we simply miss our small hometowns. But is "homesickness" just a pessimist's way of describing restlessness, a fever for frequent redeployment? Perhaps we cry because we know the secret of it all. But more often than not, queer cadets can't stop laughing.

In what are probably the three most recognizable transgender narratives in contemporary culture—*Boys Don't Cry, The Crying Game,* and *Stone Butch Blues*—even the titles signal the affect of sadness: characters move from place to place and gender to gender as readers and viewers are moved to tears by these transitions. The concurrence of these different kinds of "being moved" is not simply coincidental; Prosser notes that the "metaphoric territorializing of gender and literal territorializations of physical space have often gone hand in hand" in transgender narrative (1998, 171), an unsurprising collapse, perhaps, given that the singular site of the body is the affective space where both cycles of reification are produced and played out.

If my affective account of the relationship between transgender subjectivity and spatiality seems counterintuitive, two theorists of queer affect may help clarify the precedents as well as the stakes of such a project. Ann Cvetkovich's *An Archive of Feelings: Trauma, Sexuality, and Lesbian Public Cultures* recoups a number of ostensibly negative feelings. Cvetkovich argues: "Affect, including the affects associated with trauma, serves as the foundation for the formation of public cultures.... Rather than a model in which privatized responses displace collective or political ones, my book proposes a collapsing of these distinctions so that affective life can be seen to pervade public life" (2003, 10). Cvetkovich's text deftly illustrates the productive and creative work that can be generated by treating feelings as publicly significant acts. In her earlier text, *Mixed Feelings: Feminism, Mass Culture, and Victorian Sensationalism* (1992), she reminds readers that while the personal may be political, the political is not necessarily subversive. Thus, the affective experience of transgender may always be political, but the narratives we craft from these affects, and the actions we take in response to them, are not always or obviously resistant. The danger in this conflation of affect and action, Cvetkovich warns, is that any phenomenon that generates a specifically physical response is all too often used to affirm the supposed naturalness of that feeling—a tautological maneuver that shores up, among other things, the notion of an inborn gender identity that we "feel" to be "true."

While Prosser's work exemplifies the applicability of affect studies to trans life, it also demonstrates the liability of treating affect as an explanation for actions and identities. As he makes clear in *Second Skins: The Body Narratives of Transsexuality* (1998), the feelings associated with inhabiting the "wrong body" are the ones that have, in the manner Cvetkovich describes, formed the most accessible public narrative of transsexuality. Prosser vindicates the transsexual's desire to change sex by way of analyzing and trusting the ways in which the body feels and responds to certain procedures of gender modification, or, conversely, by the lack of such responses. Responding to the widely held assumption that transsexuals are pathological at worst, or falsely conscious Cartesian dupes at best,

Prosser states his contention "that transsexuals continue to deploy the image of wrong embodiment because being trapped in the wrong body is simply what transsexuality feels like" (69). In this account, affect is not an expression of transsexuality but is, rather, the definitive condition of it. Prosser arrives at this formulation of affect via his interest in psychoanalyst Dider Anzieu's *The Skin Ego,* which holds that one's ego is a mental projection of what one feels (as the title suggests) through one's skin. Against those who believe that transsexuals are the worst kind of body/mind dualists, Prosser argues that a self who feels accommodated by the wrong body is already corporeal through and through: "Body image...clearly already has a material force for transsexuals" (69), insofar as the ego "is ultimately derived from bodily sensations" (65).

This is a challenging formulation of affect insofar as it implies that feelings are generative rather than reflective, productive rather than derivative, and innovative rather than symptomatic of something less corporeal or more pathological. It is surprising, then, that Prosser thinks that affects "simply" (69) occur or are simply translated into the narratives and conventional procedures of gender modification. Aside from the point that living in the wrong body is certainly not "what transsexuality feels like" (69) *for everyone,* it is worth noting that no bodily sensation carries its own self-evident meaning or orders for action prior to our reformulating these affects into narratives. While the present essay is premised on Prosser's insistence that transsexuality is a matter of affect at least as much as it is a matter of certain procedures of gender transition, Prosser's defense of the wrong-body narrative runs the risk not only of settling on just one definition of the "right" trans affect, but also of figuring affect as an extremely personal phenomenon that has very little to do with others, or with places outside of one's (embodied) home.

The role of Prosser's Freudianism, which trusts that one's psyche will speak through words or through one's signifying body, is obvious in his assumption that a wrong-body narrative is simply a verbal translation of a particular affect. Prosser comes dangerously close to suggesting that wrong-body narratives emanate from our skin without the effects of other people or places, or external ideas about gender. If Freud's taken-for-granted equation of signification and affect allows the latter term to figure unproblematically in our analyses of desire, then it is entirely appropriate to turn to Deleuze and Guattari, whose complex oeuvre aims in part to formulate a specifically anti-Freudian theory of affect, to begin refiguring the relationship between affect and signification. As Freud and Prosser would have it, the formation of the self occurs when one creates a mental projection of the sensations one feels. Affects, for Deleuze and Guattari, operate in precisely the opposite way: they *undo* the subject "like weapons" (1987, 400): they "open a way out" (258) and mount a "counterattack" (400) to even our best attempts to settle on identities and desires. These dangerous bodily occurrences—"arrows," "weapons," and "projectiles" (400), as they are described—are not simply the raw or pre-verbal form of the emotions we know as love, envy, anger, or even the bodily uncanniness that inspires wrong-body narratives. Rather, for Deleuze and Guattari, these narratives of feelings are attempts to harness (and transform) the destructive quality of affect. As they write, "Affect is the active discharge of emotion, the counterattack, whereas feeling is an always displaced, retarded, resisting emotion" (400). As Bonta and Protevi note in *Deleuze and Geophilosophy*, affect is "the capacity to become" (2004, 50), whereas feeling is the reterritorialization of becoming, by means of coding and ultimately controlling it.

Deleuze and Guattari insist vehemently on "an affectability that is no longer that of subjects," but has instead to do with crafting an "assemblage," and with relationships of "symbiosis" (1987, 258). In other words, if affects are generated by proximity, movement, and symbiosis with or between other organisms and environments—a style of relationality that threatens the borders of bodies and identities—why then are they recouped, tamed, and privatized in the name of the subject? This "displaced" and "retarded" (400) harnessing of affect into feelings in fact constitutes "subjectivization," the process through which affect is controlled in order to hold the subject together. For Deleuze and Guattari, affect is the body's capacity to *undermine* our best attempts at deciding on identities and selves. If, in this account, what we call feelings are quite far from bodily sensation, and are actually attempts to maintain the coherence of the subject, then perhaps Prosser is right to say that "being trapped in the wrong body is simply what transsexuality *feels* like" (1998, 69, emphasis mine). When Prosser claims that transsexual transition is a "coming home to the self through body" (83), he describes a spatial trajectory that is the opposite of Bonta and Protevi's gloss on deterritorialization: "the process of leaving home, of altering your habits, of learning new tricks" (2004, 78), a series of exploits that sound much more like camp.

SMOOTH BODIES

January 2007, Edmonton, Alberta. In a Jasper Avenue bar connected to a Catholic church, I try to convince a pretty (and) brilliant architect that cities built on grids probably help us become straight, insofar as how we move must affect how we are moved, and that the comfortable feeling of knowing where our bodies are at all times might not in fact be a very queer feeling. His soused-up lecture on what was so radical, in the first instance, about the nonmimetic clean straight lines of modern architecture will earn him footnotes later. For now, leaning back on the men's room toilet for a pause, I see his shoes, hear his gentleman's cough at the urinal. I think about him, and his girlfriend, who has reminded me of the excitement of a reciprocated crush.

I will write about this crooked washroom moment and read it at our first drag king show at our one dank and lovely dyke bar— "the last of its kind in Canada," the owner never fails to mention. There have been other shows in years past but nobody seems to know quite when, who, or what they were. "Smooth space does not have a long-term memory with all that that entails, so only microhistories are possible" (Bonta and Protevi 2004, 145).

"You might be able to fill the [thirty] seats," a friend says before the show, but the owner has to lock the door for the first time ever, when this remote back alley bar is almost triple its legal capacity, filled with enthralling people dressed for the occasion of the first drag king show they've ever seen. At intermission I bump into the architect and his girlfriend. "Yep, this is Edmonton, all right," I think: nobody is avoidable and I almost always love this way in which rural accountability permeates our semi-urban space.

A year later, I avoid the temptation to tell the architect that Sarah Ahmed (2006) argues in Queer Phenomenology *that desire and affect are generated by our various habits of turning and directing the body, writing that "the etymology of 'direct' relates to 'being straight' or getting 'straight to the point.' To go directly is to follow a line without a detour, without mediation. Within the concept of direction is a concept of 'straightness.' To follow a line might be a way of becoming straight, by not deviating at any point" (16). But I don't call the architect, or his girlfriend. Instead, I'll smile obliquely at their summer wedding as they walk down the narrow aisle, looking gorgeously aslant.*

Insofar as Deleuze and Guattari consider the affect of a body and its surrounding environment to be mutually constitutive, it is not for rhetorical flourish alone that they continually employ geographical vocabulary and geo-oriented descriptions of the spaces in which affects occur, including their figure of the nomad who "clings to the smooth space left by the receding forest, where the steppe or the desert advances" (1987, 381). It's worth repeating that the word they use to denote the disruptive force of affect is "deterritorialization" (142). In his recent essay, "Space in the Age of Non-Place," Ian Buchanan notes that "deterritorialization names the process whereby the very basis of one's identity, the proverbial ground beneath our feet, is eroded, washed away like the bank of a river swollen by floodwater" (2005, 23). In this decidedly pastoral metaphor, Buchanan reminds us that, just as trans life seems to demand literal and figural movement, so does Deleuze and Guattari's deterritorialization of the subject implicate both body and space. In this sense, the literal shapes we impose upon bodies, buildings, or hillsides are constitutive of how we will be able to move and be moved.

If these nonurban motifs are not accidental, how might a kind of gender nomadism—of refusing home, of refusing the straightest and quickest path between two points—demand a reconfiguration of how we think and feel about space? Deleuze and Guattari's distinction between smooth and striated space suggests that, against any simple rural/urban dichotomy (which is itself instituted only through the boundary-tracing authority of the city), nomadic and radical ways of living with/in (or as) space can happen in any locale, including a rather rural city of a million dispersed people such as Edmonton. To think through the usefulness of this model of striated/smooth for trans relationships to space, I cite at length first Bonta and Protevi, then Deleuze and Guattari:

> Striated space is first griddled and delineated, then occupied, by the drawing of rigid lines that compartmentalize reality into segments, all controlled to a greater or lesser extent through a nested hierarchy of centers.... Thus striated space, because it is composed of centers, is productive of remoteness, of the entire idea that there are places of more and of less importance. Striation imparts the "truth" that "place" is an immobile point and that immobility (dwelling) is always better than "aimless" voyaging, wandering, itinerancy, and of course nomadism.... The city...is what allows the striation of a larger territory (Bonta and Protevi 2004, 154).

> Smooth space is precisely the space of the smallest deviation: there-

fore it has no homogeneity, except between infinitely proximate points, and the linking of proximity is effected independently of any determined path. It is a space of contact, of small tactile or manual actions of contact, rather than a visual space.... Smooth space is a field without conduits or channels. A field, a heterogeneous smooth space, is wedded to a very particular type of multiplicity: nonmetric, acentered, rhizomatic multiplicities that occupy space without "counting" it and can "be explored only by legwork." They do not meet the visual condition of being observable from a point in space external to them (Deleuze and Guattari 1987, 371).

With their coded roads, maps, and high straight buildings from which one might see the streets without moving, urban centers seem just what Deleuze and Guattari have in mind when they describe striated space. Perhaps their smooth or nomadic space may not be the random gay bars or drag shows to which one roves in a strange city, but instead, quite literally "a field" (371), the kind where rural queers might have first kisses or redneck trannies might roam, work, or play. In valorizing the work of *Queer Nation*, Lauren Berlant and Elizabeth Freeman suggest that this activist group succeeds in confounding the question of "where" the nation itself might be located; "it names," they say, "multiple locals and national publics; it does not look for a theoretical coherence to regulate in advance all of its tactics: all politics in the *Queer Nation* are imagined on the street" (Berlant and Freeman 1997, 151). This is all too true, insofar as *Queer Nation*'s tactics (such as claiming the public space of a shopping mall to hand out pro-queer information) are achieved by using certain versions of publicity, by assuming the possibility of anonymity, and by imagining that "the *street*" somehow belongs and speaks to all queers. Indeed, to the disapproval of Deleuze and Guattari and their privileging of smoothness, this popular model of queer nationhood—and indeed, the very institution of the Pride Parade—assumes the presence of "street" (Berlant and Freeman 1997, 151) and its "direct" centrality to bent queer life.

Interpreting Deleuze and Guattari's distinction of smooth and striated space as merely another way of saying rural and urban would be to oversimplify. To hick trannies for whom public transit is a mere abstraction, a space "explored only by legwork" (Deleuze and Guattari 1987, 371) is concretely familiar. Likewise, while a field appears meticulously organized to a farmer, or a series of landmarks may function as striations for local residents, these people "are not necessarily forces for imparting" the effect of these markings "beyond their own neighbourhood" (Bonta and Protevi 2004, 154), as urban thinkers or planners might be. Insofar as the striation of space is not conducive to becoming, this imperative needs to be actively resisted. That which is striated is, by definition, not remote. Perhaps an overarching revaluing of the very concept of "remoteness" is required to rethink the value of the rural realm and the bodies that (choose to) assemble with/in it. If, for Deleuze and Guattari, "the body or assemblage in question is co-constituted along with the space it occupies" (Bonta and Proveti 2004,146), it is clear that where one lives and moves is more than a blank space into which subjects arrive fully formed; rather, choosing where to live and how to live with/in its spaces are technologies of the (undoing of the) subject, equally as much as those surgical and hormonal technologies we recognize more easily as body/gender modification.

The suggestion that we ought to roam and fuck with the grids and codes of striated spaces deterritorializes the valorization of city dwelling, ownership, and organized urban life that often accompany representations or expectations of trans life. Regarding space and movement as constitutive of one's gender presupposes that, contra Prosser, gender identity is neither simply a matter of the psyche or the skin nor a way in which the subject ought to shore up his or her sense of body hominess. But, if our modes of moving and being moved are indeed so closely intertwined, what ethic of body modification does this reconsideration of remoteness and smooth spaces evoke? Significantly, Bonta and Protevi suggest that "we need to emphasize that striated (and smooth) can be features of non-geographic assemblages (desire, music, and cloth, to cite examples from *A Thousand Plateaus*) and so are not restricted to spaces of interest to geographical pursuits at the scale of the human or the landscape" (2004, 155). In other words, given that processes of gender modification may also be smooth or striated, how do we engage in practices of body morphology that strive toward the smooth, that aim to deterritorialize the subject rather than settle it, to become a nomad rather than come "home to the self through body" (Prosser 1998, 83)? Conceiving of practices of body modification—including gender transition—as a move from one point to another by the straightest line possible seems antithetical to that project. To striate one's body (indeed, even to regard it as so discrete as to call it that) into literal organs and imbue certain of these with a surplus of signifying power also puts one at danger for codifying embodiment in a way that creates remoteness—both of parts of one's "own" body, affect itself, and also those bodies that live elsewhere and morph in different ways. If, instead, one prioritized traits over forms, movement over stasis, and smoothness over striation, gender modification would seem to be at its most deterritorializing when we are emphatically unconcerned with moving from one fixed point to another on the path of least distance and detour. In this sense, an ethics of mobility and spatiality is entailed in and illustrated by any ethics or practice of gender modification. If, by productively unsettling the geo-affective subject, we could create new potentialities for the body, it follows that there is something lacking in our focus on reproducing existent bodies, in the very concept of transition, and in the increasingly coherent practices we pursue in transition's ubiquitously urban home.

Hopefully the applicability of such ideas to rural trans life is becoming clear. Many rural gender-fucking people find—in unconventional ways—unconventional allies, lovers, and mentors in their towns and villages, many of which don't even have geographically accessible hospitals, let alone the legion of certified psychiatrists, surgeons, and endocrinologists who preside over the processes of urban gender transition. What kind of phenomenon is "transgender" if it exists without hormones, surgery, or the extensive medical documentation that accompanies these identifiably trans procedures? Deleuze and Guattari offer resistance to those who might assume such things impossible. In one of their more (in)famous plateaus, "How Do you Make Yourself a Body without Organs?" they speak explicitly about the dangers of reducing a body to a series of cooperative organs. Their phrase "body without organs," (abbreviated BwO in specialist literature) offers resistance to the notion of bodily integrity or unity and calls to mind the dynamic character of transgender bodies—even though its dispensing of a definitive bodily organization clashes with the aspirations of those trans people for whom the acquisition or removal or certain organs constitutes the authenticity of trans subjectivity. While Deleuze and Guattari write of bodies and organs in general, their comments are especially resonant with surgical sex/gender modification. Imbuing certain parts of the body with certain meanings, what they call a focus on "part-objects," is "the approach of a demented experimenter who flays, slices, and anatomizes everything in sight, and then proceeds to sew things randomly back together again" (1987, 171). They contrast the part-object approach and its "fragmented body" (171) with the BwO by arguing that the latter neither presupposes an original unity, nor, more enigmatically, can be contained within one organism or controlled by one singular body. On this last point, they suggest that "it is not 'my' body without organs, instead the 'me' (*moi*) is on it, or what remains of me" (161). The BwO is infinitely unfinished, and it presumes that our environments move us as much as we move through them.

There is nothing necessarily deterritorializing about the gender or body of someone who lives out this kind of transgender without organs.[2] That such a configuration of transgender is possible, however—where passing, nightlife, community, and transition seem or are impossible—reminds us that policing gender identity on the basis of medical procedures also entails a policing of class, race, and a plethora of other cultural and bodily conditions, and also of location. Deterritorializing the system of subjectivity that would have us privilege certain organs and see the body as an integral whole (an idea that undermines trans life in the first instance) does not necessarily entail turning one's body into an assemblage of parts or series of seeming fragments, though this may well be involved. As Deleuze and Guattari note, functioning as a subject is necessary to effect change: "You have to keep small supplies of significance and subjectification, if only to turn them against their own systems when the circumstances demand it" (1987, 160). Transgender and transsexual subjects clearly do and will continue to exist, and for good reason—but hopefully as a way to deterritorialize gender rather than settle it, to take apart their own habits and territories, to help us experiment rather than solve a problem, and to take us wayward rather than directly from one point to the next.

IMPERCEPTIBLE TRANSGENDERS

October 2007, Los Angeles, California. Like most rural kids I feel frantic here at first, compelled to take advantage of everything offered by a new strange city—lest I not make the most of this opportunity to travel. A few hours after the hotel concierge accepts my credit card, following a ten-minute conversation about how "strange it is you use Laura as a man's name in Canada!," I visit the Los Angeles Holocaust Museum. I shuffle tentatively about the empty rooms until an older woman approaches me, introduces herself as a child survivor, and implores me to sit with her on a bench to hear her story. As she speaks about hiding with her parents in France, and tells me what a fine young man I am for coming to the museum, I think: How will I tell her my name if she asks? Might she consider the incongruence between my acceptance of her appellation, "young man," and my self-naming as "Laura" to be duplicitous? I ask whether, as a child of nine years old, she had a sense of what was going on around her, as she and her mother hid in a non-Jewish household and snuck food to her father, who lived in a cave nearby. Her response echoes one I have offered to others, when trying to explain the perils and pleasures of my new urban transgender experiences: "Do you have any idea what it's like to never know what people are thinking when they look at you? To be afraid that you'll be found out?" A staff member announcing closing time abbreviates what might have been a considerably difficult and important conversation. Later that day, I stroll a nearly deserted Sunset Boulevard and pass an establishment called Dr. Tea's. An employee on the sidewalk offers me a sample cup and says, "Sir, I'm convinced you need some tea!" I sense he's not alone in that belief. But I don't quite agree. "Could what the drug user or masochist obtains also be obtained in a different fashion...so it would even be possible to use drugs without using drugs, to get soused on pure water?" (Deleuze and Guattari 1987, 166).

I think of the way in which "passing" is a void notion in a small town where everyone knows you, and I wonder if the way in which rural people are largely ignored by urban queer theory lets us experience something more exhilarating than passing: imperceptibility. Deleuze and Guattari write: "What does becoming-imperceptible signify....A first response would be: to be like everyone else....After a real rupture, one succeeds... in being just like everyone else. To go unnoticed is by no means easy.... it is an affair of becoming" (1987, 279).[3]

If rural social lives occur in homes, backyards, and dark fields "rather than [in] a visual space" (371) like a city street, club, organization, or parade, we might ask ourselves a question that any urban postflâneur hasn't been able to ask for some time: What *is* it like to remain unseen, both by urban-centered theories of queerness and by our culture at large? While this "indiscernibility" (279) may sound like the kind of gender illegibility proffered by some postmodern theories of gender, that sort of unreadability may well be the "too-much-to-be-perceived" (279) of which Deleuze and Guattari write, though visible excess of ambiguous gender undoubtedly has its own value. Instead, the imperceptible lies beneath notice but is still only "like" (280) everybody else. In this account, imperceptibility is something entirely different from being "in the closet," as rural queers are so often read. By seeing imperceptibility as something other than a stopover on the way to a satisfying queer life, this equation of imperceptibility and becoming disrupts the teleology of coming out and transitioning. In so doing, Deleuze and Guattari offer a version of imperceptible trans life (rather than passing) that rural (or otherwise seemingly invisible) trans people might find reassuring or galvanizing: that continually navigating one's imperceptibility, rather than seeking out places where one feels readable or acknowledged as transgender[4] is not necessarily an unmitigated sign of self-loathing or the inability to move to a city; rather, it may be precisely this imperceptibility and lack of recognition that enables rural styles of transgender and the very different affects and lives that could be realized there—ones in which childhood vignettes do not add up to a narrative or to an adult, in which affects don't add up to a fully formed and settled subject, in which body parts and supposed bodily integrity are not cause for premature death, and where bodies that pass or bodies that are imperceptible each assemble in unexpectedly deterritorializing fashion, if only on the way to the next stop, the next desire, the next gender, the next . . . ?

LUCAS CASSIDY CRAWFORD is pursuing a PhD in English and film studies at the University of Alberta in Edmonton and holds an MA in English from the University of Western Ontario and a BA from Saint Francis Xavier University. Lucas thanks the Trudeau Foundation, the Killam Foundation, and the Social Sciences and Humanities Research Council of Canada for their generous support. Thanks to Susan Stryker, Ann Cvetkovich, Mark Simpson, and two anonymous peer reviewers for helpful comments on earlier drafts of this essay and to Dianne Chisholm and Cressida Heyes for their supervision and encouragement.

NOTES

1. While I use "transgender" as an umbrella term, I also understand the slippage between the terms "transgender," "transsexual," "gender-fucking," and even "queer" as an indication of the molecular, affective, unsettled and non–identity-politics version of gender modification that I try to imagine in these pages. It is also worth noting that while these words may have very specific definitions and conventions in some communities, their meanings, and even their importance, vary from place to place. For instance, in a rural maritime village of a few hundred people—where technologies of transsexuality are unavailable or largely unaffordable (financially or otherwise), is the (urban?) distinction between transsexuality and transgender a difference that

bears on the lives of local gender-fuckers in the same way? Are these definitions yet more ways to organize gender—to craft a coherent grid of identities? I follow Prosser (1998), then, in regarding different practices of place, movement, and affect as equally (and, at times, more) constitutive of trans life as are discrete operations, hormone therapies, and passing.

2. The pun here on genitals as "organs" relies on Deleuze and Guattari's "body without organs" (BwO), mentioned above, by which they hope to inspire an orientation to embodiment and assemblage that is not based on being a complete organism or focusing on "parts-objects" (1987, 171). Harnessing organs into an organism (or, in more useful words for this analysis, organizing body parts into a particular kind of coherent subject) would illustrate the kind of striation (centering, bringing home) of the body against which Deleuze and Guattari write, and which promotes the very sense of remoteness that marginalizes others genders and (their) locales. Therefore, while "organs" are not reducible to genitals, there are certainly particular orientations to (and practices of/with) genitals that may be more or less likely to strive towards the BwO. The question posed by the pun is, then, In what ways does the concept of transgender-without-organs demand that we rethink the centrality of sexual "organs" to gender?

3. There is one paragraph in *A Thousand Plateaus* in which Deleuze and Guattari address transsexuality explicitly, to suggest the differences—but also the possible connections—between transition and their phrase "becoming-woman": "What we term a molar entity is, for example, the woman as defined by her form, endowed with organs and functions and assigned as a subject. Becoming-woman is not imitating this entity or even transforming oneself into it. We are not, however, overlooking the importance of imitation, or moments of imitation, among certain homosexual males, much less the prodigious attempt at a real transformation on the part of certain transvestites. All we are saying is that these indissociable aspects of becoming-woman must first be understood as a function of something else: not imitating or assuming the female form, but emitting particles that enter the relation of movement and rest, or the zone of proximity, of a microfemininity, in other words, that produce in us a molecular woman, create the molecular woman."

Holding together this version of imperceptibility with transgender modes of passing offers a third way of interpreting the Deleuzian sense of "becoming-woman" (279), a phrase so easily either misunderstood as transsexuality or relegated to the realm of metaphor. If transgender passing has the potential to be a kind of Deleuzian imperceptibility, it is clear that their radical process of becoming-woman does, indeed, have everything to do with a literal form of gender transgression.

4. This version of imperceptibility is revisited by Kelly Oliver (2001) in her argument for a postrecognition model of subjectivity in *Witnessing: Beyond Recognition*. In the following, she could remind rural trans people to be wary of political projects that take recognition by urbanites as our main goal. As she writes, "While it seems obvious that oppressed people may engage in struggles for recognition in response to their lack of recognition from the dominant culture, it is less obvious that recognition itself is part of the pathology of oppression and domination" (23).

WORKS CITED

Ahmed, Sara. 2006. *Queer Phenomenology: Orientations, Objects, Others*. Durham: Duke University Press.

Berlant, Lauren, and Elizabeth Freeman. 1997. "Queer Nationality." In *The Queen of America Goes to Washington City: Essays on Sex and Citizenship*. Durham: Duke University Press.

Bonta, Mark, and John Protevi. 2004. *Deleuze and Geophilosophy: A Guide and Glossary*. Edinburgh: Edinburgh University Press.

Buchanan, Ian. 2005. "Space in the Age of Non-place." In *Deleuze and Space*, ed. I. Buchanan and G. Lambert. Edinburgh: Edinburgh University Press.

Cvetkovich, Ann. 1992. *Mixed Feelings: Feminism, Mass Culture, and Victorian Sensationalism*. New Brunswick: Rutgers University Press.

———. 2003. *An Archive of Feelings: Trauma, Sexuality, and Lesbian Public Cultures*. Durham: Duke University Press.

Deleuze, Gilles, and Félix Guattari. 1987. *A Thousand Plateaus: Capitalism and Schizophrenia*. Trans. Brian Massumi. London: Athlone Press.

Janoff, Douglas Victor. 2005. *Pink Blood: Homophobic Violence in Canada*. Toronto: University of Toronto Press.

Oliver, Kelly. 2001. *Witnessing: Beyond Recognition*. Minneapolis: University of Minnesota Press.

Prosser, Jay. 1998. *Second Skins: The Body Narratives of Transsexuality*. New York: Columbia University Press.

Stryker, Susan. 2007. "Transgender Feminism: Queering the Woman Question." Lecture delivered at Edmonton, University of Alberta, March 8.

Weston, Kath. 1995. "Get Thee to a Big City: Sexual Imaginary and the Great Gay Migration." *GLQ* 2(3):253–78.

AN FU TO THE MEN IN BLUE

JAMES SHULTIS

When walking down hallways we stutter + sputter in the light. The bodies, our bodies some human oddity some sort of cultural tourism we don't get tipped for, only tried. And the policeman beckons me with his badge + pistol in pocket. And do I ask you about your cock while working trying to get to know you. When really I should just let you be. But yer a cop with a pistol + it's easy to bother you right? Pad me down + tell me that it's all alright. And how lucky I am to have a girlfriend, that she's just fine with the way my body does not stand the way your body stands. That I am a boy + yes I am okay with it. What I shoulda said. What I shoulda said would've been along the lines of "FU mister New York blue, I am not what you would expect"; but instead all the lights are burning on hot, scalding skin like electroshock you shook shook me quick with all the things you shouldn'ta said.

MIDNIGHT BEEHIVE BIKE BATTLE
We are the children of that night, that eclipses into a strange circumference of moon + sun. It's when we pull our hoods on riding over time + bridges like they are our own deliverances, when I fall apart. When my feet hit the ground, suddenly synthesizing air + light + all those little poems that run through my head, some mantra, some sick trick to make me hypnotized, hit the road, fly, as quick as my feet can take me. We are a traveling kind, marking miles with scars from battles we've barely won. Raw knuckles scuff pavement. The music, that music of heavy breaths heaving over a heavier chest.

My body is your body, is a battlefield of injections + rejections + declarations of love that come to me by one million hands that want to touch.

Forget the sins that come through blinds in morning, in mourning + take forbidden pictures, that become installations, distillations of what a body, mine, is slowly forgetting its been. This boy, that girl in the dark.

[WSQ: Women's Studies Quarterly 36: 3 & 4 (Fall/Winter 2008)]
© 2008 by James Shultis. All rights reserved.

Soon the scars don't show, soon they're barely there at all + we fill our names quick on yr form, with a pen that has marked the decisions that came before. The ink running the same direction as my bike, the same way my face flies into the distance till all we've got left is this city in memory. This beehive city of too much sound.

JAMES SHULTIS is a Brooklyn-based poet with a collection of bikes and too many gardening supplies. He keeps various notebooks full of his top-fives, grocery lists, scribble-scrabble, love notes, poems + snippets of stories. He is a recent graduate of Hunter College, where he studied creative writing and gender studies. In the fall, he will be beginning an MFA in poetics at Queens College. His other work can be seen at http://www.jamesshultis.com.

PERVERSE CITIZENSHIP: DIVAS, MARGINALITY, AND PARTICIPATION IN "*LOCA*-LIZATION"

MARCIA OCHOA

Ordenanza de Convivencia Ciudadana y Sancion de Infracciones Menores

Artículo 1°. Objeto. La presente ordenanza tiene por objeto consolidar las bases de la convivencia ciudadana en el Distrito Metropolitano y la preservación de la seguridad, el orden público, el ambiente y el ornato de la ciudad, . . . y la utilización pacífica y armónica de las vías y espacios públicos del Distrito Metropolitano de Caracas.

Capítulo I. De las infracciones relativas al debido comportamiento en lugares públicos

Artículo 13 (decimotercero). Ofrecimiento de comercio sexual. El que ofrezca servicios de carácter sexual en la vía pública, será sancionado con multa de veinte (20) unidades tributarias, o la realización de algunos de los trabajos comunitarios establecidos en

el artículo 38 de la presente ordenanza por un lapso de cuarenta y ocho horas.

Ordenanza de Convivencia Ciudadana,

Caracas, Venezuela

Although sex work is not a crime in the Venezuelan penal code, on the streets of Caracas, the Ordenanza de Convivencia Ciudadana is the law of the land.[1] These few words, which happily proclaim the terms under which citizens might harmoniously live together, also condemn many women, *transformistas*, and men to live in a daily negotiation, expensive and at times violent, with the agents of the state, in this case, the Policía Metropolitana de Caracas (PM). *Convivencia ciudadana* (citizenly coexistence) implies a social harmony that respects all citizens as long as they respect the law.[2] But some citizens "live together" better than others, and the law always values some existences while marginalizing others.

I had to get to know the Ordenanza de Convivencia Ciudadana (or simply ordenanza), and its accompanying definition of "citizenship," to understand the context of Avenida Libertador in Caracas, where dozens of *transformistas* undertake sex work nightly. I had to get to know the ordinance this way because it helped me understand the structural factors that overdetermine the violence and marginalization that are produced on a daily basis on these streets and upon these bodies. But the truth is that the *ordenanza* is just a tool for the PM. Before the *ordenanza*, there was the Ley de Vagos y Maleantes, before that another law, and always Morality, Order, and Good Citizenship. If the *ordenanza* is struck down tomorrow, the PM will find another way to police these *transformistas*.

When I began my work in Venezuela, I didn't expect to engage with questions of citizenship and civil society. However, as I spent more time in an increasingly polarized political environment where mechanisms of participation and collective action became more and more contested, I began to turn to these words as ways to talk about my concerns.[3] There are some sectors of the so-called civil society (*sociedad civil*) within which I function, specifically, the work of nongovernmental organizations (NGOs) and activists to HIV/AIDS and movements to articulate identity, community, and culture for people of color in the United States. However, the limitations of "civil society," and in particular of NGOs, to respond to the concerns of queer and transgender people of color have informed the skepticism with which I approach such concepts as citizenship and civil society. Rather than approaching the survival of *transformistas* through political theory, HIV prevention, or the traditions in anthropology that attend to non-Western sexualities and gender systems, I focused my work on bodily and imaginative responses to marginalization through mass media. My fieldwork, in fact, is about these mechanisms and not about what I refer to in this essay as "GLBT civil society."

But the distinction between those who see themselves as political actors of *el ambiente* and those who are automatically excluded (or who exclude themselves) from "political" possibility recurred both in my interviews with members of GLBT civil society in Caracas, and in my work on Avenida Libertador.[4] I came to see citizenship as a tool that can be used perversely, one that actors within "civil society" (among whom I count myself) must be careful not to normalize.

In Venezuela, I collaborated on the production of a report about the problem of impunity and its impact on the "GLBT community" (Carrasco and Ochoa 2003). This study identifies a problematic relationship between the PM and the GLBT people in Caracas who responded to a short survey. When I ask a *transformista* what should be done about the PM, and if she is interested in participating in negotiations with them, she responds, "The PM?! *Ay no*. Because then when they see you on the street, just imagine." I began to understand, as I worked on Libertador, that these relations function in a climate of silence, in which the complaint filed serves not to change police behavior but rather to name the complainant and mark her for other possible aggressions. An intervention in this situation would have to be much more profound to avoid such aggressions.

This essay is based on my fieldwork with *transformista*s on the Avenida Libertador of Caracas.[5] It also draws on my experiences with a queer Latina/o HIV-prevention organization in the United States called Proyecto ContraSIDA Por Vida (PCPV) and on interviews with activists working in three GLBT NGO projects in Caracas: Alianza Lambda de Venezuela, Unión Afirmativa de Venezuela, and the nascent Divas de Venezuela. From these observations, I consider how the case of *transformista*s in Venezuela might transform our concepts of politics, citizenship, and participation.

I will begin by attending to some issues of taxonomy and translation, in which I clarify the terms and usage employed in this essay. I base my taxonomic approach on the work of anthropologist David Valentine (2007), who articulates the importance of attending to and parsing out local gender categories in ethnographic fieldwork. Then I discuss the concept of *loca*-lization, a play on words that attempts to locate the *loca* within processes of modernity, nation, and globalization.[6] I follow this discussion with sections on the concepts of citizenship and civil society as they have affected my work in Venezuela and conclude with some suggestions for a politics that honors and includes *transformista* survival strategies.[7]

TAXONOMY AND TRANSLATION

Language and naming have become central concerns to this question of citizenship and perversion, in part because citizenship in its traditional Enlightenment sense is about codifying mechanisms of recognition and participation. As Lisa Lowe (1996) has argued, the mechanisms through which noncitizens, foreigners, are made legible and thus excluded produce the conditions of possibility for a nation to define itself through the technology of citizenship. Definition, naming, confers a certain kind of visibility while obscuring that-which-will-not-be-named.

I found in Venezuela that silence, too, can be a space of possibility for *transformista*s, who often narrated their silent passage into womanhood through practices such as eyebrow plucking, hormone self-medication, and subtle shifts in wardrobe. Without asking permission, without declaring herself, a *transformista* emerges into being. By the time someone notices, by the time someone else names her difference, she has already transformed.

Throughout this work, I have encountered these problems of naming and meaning, where the stakes of specific words, even of the act of speaking, get to be very high. This is why I seek out nimble words, slippery and agile in their meanings. Terms such as "queer," *loca, de ambiente, entendido, transformista*. Those that name and define with power while refusing to be pinned down. I seek a language that honors my own slippery bilingualism, which asks you to work if you do not fully feel my form, which does not always stop to explain.

Valentine's recent "critical ethnography of the *category* 'transgender' itself" (2007, 14) attends carefully both to the politics of naming and to honoring the categories and names that people use when talking about themselves. I think about this approach as a kind of taxonomy—a faithful listing, a parsing out of particularities in the genealogies and usage of the names and categories that emerge in a given social context. Here, I work to clarify these terms very carefully because they get conflated often, despite the fact that they imply very different social realities. But I also work to register the polymorphous forms of meaning and usage I've encountered. In the following section, I will define a few key terms and clarify my usage in the languages of transgender studies and queer *Latini-*

dad (Rodríguez 2003).

TRANS TAXONOMIES

Transformista is a word used in Venezuela to refer to people who are assigned male sex at birth and who present themselves in their everyday lives as women. The word has associations with the sex work performed by many *transformista*s and is considered an insult by some, although it is also used for self-definition.

I am defining "transgender" as a general category that refers to people who make identitarian, physical, and social efforts to live as members of the gender that society says does not belong to the sex assigned to them at birth. *Transformista*s fit within this definition, but not all transgender people are *transformista*s. I think of "transgender" as an empirical category that avoids making assumptions about identity and that, as Valentine does, "avoids collapsing [self-description] or replacing [it] with 'transgender'" (2007, 25).

"Transsexual" is a clinical category, created by different medical discourses (psychiatry, endocrinology, urology) to define and treat a group of people. A transsexual person is understood to be born with a biological "sex" that is discordant with the person's identity. As a medical condition, it is treated with psychiatric, endocrinological, and surgical interventions to accomplish a "sex change." A fundamental criterion of the transsexual category is the rejection of the genitalia with which one is born. *Transformista*s are not transsexual women because (1) they are not recognized as transsexual under the diagnostic criteria, (2) may or may not desire sex reassignment surgery, and (3) may or may not have access to the medical or psychiatric care necessary to produce this category in Venezuela.

And, in case you're wondering, "travesti" and "drag queen" are words used to describe female impersonators—the *transformista*s I met on the whole did not do these kinds of performances.

QUEER *LATINIDAD*

I want to briefly clarify my use of the concept "GLBT," and how I encountered the term in Venezuela: GLBT (pronounced "*jelebeté*" in Venezuelan Spanish) is an acronym for "gay, lesbian, bisexual, and transgender or transsexual"—something I was asked to clarify for the original Spanish-language audience of this essay. Although the exercise seems unnecessary here, it is important to note that the concept has been appropriated for the purposes of activism and human rights projects in Venezuela.[8] It has come to be used as a unified concept, in the sense that it is almost invoked as a word (*jelebeté*) rather than as an acronym. Although the words *gay, lesbiana, bisexual* and *transgénero* are now used for self-identification among the people I met in Venezuela, the language is rich with other words to talk about these existences, most particularly *homosexual, marico* (gay or fag), *camionera* or *cachapera* (lesbian), and *transformista*. Of course, these are not words to be used in polite, or should I say civil, conversation. GLBT, as a concept, names specific members of what is understood to be a "community" and is different from ideas such as *el ambiente* or "in the life," which name places or environments rather than specific actors. *El ambiente* is a Latin American concept of queer sociability, sort of like the queer "scene," although it is figured more as a place and a matrix than a staging. The difference here is between being specific (gay, lesbian, bisexual, or transgender people) or ambiguous (queer, *de ambiente*). In the end, I choose to go with ambiguity over naming, preferring slippery signifiers over reified categories.

LOCAS, FABULOUSNESS, PERVERSION, AND MODERNITY

> "Holly, what's it like to be a woman trapped in a man's body?"
> "I'm not trapped in a man's body, I'm trapped in New York City!"
> I quipped.
> "But what are you? Are you a man, are you a woman—"
> "Honey," I shot back. "What difference does it make, just so long as you're fabulous!"
>
> Holly Woodlawn, narrating an experience on the *Geraldo Rivera Show*, in *A Low Life in High Heels: The Holly Woodlawn Story*

First, "*loca*-lization." The diverse and imaginative strategies of survival that we invent continue to impress me. Among them is the talent of being "fabulous." How do people manage to make themselves "fabulous" despite great social resistance and material constraints? In talking about melodrama, Ian Ang calls this "the expression of a refusal, or inability, to accept insignificant everyday life as banal and meaningless" (1989, 79). Those who are "fabulous" sometimes appear as divas or *locas*. Of course, I use *loca* in its most generous and honorific sense, as a category used in many places *de ambiente* to refer to its boldest and most scandalous actors. The word is used to refer to effeminate gay men and also to *transformista*s and transgender women.

I would like to do several things with the idea of "*loca*-lization." First, I want to "*loca*-lize" myself, or rather I want to explain to you how and from where I arrive at this inquiry. Second, I want to signal the intersecting and transnational pathways that underscore the political and social environment where *las locas* are found. Third, I want to invoke the process called "globalization" as a very local and contingent one, to highlight that there is negotiation between transnational and local realities. Finally, I want to privilege in my analysis those citizens—good, bad or undocumented—whom I have called *locas*, who are excluded from the political imaginary, to suggest a few ways to make *política* a bit more *loca* and learn from the micropolitics of *locas*.

I "*loca*-lize" myself as a butch dyke baby of the Colombian brain drain, coming to consciousness as a gender-nonconforming "foreigner" in the United States of America. In this negotiation of difference, I found my base in the confluence of *jotería* in the San Francisco Bay Area—primarily (but not exclusively) Latinas and Latinos *de ambiente* surrounding the cultural project of Proyecto ContraSIDA Por Vida. At PCPV, *jotería*, an idea based in Chicana/o movement and culture and its queer participants, articulated with the idea of queerness and the people of color who found ourselves in the Mission District of San Francisco in the mid-1990s.

I am drawn to *locas* because although I fit quite easily into a "good" citizenship, I too have experienced the process of marginalization, and I want to understand how power and marginalization work so that we can begin to imagine the possibilities of our collective survival. I am drawn to *peluqueras* (hairdressers), *divas, locas,* and *putas* both because in my experience I have always been legible to them and because they often scandalize me. In my community, they have been those willing to take risks, *las atrevidas*. These trans women are important to me precisely because they complicate the political project; they are the ones who bring shame upon themselves, their families, the nation. And they are not afraid of this shame; rather, they embrace it, turn it around, use it as a weapon. If we want to elaborate a truly inclusive social project, we have to imagine that not all its citizens will be good or conform to the expectations for social participation (be educated, interested, rational, not frivolous). A project that strives for social transformation must embrace and negotiate both complexity and frustrating political subjects.

What draws my attention is a question of power; over the bodies of these divas, society violently demarcates the territory of gender. This demarcation results in their social, economic, judicial, political, and interpersonal exclusion. "Citizenship" has been a mechanism used to exclude them. They are denied social participation, their rights are violated (both as citizens and as humans), and many times they themselves refuse to participate in what could be considered a "good" citizenship. So although "citizenship" and "civil society" have not been central to the formation of my work, they are mechanisms for exercising social power.

In my research, I encountered two areas that have come to frame my understanding of the complexities of *transformista* citizenship: the relationship between perversion, modernity, and nature, and the situation of policing *transformista*s performing sex work on Avenida Libertador in Caracas.

PERVERSION, MODERNITY, POLICING

The idea of perversion came up many times during my stay in Venezuela, but not the sort of celebratory perversion that I live and embrace in San Francisco. The idea of perversion that pervaded was more like an unintended or undesired effect. A perversion of democracy. Corruption and police abuse as perverse. Perversion—like diversion, subversion, inversion—as a directional metaphor, the place reached by a trajectory intended for somewhere else. During my time in Venezuela, I began to see the country as a profoundly and perversely modern place. I came to understand the project of being modern as inherently productive of perversions of all sorts, including my own fabulous and charming perversions. What I am trying to find is a point of reconciliation within the idea that the lives we make are embedded in a cultural logic that seeks to destroy us. That sometimes riding that razor edge between our perverse existences and the perversions of modern institutions—such as the police state, democracy, or science—is part of the fun.

There is a fundamental contradiction at work here—the process of modernity extinguishes humanity yet creates other possibilities for existence. It is the same mechanism that allows us to understand nature as a legitimizing force while at the same time it becomes the thing upon which order and civilization must be imposed, and violently. I felt this contradiction most during a conference I organized in Caracas—TRANSforo—which brought together physicians, psychiatrists, legal scholars, and transgender people to open a dialogue and exchange information. One of the presentations was of two transgender women (who do not identify as *transformistas*), Rummie Quintero and Estrella Cerezo, and their mothers. Rummie's mother, Gisela, talked about her experience of her now-daughter in the womb, how she always "knew" that she was different. Someone asked her what it was like, watching her son transition into a daughter, and she said: "Bueno, si se opone la naturaleza lucharemos contra ella y haremos que nos obedezca" (If nature opposes us, we will fight against her and we will make her obey us).

These words were delivered by Simón Bolívar, called "the Liberator," on March 26, 1812, in Caracas (Avenida Libertador is named after Bolívar). A massive earthquake had decimated an already struggling and war-torn Caracas. Bolívar's followers began to fear that this earthquake was God's retribution for rising up against their king. Bolívar reassured his compatriots that their struggle to impose a new order, in the land that would become the nation of La Gran Colombia and later Venezuela, was righteous, and not in a godly way. That righteousness could come from imposing order, from shaping nature and making her obey. The project of citizenship then, in nineteenth-century Venezuela, became, for people like Bolívar, the shaping of the nature of *el pueblo* to conform to the functioning of a modern nation-state. That Rummie's mother could employ this foundational bit of national ideology to describe her daughter's need to discipline a "male" body with unruly hair and testosterone into a "female" body through whatever means she had available to her seemed to me profoundly perverse. It is an appropriation of the discourses of modernity and nature employed in Venezuela precisely to *exclude transformistas*, and yet which make their existence possible, feasible, even legible.

The modern project of disciplining nature and bodies produces an aesthetic to include or exclude subjects from its realm of comprehension. As the Venezuelan political crisis unfurled before me during my fieldwork, I became particularly interested in the process of inclusion or exclusion of subjects in the project of citizenship. As undesirable citizens are culled out of civil society projects to legitimize claims within a liberal political aesthetic—as was the case with the *transformistas* and the GLBT organizing going on in Venezuela at the time—I am concerned with building the basis for interventions that privilege *transformista* strategies within their own contexts. An incident that I describe in what follows sparked my concern with the project of what I now call "perverse citizenship."

One evening on Avenida Libertador in Caracas, my outreach companion and I saw five Venezuelan national guardsmen with machine guns escort two *transformista*s under a bridge and disappear. The escort walked in silence: neither we civilians, nor the *guardias*, nor the *transformista*s in their custody spoke while they walked by. When they passed by me, I exchanged glances with one of the girls, who seemed to be saying, "*Ahora sí que estamos jodidas*,"—"Now we're really screwed"—with a faint, cynical smile and an eyebrow arched as if it were a challenge. The *guardias* took them under the bridge, we stood frozen as silent firepower paraded past us. After they passed, we slowly edged toward the bridge to see if we could see where they had gone. Not wanting to leave, I began scribbling notes about the incident on my memo pad. We couldn't see what was going on under the bridge. Five minutes passed. Everything was quiet except the passing cars. One of the soldiers had remained above as a lookout. He spotted us, and we began to edge back, not sure if our presence would help or hurt the fate of the *transformista*s. I never found out what happened to the girls—no bodies turned up, no shots were heard, the best case scenario I could imagine is that they had to perform some sexual favor for the *guardias* and then were let go. We don't know because we hailed the next cab that came by after the *guardia* saw us.

These kinds of things happen all the time on Libertador, not just with the Guardia (in fact, this was the first time I had seen them take *transformista*s in custody), but also with the Policía Metropolitana. These things happen because there are silences in which they can happen—people who are not subjects of rights are regularly subject to violations of their integrity as human beings and citizens. No complaints are filed because the complaint is not a useful tool for them. At that moment they are really, irreverently, screwed. So at any moment, some men with guns can do what they please, and if there is silence, they can continue to do so. In Venezuela I learned that this problem has a name: impunity. There are few negative consequences for these actions (which are presumably worth the risk for a free blow job).

If one were to try to produce an utterance that brought consequences—a sound in the night or a complaint filed and prosecuted the morning after—one would be attempting to intervene in the situation. But the problem is that the situation works within its spaces of silence and that the same people who are subject to its abuses have learned to take advantage of these silences. If they wanted to fight for their "rights" they would be doing so already—because they already know how to fight. While there is no such discourse that makes explicit the terms of interaction within what is now a space of silence, the parties coexist in a daily negotiation, lubricated by that very silence. The problem is that sometimes they don't coexist, and one of them ends up dead under a bridge. For those of us who, coming from another place, happen upon these realities and want to intervene, the task is not to bring "light" or "voice" somehow, presuming there was none before; it is to use the social mobility of our bodies and our language to transform relations—to treat people as legitimate subjects of rights, to mobilize the resources necessary for an intervention that makes sense to the people directly involved.

CITIZENSHIP AND PARTICIPATION

This brings me back to the problem of citizenship. There are several ways to consider the idea. Citizenship can be a disciplinary structure (González Stephan 1996) that crystallizes identities through the control of state and ideological mechanisms, or a political structure within which the subjects of rights and political actors capable of intervening in governance are recognized (as it is defined by the Real Academia Española). "Citizenship," as an idea that refers to the subject position of individuals with respect to governance, contains both structural components (the law and other practices of citizenship, such as carrying a national ID card, getting a birth certificate, being recognized by the state, and voting) and affective components (feelings of belonging, participation, one's stance with respect to state recognition or lack thereof). Both structures and affect will condense into practice. Ultimately, addressing issues of citizenship requires changes in all three. I engage in this discussion about citizenship and civil society with deep ambivalence. While in many ways such a discussion can inform the development of policy and political strategy, as concepts profoundly embedded in a liberal Enlightenment ideology they may not be very useful to projects rooted in radical otherness. I have found Nira Yuval-Davis's approach to citizenship very productive: "On its own, the notion of citizenship cannot encapsulate adequately all the dimensions of control and negotiations which take place in different areas of social life, nor can it adequately address the ways the state itself forms its political project" (1997, 5–6).

Citizenship has an affective component that is as important as its structural one. Both dimensions necessarily marginalize *transformista*s. The important thing about citizenship for my work is that it facilitates logics, aesthetics, practices, and structures of *participation*. For citizenship to be useful to *transformista*s, the very notions of politics and citizen must be transformed. To put it another way, for a person to imagine herself the "subject of rights" and to participate in the exercise of those rights there has to exist a process that *produces* this subjectivity, at the same time as there is a struggle for structural recognition in other spheres.

So, if we define a citizen as a subject of rights who exercises them, and if rights and recognition actually have any impact on the situation of social marginality, I have then proposed the idea that it would be a useful intervention for *transformista*s to cultivate a kind of citizenship. I am interested in some strategies to materialize this proposed social transformation, something that seems to me to be a very long term project with little ability to intervene in immediate problems. For example, to intervene in the moment that the Policía Metropolitana is trying to put you in the *perolón* it is much more useful to take off your acrylic heels and start running, not think about fostering your sense of citizenship.

The disciplinary vision of citizenship as elaborated by Beatriz Gonzalez Stephan (1996) indicates the depth of transformation necessary, given that the process of creating citizenship is a process of *enculturation*. Writing about forms of creating citizenship in the national period in Venezuela, she explains: "The foundational project of the nation is civilizing in the sense of giving, on one hand, a power to writing that legitimates and normalizes practices and subjects whose identity is circumscribed by the space of writing; and on the other hand, organizing *power*—multiple, automatic and anonymous—that incessantly and directly controls individuals, making them into citizens of the *polis*" (19–20).

The problem of *transformista* citizenship must be seen from two vantage points: from the integration of *transformista*s into the concept of citizenship and from the transformation of the concept of citizenship. This is how Rummie Quintero puts it. Through her dance and sport activities in her barrio, an expansive 1950s-Soviet-style concrete housing project in Caracas called 23 de Enero, Quintero brings visibility to transgender women in Venezuela. To be clear, Quintero is a transgender woman who is proposing to work with *transformista*s. She does not identify herself or work as a *transformista*. She formed an NGO project called Divas de Venezuela, an organization for transgenders, transsexuals, and *transformistas* in Venezuela. She remarks:

> From the time I began my projection as a person and dancer, I began, at the same time, that social piece. Always working with communities because I always saw the respect that you win by adapting yourself, and many times, you have to adapt to the society so that you can then adapt society to yourself. That is what I'm doing now. Now I'm adapting society. First I adapted myself to the society, now I'm adapting the society to me. (2003)

For however much one can try to "polish" *transformistas* to become exemplary citizens (the normative project), so they can coexist with, for example, the residents of Avenida Libertador who always call the Policía Metropolitana to run them off, or so they begin to file complaints when their rights are violated, one would be naïve to assume that opening the door to dialogue or taking complaints would actually receive any sort of response. The years of active state and social repression have to be countered by some other sort of intervention. Quintero comes from a position that recognizes the legitimacy of society and of her community, a position that is not common among many of the *transformistas* I talked to, but that I have found among people who identify as transgender or transsexual, and not as *transformista*.

Quintero recognizes that one strategy for transforming society's views of transgender people is to respect the norms of the society, and in her experience, to stand out on your artistic merits wins you respect. This strategy works well for her, and I have been quite impressed with her ability to project a positive image of transgender people to a very wide audience of people who one might assume at first to be hostile to transgender people. But the strategy doesn't work in the criminalized and stigmatized environment of publicly visible sex work. Here I have found an aesthetic that privileges shock, scandal, and at times abjection.[9] The aesthetic involves "scandalous" activities such as sex work, aggression, public nudity, stealing, and alcohol and drug use, to name a few. But in the words of one male sex worker on Avenida Solano, a block from Libertador, "I know this is illegal and all, but the fact that I'm a human being—they shouldn't mistreat you."[10] Being a subject of rights is conditioned by the accomplishment of the aesthetics and behavior of a "good citizen." The sex worker refers to a subject of rights who has these rights based on the condition of being a human being, not a citizen. He is, of course, employing the language of international human rights advocacy and, at the same time, indicating another way of understanding the question of citizenship.

The Brazilian political scientist Evelina Dagnino identifies a difference in struggles for rights in Brazil; the sex worker's statement indicates not a struggle *for rights,* but rather a struggle for *the right to have rights*. According to Dagnino, "Poverty is a mark of inferiority, a way of being in which individuals lose their ability to exercise their rights. This cultural deprivation, imposed by the absolute absence of law and rights, which expresses itself as a suppression of human dignity, becomes constitutive of the material deprivation and political exclusion [to which these individuals are subject]" (1998, 48). Dagnino identifies two types of rights: the right to equality and the right to difference. The right to equality corresponds to the liberal definition of citizenship, while the right to difference corresponds to what she calls the "new citizenship" (50). The new citizenship is defined outside the relationship between the state and the individual. This implies not only "access, inclusion, membership and belonging in a political system," but also "the right to participate in the definition of that system" (51). In the redefinition of citizenship, it is seen as both a political strategy and a cultural politics.

What Dagnino calls new citizenship intersects with Laclau and Mouffe's concept of "radical democracy."[11] Both are based in the "struggles against different forms of subordination—class, sex, and race-based as well as those opposed by ecological, anti-nuclear and anti-institutional movements" (Laclau and Mouffe 1989, IX). Dagnino also includes the GLBT movement in these struggles. But to what extent are the liberal concepts of citizenship, in fact, reproduced within new social movement struggles? Based on my experience with the "GLBT movement" in the United States, and now in Venezuela, it seems that the categorization of these actors as participants in the creation of "new citizenship" occludes the exclusionary practices and limitations in the political imaginaries that we use within the same movement.

I would like to suggest two ways to see the possibility of equality: one in which I am equal to you and another in which you are equal to me. From a position of abjection, or from absolute societal rejection, this difference implies different strategies—if I am equal to you, I conform to your aesthetic to make myself a subject of rights. If you are equal to me, and I am a person rejected in society, then you, too, in the moment of equivalence, are polluted.

In an article called "Scandalous Acts," Don Kulick and Charles Klein (2001) analyze Brazilian *travesti* scandal to understand its political possibilities. For Kulick and Klein, *travesti* scandal as a transformative distribution strategy "reterritorializes shame," that is to say, the *travesti* uses her power to contaminate, implicating the object of her scandal (a client accused of being a *maricón* and taking pleasure in being penetrated by the *travesti*), thus transforming the "battlefield" and getting what she wants. This strategy works to produce the desired effect, which in the case illustrated in the article is getting the client to pay more money. *Travesti* scandal is a resignifying strategy: "*travestis* transgress public decorum and civil society not by rejecting shame (and championing something like 'Travesti Pride'), but by inhabiting shame as a place from which to interpellate others and thereby incriminate those others" (2). Upon being incriminated, the object of the scandal feels shame enough to quiet the scandal by acquiescing to its demands. Kulick and Klein suggest that this strategy at times extends beyond the micropolitical sphere of *travesti*-client relations into "battlefields" of an organized, collective arena.

SOCIEDAD CIVIL

If it can be said that the "economic and political direction of society" can be constructed through a consensus (Robles Gil 1998, 117), then civil society can be seen as the field of that construction, negotiation, and reelaboration. Robles Gil contrasts this (Gramscian) sense of civil society with the Habermasian sense: civil society as the "institutional level of life, in which associative practices develop and culture is formed" (120). The Habermasian sense of civil society, he says, isn't as helpful in "understanding the complex articulations between the cultural world, on the one hand, and the economic and political world on the other" (121). What is certain is that to design interventions, it is important to understand and respect the symbolic, economic, political, and interpersonal environments that are pertinent to the transformation one wants to effect.

At various moments in the elaboration of this essay, I have asked myself: is civil society useful at all? And increasingly, I have found myself very frustrated with the whole question and landing on the idea that it is more important to know how to imagine and manifest interventions than to relate them to some idea called "civil society." But Roitter points out one way to think of the operability of the concept of civil society: "We consider that the reintroduction of this theme in the social sciences also signifies another opportunity to pay attention to how people organize themselves in autonomous ways to influence the State and the market, and confront the growing levels of exclusion and fragmentation in society" (2003).

The idea of looking at ways of organizing to make one's presence felt seems important, but I wonder how we deal with those social elements one would want to resist that are neither of the state nor of the market: for example, domestic violence, religious prohibitions on sexuality, or the cultural mechanisms for imposing racism and xenophobia. These things are beyond the state; they bear upon the market. Are the state and the market the only sites for transformation? Where can we locate internal transformations, conceptual transformations that change the way we see a problem, the place of faith, creativity, pride, shame? How do we approach the affective and imaginative dimensions of social transformation? To put it succinctly, how do we go from the intimate (and sometimes public) space of pleasure and feeling (*la rumba*) to the often very public and alienating space of political determination (*el rumbo*)?[12] In my interviews with LGBT NGO representatives in Caracas, there was a separation between "social" space and legal or juridical space.[13] For Jesús Medina, executive director of Asociación Lambda de Venezuela, the two kinds of space form part of and "an 'integral' approach" to defending LGBT rights: "You can attack a violation of rights from the juridical point of view, but also from the educational. Maybe there is also something worth looking at in health, and the social part. You can do a sports event to get a group of people together, have them meet each other, interact. And this will allow you to bring a strong group together so that when you try to attack a problem like discrimination you'll have that strong group that you created through sports" (Medina 2003).

Jesús Raveloof Unión Afirmativa (UnAf) characterizes his experiences at the Lambda meetings as having the quality of a "social encounter," or of "community."[14] Speaking about the difference between Lambda and UnAf, he remarks: "We saw in practice that…Lambda, the couple of times that I visited them, they had their cinema group every Tuesday, and chévere, because the times I went I felt like...there's community, or at least a part of the community is forming there. But then in these kinds of activities, I feel like it's important...to educate" (Ravelo 2003).

This distinction is reaffirmed in the work that Lambda does to put on Orgullo GLBT (GLBT Pride) in Caracas. Orgullo is an event that convenes the "community" to promote visibility, pride, and rights for GLBT people. Lambda became the main organizer of Orgullo after a split with an HIV-services organization and the Red GLBT (GLBT Network) in 2002. The primary reason I point out this distinction is that the two spaces, social and political, are seen as spaces *apart*. In this division, Lambda becomes the organization that puts together more "social" activities (although they clearly see the political dimensions of these kinds of activities), and UnAf becomes the organization that does more "legal" or political activities. The division is also created in a context in which UnAf comes to be known not only for its activities but also for its members, as the organization for professionals and intellectuals (university professors, lawyers, political scientists, and so on). The separation created between social and political space, between doing and thinking, is an aesthetic distinction, in which the social is fun and the political is *pesado* (heavy or serious).

The problem of being serious is like plucking your eyebrows. One of the first things that many *transformista*s I talked to did when they began to recognize their femininity was to look in the mirror and find those features they liked about their bodies, then to work them to attain "perfection." When it comes to eyebrows—and this is true of almost every *transformista* I have interviewed—they begin to pluck them out with tweezers until they took on the desired profile: an eyebrow that can arch as though it were a challenge. To be taken "seriously" in the political sphere, one must cultivate a certain aesthetic and pluck out the inconvenient stray hairs. But in this refinement of a political aesthetic, we run the risk of *cayendo pesado*—of rejecting desire. This section of the Ordenanza governs behavior in public places, criminalizes the offering of sexual services in public, and penalizes this behavior as a petty crime. Ravelo relates an experience that the UnAf people had, on Republicagay.com, a Venezuelan GLBT Web site:

In fact in *Republica Gay*, over about a year we had a column...every two months. But the column apparently was the least visited in the entire Web site [Author: The what? The least visited? (laughter)] The least visited, yes, yes. Because there was all the rumba (party) and all the interesting news...and the Galería [the site's photo and video area, which provides free soft porn] and the Cuarto Oscuro [Dark Room, the sexually explicit photo and video area of the site]. No one wanted to hear us talk politics [laughs] no way! (Ravelo 2003).

One of the most often repeated complaints of my friends in the "GLBT civil society" of Caracas pertained to the lack of *participation* of members of the "community." Jesús Ravelo's experience indicates that the readers of Republicagay.com have many more things that interest them besides "politics," and it is in these activities that they choose to participate.

Now I would like to return to Rummie Quintero, founder of Divas de Venezuela, who you may recall also works what she calls the "social," and who shares Jesús Medina's vision of the social as something integral to a larger project of exercising rights for GLBT people. The reasons that Quintero gives for not participating in the other GLBT organizations illustrate as much the aesthetic problem as the problem of participation for transgender and *transformista* subjects, particularly in the frustration she felt from how she was received by other NGOs:

> I have been in many sports organizations, I've been in others, and yet...there's been that...like that not hearing, no? Because all of the sudden you might see that lack of respect toward transgender people, or that lack of valuing [our contributions]. I have also found that...there are choques [clashes] with people who are not as prepared as you are, or as one is, to take on a role, and sometimes that gets to people. In other words, that is why I decided to start this NGO [Divas]. As far as organizations where there are heterosexual people, I have experienced a lot of openness. My areas they leave to me, and I handle them. And well, whenever I was the one handling them, thank God, it's gone well for me. (Quintero 2003)

Quintero feels as though she gets more respect for her organizing abilities in a *non*-GLBT environment. Although it can be said that Lambda and UnAf accept the participation of transgender people, there are frustrations and self-exclusions:

> You would get, "Well, we won't reject you outright because you're also with the GLB…you're the 'T'" Or rather, the gay community. But no…I actually got a *cargo* [position], in Lambda de Venezuela as cultural and sports coordinator, a position that I never really occupied, as they say, it was something very fictitious, and that was a disappointment to me, really, because, well, if they give you a *cargo*, they should give you the importance of that *cargo*. (Quintero 2003)

But Quintero and I have also encountered the problem of participation in trying to convene groups of transgender women and *transformistas*, and it seems to me that the act of "convening" is precisely where we encounter the problem. If Quintero herself can function within a more or less normative political model ("conform herself to society"), then there are many more transgender women and *transformistas* in particular who can't or won't.

La rumba, *locas*, and scandal are not always productive sites from which to build interventions. When I say we have to imagine a politics from the *rumba* I am not saying that it should only be imagined in that way, but rather that it is necessary to transcend the aesthetic distinctions that marginalize or cause specific actors to exclude themselves. If the idea is to bear upon those grave moments and silences in which rights are violated, we have to transform politics so that it exists in those spaces and is employed by the subjects that transit them.

CONCLUSION

Since I wrote the first version of this essay, the landscape of organizing for transgender and GLBT people in Caracas has changed quite a bit. While the "GLBT civil society" of Caracas (that is, those who imagine themselves as the "political" actors of *el ambiente*, who attempt to intervene in situations of abuse and inequality for GLBT people) has suffered some setbacks and divisions, particularly around Venezuela's political situation and the tensions between programs that are funded to provide HIV-prevention and -treatment services and those that are not, there has also been a significant expansion in the landscape of activism and advocacy by and for LGBT people in Caracas, as well as the rest of Venezuela. Two transgender organizations were registered in 2004 with the goal of advocating for transsexuals, transgender women, and *transformista*s.

While initially Rummie Quintero and Estrella Cerezo proposed to start one organization, *Divas de Venezuela*, the differences in their approaches made it clear that their efforts would best be served by establishing two organizations. For Quintero, cultural activities such as sporting events, aerobics, and beauty pageants are of more interest. Informed by her (very successful) efforts in barrio organizing in Caracas's 23 de Enero housing projects, Quintero privileged "self-esteem," "cultural expression," and "alternatives to delinquency" programming based on her experience with youth movements in Caracas. Quintero's work as a neighborhood and youth activist marked her approach to transgender organizing. She actively tried to counter the stereotype of *transformista*s as hairdressers or prostitutes, and this stance meant that some of the *transformista*s I worked with on Avenida Libertador disliked her and refused to participate in Divas because she did not accept their sex work as a legitimate vocation.

Cerezo's approach to organizing was based in her experiences with political parties, including a huge effort during the 1998 presidential elections (when current president Hugo Chávez Frías was elected) and the subsequent Constitutional Convention in 1999. Cerezo was also a founding member of Movimiento Ambiente de Venezuela (MAV), a GLBT organization founded by Oswaldo Reyes, who registered MAV with the National Electoral Commission and ran as an openly gay candidate to the 1999 Constitutional Assembly. Cerezo worked closely with Reyes on this campaign, but complained bitterly about her exclusion from MAV's charter at the time of its registration, claiming she had been excluded from the leadership of the organization for being transgender. When MAV was dissolved, she decided not to continue working with the primarily gay-male-led organizations that emerged—Unión Afirmativa and Alianza Lambda de Venezuela, suspicious that she would suffer the same treatment with them. Both Quintero and Cerezo complained about gay men's misogyny and transphobia in the Venezuelan GLBT movement. Although Cerezo had not been a sex worker (she was trained as a nurse but was turned away from every place she applied for a job after graduating), several of her friends and acquaintances were sex workers, and she was concerned about their health. She and artist Argelia Bravo began accompanying me to Avenida Libertador in the summer of 2003, having expressed curiosity about my work on the street. After investigating the possibility of joining Divas, Estrella decided to found her own organization, which she called TransVenus de Venezuela. Bravo and Cerezo decided to work together on the organization, and TransVenus was registered in April 2004. With great dedication, they have developed and maintained close relationships with many of the *transformistas* who work on Avenida Libertador, providing condoms, medical visits (in collaboration with volunteer physicians), and vigilance toward human rights violations. After collaborating with the HIV/AIDS service organization ASES de Venezuela, TransVenus applied for and received funding from the Ministry of Health and Development (MSDS) to continue its condom distribution and medical attention to *transformistas* on Avenida Libertador. Cerezo also began giving hairdressing classes to *transformistas* doing sex work. This work was supported by Fundación Artistas Emergentes.

On June 25, 2004, in conjunction with a month of Orgullo GLBT programming put on by various organizations, TransVenus organized a vigil for the human rights of *transformistas* on Avenida Libertador. Forty people attended and stood with *transformistas* where they do sex work every day, everyone holding up placards bearing the points of the United Nation's Universal Declaration of Human Rights and waving them at passing cars. The event resulted in two full pages of coverage on transgender issues in *El Nacional*, one of Venezuela's newspapers of record. As transgender people and *transformistas* begin to articulate individual and collective responses to the problems they face in Venezuelan society, I am inspired to see them analyzing *transformistas*' existing survival strategies and resisting the pressure to conform their demands and political imaginaries to a liberal model that fundamentally excludes many *transformistas*.

MARCIA OCHOA is assistant professor of community studies at the University of California, Santa Cruz. Her book *Queen for a Day: Transformistas, Misses, and Mass Media in Venezuela* is under contract with Duke University Press. Her field research explores the strategic use of beauty and femininity by beauty pageant contestants and transgender women. She currently supervises the El/La Transgender Latina HIV Prevention Program, which promotes the health and survival of transgender Latina immigrants in San Francisco's Mission district. Ochoa has done extensive work on HIV-prevention media campaigns, media literacy, and human rights for Latin American transgender people in Venezuela and the United States.

NOTES

1. The preceding epigraph is chapter and verse from the Ordenanza de Convivencia Ciudadana of the city of Caracas. In the tradition of the Spanish Requerimiento, which was read in Spanish to populations of indigenous people in what was then called Yndias on the eve of conquest, I leave it untranslated. I dedicate this essay to Estrella Cerezo, Argelia Bravo, and TransVenus de Venezuela, with whom I have worked to establish condom distribution and HIV-prevention education on Avenida Libertador.

2. *Transformista* is a term used in Venezuela to refer to someone who is assigned male sex at birth and who presents herself in her life as a woman, using technologies related to hair, cosmetics, clothing, diet, hormones and implants to accomplish her femininity. The term is at times considered an insult, but is also used for in-group identification. It also implies, more often than not, the practice of publicly visible sex work as part of one's identity. Not all transgender women in Venezuela do sex work or identify as *transformista*s.

3. Note that in the polarization between the Chávez government and the opposition, the words *ciudadano* and *sociedad civil* have been taken up by the different sides to signify participation. *Ciudadano* has become the parlance of the Chávez administration, and of the Movimiento Quinta Republica (MVR) as it struggles to include marginalized Venezuelans in the political process. *Sociedad civil* has been appropriated by the opposition to signify dissent from an authoritarian regime, as it came to be used in Brazil, Argentina, and Chile in the late twentieth century.

4. "GLBT" refers to a kind of queer "scene" and is a term used for LGBT communities and spaces throughout Latin America. I will further define this and other terms below.

5. This fieldwork was generously supported by a Dissertation Fieldwork Grant from the Wenner Gren Foundation for Anthropological Research in 2002–3. The original Spanish version of this article was developed through my participation in the Programa de Cultura, Globalización y Transformaciones Sociales at the Universidad Central de Venezuela, Centro de Estudios Post-Doctorales (CIPOST), Facultad de Ciencias Económicas y Sociales (FACES). For the original version of this essay, see Ochoa 2004. This is a translation of the original essay, which I have adapted to a U.S. audience. My thanks to Professor Daniel Mato and all the participants in the Grupo de Trabajo Ciudadanía y Sociedad Civil en Tiempos de Globalización. Thanks in particular to Afef Bennasieh and Judith Halberstam for their contributions to my development of this title. Thanks also to an anonymous reader, who provided important comments for this revision.

6. Although my usage of the term *loca* emerged from my experience with gay, queer, and trans (Latino) communities in the United States, Colombia, and Venezuela, it is very much resonant with Lawrence La Fountain-Stokes's (2008) beautiful riff on *locas* and *locura* in this issue of *WSQ*. I use the term to refer to a variety of people and will discuss this in the section on taxonomy and translation.

7. In an expanded version of this essay as well as in the original Spanish-language version, I discuss in more detail the relationship of this work to my experience with the San Francisco–based Proyecto ContraSIDA Por Vida. See Ochoa 2004, 2006.

8. For a critique of the "Gay International," see Masad 2002. Extensive debates on the globalization of LGBT political categories have emerged in the past decade, and I will not summarize them here. For important contributions to and documentation of these debates, see Cruz-Malavé and Manalansan 2002; Boelstorff 2005, 2007.

9. Márquez (1999, 46-47) describes the cultivation and use of an abject aesthetic among the "chupapegas" (glue-sniffers, generally boys eight to twelve years old) in Sabana Grande, the area of Caracas where the *transformista*s and other sex workers do their work.

10. "Yo sé que esto es ilegal y todo pero el hecho de ser un ser humano—no te deben maltratar" (Carrasco and Ochoa 2003; translation mine).

11. Thanks to Cristina Bloj for suggesting this line of thought.

12. *La rumba* translates as "the party"; *el rumbo* is "the direction," or "the sense" in which something or someone is going.

13. For one take on Movimiento Ambiente de Venezuela (MAV), see Muñoz 2003. Muñoz's article includes a content analysis of MAV's publication *Igual Género*, national press coverage, Web pages, and interviews with Jesús Medina (identified as "Jesús Rovelo") of Lambda de Venezuela and José Ramon Merentes of Unión Afirmativa. Muñoz places MAV in a previous "generation" of GLBT organizing, one before the current generation, in which Lambda and Unión Afirmativa emerge from the ashes of MAV (indeed, they are called the "sons" of MAV). The world of LGBT NGOs, and notably the work of Oswaldo Reyes, was profoundly affected and defined by MAV. All the interviews for this essay in one way or another came back to the MAV scandal, a misappropriation of European Union funds in 1997 that led to MAV's gradual decline. By 2000, MAV and Oswaldo Reyes no longer had any political life in Caracas. Neither surfaced in the year I spent in Venezuela.

14. Muñoz may have transposed and misspelled names. I know of no Jesús Rovelo associated with Lambda. Jesús Ravelo has not, to my knowledge, ever been part of the leadership of Lambda de Venezuela, though he has participated in Lambda events and workshops.

WORKS CITED

Ang, Ian. 1989. *Watching* Dallas: *Soap Opera and the Melodramatic Imagination*. New York: Routledge.

Boellstorff, Tom. 2005. *The Gay Archipelago: Sexuality and Nation in Indonesia*. Princeton: Princeton U Press.

———. 2007. *A Coincidence of Desires: Anthropology, Queer Studies, Indonesia*. Durham: Duke University Press.

Carrasco, Edgar, and Marcia Ochoa. 2003. "Informe sobre impunidad: Venezuela." Proyecto ILGALAC-OASIS-Unión Europea. Caracas: Acción Ciudadana Contra el SIDA.

Dagnino, Evelina. 1998. "Culture, Citizenship, and Democracy: Changing Discourses and Practices of the Latin American Left." In *Culture of Politics/Politics of Culture: Revisioning Latin American social movements*, ed. Sonia E. Alvarez, Evelina Dagnino, and Arturo Escobar. Boulder, CO: Westview Press.

González Stephan, Beatriz. 1996. "Economías fundacionales: Diseño del cuerpo ciudadano." In *Cultura y Tercer Mundo 2: Nuevas identidades y ciudadanías*, comp. Beatriz González Stephan. Serie Nubes y Tierra. Caracas: Editorial Nueva Sociedad.

Kulick, Don, and Charles Klein. 2001. "Scandalous Acts: The Politics of Shame Among Brazilian Travesti Prostitutes." http://www.sociology.su.se/cgs/Conference/Klein%20and%20Kulick2001.pdf(accessed 16 April, 2003).

Laclau, Ernesto, and Chantal Mouffe. 1989. *Hegemonía y estrategia socialista. Hacia una radicalización de la democracia*. Madrid: Siglo XXI.

La Fountain-Stokes, Lawrence. 2008. "Trans/Bolero/Drag/Migration: Diasporic Puerto Rican Theatricalities." *WSQ: Trans-* Special Issue.

Lowe, Lisa. 1996. *Immigrant Acts: On Asian American Cultural Politics*. Durham: Duke University Press.

Márquez, Patricia. 1999. *The Street Is My Home: Youth and Violence in Caracas*. Stanford: Stanford University Press.

Massad, Joseph. 2002. "Re-Orienting Desire: The Gay International and the Arab World." *Public Culture* 14(2): 361–385.

Medina, Jesús, executive director, Lambda de Venezuela. 2003. Interview by the author, May 6, Caracas, Venezuela. Minidisc recording.

Muñoz, Carlos. 2003. "Identidades translocales y orientación sexual en Caracas: (arqueología, geneología y tecnologías de la orientación sexual." In *Políticas de identidades y diferencias sociales en tiempos de globalización*, coord. Daniel Mato. Caracas: FACES, Universidad Central de Venezuela.

Ochoa, Marcia. 2004. "Ciudadanía perversa: Divas, marginación y participación en la 'loca-lización.'" In *Políticas de ciudadanía y sociedad civil en tiempos de globalización*, coord. Daniel Mato. Caracas: FACES, Universidad Central de Venezuela.

———. 2006. "Queen for a Day: *Transformista*s, Misses, and Mass Media in Venezuela." PhD diss., Stanford University.

Quintero, Rummie, founder, Divas de Venezuela. 2003. Interview by the author. Minidisc recording. May 5, Caracas, Venezuela.

Ravelo, Jesús, general coordinator, Unión Afirmativa. 2003. Interview by the author. Minidisc recording. May 8, Caracas, Venezuela.

Robles Gil, Rafael Reygadas. 1998. *Abriendo veredas: Iniciativas públicas y socials de las redes de organizaciones civiles*. México: Convergencia de Organismos Civiles por la Democracia.

Rodríguez, Juana María. 2003. *Queer Latinidad: Identity Practices, Discursive Spaces*. New York: New York University Press.

Roitter, Mario. 2003. "El tercer sector como representación topográfica de la sociedad civil." Paper presented at the *Coloquio Internacional Políticas de Ciudadanía y Sociedad Civil en Tiempos de Globalización. Más Allá de los Debates sobre la Coyuntura en Venezuela*. Caracas, May 23–24, 2004.

Valentine, David. 2007. *Imagining Transgender*. Durham: Duke University Press.

Yuval-Davis, Nira. 1997. "Women, Citizenship, and Difference." *Feminist Review* (57):4–27.

ELECTRIC BRILLIANCY: CROSS-DRESSING LAW AND FREAK SHOW DISPLAYS IN NINETEENTH-CENTURY SAN FRANCISCO

CLARE SEARS

In 1863, midway through the Civil War, the San Francisco Board of Supervisors passed a local law against cross-dressing that prohibited public appearance "in a dress not belonging to his or her sex" (*Revised Orders* 1863). That city was not alone in this action: between 1848 and 1900, thirty-four cities in twenty-one states passed laws against cross-dressing, as did eleven additional cities before World War I (Eskridge 1999). Far from being a nineteenth-century anachronism, cross-dressing laws had remarkable longevity and became a key tool for policing transgender and queer communities in the 1950s and 1960s. However, although studies have documented the frequent enforcement of these laws in the mid-twentieth century, far less is known about their operations in the nineteenth century, when they were initially passed. In this essay, I examine the legal and cultural history of cross-dressing law in one city—San Francisco—from the 1860s to 1900s. In particular, I explore cross-dressing law's relationship with another nineteenth-century institution that was centrally concerned with cross-gender practices—the dime museum freak show.

Focusing on the complex, contradictory, and sometimes unpredictable relationships between legal regulation, cultural fascination, and gender transgressions, I develop three main arguments. First, I examine the legal work of cross-dressing law, documenting the range of practices criminalized, people arrested, and punishments faced. Observing that the law exclusively targeted public cross-dressing practices, I argue that it did much more than police the types of clothing that "belonged" to each sex; it also used the visible marker of clothing to police the types of people who "belonged" in public space. Second, I explore the relationship between cross-dressing law and a host of other local laws that targeted human bodies as public nuisances. In doing so, I argue that cross-dressing law was not an isolated act of government, exclusively concerned with gender, but one part of a broader regulatory project that was also concerned with sex, race, citizenship, and city space. Finally, I analyze the case of Milton Matson, a female-bodied man who was recruited from a jail cell to appear in a dime museum freak show in 1890s San Francisco. Based on this analysis, I argue that cross-dressing law and the freak show had similar disciplinary effects, producing and policing the boundaries of normative gender, albeit in incomplete ways.

A DRESS NOT BELONGING

San Francisco's Board of Supervisors did not initially criminalize cross-dressing as a distinct offense, but as one manifestation of the broader offense of indecency. The full legal text stated:

> If any person shall appear in a public place in a state of nudity, or in a dress not belonging to his or her sex, or in an indecent or lewd dress, or shall make any indecent exposure of his or her person, or be guilty of any lewd or indecent act or behavior, or shall exhibit or perform any indecent, immoral or lewd play, or other representation, he should be guilty of a misdemeanor, and on conviction, shall pay a fine not exceeding five hundred dollars (*Revised Orders* 1863).

In turn, this wide-reaching indecency law was not a stand-alone prohibition, but one part of a new chapter of the municipal codebook, titled *Offenses Against Good Morals And Decency*, which also criminalized public intoxication, profane language, and bathing in San Francisco Bay without appropriate clothing. Alongside these newly designated crimes, cross-dressing was one of the very first "offenses against good morals" to be outlawed in the city. In 1866, the original five-hundred-dollar penalty was revised to a five-hundred-dollar fine or six months in jail; in 1875, it increased to a one-thousand-dollar fine, six months in jail, or both (*General Orders* 1866, 1875).

Despite its roots in indecency law, San Francisco's cross-dressing law soon became a flexible tool for policing multiple gender transgressions. Before the end of the nineteenth century, San Francisco police made more than one hundred arrests for the crime of cross-dressing (*Municipal Reports* 1863–64 to 1899–1900).[1] A wide variety of people fell afoul of this law, including feminist dress reformers, female impersonators, "fast" young women who dressed as men for a night on the town, and people whose gender identifications did not match their anatomical sex in legally acceptable ways (people who today would probably—although not definitely—identify as transgender). Those arrested faced police harassment, public exposure, and six months in jail; by the early twentieth century, they also risked psychiatric institutionalization or deportation if they were not U.S. citizens. For example, in 1917, a female-bodied man named Jack Garland was involuntarily institutionalized in a psychiatric ward for refusing to wear women's clothing (Stryker and Van Buskirk 1996), while a male-bodied woman named Geraldine Portica was arrested for violating San Francisco's cross-dressing law and subsequently deported to Mexico (Jesse Brown Cook Scrapbooks n.d.).

San Francisco's cross-dressing law marked the start of a new regulatory approach toward gender transgressions, and it attempted to draw and fix the boundaries of normative gender during a period of rapid social change. However, cross-dressing law signaled not only a new object of regulation, but also a new mechanism of regulation—exclusion from public space. From its inception, cross-dressing law was specifically concerned with public gender displays, and it targeted cross-dressing in public places. Notably, the law made it a crime for someone to "appear *in a public place*...in a dress not belonging to his or her sex," and any clothing practices that occurred in private were beyond its scope (*Revised Orders* 1863; italics mine). As a result, some people confined their cross-dressing practices to private spaces and modified their appearance when in public for fear of arrest.

For example, in the 1890s, a male-bodied San Franciscan who identified as a woman named Jenny reported that although she preferred to wear women's clothing, she only dared do so in private, for fear of arrest on the city streets. In a letter to German sexologist Magnus Hirschfeld, Jenny wrote: "Only because of the arbitrary actions of the police do I wear men's clothing outside of the house. Skirts are a sanctuary to me, and I would rather keep on women's clothing forever if it were allowed on the street" (Hirschfeld 1991, 84). Her fears were not unfounded. In 1895, the police arrested a middle-aged carpenter named Ferdinand Haisch for "masquerading in female attire," after Hayes Valley residents called the cops on the "strange appearing woman" who walked through their neighborhood every evening ("Masqueraded as a Woman," *San Francisco Examiner*, April 16, 1895, 4).[2] The police staked out the neighborhood for several weeks before arresting Haisch, who was wearing the latest women's fashions—a three-quarter-length melton coat, green silk skirt, red stockings, silver-buckled garters, high-heeled shoes, and stylish hat. Following a brief stint in the city prison, Haisch was released by the police court judge on the condition that Haisch ceased wearing these clothes in public. Haisch apparently complied, but her ever-vigilant neighbors were still not satisfied, and they demanded her rearrest for wearing women's clothing at home. However, while predictably sympathetic to the neighbors' complaints, the police admitted that they were powerless to intervene, because the law permitted cross-dressing in private ("Crazy on Female Attire," *The Call*, July 3, 1895, 8).

The exclusion of cross-dressing practices from public space—and their concurrent confinement to private spaces—was a form of legal segregation that had significant political consequences, both for individuals whose public appearance constituted a crime and for the "general" public. First, for people excluded from public space, participation in day-to-day city life was curtailed. Everyday activities, such as going to the shops, enjoying a night on the town, or even walking through one's own neighborhood brought surveillance and arrest. As such, cross-dressing was marked as a deviant and secretive practice, rather than a public activity and identification. Second, by excluding cross-dressing practices from public space, the law also severely restricted people's access to the public sphere, which twentieth-century critical theorist Jürgen Habermas (1991) identified as a fundamental precondition of democracy. In Habermas's influential formulation, the public sphere consisted of multiple public venues where individuals came together to discuss common public and political affairs, these spaces including coffee houses, saloons, bars, and meeting halls, as well as the mediated venues of newspapers and journals. By restricting access to these public venues, cross-dressing law effectively excluded multiple people with non-normative gender from civic participation and the democratic life of the city. Finally, cross-dressing law was not only consequential for those excluded from everyday public and political life, but also for the "general" gender-normative public, who faced an artificially narrow range of gender identities in city space. After all, when in public, there were only two ways that people with non-normative gender presentation could avoid arrest—either changing their clothing to comply with the law or evading police detection by fully "passing." Clearly involving different risks and benefits, these strategies nonetheless had a similar effect on city space, removing different-gender appearances and identities from public view. Indeed, by policing gender hierarchies through public exclusion, cross-dressing law reinforced the very notion of "difference" as anomalous by exaggerating the prevalence of the "norm."

PROBLEM BODIES, PUBLIC SPACE

Although cross-dressing law marked a particularly literal attempt to produce and police normative gender, it was not an isolated or idiosyncratic act of government. Instead, it was one part of a broader legal matrix that targeted the public visibility of multiple "problem bodies," including those of Chinese immigrants, prostitutes, and individuals deemed maimed or diseased.[3] These local orders constituted a body of law that targeted the atypical human body as a potential public nuisance, and they appeared in the municipal codebook alongside laws that regulated sewage, slaughterhouses, and the keeping of hogs. However, while these nineteenth-century laws differed significantly from each other in their object of concern, their mechanisms of control were very similar, seeking to manage public nuisances—animal, object, or human body—through regulating city space.

Mirroring the regulatory logic of cross-dressing law, some of these laws sought to directly *exclude* problem bodies from public space. For example, in 1867, the Board of Supervisors passed a law that prohibited anyone who was "diseased, maimed, mutilated," or an otherwise "unsightly or disgusting object" from appearing in public (*General Orders* 1869). One part of a broader law, with the name "To Prohibit Street Begging, and to Restrain Certain Persons from Appearing in Streets and Public Places," this law focused on the intersection of disability and poverty, seeking to exclude the potentially sympathetic figure of the disabled beggar from San Francisco streets (Schweik 2007). Two years later, in 1869, the supervisors passed another law that prohibited persons from carrying baskets or bags on poles on the city streets—this way of moving through public space being common among some Chinese immigrant workers (*General Orders* 1872). Similar to cross-dressing law, these laws focused on public appearances and movements and simultaneously policed problem bodies while producing governable city space.

A second set of laws operated through *confinement*, rather than exclusion, seeking to ban problem bodies from particular neighborhoods, rather than from generic public space. A series of laws in the 1880s and 1890s, for example, targeted houses of prostitution on middle-class, residential streets, in an effort to reduce the visibility of commercial sex work for "respectable," middle-class, Anglo-American women and children, through its confinement in carefully designated, racialized vice districts (*General Orders* 1890, 1892, 1898). Subsequent laws and policies went even further in endeavors to confine vice to specific areas. For example, when the owner of a Barbary Coast "den" attempted to buy property in the upscale Pacific Heights neighborhood, following the 1906 earthquake and fire, the police captain promised to block the sale: "This section of the city must be kept free of such places. They have no business outside of the burned district and I propose to drive them back to where they belong" ("Barbary Coast Harpies Seek to Settle Among Homes of Pacific Heights," *The Call*, September 15, 1906, 3). Two years later, even more dramatically, the chief of police drew territorial boundaries around the Barbary Coast, ordering the district's female residents to remain east of Powell Street and north of Bush Street or face arrest and jailing under vagrancy laws ("Biggy Marks Deadline for Tenderloin Women," *The Call*, January 12, 1908, 32).

A third type of legal intervention required the *concealment,* rather than exclusion or confinement, of problem bodies from the "respectable" public's view. Specifically, in 1863, as the Board of Supervisors enacted its wide-ranging indecency law, the local chief of police, Martin Burke, attempted to reduce the visibility of prostitution in Chinatown by requiring the owners of "cribs" (small, street-level rooms from which women solicited sex) to buy and erect large screens at the entrance of the streets that housed them (Burke 1887). This specified not only the geographic spaces of concern (namely, Chinatown), but also the characteristics of "the public" that needed to be shielded from these sights. Burke made this explicit in a subsequent annual report, stating that his purpose was to "hide the degradation and vice…from the view of women and children who ride the streetcar" through the newly developing downtown area (*Municipal Reports* 1865–66).

Finally, there were several legal attempts to bypass intracity boundaries and *remove* problem bodies from the city entirely, aimed exclusively at Chinese immigrants. In 1865, for example, the Board of Supervisors passed an "Order to Remove Chinese Women of Ill-Fame from Certain Limits of the City" (*General Orders* 1866). This was the first local law to explicitly target a single nationality, and under the advice of the city attorney, the supervisors removed the word "Chinese" from the legal text, prior to publication. The intent of the law, however, remained unchanged, and the following year, 137 women—virtually all Chinese—were arrested as "common prostitutes," an enormous increase over the previous year, when there had been one arrest. These women were subsequently removed from the city, and the chief of police boasted that he had used the law to expel three hundred Chinese women, with fewer than two hundred remaining (*Municipal Reports* 1865–66). Additionally, the Board of Supervisors made numerous attempts to harness the power granted by nuisance law to remove all Chinese residents from San Francisco. This possibility had circulated in anti-Chinese political discourse since at least the mid-1850s and reached its peak in 1880, when an investigative committee of the San Francisco Board of Health published a report declaring Chinatown a nuisance and calling for all Chinese residents to be removed from the city (*Chinatown Declared a Nuisance!* 1880, 6). Judicial restraints ultimately rendered this effort ineffective, but not before the Board of Health unanimously accepted the committee's recommendations, signaling local government's investments in using nuisance law for racialized removal.

Undoubtedly, there were important differences between these laws, as well as between the processes through which cross-dressed, indecent, unsightly, and racialized immigrant bodies were defined as problems and targeted for legal intervention. Nonetheless, I bring these particular laws together here—as they were brought together in nineteenth-century municipal codebooks—for two specific reasons.

First, when these laws are considered together, it becomes clear that cross-dressing law was not alone in its attempt to minimize the public visibility of problem bodies. Instead, it was one part of a broader legal matrix that was concerned not only with gender transgressions, but also with race, citizenship, and disease. Moreover, these were not independent concerns. As numerous scholars have argued, accusations of gender and sexual deviance have frequently been deployed in processes of racialization, while racialized anxieties have informed the policing of gender and sex. In turn, race, gender, and sex have all been linked to disease, and in nineteenth-century San Francisco, the management of public health was key to policing Chinese immigrants and prostitutes. In short, there were numerous intersecting cultural anxieties during this period that become more apparent when cross-dressing law is situated in its broader legal context.

Analyzing cross-dressing law within this context also makes clearer the ways that the law sought to manage not only gender but also city space. As legal historian Lawrence Friedman has stated about nineteenth-century morality laws in general: "What was illegal, then, was not sin itself—and certainly not secret sin—but sin that offended public morality. This was what we might call the Victorian compromise: a certain toleration for vice, or at least a resigned acceptance, so long as it remained in an underground state" (1985, 585). However, before vice in San Francisco could "remain in an underground state," such spaces had to be created. Indecency and nuisance laws were instrumental to this process, creating urban zones where problem bodies could be contained—primarily the racialized vice districts of Chinatown and the Barbary Coast. Consequently, these laws affected not only the public visibility of problem bodies, but also the sociospatial order of the city, drawing a series of territorial boundaries between public and private, visible and concealed, and respectable and vice districts.

FASCINATION AND FREAKERY

Laws that sought to reduce the visibility of problem bodies—including cross-dressing law—constituted a dense legal matrix that dictated the types of bodies that could move freely through city space and the types of bodies that could not. However, such laws could also incite cultural fascination and the desire to see, which entrepreneurs could exploit. One manifestation of this was the popular commercial "slumming tour," in which tourists were guided through the Barbary Coast and Chinatown, to glimpse the bodies that the law sought to conceal. These tours took in brothels, opium dens, dive bars, and sick rooms housing Chinese patients who were banned from the city's hospital (Evans 1873). Another manifestation was the newspaper scandal, which splashed cross-dressing practices across the front page, as local editors ran sensational stories and interviews with those who broke the law. These scandals publicized normative gender boundaries and ridiculed transgressors, representing gender difference as a titillating private eccentricity or individual moral flaw (Duggan 2000; Sears 2005). However, the starkest manifestation of this cultural fascination was the dime museum freak show, which displayed non-normative bodies and cross-gender performances in seeming conflict with the law.

Dime museum freak shows emerged as a popular form of entertainment in most major U.S. cities after the Civil War, peaking in popularity during the 1880s and 1890s. As one component of the era's new mass entertainment industry, dime museums had their socioeconomic roots in technological, demographic, and economic changes that led to an unprecedented rise in leisure time among working-class and middle-class city residents (Adams 2001).[4] Similar to municipal law, the dime museum freak show was preoccupied with the public appearance of non-normative bodies and offered a variety of attractions for the low price of a dime, including human anatomy exhibits, lectures on morality, sideshow circus artists, and freak show performers. Most studies of dime museums and freak shows have focused on East Coast institutions, with particular emphasis on P. T. Barnum's American Museum in New York (Bogdan 1988; Dennet 1997; McNamara 1974). San Francisco, however, boasted numerous freak shows of its own, ranging from the short-lived Museum of Living Wonders, which operated out of a "leaky tent on Kearny Street" in the early 1870s ("A Shocking Exhibition," *The Call*, December 17, 1873), to the grand exhibitions held at Woodward's Gardens, an expansive family amusement resort that occupied two city blocks in the Mission district from 1866 to 1891 ("Where the 'Old Town' Frolicked," *San Francisco Chronicle*, November 9, 1913, 25). Most of the city's freak shows, however, were clustered on Market Street, operating out of small, seedy, rented storefronts (Asbury 1933; Cowan 1938). Market Street was also home to the Pacific Museum of Anatomy and Science, the city's longest-running dime museum, which claimed to be the "largest anatomical museum in the world" ("Visit Dr. Jordan's Great Museum of Anatomy," *The Call*, September 11, 1902, 2).

In San Francisco, as elsewhere, dime museum entertainment centered upon performances of bodily difference and paid particularly close attention to bodies that challenged gender, racial, and national boundaries or that ostensibly revealed the somatic penalties of immorality through spectacles of disease or deformity. For example, freak shows typically featured a Bearded Lady or Half-Man/Half-Woman character, while anatomy exhibits included hermaphrodite bodies, such as that of the Pacific Museum's display of "a beautiful dissection" of a hermaphrodite cadaver, featuring "the internal arrangements and dissections of this wonderful freak of nature" (Jordan 1868, 19). Another staple attraction was the popular "Missing Link" or "What-Is-It?" exhibit, which usually featured an African American or a white man in blackface who was presented as the "missing link" between man and animal (Cook 1996). Many dime museums also featured pathology rooms that contained displays of diseased sexual organs and other body parts, damaged by syphilis, gonorrhea, and "the filthy habit of self-abuse" (Jordan 1868, 36). Finally, dime museums regularly staged performances of racialized national dominance that corresponded to contemporary wars. One of the first crowd-drawing exhibits at the Pacific Museum of Anatomy and Science, for example, was the preserved head of Joaquin Murietta, the notorious Mexican "bandit" who fought against Anglo dominance and violence in the southern California gold mines, before being killed by state-sponsored rangers in 1853 (Asbury 1933). Murietta was a popular symbol of Mexican resistance, and the display of his severed head graphically dramatized a narrative of Anglo dominance and Mexican defeat, against the backdrop of the Mexican War. Occasionally, dime museum exhibits explicitly linked gender and national boundary transgressions, as when Barnum's American Museum displayed a waxwork figure of Jefferson Davis, the defeated leader of the Southern Confederacy, wearing women's clothing, at the close of the Civil War. This exhibit dramatized rumors that Davis had disguised himself in hoopskirts when trying to escape his northern captors, deploying cultural anxieties about cross-gender practices to emasculate the defeated South, fortify territorial boundaries, and reconsolidate the postwar nation (Silber 1989).[5]

As this brief review suggests, the freak show and the law shared a set of cultural anxieties concerning the shifting boundaries of gender, race, health, and the nation, and the disparate bodies gathered on the freak show stage eerily mirrored the bodies targeted by municipal law—the sexually ambiguous, the indecent, the racialized, and the diseased. However, the relationship between the two institutions was complex, not least because the law prohibited the public visibility of problem bodies while the freak show required their public display. These complexities are illustrated by the case of one man who navigated both legal proscriptions and freak show visibility in 1890s San Francisco—Milton Matson.

In early January 1895, Matson was arrested in San Francisco, in the room of his fiancée, Ellen Fairweather, and charged with obtaining money under false pretenses. Matson was taken to San Jose County Jail and locked up in a cell with several other men, where he remained for two weeks, until the jailer received a bank telegraph, addressed to Miss Luisa Matson, and realized that Matson was female.[6] After complicated legal wrangling, charges against Matson were dropped, and he walked free from the jail in men's clothing, returning to San Francisco the following month.

The exposure of Matson's "true sex" generated a mass of newspaper coverage and the San Francisco dailies ran numerous stories on this "male impersonator" or "pretender," as Matson was described ("Louisa Has Her Say," *The Call*, January 28, 1895, 1; "Will Again Don Woman's Garb," *San Francisco Examiner*, January 30, 1895, 3). In these stories, the press excitedly debated the possibility of Matson's arrest under cross-dressing law and reported that he publicly dared the police to arrest him. Before this could happen, Matson was approached by a local dime museum manager, Frank Clifton, and offered work, sitting upon a museum platform, wearing men's clothing, for the public to view. In need of employment and money, particularly since the press had undermined his ability to live as a man, Matson accepted Clifton's offer. The strangeness of this transition—"from a cell in the San Jose prison to the electric brilliancy of an amusement resort"—was not lost on Matson, who commented: "Funniest thing...I'm getting letters from all sorts of showmen offering good salaries if I will exhibit myself. It amuses me very much....I'm beginning to think it pays to be notorious. It certainly does not seem to be a detriment to people in America" ("Has No Love for Petticoats," *San Francisco Examiner*, February 7, 1895, 16). The appeal of Matson's notoriety proved so popular that several other local freak shows began featuring cross-dressed performers, deceptively advertised as "the only genuine Miss Martson [sic] in male attire" ("Louisa Matson's Double Sued," *The Call*, February 15, 1895, 12).

Given the punitive forces impinging on cross-dressing practices in nineteenth-century San Francisco, and the law's insistence on removing them from public view, the concurrent display of cross-dressing performers in city freak shows is initially perplexing. On the one hand, these institutions operated according to very different logics. The law imprisoned, the freak show displayed; the law deprived its subject, the freak show offered a salary; the law disapproved and sought to reduce its subjects' "deviance," the freak show was fascinated and sought to exaggerate and increase it.

On the other hand, the operations of cross-dressing law and the freak show overlapped. After all, Matson was recruited into freak show entertainment directly from a jail cell, following a path that other San Francisco performers had walked before him.[7] Moreover, Matson's participation in a freak show exhibition regulated his offstage behavior in a very direct way; his contract forbade him to wear men's clothing on San Francisco's streets, to preserve the mystique—and profitability—of his show ("She Has Been a Man of the World for Over Twenty-six Years," *San Francisco Examiner*, February 10, 1895, 26). Consequently, although the law and the freak show operated through distinct logics of concealment and display, they could have similar regulatory effects on freak show performers.

The freak show also paralleled cross-dressing law as a normalizing discourse that communicated to audiences, in starkly visual terms, the parameters of acceptable behavior and the penalties for violating these norms. While there are few historical records that speak to the disciplinary impact of cross-dressing performers on freak show audiences, a popular 1890s dime novel is highly suggestive of possible effects. In Archibald Gunter and Fergus Redmond's *A Florida Enchantment*, of 1891, a wealthy white woman, Lillian Travers, purchases a box of African sex change seeds from a dime museum in Florida.[8] Following an argument with her fiancé, she swallows a seed and transitions into a man named Lawrence Talbot. Realizing that a wealthy man needs a male valet, rather than a female housekeeper, Lawrence forces his "mulatto maid," Jane, to also swallow a seed and become a man named Jack. Lawrence later realizes with "fearful horror" that dime museums would love to exhibit him as a freak and he has a nightmare in which the city is covered in gigantic dime museum posters, advertising him as "The Freak of All Ages" and "The Woman Man," appearing alongside "The Living Skeleton" and "The Missing Link." Although doubly fictional (first as appearing in a novel, second as appearing as a dream), this scene illuminates the operations of the freak show in two specific ways.

First, by illustrating Lawrence's horror at the prospect of being displayed as a freak, the nightmare suggests that freak show visibility could have disciplinary effects, operating as a threat against gender transgression and an inducement to conform. Second, the context of Lawrence's nightmare, within the novel, suggests that the disciplinary effects of freak show visibility were informed by racialized anxieties, rather than by a universal fear of being labeled "freak." Specifically, Lawrence's nightmare occurs after he has already entered a dime museum to purchase sex change seeds from Africa and after he has learned that his former maid, now Jack, has begun working at a dime museum as "the greatest freak on earth." Additionally, the poster from his nightmare suggests that part of the horror of being displayed as "The Woman Man" is appearing alongside and in association with the racialized "Missing Link" character and the deformed "Living Skeleton." Indeed, throughout the novel, the dime museum appears as a racialized site that serves as both the source of gender transgression (sex change seeds from Africa) and the space of its containment. This suggests that the potential disciplinary effects of freak show visibility were intricately connected to its association with imperial exoticism and racialized difference.

Finally, freak shows worked in tandem with cross-dressing law by producing not only disciplined audiences schooled in gender normativity, but also vigilant audiences trained in the pleasures of suspicion. The possibility of being duped was central to dime museum entertainment, and show managers encouraged audiences to gain pleasure from suspecting, confronting, and unmasking frauds. Performances of sexual and gender ambiguity were particularly susceptible to this suspicion. For example, the Bearded Lady's combination of feminine dress and masculine facial hair confronted audiences with a fascinating gender dilemma—was this a woman who pushed the female body beyond recognizable femininity or was this a man in drag? Visitors sought to resolve this dilemma by prodding at flesh, tugging at beards, and demanding to know the Bearded Lady's marital and maternal status (Wood 1885). Freak show managers encouraged this questioning and occasionally brought in experts to heighten the drama. At New York's American Museum, for example, P. T. Barnum instigated a confrontation, one that ended in court, in which a freak show visitor accused a Bearded Lady of being male, only to be rebuffed by the latter's husband, father, and numerous doctors who testified that she was, indeed, female. Back in San Francisco, Matson's manager also went to court, to sue rivals of his who allegedly featured "fake" Matsons in their shows. Far from resolving the gender confusion at hand, such events reminded audiences of their susceptibility to being duped. As such, freak shows not only reproduced the boundary between permissible and criminal gender displays that cross-dressing law policed—they also popularized and democratized this boundary, turning audiences into aware and vigilant judges of possible gender "fraud."

Despite their different modes of operation, cross-dressing law and the freak show performed similar cultural work in nineteenth-century San

Francisco, as techniques of normalization that strove to produce clear, recognizable boundaries between normative and non-normative gender. Additionally, their mutual preoccupation with cross-dressing bodies did not occur in a vacuum, but was one part of a broader set of cultural concerns about the public visibility of problem bodies, particularly those marked by sexual immorality, race, and disease/deformity.

At the same time, however, freak show displays may have had unintended or ironic effects, particularly when the carefully managed distance between viewer and viewed broke down. As cultural scholar Rachel Adams (2001) has argued, freak shows were not only sites of disidentification and disavowal, where audiences secured a sense of normality through their spatial and existential distance from the freaks on stage, but were also sites of identification, where audiences recognized themselves in the freaks and the freaks in themselves. In part, this occurred because the meaning of the freak show performance (like the meaning of any text) was never completely fixed, but was open to multiple interpretations by different audiences. Moreover, as Adams points out, the interactive format of the freak show amplified the possibility of unintended interpretations, as it facilitated unscripted exchanges between disruptive audience members and the freaks who talked back. Such exchanges encouraged alternative readings of the freak show not only among those who participated in them, but also among the wider audience who collectively observed an unintended show.

Adams makes this argument in the context of discussing African American audiences who identified and unmasked racialized freak show performers as local people of color. Such identification, she claims, undermined the fantasy of complete otherness on which the freak show depended and dissolved the boundary between audience and performer, "relocating [the freak] within the community of onlookers" (2001, 170). However, in the context of gender freaks, particularly Matson, the politics of identification could take a slightly different turn, through identifications and desires that did not relocate the freak within the audience but attracted the onlooker to the cross-gender performer on stage. This attraction could be fueled by a shared sense of female masculinity—after all, Matson was not the only female-bodied person to live as a man in 1890s San Francisco.[9] It could also be fueled by an erotic desire for the cross-gender performer, particularly one such as Matson who had described the pleasures of courting women in the pages of the city press.

There is, unfortunately, scant evidence of such identifications and desires in relation to Matson or other cross-dressed freak show performers, as the voices of those who may have appropriated freak discourse in this manner have not made their way into the archive. However, neglecting this possibility because of insufficient evidence may be more problematic than raising it unsupported by positive proof, as it replicates the structure of the archive, amplifying some voices and silencing others. Within the archive, the voice of the newspaper reporter is prominent; a *San Francisco Examiner* reporter described Matson's dime museum exhibit as follows: "Her part will not be a difficult one. She will be faultlessly attired in patent leathers, a handsome dress suit, embroidered linen and a white tie. She will recline in an easy-chair on a little platform and chat with the socially inclined, but whether she will divulge any of the interesting secrets connected with her numerous love episodes is not definitely known" ("Has No Love for Petticoats," *San Francisco Examiner*, February 7, 1895, 16). Consequently, we can imagine the different ways that different audiences may have interacted with Matson—with fascination and titillation, perhaps; with discomfort and disdain; but also perhaps with identification, attraction, and desire.

CONCLUSION

Through its focus on cross-dressing law, this essay has demonstrated the centrality of gender regulation to nineteenth-century city life and unearthed the hidden history of a law that has appeared in the footnotes of twentieth-century studies, but has not yet been brought to the fore. The essay has also brought together subjects that rarely share the pages of academic inquiry, despite sharing San Francisco streets: male-bodied women and "unsightly" beggars; female-bodied men and sex workers; freak show managers and city police. In doing so I have argued that the policing of gender transgressions needs to be analyzed in relation to the policing of multiple forms of bodily difference and that legal regulations need to be studied alongside cultural fascination. These analytic insights are crucial not only for a study of nineteenth-century cross-dressing law, but also for future studies of the production and regulation of normative gender.

CLARE SEARS is an assistant professor in sociology at San Francisco State University, where she teaches courses in law, punishment, and social control.

She received the Kevin Starr Postdoctoral Fellowship in California Studies (University of California Humanities Research Institute, 2005–6) and she is currently completing a book titled *Arresting Dress: Cross-Dressing Law in Nineteenth-Century San Francisco* (forthcoming, University of California Press).

NOTES

1. Arrest records were not broken down by gender, but in 1867–68, arrests were reported separately for "wearing female attire" and "wearing male attire." During this year, four people (presumably male bodied) were arrested for "wearing female attire" and two people (presumably female bodied) were arrested "wearing male attire" (*Municipal Reports* 1867–68).

2. Newspapers did not report on Haisch's own gender identification, but they did describe her going to considerable lengths to publicly present as a woman. Consequently, I use female pronouns when discussing Haisch.

3. I use the term "problem bodies" to collectively refer to the multiple sets of bodies that local government officials defined as social problems and targeted for legal intervention in nineteenth-century San Francisco. In particular, I use "problem bodies" as a term that conceptually precedes the related, but narrower, term "deviant bodies" (Terry and Urla 1995), because I identify the construction of deviance, through processes of normalization, as only one of several different strategies used to manage social, political, and economic conflicts. The concept of problem bodies thus allows a wider range of bodies—and a wider range of conflicts—to be brought into view.

4. Vaudeville theater and minstrel shows were also central components of the new entertainment industry and they shared the freak show's emphasis on cross-gender and cross-racial performances (Lott, 1993; Toll, 1976).

5. Thanks to Susan Stryker for pointing me to the Jefferson Davis reference.

6. Matson was accused of committing this crime in Los Gatos, fifty miles south of San Francisco, and was consequently jailed in San Jose.

7. In 1888, freak show managers recruited another San Francisco performer, "Big Bertha the Queen of Confidence Women," directly from jail, literally paying her bail so as to secure her performance in their Market Street show ("Madame Stanley," *Morning Call*, June 11, 1888, 4).

8. In my discussion of this novel, I draw upon and extend Siobhan Somerville's (2000) earlier analysis.

9. For example, Lou Sullivan (1990) documented the life of Jack Garland (aka Babe Bean), a female-bodied man who lived in or near San Francisco in the late 1890s and 1900s.

WORKS CITED

Adams, Rachel. 2001. *Sideshow USA: Freaks and the American Cultural Imagination.* Chicago: University of Chicago Press.

Asbury, Herbert. 1933. *The Barbary Coast: An Informal History of the San Francisco*

Underworld. New York: A. A. Knopf.

Bogdan, Robert. 1988. *Freak Show: Presenting Human Oddities for Amusement and Profit*. Chicago: University of Chicago Press.

Burke, Martin J. 1887. "The San Francisco Police." Bancroft Library, University of California, Berkeley.

Chinatown Declared a Nuisance! 1880. San Francisco: Workingmen's Party of California.

Cook, James W. 1996. "Of Men, Missing Links, and Nondescripts: The Strange Career of P. T. Barnum's 'What Is It?' Exhibition." In *Freakery: Cultural Spectacles of the Extraordinary Body*, ed. R. G. Thomson. New York: New York University Press.

Cowan, Robert Ernest. 1938. *Forgotten Characters of Old San Francisco, 1850–1870*. Los Angeles: Ward Ritchie Press.

Dennett, Andrea Stulman. 1997. *Weird and Wonderful: The Dime Museum in America*. New York: New York University Press.

Duggan, Lisa. 2000. *Sapphic Slashers: Sex, Violence, and American Modernity*. Durham: Duke University Press.

Eskridge, William N. 1999. *Gaylaw: Challenging the Apartheid of the Closet*. Cambridge: Harvard University Press.

Evans, Albert S. 1873. *A la California: Sketch of Life in the Golden State*. San Francisco: A. L. Bancroft.

Friedman, Lawrence Meir. 1985. *A History of American Law*. 2nd ed. New York: Simon and Schuster. (1st ed. pub. 1973.)

General Orders of the Board of Supervisors. 1866–98. San Francisco: San Francisco Board of Supervisors.

Habermas, Jürgen. 1991. *The Structural Transformation of the Public Sphere: An Inquiry into a Category of Bourgeois Society*. Cambridge: MIT Press (Orig. pub. 1962.)

Hirschfeld, Magnus. 1991. *Transvestites: The Erotic Drive to Cross-Dress*. Buffalo: Prometheus Books (Orig. pub. 1910).

Jesse Brown Cook Scrapbooks Documenting San Francisco History and Law Enforcement. n.d. Vol. 4. The Bancroft Library. University of California, Berkeley. Unit ID: 184.

Jordan, Louis J. 1868. *Handbook of the Pacific Museum of Anatomy and Science*. San Francisco: Francis and Valentine.

Lott, Eric. 1993. *Love and Theft: Blackface Minstrelsy and the American Working Class*. New York: Oxford University Press.

McNamara, Brooks. 1974. "'A Congress of Wonders': The Rise and Fall of the Dime Museum." *ESQ* 20(3):216–31.

Municipal Reports. 1863–64 to 1899–1900. San Francisco: San Francisco Board of Supervisors.

Schweik, Susan. 2007. "Begging the Question: Disability, Mendicancy, Speech and the Law." *Narrative* 15(1):58–70.

Sears, Clare. 2005. "A Tremendous Sensation: Cross-Dressing in the Nineteenth Century San Francisco Press." In *News and Sexuality: Media Portraits of Diversity*,

ed. L. Casteñada and S. Campbell. Thousand Oaks, CA: Sage Press.
Silber, Nina. 1989. "Intemperate Men, Spiteful Women, and Jefferson Davis: Northern Views of the Defeated South." *American Quarterly* 41(4):614–35.
Somerville, Siobhan. 2000. *Queering the Color Line: Race and the Invention of Homosexuality in American Culture.* Durham: Duke University Press.
Sullivan, Lou. 1990. *From Female to Male: The Life of Jack Bee Garland.* Boston: Alyson.
Stryker, Susan, and Jim Van Buskirk. 1996. *Gay by the Bay: A History of Queer Culture in the San Francisco Bay Area.* San Francisco: Chronicle Books.
Revised Orders of the City and County of San Francisco. 1863. San Francisco: San Francisco Board of Supervisors.
Terry, Jennifer, and Jacqueline Urla. 1995. *Deviant Bodies.* Bloomington: Indiana University Press.
Toll, Robert. 1976. *On with the Show! The First Century of Show Business in America.* New York: Oxford University Press.
Wood, J. G. 1885. "Dime Museums." *Atlantic Monthly* 55 (January–June):759–65.

ZAMBONI
AFTER PEGGY MUNSON'S *ORIGAMI STRIPTEASE*

NOELLE KOCOT

Richard liked transsexuals,
Female to male transsexuals.
He'd invite them over to play
Bridge every Saturday night.
Jack was a boi who also went to
The games and who liked
Zamboni machines. "Ice,
Ice, winter, ice," is what he'd
Tell everyone between hands.
One day Richard and Jack
Went to see the Ice-capades,
Then high-tailed it over to a
Hockey game. Jack was in
His glory, and expressed deep
Gratitude to Richard for taking
Him. Richard loved Jack,
In a completely friendly kind
Of way, and they were happy.
Richard bought Jack a Zamboni
Machine for his birthday,
And Jack built an ice-rink
In his yard. In the winter, he
Made ice sculptures of exotic
Plants and gave them to Richard,
Which Richard kept until they
Melted. One night at a bridge
Game, someone asked Jack
What he did for a living. "Ice,
Ice, winter, ice" is all he'd say.
Richard interjected, "Jack's love

For all things frozen touches
Me. He tumbles in the wood,
The birth pangs of his labor
Are fine for anyone to see, and
We are bound forevermore by
This pact of cold and subtle conduct."
Jack smiled, which he rarely did.
Adam and Steve looked up from
Their hands with deep approval.
There seemed nothing left to say.
Winter had fallen on the green green wood.

NOELLE KOCOT has received awards from the Academy of American Poets, the *American Poetry Review*, the National Endowment for the Arts, and the Fund for Poetry. Her third book, *Poem for the End of Time and Other Poems*, was published by WAVE Books in 2006, and her next book, *Sunny Wednesday*, is forthcoming from WAVE in 2009.

TRANS/BOLERO/DRAG/MIGRATION: MUSIC, CULTURAL TRANSLATION, AND DIASPORIC PUERTO RICAN THEATRICALITIES

LAWRENCE LA FOUNTAIN-STOKES

Bolero is a music of seduction. Wong Kar-wai knows it well, and that is why boleros accompany Maggie Cheung and Tony Leung extradiegetically as they become desperate lovers in Wong's *In the Mood for Love* (2000), a nostalgic film set in 1960s Hong Kong and interlaced with classic Latin American songs, interpreted by none other than Nat King Cole in a heavily accented Spanish. A movie for the new millennium, marked by its postmodern vanguardist style, but at the same time profoundly conservative, as Stephen Teo (2001) points out in relation to its traditional melodramatic romantic plot; a film in Cantonese and Shanghainese, with a soundtrack performed by an African American heartthrob well known for conquering many hearts, here and there.[1]

Wong's attraction to all things Latin American is well known. Earlier, in his deceivingly titled 1997 film *Happy Together*, the director had presented Leslie Cheung and Tony Leung as two melancholy gay male Hong Kong expatriates in Buenos Aires whose amorous travails anticipate those of *In the Mood for Love*. Among the first images in *Happy Together* is a stunning aerial shot of the imposing Iguazú waterfalls, accompanied by the music of the Brazilian Caetano Veloso, singing not in Portuguese, but in Spanish, as he does in his album *Fina estampa*. This linguistic gesture is reproduced by the Spanish film director Pedro Almodóvar—a faithful lover of the bolero and of Latin American songs—in *Talk to Her*, of 2002, where we see a Spanish lady bullfighter and her male Argentinean reporter friend listening to Caetano, who sings "Cucurrucucú Paloma" in Spanish before their eyes. It is noticeable that it is the same *huapango* in the Spanish film as that in Wong's movie—a song by the Zacatecan composer Tomás Méndez that was immortalized by the great Lola Beltrán. But here it is the androgynous Caetano, who years before had openly declared his attraction to a young, sun-drenched, male Bahian surfer in his song "O leãozinho" (The Little Lion), the same Brazilian singer whose large musical production is marked by ambiguity and sexu-

[WSQ: Women's Studies Quarterly 36: 3 & 4 (Fall/Winter 2008)]
© 2008 by Lawrence La Fountain-Stokes. All rights reserved.

al/gender games, as César Braga-Pinto (2002) has observed; the same Caetano who sang in English, with Lila Downs, in Julie Taymor's 2002 film *Frida*, in which the grande dame of female masculine androgyny Chavela Vargas also appeared.² In "Cucurrucucú," Caetano sings of a lover's lament for his absent love, crying, suffering, singing, moaning, passing through hunger, and finally dying of "mortal passion," after which his soul turns into a bird—love and death, tied together by the musical form.

Accompanied by Caetano and the tango, the homosexual lovers of *Happy Together* reconstruct their lives as fleeting immigrants in Argentina and become local in their passion for *fútbol* (soccer), *mate* (the herbal infusion), and beef, although, as Francine Masiello points out, the process is marked by the disjunctures experienced by Asian migrant workers, suffering from linguistic alienation and economic poverty, in the Southern Cone (2001, 141–43). The homoerotic passion itself is mediated by the dance in which the protagonists wordlessly engage in the privacy of their small rented room: a dance similar to that of Salma Hayek (in the character of Frida) and Ashley Judd (playing Tina Modotti) in a scene from *Frida* in which the two women dance while Lila Downs sings "Alcoba Azul," with the difference that in the latter, their public watches and desires them in silence.

This musical passion is no coincidence: the tango, in many erotic and sentimental ways, is the Buenos Airean equivalent of the Mexican-Caribbean bolero, of the Portuguese fado, of the Southern blues, and of many other genres producing explicit songs of passion, as Iris Zavala (2000) suggests in *El bolero: Historia de un amor*. All these twentieth-century musical forms, clear markers of modernity (and of its inherent contradictions), are intercrossed with a profound desire for the impossible, for the perfect love: the longing for the painful recognition of that which is beyond reach. The bolero is the music of the androgynous voice—deep, in the case of women; ethereal, almost falsetto, when performed by men (think of Bola de Nieve)—a music of indeterminate love objects, of ambiguity, of the you and the me, in spite of your sex, or precisely because of your unnamable sex. For José Quiroga, the bolero is a nostalgic diasporic recuperation of a Cuba that no longer exists, the musical equivalent of the homoerotic photo by Benno Thoma that graces the cover of Quiroga's *Tropics of Desire* (2000). For the Puerto Rican Luis Rafael Sánchez, in his novel (or *fabulation*, as he prefers to call it) *La importancia de llamarse Daniel*

Santos (1988), the bolero is transformed into the motivation for a homosexual pilgrimage through the Caribbean, which is to say, as my good friend Ben. Sifuentes-Jáuregui put it to me, the importance of being, or rather loving, not the Ernest of Oscar Wilde, but a tropical music singer.

Some time ago, an Italian American artist turned poet from New Jersey broke my heart; let's say he was something between an angel and a demon. I confess that in my state of profound depression, I couldn't find a greater relief than by listening to recordings by Paquita la del Barrio, that Mexican institution who sings about squashing men as if they were vile insects. Unlike Zavala, who views Paquita as a pseudo- or counter-bolero singer ("one who elaborates the transvestism of the bolero" [2000]), I see Paquita's art as pure emotion, by which I mean the distilled or condensed intensity of affect that breaks forth, free of social convention, and speaks its truth as cruel hyperbole and that sees the world as a stage for the taking and the subject as a star. Who knows: perhaps it is precisely Paquita's inversion or transvestism that attracts me so much. "Tres veces te engañé, tres veces te engañé, tres veces te engañé: la primera por coraje, la segunda por capricho, la tercera por placer."[3] But of course I didn't deceive him, at least not that I remember (and certainly not three times!), although it doesn't really matter. The only thing that does is that I felt that Paquita could say all those things that I couldn't, such as, "¿Me estás oyendo, inútil?" (Are you listening to me, you good-for-nothing?) And suddenly, I felt myself back in Monterrey, Nuevo León, attending the "Shakira" drag queen cabaret that Jorge Merced had mentioned to me, seated at a lonely table in the nearly empty Fréber Concert Theater, hypnotized by a drag queen identical to Paquita who impeccably lip-synced her songs to the great delight of the small audience. So much so that for me, Mexico became a world all about women: not only María Félix—may she rest in peace, she who died in her sleep on her eighty-eighth birthday; she who played Doña Bárbara and also became Agustín Lara's María Bonita and whom some believe is to blame for poor Jorge Negrete's burning in hell—but also Paquita la del Barrio and Paulina Rubio, La Pau, whom I saw much later, in 2001, interpreted by another, rather ugly drag queen, on a stage in El Zócalo, directly across from the cathedral and under the shade of an enormous tricolored flag, after Mexico City's twenty-third annual gay pride parade. The bolero is thus about memory: of body, place, space, and time. It marks our lives and organizes our experiences, creating a referential transcription of love. Transvestism itself (and especially the drag queen who sings or lip-syncs boleros) re-creates and reanimates these worlds using deceit as an accessory: it makes us live them again, with some distance, without a doubt, but with great emotion and intensity, with the enthusiasm that marks the affective ties of a good spectator.

In *El bolero fue mi ruina* (The Bolero Was My Downfall), Jorge Merced and the Pregones Theater of the Bronx present a play with musical accompaniment centering on the experiences of the unforgettable Loca la de la Locura (The Queen of Madness), a murderous transvestite bolero singer and teller of love stories. Jailed in Puerto Rico, Loca meditates in her cell in the Oso Blanco State Penitentiary about why she killed her lover Nene Lindo (Pretty Baby), a *bugarrón* (a masculine-acting man who has sex with men and identifies as heterosexual) whom she was afraid would abandon her.[4] The play is a faithful adaptation of the story "Loca la de la locura" by Manuel Ramos Otero (1948–90), the most important openly gay Puerto Rican author of the twentieth century, who lived in self-imposed exile in New York City for most of the last twenty-two years of his life. The story was published in the Puerto Rican magazine *Reintegro* in the early 1980s and reprinted posthumously in *Cuentos de buena tinta* (Ramos Otero 1992). Ramos Otero's story arrived at the Pregones Theater via José Olmo Olmo, who was a friend of the deceased author and gave the manuscript to Merced, the company's artistic director. The play, which premiered in 1997, was in repertory until 2002 and was later restaged (with new costumes and backdrops) in 2005.

An analysis of *El bolero fue mi ruina* allows me to further expand the discussion of music, transgenderedness, and translocality with which I opened this essay. It opens a discussion of migration, sexual and erotic games, auditory and stereophonic stimuli, and desire, in the context of theater, of the Puerto Rican diaspora, and of the redefinition of the sexual and affective (emotional) identities that have become characteristic of the past four decades, specifically since 1968, when Ramos Otero first arrived in New York. To speak of *El bolero* is to summarize personal stories of music, transvestism, and translocality, mine and others, and that's why I have begun this essay with so many digressions, with the maps of my own migratory musical, performative, and geographic emotiveness.

JORGE MERCED AS TRANSLOCA

I consider Jorge Merced to be part of a group of gay and trans Puerto

Fig. 1. Jorge Merced as Loca la de la Locura in Pregones Theater's *El bolero fue mi ruina*. Photo by Erika Rojas, courtesy of Pregones Theater.

Rican and Nuyorican contemporary performers whom I have affectionately nicknamed *translocas* because of their exploration of homosexuality, transvestism, and spatial displacement (La Fountain-Stokes 2005b; forthcoming). The word *transloca* itself consists of the polysemic prefix "trans-" (from the Latin for "across" or "over") and the Spanish word *loca*, meaning "madwoman" and widely used in slang as a synonym for "effeminate homosexual." With the neologism "*transloca*," I wish to offer an enabling vernacular critical term that accounts for the intersection of space (geography) and sexuality in the work and lived experience of queer diasporic artists who engage in male-to-female drag, including Merced, Freddie Mercado, Eduardo Alegría, Javier Cardona, and Arthur Avilés. It is a similar critical move to that of the queer anthropologist Martin Manalansan (2003), who analyzes the lived experience and performances of queer and trans Filipino men under the framework of "global divas," a term that plays with polyvalent linguistic associations (in Tagalog and English) and with the shifts and continuities brought about by migration.[5]

Translocas are many things, contradictory ones, to be sure: performers, queers, innovators, marginals, exiles, eccentrics, beauties, troublemakers, lovers, loners, and friends. To be a transloca is to disidentify with dominant social mores in the sense advanced by José Esteban Muñoz (1999): to tread dangerous ground, make and break allegiances, and redefine meanings and sensibilities. What does this neologism respond to, this interest in integrating the concepts of migration and transvestism, of creating a new form of identification? It is clear that translocas are an enormously diverse and heterogeneous group, one that might not self-identify with this neologism. Yet I find the term fascinating, as it serves to perform a type of Fernando Ortizean performative drag *sancocho* (stew)—*por no decir ajiaco*—bringing together individuals with rather divergent styles. As such, I propose that the concept of *transloca* (or the transloca state) is a (queer) extension of the historically important (and culturally and geographically specific) concept of *transculturación* (transculturation), developed by Cuban ethnographer Fernando Ortiz in his 1940s classic, *Cuban Counterpoint: Tobacco and Sugar*.

For Ortiz, cultures that come in contact do not erase or substitute each other, but rather find a dynamic balance, in which elements of each persist but more important, are transformed and coexist as a new formation. While Ortiz was most interested in the particular situation of Cuba, with its predominantly European, African, and Chinese elements, I will focus on a Puerto Rican context in which Anglo, Hispanic, and African elements predominate and where new notions of sexuality and space have radically transformed understandings of self.[6] And while Ortiz clearly felt that European (and, need we say, heterosexual) culture was superior and would dominate the mix, contemporary developments and social movements allow us to envision a radically different Puerto Rican case.

I suggest that the prefix "trans-" be understood as linked to these differences in the context of the translocal and the transgender. I see that which is "trans" not necessarily under the optic of the unstable, or in between, or in the middle of things, but rather as the core of transformation—change, the power or ability to mold, reorganize, reconstruct, construct—and of longitude: the transcontinental, transatlantic, but also transversal (oblique and not direct). I also see it as related to Juan Flores and George Yúdice's "trans-creation" (Flores 1993) and Guillermo Gómez-Peña's (1996) global transculture. This transgeneric transitoriness implies several challenges to dominant notions of Puerto Ricanness (and Latin Americanness) that do not incorporate or accept either migration (the migrant diasporic community, immigrants in Puerto Rico, or both) or homosexuality or other marginalized sexualities. It also has to do with the instability that Meg Wesling (2002) hints at when she asks, in reference to the Cuban drag queens portrayed in the documentary *Butterflies on the Scaffold*, if the "trans" in "transsexual" (and, we could add, "transvestite" and "transgender") is the same as the "trans" in "transnational" (or "translocal"). It also relates to Marcia Ochoa's (2004) playful ethnographic theorization of "*loca*-lization" as the confluence of queer sexuality, space, and place among Venezuelan drag queens in Caracas (see her essay in this issue).

Loca, in its own right, also suggests a form of hysterical identity (that of individuals lacking sanity, composure, or ascription to dominant norms) that is pathologized at the clinical level, seen as scandalous at the popular one, and celebrated as a site of knowledge and resistance in psychoanalytically inspired cultural critique. *Locas* include effeminate homosexuals, madwomen, rebels for any cause. These are marginalized categories that in an ironic and playful gesture I would like to resemanticize in the style of the Anglo-American term "queer": *loca* as *maricón* (faggot), a name that friends call one another as a sign of complicity and understanding; as a sign of being *entendidos* (those in the know, in the life); not necessarily as a joke or hostile insult, although perhaps that too, if one is to do justice to cruelty as an art or strategy for survival; or simply as an acknowledgment of self-hatred. *Loca* can also be seen as the felicitous coming together of Susan Sontag and Esther Newton's (m/other) camp, with the good grace of Judith Butler, Marjorie Garber, and Ben. Sifuentes-Jáuregui; as a high-camp extravaganza; or as a homage to the drag house system, the ladies of *Paris Is Burning* and the drag queens of Latin American literature. Or perhaps as a hallucination of the radical French philosophers Gilles Deleuze (bursting in nomadic rhizomes) and Guy Hocquenghem through the filter of the Argentinean anthropologist Néstor Perlongher, which is to say, as radical and profoundly Latin American term that engages with postmodernism and queer liberation. It can also be seen as reminiscent of Gilles Deleuze and Luce Irigaray, as read by Elizabeth Grosz, which is to say, as a radical term of destabilization and decentering; or as suggested by Erasmus's *In Praise of Folly* (a defense of madness or *locura*, precisely, as a state of knowledge), read as a foundational Latin American text (as European invention) in the spirit of Cervantes's *Don Quixote* (the brilliant mad Renaissance seer par excellence) as seen by the Mexican novelist Carlos Fuentes, who argues for the centrality of both thinkers (Erasmus and Cervantes) in our conceptualizations of the Americas. Finally, the *loca* as literary critics Susan Gilbert and Sandra Gubar's madwoman in the attic (madness as the symbol of the subjugation of women) or the character in novelist Jean Rhys's *Wide Sargasso Sea* (madness as feminist liberation and an anticolonial gesture) or as theoretical and political meld of lived experience and brains, like something imagined by transgender theorists Susan Stryker and Sandy Stone.

It is in this context that I discuss *El bolero fue mi ruina*. In what follows (reelaborations of La Fountain-Stokes 2005b, as are all that precedes), I elucidate the process by which Ramos Otero's "Loca de la locura" was transformed into a theatrical work. I examine the experience of Jorge Merced as an actor and dramatist (together with Rosalba Rolón) who transformed the story into a particular type of solo show, with live, interactive musical accompaniment, and the final result as a play that has generated multiple possible reactions and interpretations. Within this framework, certain points should be emphasized: first, the profoundly migratory character of Manuel Ramos Otero's writing; second, the story's drag or trans specificity, as a narrative experiment in the first person; and third, the process by which Ramos Otero's body (as that of writer/performer/icon) and his work (the story "Loca de la locura") become the body of the actor Jorge Merced (his embodiment, gestures, and physical presence) and also the articulation of his discourse (his voice, the text of *El bolero fue mi ruina*) as part of a collective theatrical piece. Merced's performance of the roles of Loca la de la Locura and Nene Lindo lead me to

Fig. 2. Jorge Merced as Nene Lindo in Pregones Theater's *El bolero fue mi ruina*. Photo by Erika Rojas, courtesy of Pregones Theater.

think of Merced as a *transloca* (in the case of the former) and as what we could refer to as a *transmacho* (in the case of the latter), in his hyperaestheticized representation of the performative quality of masculinity. Merced's embodiment as *transmacho* (privileging loud, expressive, yet also suave and seductive hypermasculinity as a function of machismo, sexuality, and vulnerability) sharpens the performative and signifying valence of his *transloca* (feminine) enactment.

The analysis that I propose is that of Merced as a performer and author/translator/interpreter/actor: of the spiritual transference of the written modality from the page to the space of the stage, where it is complemented by two musicians and the recordings of bolero as a manifestation of the space of cabaret and of musical theater. Merced bases his work as an actor on his personal experience, his contact with drag queens and transvestites, Puerto Rican homosexuality, bolero, melodrama, and migration, to achieve a process of *transubstantiation*, one that focuses on the reproduction of bolero, in the shared delight of the audience and the performers onstage. As several Puerto Rican spectators have pointed out to me, to see Merced perform this role is to relive memories of Ramos Otero in his bohemian nights or even in his drag escapades in the Condado (an area of San Juan), where he was nicknamed "Miss Condominio" because of his statuesque height in and out of heels. To see and hear Merced is to recall a series of boleros, and the role of the bolero, in the darkness of the theatrical night.

TRANS/FORMING THE DRAG QUEEN: A CONVERSATION WITH JORGE MERCED

In her extraordinary book *El Teatro Campesino*, the feminist Chicana scholar Yolanda Broyles-González (1994) presents a detailed history of the eponymous Chicana/o theater collective and the collaborative creative process that characterized its work in the 1960s and 1970s, before the supposed "professionalization" of the group radically altered its nature as a political theater of protest, founded on a commitment to and direct relationship with its community. I want to emulate Broyles-González in her feminist critical methodology, centered as it is on documenting the collective process of creation and highlighting the contributions of the actors as individuals, a different strategy from that of Jorge Huerta (1992), who favors the canonization of Luis Valdez's authorial figure as a singular "genius" and neglects the communal dimensions of El Teatro Campesino's work. It is for these reasons that I want to point out not only the importance of Manuel Ramos Otero as author of the text but also and especially that of Jorge Merced, together with Rosalba Rolón and the musicians and creative team members who participated in this piece.

As I mentioned, I propose that *El bolero* be understood as at least three things—the adaptation of a story by Ramos Otero, a work created and collectively produced by the Pregones Theater, and a performance by Jorge Merced. The New York–based Puerto Rican actor's role was key for several reasons: Merced brought the text to the theatrical collective (of which he is an integral member), his own personal background and experiential repertoire informed the entire process, and his concrete physical presence grounds and gives meaning to the play. To a large extent, my analysis concentrates on Merced's staging, which is to say, the specific weight and impact of his body, voice, and gestures. This doesn't deny the possibility that other actors will interpret the same role in the future, which would require a different analysis. As such, I propose that we read Merced's concrete presence and "choreography" and give weight to the specificity of his body and person, as a way of recognizing and documenting his work.

I understand that the dramatic force of *El bolero* depends on and is nourished by Merced's life experiences, very concretely in his personal approximation to Latino/a drag or transvestism in New York City, and his experience of being (just as Ramos Otero) a Puerto Rican first-generation gay migrant who left the island in 1982 in part because of his sexuality. For Merced, *El bolero* functions as a re-creation of the gay Latino world of the big city, even when the text centers on the island of Puerto Rico. As such, the text and musical play represent what Jossianna Arroyo (2001) has described as a "transit between Norzagaray and Christopher Street" in reference to Ramos Otero's work: a multiple referentiality toward two localities or central points, Norzagaray Street being an important thoroughfare or perimeter marker of the colonial city of Old San Juan, while New York's Christopher Street (the location of the Stonewall Bar) is a historic site of gay North American culture and resistance. In this sense, the parallel between Merced and Ramos Otero is crucial.

I propose that we understand the relationship between Merced and drag/transvestism as a double process of *approximation* and *incorporation*, which occurs simultaneously in the transit between Puerto Rico and New York and that culminates in *El bolero*. By "approximation" I mean to reference a concrete, visual, and emotional repertoire and archive of feelings, that is to say, the experience of seeing drag queens and trans women (either on television or in person) as much as to the personal contact that occurs through conversations and friendship. By "incorporation" I mean the bodily process of transvestism in the flesh, through one's own praxis: the corporealization or embodiment that occurs when one cross-dresses, as one partakes in a potentially transgressive action. A chronological retelling of Merced's experiences reveals that both phenomena occur simultaneously, with very particular meanings for the actor. We can divide this progression in two fundamental moments: before and after his migration to New York.

Merced's early life in Puerto Rico was marked by his childhood experimentation or play with his mother's clothes (a game he sees as typical of homosexual boys)—what we could refer to as an early stage of *incorporation*—as well as by a later experience of *approximation*, that of viewing a television show hosted by Antonio Pantojas, the island's best-known drag performer of the 1970s (Laureano 2007). Watching this show, in fact, became the catalyst for a major family confrontation, when Merced's father angrily turned off the TV and actually went on to slap his son, after Merced defended Pantojas's performance as a legitimate way to earn a living and compared Pantojas to his own father. As Merced has stated, "That was the only *galleta* [slap] that my father has ever given me in my life. And as soon as he did it, I looked at him and told him: 'I hope you remember this moment for the rest of your life and never forget!' and then I left" (Merced, interview by the author, Bronx, New York, March 15, 2002). This "I left," of course, becomes a direct precursor of Merced's migration or sexile to the United States and of the symbolic vengeance that he carries out against his father when he stages *El bolero*. The physical and psychic pain provoked by the father's aggression also serves to transform this episode from one of *approximation* (one that corresponds to the world of ideas) to one of *incorporation* (the corporeal pain produced by the defense of the right to watch and enjoy a performance of transvestism in one's own house). Merced's retelling of this story reenacts complex personal and family dynamics; his staging of *El bolero* can be seen (in part) as a psychic response to the violence his father exerted at that moment.[7]

Merced's experiences in New York offer us two different, though interrelated, approaches to transvestism. *Incorporation* occurs through three specific events: Merced's participation in the 1986 Greenwich Village

Halloween celebration, where he dressed up as Miss Piggy (his first act of public cross-dressing); his participation in Pregones Theater's play *Migrants*, where he portrayed a City Hall (as a speaking building) along with Alban Colón and José García; and finally, his role in *El bolero*. His process of *approximation*, however, is more complex and diverse, and has to do with Merced's frequenting La Escuelita, one of the most important Latino gay clubs in New York, and later GT's Bar in the Bronx, as well as with his participation in activist and social groups such as Boricua Gay and Lesbian Forum (BGLF), Latino Gay Men of New York (LGMNY), and Gay Men of the Bronx (GMOB), and with his extensive contact and friendship with Latina drag queens and trans women, especially with Barbara Kent.[8]

Merced feels that these shared experiences with drag queens and trans women are the sources of his character (Loca), and that what occurs in *El bolero* is the re-creation or reconstitution of a queer, gay/trans Puerto Rican space in New York, a type of space that the actor never experienced during his youth in Puerto Rico except through TV and childhood cross-dressing games. Thus, his referential frame is the queer, trans Puerto Rican world of Manhattan and Queens, and later of the Bronx, so much so that when he finally saw his first drag show in Puerto Rico in 1994, what he felt was nostalgia for New York. Merced arrives at Ramos Otero's short story as the direct result of his experiences "abroad": the "local" is "translocal" and queer in its conception and elaboration. This point bears repeating, as it is in no way self-evident: the construction of Puerto Rican "authenticity" in this play is a direct reflection of the existence of these "authentic" (vernacular, autochthonous) practices among New York Puerto Ricans and of the actor and theater company's ability to tap into this rich cultural and performative repertoire.

Finally, it is worthwhile highlighting Merced's perception that *El bolero* is a profoundly diasporic, New York–based work, because it is precisely the distance of exile, that space outside Puerto Rico, that allows for the telling of such tales. This is true as much for the conditions of production of Ramos Otero's story as for the professional and cultural formation of Merced in the gay Latino bars and nightclubs in New York (from where he obtains the gestures and the conceptual imaginary of the piece), his gay Latino activism, and his friendships with Puerto Rican and other Latina drag queens and trans women in that city. It is also particularly true when it is compared with the largely imitative, derivative works of gay theater produced in the 1990s in Puerto Rico, which were to a great extent translations and adaptations of white, mainstream American and European shows and not original works based on texts by Puerto Rican playwrights.

THE REPEATING ISLAND: PREGONERO TRANSVESTISM

As I have pointed out, *El bolero fue mi ruina* is a "solo" performance centered on Loca la de la Locura's divergent inner monologues and mental reenactments. Premiered in 1997 under the direction of Rosalba Rolón, the piece was adapted by Rolón and Merced and has a musical score by Ricardo Pons, arrangements and musical direction by Desmar Guevara, set design by Regina García (and more recently, by Yanko Bakulic, based on García's original design [2006]), costumes by Harry Nadal (2006), lighting by Alvan Colón Lespier and Esteban Lima, and two musicians who perform live (Ricardo Pons and Desmar Guevara in the initial performances) and interact with the actor on stage.[9] Why was this play made in the Bronx and not in Puerto Rico? What is diasporic about this play?

To fully understand *El bolero* it is important to keep in mind the specific context of the Pregones Theater, a celebrated company established in 1979 that has been a bastion of Puerto Rican artistic production in New York City, and particularly in the South Bronx.[10] It is also important to mention that Pregones has had and has other theatrical initiatives that deal directly with issues of queer (and other) sexualities, such as the theater-forum piece *El abrazo/The Embrace*, an AIDS community education project based on the theories of Augusto Boal that ran from 1987 to 1993 and was carefully examined by Eva C. Vásquez (2003, 86–93), as well as *Máscaras*, a piece for women audiences dealing with sexual violence and abuse.[11] The Asunción Playwrights Laboratory, which seeks to promote and develop Latino/a playwrights with innovative projects on gender and sexuality, has also been a major contribution by Pregones since 2003.[12] Pregones has consistently focused on issues of women's experience, as in *Máscaras*, mentioned above, and in the 1995 *Translated Woman*, based on Ruth Behar's eponymous experimental ethnography.

During its initial five-year run, *El bolero* traveled extensively throughout the United States, Europe, and Latin America. During this time, the large number of viewers who saw it had surprisingly divergent reactions. In Denver, Colorado, people tried to get onstage in the midst of the production to tip the actor (typical audience behavior at drag queen shows);

there was an extraordinary reception among Puerto Rican and Latina/o immigrants in the South Bronx and a warm response from Parisian audience members who did not even speak Spanish; there was devotion from some in Lima, Peru, and at the University of Puerto Rico, Río Piedras, while others criticized the play for being too "gay" and not queer and radical enough. Among the best-documented responses is that of the open hostility and indifference that the play received at an international festival and conference on performance in the Americas held in Monterrey, Mexico.[13] This performance caused a debate in the Mexican press, where a somewhat conservative Mexican critic, Fernando de Ita (2001), who was more accustomed to theater than to performance, accused *El bolero* of inferior quality, while Antonio Prieto Stambaugh insisted on the need to understand the context of the play's production and reception to be able to appreciate it and pointed out the ways in which the play's Puerto Rican linguistic and cultural particularities were not immediately translatable or apparent to the Mexican university audience.

In what ways is *El bolero* a diasporic work, besides being the product of a Bronx-based theater company and of the imagination and theatrical talent of two queer exiled men? The recuperation of the drag world we witness, that of transvestite cabaret chanteuses and *bugarrones*, forms a curious juxtaposition with the more common nostalgic memory of a tropical paradise marked by an exuberant nature. We can interpret this play as a simple incursion into Puerto Rican or Latin American themes; however, to see it as a diasporic production means to establish an alternate relation to the country of origin, one where notably different social phenomena and realities exist. The play attracts a varied, remarkably faithful audience, including those who identify with it because of the nostalgic music (the bolero) as much as those for whom the affective sexual system results are particularly well known, attractive, or intriguing. In fact, it is not rare to find people who have seen the play more than once during the many years it has been shown. (Here, it is worth pointing out the very low prices of admission that Pregones Theater charges, facilitating working- and middle-class attendance to their shows.)

It is evident that *El bolero* has more to do with what theorists such as Juan Flores (1993) have identified as early cultural stages of migration, which favor referencing the country of origin, than with second- and third-generation productions, in which there is a more marked use of English and a U.S. geographic specificity. What is interesting is that Pregones Theater has not only works such as *El bolero* in its repertoire, but also plays that are more clearly anchored in the new experience, located concretely in New York and in the Bronx. At the same time, if, like Ruth Glasser (1995), we privilege music as a space or medium for the construction or maintenance of diasporic Puerto Rican identities, as she suggests in her enormously valuable book *My Music Is My Flag*, then perhaps it is not so important to verify whether there is a specific, explicit mention of the migratory condition itself, an overdetermination, as the very enactment (or reenactment) of the music has its own social purpose and end. Here it is also useful to insist on the different ways in which music interpellates audience members according to their age, sex, gender, sexual orientation, and migration history.

In *El bolero*, Loca is in prison with her scarce possessions, which include a small makeup kit and a pink satin photo album embroidered with lace, where she keeps photos, press clippings about her case, and the braids of her mad (*loca*) deceased mother. The solitary bed and the empty cell—the narrative space—are framed by features of other environments: a stage with sparkling stars, a moon, and a golden palm tree between the two musicians who accompany Loca and Nene Lindo in their performative musical remembrances as well as a profusion of plastic flowers and small white crosses that delineate a cemetery, the space where the play begins and ends.

Jorge Merced's chameleon-like ability before the audience is truly remarkable; he transforms himself from an aging convict into a ladies' man and then into a glamorous transvestite cabaret performer. His mutations conclude with an androgynous figure clad in black that visits the cemetery. In *El bolero*, the hirsute body of the actor, and his bald head, while ultramasculine in certain respects, becomes that of a Puerto Rican drag queen, an icon of sexualized musicality, as well as a masculine, seductive lover. Thus, the actor cross-dresses into masculinity as much as into femininity, creating both gender presentations on the basis of a corporal performance that recalls Judith Butler's (1990) theorizations on the performativity of gender. This, perhaps, is one of the most valuable conceptual insights that the play offers through its staging, as we witness the literal act of one individual "becoming" male and female in Caribbean terms: two identities or poses that are presented as eminently performative, expressive, and loud, at least in these very specific, class-delimited locations of bolero diva (loca/chanteuse) and macho (*bugarrón*).

While in Ramos Otero's story we mainly hear the tale through the protagonist's voice and the citations that Loca offers of Nene Lindo, in the staged adaptation we see the myriad transformations of the convict who becomes a multiplicity of characters, bringing numerous memories to life. Frequently, it is the stereotypical figure of the sexist, "macho" *bugarrón* Nene Lindo that receives the loudest approval from the audience. However, the audience's clearly evident display of enthusiasm is not diminished when Loca performs boleros by Toña La Negra, Lucho Gatica, or Myrta Silva; particularly when Loca changes into a spectacular silver or gold outfit, crowned by a *rumbera*-style headwrap, carrying shiny, bejeweled maracas, and lures the audience into clapping and singing along the chorus: "La vida es un problema, yo sí lo sé" (Life is a problem, I really know it).

Ultimately, the protagonist's recovery of these memories is accompanied by revelations about the causes of the tragic ending of her love story: fear of aging and of being left alone, her having dreamed of eternal youth; envy of the male lover's appearance, and concern that he would leave her if she didn't look good; and the *bugarrón*'s resistance to being anally penetrated by the supposedly "passive" transvestite, a gesture that would seem to effect an inversion of dominant power and gender relations (Cruz Malavé 1993). At the play's climax, the protagonist savagely attacks the air with a knife, tracing the fury of her memories, cleansing her thoughts, revisiting her crime of passion.

This successful adaptation of one of Ramos Otero's most notable stories presents a no-holds-barred account of the complexities of same-sex love (specifically, between an effeminate trans subject and a masculine-acting man), particularly when it is circumscribed within rigid social norms that hinder the fluidity and evolution of a relationship; it also shows the survival and triumph of a "marginal" character. It is firmly placed within the world of the bolero, a space that offers possibilities for masculine sentimentality and hidden tears, as Luis Rafael Sánchez (1989) points out; it is a space that builds a dramatic stage for unbridled passion and frustrated love, similar to the world of Hollywood's classic movies or the great films of Mexico's golden era. Rosalba Rolón's direction underlines the connections between the collective imaginary and popular culture, between how we perceive love based on what we sing about and what we want to listen to, through idealized notions and different levels of affect. The play transits these spaces of desire, grounded in nostalgia, false illusions, and reality's terrible violence.

El bolero fue mi ruina is a play that has marked my life as well as that of many other Puerto Ricans and Latinas/os, particularly queer ones in New York. While Wong Kar-wai's cinematographic meditations and Caetano Veloso and Chabela Vargas's film performances have undoubtedly moved me, the experience of sitting in Pregones's Bronx performance space or at Hostos Community College watching this show with large numbers of diasporic Puerto Rican and Latino/a queer men and women has made me and others feel profoundly connected—in part precisely through abjection. Bolero is a musical form that confuses; it tugs at the soul and reformulates our emotive map. Jorge Merced, Manuel Ramos Otero, and the Pregones Theater reorient our queer diasporic Puerto Rican sensibilities and tune us into the transdiasporic body/mindspace of sound.

LAWRENCE LA FOUNTAIN-STOKES is an assistant professor of Latina/o studies, American culture, and Romance languages and literatures at the University of Michigan, Ann Arbor. His book *Queer Ricans: Cultures and Sexualities in the Diaspora* is forthcoming from the University of Minnesota Press in 2009. His volume of short stories, *Uñas pintadas de azul/Blue Fingernails*, is forthcoming from Bilingual Press, Arizona.

ACKNOWLEDGMENT

An earlier (and much longer) version of this essay was published in Spanish in 2005 in *Revista Iberoamericana*. The essay as it appears here is my translation.

NOTES

1. In fact, Teo identifies several elements of the film beyond the plot (including the musical score, costume, and mise-en-scène) as agents of "aesthetic abstraction" that acquire equal if not greater importance with regards to the development of a dreamlike, nostalgic atmosphere.

2. For Vargas, see Yarbro-Bejarano 1997.

3. "Three times I fooled you, three times I fooled you, three times I fooled you: the first, out of rage, the second, for whimsy, the third, for pleasure." The song is by R. Macedo.

4. On *bugarrones*, see Ramírez 1999.

5. Manalansan (2003) explores the differences between the vernacular Filipino term *bakla* and "gay/homosexual" in the way I explore the specificity of the Spanish-language word and cultural concept of *loca*.

6. The notable omission or minor role of indigenous heritage has to do with the genocide of Taíno populations in the Caribbean in the early sixteenth century. For a

discussion of contemporary reaffirmations of Taíno culture, see Haslip-Viera 2001. For discussions of contemporary developments in Puerto Rico and its diaspora regarding queer culture, see Aponte-Parés et al. 2007 and La Fountain-Stokes 2005a.

7. For a much lengthier analysis of this episode in the context of a Freudian primal scene, see La Fountain-Stokes 2005b.

8. For a detailed ethnographic account of La Escuelita, see Guzmán 1997. Aponte-Parés (2001) and Aponte-Parés and Merced (1998) offer a history and analysis of early Puerto Rican gay activism in New York and Boston.

9. Desmar Guevara was musical director from 2000 to 2002, and once again in 2006. Ricardo Pons served as musical director from 1997 to 1999. Roxanna Riera and Anaida Hernández collaborated with Regina García in the assembly and installation of dozens of small crosses and "capias" for the Campo Santo (holy ground or cemetery) platform. Costumes used from 1997 to 2002 were the collective creation of Pregones Theater. Alvan Colón Lespier initially designed the lighting (1997–99) and was later replaced by Esteban Lima (2000–2002, 2006). (Information provided by Arnaldo López Maldonado for Pregones Theater.)

10. For a history of Pregones Theater, see Vásquez 2003 and Pregones's Web site, www.pregones.org.

11. Merced discusses his participation in *El abrazo* and *Máscaras* in his interview with Vásquez (2003, 147–53).

12. See Pregones's website and La Fountain-Stokes (2004) for more information on the Asunción project.

13. The play was presented as part of the Second Encuentro of the Hemispheric Institute of Performance and Politics, which is based at the Department of Performance Studies at New York University's Tisch School of the Arts. The conference and festival were organized by New York University in collaboration with the Autonomous University of Nuevo León.

WORKS CITED

Aponte-Parés, Luis. 2001. "*Outside/In*: Crossing Queer and Latino Boundaries." In *Mambo Montage: The Latinization of New York*, ed. Agustín Laó-Montes and Arlene Dávila. New York: Columbia University Press.

Aponte-Parés, Luis, Jossianna Arroyo, Elizabeth Crespo-Kebler, Lawrence La Fountain-Stokes, and Frances Negrón-Muntaner. 2007. "Puerto Rican Queer Sexualities: Introduction." *CENTRO Journal* 19(1):4–24.

Aponte-Parés, Luis, and Jorge B. Merced. 1998. "*Páginas Omitidas*: The Gay and Lesbian Presence." In *The Puerto Rican Movement: Voices from the Diaspora*, ed. Andrés Torres and José E. Velázquez. Philadelphia: Temple University Press.

Arroyo, Jossianna. 2001. "Exilio y tránsitos entre la Norzagaray y Christopher Street: acercamientos a una poética del deseo homosexual en Manuel Ramos Otero." *Revista Iberoamericana* 67(194–95):31–54.

Braga-Pinto, César. 2002. "Supermen and Chiquita Bacana's Daughters: Transgendered Voices in Brazilian Popular Music." In *Lusosex: Gender and Sexuality in the Portuguese-Speaking Word*, ed. Susan Canty Quinlan and Fernando Arenas. Minneapolis: University of Minnesota Press.

Broyles-González, Yolanda. 1994. *El Teatro Campesino: Theater in the Chicano Movement*. Austin: University of Texas Press.

Butler, Judith. 1990. *Gender Trouble: Feminism and the Subversion of Identity*. New York: Routledge.

Cruz Malavé, Arnaldo. 1993. "Para virar al macho: La autobiografía como subversión en la cuentística de Manuel Ramos Otero." *Revista Iberoamericana* 59(162–63):239–63.

de Ita, Fernando. 2001. "Encuentro Monterrey 2001: Memoria, atrocidad y resistencia." *Revista Cultural El Angel, Periódico Reforma* (Mexico), June 24, n.p.

Flores, Juan. 1993. *Divided Borders: Essays on Puerto Rican Identity*. Houston: Arte Público Press.

Glasser, Ruth. 1995. *My Music Is My Flag: Puerto Rican Musicians and their New York Communities, 1917–1940*. Berkeley and Los Angeles: University of California Press.

Gómez-Peña, Guillermo. 1996. *The New World Border: Prophecies, Poems, and Loqueras for the End of the Century*. San Francisco: City Lights.

Guzmán, Manolo. 1997. "Pa' la Escuelita con mucho cuidao' y por la orillita: A Journey Throught the Contested Terrains of the Nation and Sexual Orientation." In *Puerto Rican Jam: Essays on Culture and Politics*, ed. Frances Negrón-Muntaner and Ramón Grosfoguel. Minneapolis: University of Minnesota Press.

Haslip-Viera, Gabriel, ed. 2001. *Taíno Revival: Critical Perspectives on Puerto Rican Identity and Cultural Politics*. Princeton, NJ: Markus Wiener.

Huerta, Jorge. 1992. Introduction. In *Zoot Suit and Other Plays* by Luis Valdez. Houston: Arte Público Press.

La Fountain-Stokes, Lawrence. 2004. "Pregones Theater's 2003 Asunción Playwrights Project." *Latin American Theatre Review* 37(2):141–46.

———. 2005a. "Cultures of the Puerto Rican Queer Diaspora." In *Passing Lines: Sexuality and Immigration*, ed. Brad Epps, Keja Valens, and Bill Johnson González. Cambridge, MA: David Rockefeller Center for Latin American Studies and Harvard University Press.

———. 2005b. "Entre boleros, travestismos y migraciones translocales: Manuel Ramos Otero, Jorge Merced y *El bolero fue mi ruina* del Teatro Pregones del Bronx." *Revista Iberoamericana* 71(212):887–907.

———. Forthcoming. "Translocas: Migration, Homosexuality, and Transvestism in Recent Puerto Rican Performance." In *Theatre and Performance in Latin America*, ed. Jill Lane. London: Routledge.

Laureano, Javier E. 2007. "Antonio Pantojas se abre el traje para que escuchemos el mar: una historia de vida trasformista." *CENTRO Journal* 19(1):330–49.

Manalansan IV, Martin F. 2003. *Global Divas: Filipino Gay Men in the Diaspora*. Durham: Duke University Press.

Masiello, Francine. 2001. *The Art of Transition: Latin American Culture and Neoliberal Crisis*. Durham: Duke University Press.

Muñoz, José Esteban. 1999. *Disidentifications: Queers of Color and the Performance of Politics*. Minneapolis: University of Minnesota Press.

Ochoa, Marcia. 2004. "Ciudadanía perversa: divas, marginación y participación en la 'loca-lización.'" In *Políticas de la ciudadanía y sociedad civil en tiempos de globalización*, ed. Daniel Mato. Caracas: FACES, Universidad Central de Venezuela.

Ortiz, Fernando. 1947. *Cuban Counterpoint: Tobacco and Sugar*. Trans. Harriet de Onis, introduction by Bronislaw Malinowski. New York: Knopf.

Paquita la del Barrio. 1993. *Tres veces te engañé*. Discos Musart, CDP-1052.

Prieto Stambaugh, Antonio. 2001. "Las ex-centricidades del performance: un encuentro en las fronteras del hemisferio." *Conjunto* 122:108–10.

Quiroga, José. 2000. *Tropics of Desire: Interventions from Queer Latin/o America*. New York: New York University Press.

Ramírez, Rafael L. 1999. *What It Means to Be a Man: Reflections on Puerto Rican Masculinity*, trans. Rosa E. Casper. New Brunswick, NJ: Rutgers University Press.

Ramos Otero, Manuel. 1992. "Loca la de la locura." In *Cuentos de buena tinta*. San Juan: Instituto de Cultura Puertorriqueña. Translated as "The Queen of Madness" by Amy Prince. 1990. *The Portable Lower East Side* 7(1):113–23.

Sánchez, Luis Rafael. 1988. *La importancia de llamarse Daniel Santos*. México: Editorial Diana.

Teo, Stephen. 2001. "Wong Kar-wai's *In the Mood for Love*: Like a Ritual in Transfigured Time." *Senses of Cinema*. http://www.sensesofcinema.com/contents/01/13/mood.html.

Vásquez, Eva C. 2003. *Pregones Theatre: A Theatre for Social Change in the South Bronx*. New York: Routledge.

Wesling, Meg. 2002. "Is the 'Trans' in Transsexual the 'Trans' in Transnational?" Paper presented at the American Comparative Literature Association Conference, San Juan, Puerto Rico, April 11–14.

Yarbro-Bejarano, Yvonne. 1997. "Crossing the Border with Chabela Vargas: A Chicana Femme's Tribute." In *Sex and Sexuality in Latin America*, eds. Daniel Balderston and Donna J. Guy. New York: New York University Press.

Zavala, Iris M. 2000. *El bolero: historia de un amor*. Madrid: Celeste.

RECONSTRUCTING THE TRANSGENDERED SELF AS A MUSLIM, NATIONALIST, UPPER-CLASS WOMAN: THE CASE OF BULENT ERSOY

RUSTEM ERTUG ALTINAY

Winter of 2007. Another Sunday night, a new episode of *Popstar Alaturka*, a Turkish version of *Pop Idol*. Minority and human rights activist Hrant Dink has recently been assassinated by an ultranationalist youth and Turkey is experiencing one of the few notable instances of spontaneous collective action in the past two decades.[1] It has been only days since tens of thousands of people marched in the streets, chanting, "We are all Armenians!" to express their sympathy for Dink and the Armenian community. Hence, the TV show opens with the popular Armenian folk song "Sari Gelin"—which, later in the evening, will lead to a rather long and interesting monologue by one of the jury members. This member is a glamorous lady in her fifties, wearing a haute couture dress revealing her long legs and shapely breasts. She expresses her discontent with the slogan "We are all Armenians!" Underlining the fact that she is "the Muslim daughter of Muslim parents," she emphasizes that no one can ever make her say she is Armenian or Christian. Claiming that it would be more acceptable if the slogan had been "We are all Hrant," she deems it intolerable for a Muslim person to say that s/he is Armenian—and therefore Christian.

But who is this glamorous woman who seems in desperate need to underline her Muslim, nationalist identity? For readers who take an even slight interest in Turkish popular culture, the answer would be quite obvious. The person is Bulent Ersoy: a self-proclaimed expert on classical Ottoman music—though a singer of the popular genre arabesk—one of the first Turkish men to undergo sex change and the very first one to ask for a female passport, and a hater of transgendered prostitutes. Ersoy has been an extremely popular public figure in Turkey since the early 1970s and is very likely to remain so.

Following Simone de Beauvoir's claim that "one is not born, but, rather, *becomes* a woman," in this essay I seek to trace how Bulent Ersoy

[WSQ: Women's Studies Quarterly 36: 3 & 4 (Fall/Winter 2008)]
© 2008 by Rustem Ertug Altinay. All rights reserved.

has "become" a Muslim, nationalist, upper-class woman. In doing so, I aim to understand the strategies that define spaces of abjection reserved for transgendered individuals in Turkey in the post-1980s and examine the tactics for survival that are available to them.[2] I will try to explore Ersoy's personal history in the context of events in Turkey since the 1970s and discuss the cultural atmosphere and dynamics of gender in the country in the light of Ersoy's narrative.

A YOUNG, FLAMBOYANT MALE SINGER

The renowned singer of classical Turkish music Bulent Ersoy was born as Bulent Erkoc in 1952 in Istanbul. Named after a soccer player, Bulent was the only son of an urban middle-class family. He was introduced to classical Turkish music by his grandfather, who played the zither, and his grandmother, who played the lute. Shown to have talent, he took private lessons with acclaimed musicians at an early age and later attended the conservatory. While he was still a student, he began singing professionally under the stage name Bulent Ersoy—the name Erkoc, meaning "brave ram," was probably too masculine for this rather androgynous young man, so it was replaced by Ersoy, "brave lineage." Ersoy is also easier on the tongue.

Ersoy's first record came out in 1971. At that time, nightlife in the big cities, especially Istanbul, mainly consisted of Greek tavernas and nightclubs called *gazinos*. Those nightclubs provided the middle- and upper-classes with hours-long programs bringing together several singers as well as comedians and belly dancers. There would often be one lead singer, called an *assolist*, who would take the stage last and sing classical Turkish music. The extremely competitive atmosphere made it difficult to become a lead singer. At the time, many established lead singers sang arabesk, a genre influenced by Turkish folk and Middle Eastern music, that had come out in Turkey in the 1950s and 1960s. Martin Stokes, one of the leading experts on arabesk, claims that it is "a music inextricably linked with the culture of the *gecekondu*, literally the "night settlements" which mushroomed around Turkey's large industrial cities after the Menderes government program of rural regeneration in the 1950s produced a large rural labor surplus" (1989, 27). To the urban elite, arabesk was a new and lower-quality musical form. In this context, Ersoy decided to use this dissatisfaction with arabesk and constructed his public image as a "classicist." In other words, he appropriated Turkish classical music and made it his trademark so as to win a place in a highly competitive market. He catered to an audience that wanted to consume "authentic" or "elite" classical Turkish music as opposed to the "popular," "commercial" variety. With a singing style extremely similar to that of Muzeyyen Senar—a popular singer of classical Turkish music who at the time was at the height of her career and, in some sense, Ersoy's patron—he became the lead singer at Maksim, the most prestigious nightclub in the country. He was the second lead male singer at that time, after Zeki Muren (1931–96)—a flamboyant queer male singer, as was Ersoy. In fact, one could argue that Ersoy had appropriated an image with which the audience was already familiar, through Zeki Muren, who maintained it until the late 1960s, when he adopted a style that was an interesting combination of Elvis and Liberace. In other words, while Muren was adopting a new image, Ersoy was taking on Muren's previous one. After Ersoy established his name in the Turkish music scene, he started singing arabesk, for financial reasons (Tulgar 2004). This increased his both popularity and income immensely.

As was customary for such singers, Ersoy, like Muren, also made a number of movies with popular female stars of the Turkish cinema. In these mainstream love stories, Ersoy would act the young, naive, maybe somewhat androgynous, yet heterosexual, man. This accorded with his public image. Even though, later, Ersoy would claim that her friends had always seen her as a woman, at the time Ersoy would be visible in the press with his fake fiancées, constructing his image as heterosexual and male. Yet, as Pinar Selek argues, Ersoy and Muren challenged the codes of masculinity in Turkey with their public personas (2007, 111). They did not have the masculinity of other male singers such as Munir Nureddin Selcuk, Orhan Gencebay, or later, Ibrahim Tatlises. Ersoy's most significant attributes were probably his rather naive politeness and somewhat androgynous style. Thus, through a bodily and linguistic performance as a man who was openly gay in his private life, yet with a heterosexual public image, Bulent Ersoy opened a liminal sphere that challenged the codes of masculinity. According to Selek, this was why he was loved by women. In the Turkish movie *Evlidir Ne Yapsa Yeridir*, from 1978, women embark on a kind of feminist revolution; among their demands are male domestic help, new clothes, and listening to Bulent Ersoy.

EARLY POST-OPERATION YEARS

When Ersoy was physiologically male, he would usually wear a white tuxedo or a dark suit and bow tie. Unlike Muren, at the time, he never appeared in garments or accessories that challenged established masculine dress codes, such as mini-shorts, ostrich feathers, or sequins or wore hairstyles or jewelery that were normally seen on women. It was only after his hormone treatment began that he started to appear on stage in female attire. Arguably because Ersoy wanted to claim the female body, his costumes were particularly revealing. In 1980, after the military coup, when she was singing in a nightclub at the Izmir International Fair, Ersoy did not deny the audience its desire to see her newly developing breasts. Proving her femininity in this way resulted in her arrest and she served forty-five days in prison. In 1981, she underwent a sex change operation in London. This would change her life in ways that she probably never expected. Being a transsexual was not easy during the notoriously oppressive military regime. She had to go through several physical examinations as well as an exhausting legal case to be recognized as a woman. Her court defense was very significant for the construction of her public image as a transgender individual. She underlined that she was not an anarchist, but a loyal citizen who did not aim to do anything against the social order. By emphasizing her patriotism, she intended to avoid the fate of other victims of the military regime, during which 650,000 people were taken into custody, 230,000 were tried, fifty were executed, and 229 "died of unnatural causes" while in custody (Gunersel 2007).

Ersoy was not the only transgendered person who was at risk following the coup; and in fact, the trans community had been suffering from state violence since the 1960s. Back then, the community was quite small and most of its members lived in Istanbul (Cingoz 2007). As their chances for employment were extremely limited, they tried to survive by either doing odd jobs or taking up prostitution. As prostitutes working in the streets, they were always easy targets for the police. In 1973, the first brothels for transgendered prostitutes was opened in Istanbul's Beyoglu district. There, transgender people enjoyed relative security and regular health checks. In the late 1970s, the "social democratic" CHP government started a war against these brothels. It provided no alternative employment opportunity or any other support for the trans community, it just tore down the brothels—only for them to be reconstructed by the brothel workers. Transphobic policies intensified with the military coup of 1980. For one thing, the brothels were closed down for good. It was extremely difficult for a member of the trans community to find an apartment; they therefore had to share hotel rooms. When the brothels were closed down, many of the workers were subjected to verbal and physical abuse. Some were held in custody for weeks, and some were reportedly killed by police and their bodies were thrown into a river (Gunersel 2007). The approach of the military regime toward transgendered prostitutes was similar to that of the social democrats, but harsher: not only were the brothels closed down, but the doors of the only other sector that employed transgendered people, entertainment, was now closed to them. Performances by all transgendered entertainers were banned, and many had to take up prostitution as well.

In this political atmosphere, Ersoy was the only person who had the power to have her voice heard. What was striking in her attitude was that she was not making a claim in the name of queer people or the trans community—she was only trying to save herself. For one thing, she had found an interesting way to explain her gender status as a woman: "My mother thought I was a girl when she was pregnant with me. Maybe that is the reason why my male hormones did not develop." With such comments, she was clearly rejecting transgenderism as an opportunity to deny established gender codes. She desired only to be accepted as a woman. She did not have any intention to fight against heterosexism either. In an interview with the newspaper Gunaydin April 1981, Ersoy said: "The people whom I find most disgusting are homosexuals. I am so glad that I am not one" (Ersoy qtd in Isiguzel 2000). With these statements and her own pseudoscientific theories, Ersoy claimed a female identity, and a strikingly homophobic one. But as far as the court was concerned, her efforts were in vain: her performances were banned, and she was unable to work in Turkey. Her right to work—a human right—had been violated. During this period, she had to work in Germany and France. She performed for Turkish migrant workers, singing what she now calls "market music," a position of lower status for a singer who had worked at the most exclusive nightclubs in Turkey. Among other things, she had to sell her jewelery, and at one point, she attempted suicide. While her public performances were banned, she still made albums and low-budget films for video. In Turkey, she would occasionally perform in nightclubs, where she would pretend to be part of the audience and sing from her table. She also worked as a model and continued giving interviews. Thus, she not only remained a popular public figure, keeping her fans remembering and missing her, but also persisted in affirming her female identity, in the clichéd heterosexual romances in which she acted, now taking the woman's part, and in the erotic photographs for which she posed.

In 1988, Ersoy was permitted by the neoliberal government of Turgut Özal to obtain a female ID and work in Turkey. It is worth noting that she had become a showpiece for the government. Before her sex change, he was a very popular singer and the public had been longing for her comeback. By giving her a female ID and allowing her to perform in Turkey, the government achieved two goals. First, to increase their own legitimacy, they presented the case of Ersoy as expressing the epitome of personal freedom.[3] Second, by granting Ersoy her work permit the Özal regime differentiated itself from the highly unpopular military regime that had preceded it. Thus, the neoliberal regime and its laissez-faire economic policies were legitimized in the eyes of Ersoy's fans, especially Turkey's new bourgeoisie, to whose tastes Ersoy catered, but also the general public. She had become the signifier of an era of freedom and tolerance.

The discourse of tolerance is crucial to understanding this process. Ersoy was given a female passport and the right to work not because this was her "right," but because she was "tolerated" by the regime. The discourse of tolerance is strongly related to the construction of spaces of abjection and their use for the definition and celebration of the "normal" or "legitimate" spheres as well as the nation or the state. Ersoy, as a transgendered individual, was the Other who was to remain in an abject space, yet enjoy the "tolerance" of the regime.[4]

Stokes notes that Ersoy made an album of classical Turkish music in 1987 "when the debate over the stage performance on [her] was at its height" and "this undoubtedly strengthened the case for the repeal of the ban" (1992, 227). After the ban was repealed, Ersoy again made a number of arabesk albums. It is feasible that Ersoy instrumentalized classical Turkish music to legitimize her singing in the eyes of people who did not enjoy arabesk.

When she managed to return to the stage, Ersoy climbed back to the top in no time. She resumed her work in prestigious nightclubs and gave concerts all over the country. Many of her songs became instant hits, and her films enjoyed success at the box office. The Turkish people had gladly accepted her back, and she enjoyed the support of the Özal family, particularly Semra Özal, the prime minister's wife, leading to Ersoy's appearing in a televised official celebration even though arabesk singers were rarely given the opportunity to appear on state-owned television at the time (Stokes 1989, 29). But this time, Bulent Ersoy was neither a young flamboyant boy nor the femme fatale of her early post-operation years. Although she was still loved dearly by her fans, her sex change operation was seen as a threat to the heterosexist patriarchal state hegemony during the military regime. She was cornered and had to face the tools of the homophobic and transphobic regime, from medicine to law. When she was back on the stage, she refused to use her transgendered status as a way to challenge gender codes, heterosexism, patriarchy, nationalism, capitalism, or conservatism. Rather, she refused to acknowledge her transgendered status and gradually started to advance an identity as a conservative, Muslim, nationalist, upper-class woman.

While she continued to sing at the most popular clubs and was dressed by some of the most prominent fashion designers, a significant change in her style became evident. Although glamorous, her costumes were not as revealing as they had been. She did not pose in lingerie or bathing suits anymore. She started to make films with important stars again.[5] But unlike her actions in the low-budget films in which she acted in her early post-operation years, when she would appear in lingerie, she did not even kiss the male lead. It would be plausible to say that she was following in the footsteps of Turkan Soray. Arguably the most popular actress in the history of Turkish cinema, Soray had adopted what came to be known as "Soray's rules": Don't undress, don't kiss, don't have sex in front of the camera (Buker 2002). Like Soray, Ersoy sought to present her sexuality as that of a woman, yet do it in a more discrete, almost "chaste" way to enjoy greater public acceptance in Turkey, where conservative Islam was on the rise, with the educational policies of the past three decades and the empowerment of the conservative Muslim small capital holders during the Özal regime. Her getting engaged with her boyfriend, Birol Gurkanli, in her early post-operation years also served to project the image that she adhered to the conservative heterosexual norms. Years later, in 1998, when she would marry the much younger Cem Adler, the public discussion would revolve around the age difference between the couple, rather than Ersoy's transsexualism.

In the late 1980s, Ersoy began to emphasize her Muslim identity, including references to Allah in her songs and during her performances, and she continues to wear a veil when she attends funerals. Her emphasis on this aspect of her identity peaked in 1995, when she recited the *adhan*, the Islamic call for prayer, in her album *Alaturka 95* and sparked a heated debate.

Normally, the *adhan* is called out by a muezzin from a minaret of a mosque five times a day to summon Muslims for prayers. In 1932, the Atatürk government imposed a Turkish-language *adhan* to replace the traditional Arabic, to promote Turkish as a liturgical language. This highly unpopular policy, implemented as part of the Kemalist project of modernization, was repealed in 1950. Today, although there are defenders of the policy among the Kemalist modernists, it is virtually impossible to hear the Turkish adhan.

By reciting the *adhan* in Arabic, Ersoy asserted her identity as a conservative Muslim. If she had recited the call to prayer in Turkish, she would have not only expressed her identity as a Kemalist/modernist but also led the media to focus on the language of the adhan. Instead, the media's focus was Ersoy's gender, and a huge debate started on whether a woman can recite the adhan or not. This gave Ersoy the opportunity to reaffirm her faith in Islam and also have others reaffirm her gender identity as a woman.

Ersoy's use of language, especially her choice of vocabulary, was also significant for the performance of her identity. What makes her vocabulary choices significant is her extensive use of Ottoman words. Having been virtually eliminated from the Turkish language with the modernizing Kemalist language reforms, this vocabulary is normally available to only a few elderly people who come from families that have social, cultural, and economic capital, or to people who learned it in university Turkish or history departments or in one of the few private language courses. In any case, it is an indicator of status and, to some extent, class. However, as this vocabulary was eliminated by the modernization project, its use has conservative connotations as well. As these words are borrowed from Arabic or Persian, they may also have a religious connotation. It is also possible to interpret this vocabulary choice as playing with the past. Ersoy aims to use a language that has been forgotten. When she uses this particular vocabulary, she seeks to perform her identity in a particular way. She reconstructs the time, and performs her identity not only as a person who brings a long forgotten knowledge from the past but also as someone who belongs to that past.[6] By constructing herself as an element of the past, she probably contests the social rejection that she faced because of her new status as a transsexual woman. This rejection of modernity is ironic because her sex change was made possible by modern medical technologies. By performing her identity as a conservative Muslim woman, Ersoy contests social rejection not only by rejecting a queer or transgender identity, but also by rejecting "modernity."

The developments in Turkish media were particularly instrumental in Ersoy's promoting her new public image. Previously, there was only state television; because her public performances were banned, Ersoy could not appear on television. Nor were there any private radio stations. Later, with the establishment of private stations for both television and radio, Ersoy started to appear frequently on television and radio. In fact, she even had her own talk show in one of the earliest private television channels, Kanal 6, owned by the Özal family. With the aid of these developments, Ersoy's new public image was established quite firmly by the mid-1990s.

THE OLDER SISTER

In 1992, Ersoy made one of her most successful albums. There was a song in the album that would turn out to be very important for Ersoy's personal history: "Ablan Kurban Olsun Sana" (Your Older Sister Would Sacrifice Herself for You). The song was about the sexual interest of an older woman in a younger person, but the most significant words it contained were those that formed the title. Using these lyrics as a term of affection in addressing her public, Ersoy was soon awarded the nickname *abla* (older sister). As noted by Sirman, while persons of the same generation and the same parents who are older than one are referred to as *agabey* (older brother) or *abla* (older sister) in Turkish, these words also serve as terms of address "not only with regard to persons one has filial and affinial ties to, but also with complete strangers. These terms provide a means of regulating relations between non-kin, thus extending the language of hierarchy and respect, age, and gender to cover a whole range of relationships within the society in general" (2004, 44). Ersoy's being given the nickname *abla* meant two things. First, her gender status as a woman had been strongly affirmed by her public. Second, she had managed to gain respect. Even though Ersoy did manage to gain the respect and love of her public as a popular singer, this would not be the ultimate status she would aim at.

THE DIVA

In the summer of 2004, Ersoy gave a concert in the Cemil Topuzlu open air theater in Istanbul. In this concert, she sang only classical Ottoman songs that were familiar to few people. In fact, she claimed that the scores for some of the songs could not be found in archives and she had had to make transcriptions from memory. She wore a dress inspired by the caftans of the Ottoman sultans and a headpiece that resembled an Ottoman turban. Ersoy did not earn any money from this concert. What she gained was social status.

Before the concert, she accepted an interview with the well-known journalist Ahmet Tulgar from the daily newspaper Milliyet. Ersoy was rarely giving interviews at the time, so even the existence of the interview was a sign of something important. In this interview, Ersoy claimed that she had caused a revolution in the 1970s by singing classical Ottoman music in nightclubs, yet betrayed her revolution as well as classical music by singing arabesk to be more popular and earn more money. Her desire was to "apologize to music." In other words, she was no longer satisfied with her status as an arabesk singer. She had earned enough money and could afford her albums to be less popular—which did not really matter at a time when most people could download music from the Internet anyway—but she wanted to regain her status as a classicist. This concert project was a result of this concern. With the costume as well as the songs she chose to sing in one of the most prestigious concert halls in Istanbul, underlining her status as a singer who could sing songs from the thirteenth-century that were known and understood by few, yet could fill that concert hall. With this performance, she claimed the past; just as she was legitimizing her identity with reference to the past in her use of Ottoman vocabulary while trying to avoid the rejection she might experience because of her transsexual identity, which is a modern, present-day possibility.

This was the beginning of a new era for Ersoy's public image. To the amusement of some, a term from classical music of the West was appropriated, and Ersoy became "the Diva" of Turkey. In many respects, not much had changed in the way she performed her identity. Yet things had intensified and her new title and her role as a member of the jury in *Popstar Alaturka* had provided her with a new forum to perform her identity.

Probably, the biggest change in Ersoy's public image was her approachability. She had already gained respect as the Older Sister, but being the Diva was something else. There was no real change in her music after the concert in which she sang classical Ottoman songs. In her television show as well as her concerts, Ersoy kept singing arabesk and pop music. But her expertise in a musical form that her public neither really knew nor could really stand, yet recognized as an indicator of status, as it was appreciated by a small elite group, did improve Ersoy's status.

In the construction of the Diva, class was also a key issue. Among signifiers of class were gift giving, conspicuous consumption, and discourses concerning consumption. Beginning with her relationship with Gurkanli, Ersoy had been famous for her lavish gifts. These became more and more visible after she became the Diva. Although expensive, some, such as the ring she gave her close friend Oya Aydogan on her birthday, fit within the established norms of gift giving in contemporary Turkish society; others, such as the bracelet she gave her patron Muzeyyen Senar when she was hospitalized, did not. All these sumptuous gifts helped to construct Ersoy's identity as an upper-class person. Her own expensive jewelry and clothing as well as shopping trips to Europe added to the indicators of class, yet the discourses concerning her consumption practices were even more influential. It was especially so in the case of jewelery. Even though jewelery has traditionally been a signifier of class, it is not always possible to tell whether it is real or fake. Ersoy started to insist that she never wears fake jewelery and to reveal the price of each and every piece she has.

As the importance of nationalism and Islam in Turkish public discourse has increased since the 1980s, the significance of these elements in Ersoy's construction of her identity has increased as well. Since the 1980s, Ersoy has been telling stories of rejecting European offers of citizenship. In 1997, she scolded a French interviewer who asked her about the ban on her public performances, saying that "it is a matter of domestic policy." But her aggressive response to the Dink incident, described at the beginning of this essay, was unprecedented. With it, she allied herself with the ultranationalists at a critical time in Turkish history as well as expressed her identity as a nationalist Muslim. With practices such as breaking her Ramadan fast on a live broadcast, she persisted in constructing a Muslim identity.

The last key aspect of the identity of the Diva was her womanhood.

Even though her gender identity as a woman had largely been accepted, she still had a past to deal with. When her old friend, and new enemy, Sacit Aslan said that Ersoy had done her military service—which is compulsory for all men and only men—she furiously rejected the claim. She asserted that "her status" did not allow her to do military service, and waving her pink identity card, she said that she was "as female as Semra Özal." Here, she was using the female identity card (that was begrudged to her for so long) as a weapon with which to claim her womanhood. The reference to Semra Özal is also striking. By saying that she was "as female as Semra Özal," Ersoy not only claimed womanhood but also made a claim for power by equating herself with the former first lady, with whose help she had managed to get her pink identity card and work in Turkey.

The media helped Ersoy in the reconstruction of her past. In *Canli Hayat*, a television show presenting interviews with famous people and reenactments of important moments in their lives, Ersoy's pre-operation years were played by a young girl. Since her early post-operation years, Ersoy had been telling stories of how she would perform a female identity as a child. When he was alone at home, he would put on makeup, wear his mother's clothes, and take her cigarettes and cigarette holder and "pose like a woman" in front of the mirror (Tanis 2005). She would also claim that her friends had always seen her as a woman. In this show, the past had been reconstructed and the biggest "mistake" in Ersoy's life had been corrected: she had never been a man.

In an episode of *Popstar Alaturka*, Ersoy proved that she could not only claim a female identity but also claim the body of a particular woman. Like most stars, Ersoy occasionally undergoes plastic surgery, such as liposuction and face-lifting. In one episode of the show, she had recently undergone a series of plastic surgery. Having also borrowed the makeup artist of fellow singer Ebru Gundes, Bulent Ersoy had a striking resemblance to Gundes, a member of the jury on the show. Her class and status had enabled Ersoy to undergo plastic surgery in Germany, and also to borrow this makeup artist, which made it possible for her to claim not only womanhood but also the body of a much younger woman.

Popstar Alaturka also provided Ersoy with a new tactic to construct her identity. As a member of the jury, Ersoy was given the opportunity to criticize the contestants. Her comments were not limited to their singing. She would make sometimes friendly, sometimes harsh comments about their bodies and physical practices. She would often give examples from her own body. When the jury was discussing why one of the contestants preferred costumes that they found too conservative, Ersoy said that some women cannot wear dresses with a deep cleavage, as their bodies were not as fit for it as was hers. Later, she called a girl over and made her bend over, examining her body. Through these practices of criticism and evaluation, Ersoy constructed herself as an expert on the "ideal" female body and bodily practices and deemed her own body, at least in some respects, as the ideal body for a woman. It seems clear that Ersoy has internalized the restrictive discourses on gender and the body rather than resisting them. She constantly reproduces them while she constructs her body as desirable if not perfect and criticizes the bodies of the contestants of *Popstar Alaturka* as well as of other women, including the guests on her talk show, within the framework of stereotypes about gender and the body.

THE ANTI-MILITARIST MOTHER WITH NO CHILDREN

Although the preceding section was intended to be followed by the conclusion, a very significant incident in Ersoy's life occurred while this essay was in review and has led me to add one more section on Ersoy, as the anti-militarist mother with no children—an identity she briefly seemed to claim, then abandoned in haste.

An episode of *Popstar Alaturka* in February 2008 was devoted to soldiers who died in an operation to northern Iraq. While the host of the show and Ersoy's fellow singers sent their condolences to the soldiers' families, along with nationalistic and militaristic messages, Ersoy took an unexpected stance. Acknowledging that she could never be a mother, she stated that if she had a son, she would never send him to the army. This is a fairly popular discourse among Turkish mothers. Although they can't say it in public, as it is a crime punishable not only by the law but also by nationalists, many Turkish mothers tell their friends, relatives, or sons that they would never let them perform compulsory military service. In other words, while expressing her feelings about a war in which "Turkey has been instrumentalized by big powers," Ersoy sought to perform her identity as a mother by shifting the focus from reproductivity to feelings. This was a quite dangerous move, especially when combined with an anti-militarist comment. Fellow singer Ebru Gundes took the microphone to say that she could be a mother and she would only be happy to be the mother of a martyr if it was her destiny. Ersoy had opened a position that she could not fulfill and Gundes had used the opportunity to perform her identity as a nationalist mother, although she had no children either. But this would not be all. A public prosecutor filed charges against Ersoy for disparaging the military (Bax 2008). Interestingly, Ersoy enjoyed the support of many Turkish intellectuals, as well as—to her distress—the Democratic Society Party (DTP). As an antinationalist party that represents Kurdish people in the parliament, DTP was probably the last party whose support Ersoy would appreciate and enjoy. Still, the party's parliamentary group's deputy chairman, Ahmet Turk, praised her courage, the mayor of Batman offered to name a street after Ersoy, and her albums started to fly off the shelves in the southeast, where the majority of the population is Kurdish (DHA 2008). By contrast, a member of parliament from the ruling Justice and Welfare Party made fun of Turk and Ersoy, remarking that had Turk been as brave as Ersoy, he would "have his thing cut off" as well. This attitude was not unique to him. Thousands of people were making fun of Ersoy's transgenderism on the Internet. The one time she tried to perform her identity in a slightly different way, she was insulted by a member of parliament and thousands of people, and faced time in prison.

Ersoy was cornered once more, this time by the wrath of the government and nationalists, and the love of the Kurds. Therefore, she held a press conference. Stating that all she wanted was a "solution, instead of death" Ersoy reaffirmed her loyalty to the republic of Turkey. Arguing that "Turks are a soldier nation" and "one may give the God-given life for the motherland, for the nation" she stressed that she was not the public face or supporter of any group. Thus, she reembraced nationalism and militarism while rejecting any affiliation with or sympathy for the Kurdish community. Later, she stated once more that she was going to leave her wealth to the Turkish Educational Foundation (a secularist, nationalist foundation for education) and the Mehmetcik Foundation (a militarist, nationalist foundation that caters to the needs of disabled war veterans and the families of soldiers who lost their lives). Ersoy's choice of institutions was of particular significance, as the other queer star of Turkish music, Zeki Muren, had also left his considerable wealth to the same institutions. It appears that Ersoy was aiming at the acceptance that Muren always enjoyed in regard to the state and the military.

This example shows that while identity may not be a mere survival tactic, Ersoy's public performance of her identity is strongly related to survival in an hostile environment. Her transgenderism was such a sensitive issue that whenever she would do something that might challenge her established public image, she would be dispossessed of her womanhood and relive past stigmatization and humiliation.

CONCLUSION

This essay is being written in late 2007, twenty-six years after Ersoy's sex change operation. According to a recent study, 23 percent of urban gay/lesbian/bisexual identified people confirmed having been subjected to physical harassment and a distressing 87 percent confirmed having been subjected to verbal harassment (Ercivan et al. 2006, 112). On the cultural level, the popular drag performances of Seyfi Dursunoglu, which he has been presenting for more than forty years in nightclubs and more than thirty years on television, have been banned from television by the Radio and Television Supreme Council (Dundar 2007). The charge was that he promoted homosexuality to youth. This was not the only homophobic act by the council. Gay fashion designer Barbaros Sansal's talk show *Toplu Igne* was banned for the same reason. Virtually all depictions of homosexual physical intimacy on television, including kissing, are penal offenses. As a result, foreign shows such as *Dawson's Creek* or *Six Degrees* are often censored and Turkish productions have very few queer characters. As far as politics are concerned, there have been no openly gay politicians who have entered parliament in the history of the country. Even though the population is quite high in the big cities, only a handful of transgendered individuals work in the professions and, to my knowledge, none work in the public sector. All others work as indirectly forced sex workers.[7] And, leaving any affirmative action aside, the government even refused to ban "discrimination based on sexual orientation" in the new draft constitution.

In this sociopolitical and cultural context, there is only one transgendered person who enjoys success and popularity. Bulent Ersoy has two shows on prime-time television and earns millions of dollars every year, adding to her significant wealth. While she is indeed a talented singer and is highly knowledgeable about classical Turkish music, I contend that she owes her popularity, at least to some extent, to her earlier image as a heterosexual man and the tactics she employs against the strategies of the hegemony in contemporary Turkish society.

Like the first queer star of Turkey, Zeki Muren, Ersoy started her career with a heterosexual male image. Yes, he did not have the masculinity of other male singers, but he was in the press with his fake fiancées, and he acted as heterosexual men in movies. He attained fame as a heterosexual man. Muren had never dared to deny heterosexuality in public, although he was openly gay in his private life. His first stage performance was 1950, wearing a tuxedo. He had to wait for twenty years to become arguably the most popular and respected singer in the country to challenge the established dress codes for men with a costume he named "The Prince from Outer Space": platform heels, a miniskirt, and a sheer cape, with earrings and a kind of tiara. Muren had probably expected to use science fiction as an excuse for drag. If the prince was from outer space, it wasn't plausible to expect him to share the same codes of masculinity with earthlings. But things did not exactly work out that way. Muren had created a huge scandal and journalists were saying that he was "wearing women's clothes" (Alpman 2006). People had started to question his masculinity. At that time, Muren took an interesting turn and, leaving science fiction aside, chose to legitimize drag with the aid of history and nationalism. He said that his costume was inspired by Turkish heroes such as Baytekin and referred to Sultan Selim 1, who allegedly wore earrings. After that incident, Muren never performed in drag again, and even in his fifties he was holding meetings with the press at which he declared that he had "had affairs with 104 women" and that the allegations of homosexuality were nothing but ugly lies.

The sex change operation did not allow Ersoy to stick to a heterosexual male identity. Interestingly, when her hormone treatment began, Muren insulted her by asking, "I can walk with my head up, can Ersoy?" Being more successful in his bargain with the heterosexist hegemony, Muren did not refrain from allying with it to mock his rival. Soon, Ersoy was also going to adopt the language of the heterosexist hegemony, develop survival tactics that actually reproduce this hegemony and its strategies rather than resisting them. This can be interpreted as a bargain with the hegemony. I believe that this bargain is what gives Ersoy's story its particular significance. With the aid of the power she gained as a "heterosexual" man, Ersoy had the privilege to bargain with the heterosexual hegemony. This seems rather different from what Duggan calls "homonormativity" or Puar's concept of "homonationalism," as the privileges Ersoy enjoys as well as the political views she defends are far from reflecting anything about the trans community in Turkey. While Ersoy enjoyed the support of the first lady, transgendered prostitutes were being tortured by the police, and they were being killed in the streets of Istanbul, Ankara, and Izmir. While Ersoy had two shows in prime time, LGBT organizations were being closed down by the state. Other than recognizing their new gender identity, the state has done nothing for members of the trans community. As noted earlier, there are only a handful of transgendered individuals in Turkey who are employed in any sector other than prostitution (Ogunc 2007).

Because of limited prior research, it is difficult to make any general statement about the political affiliations of the trans community. Berghan (2007) shows that they either tend to be apolitical or affiliate themselves with the Left. In fact, there are a couple of well-known leftist transgendered activists, among them Demet Demir, who was a candidate for parliament from a small leftist party, and Esmeray, who defines herself as a Kurdish feminist. LGBT organizations in Turkey, such as KAOS-GL and Lambdaistanbul, also tend to affiliate themselves with the Left. By performing her identity in the way that she does, Ersoy differentiates herself from contemporary leftist Turkish transgendered activists, as well as from transgendered performers such as Dana International, who embraces her transgender identity and openly supports the community, and performance artists, such as Kate Bornstein, who use their status to criticize heteronormative society and its tools, particularly medicine and law. Here, it is worth noting that while Ersoy has been embraced by the state and her public, she is openly rejected by one particular group: the trans community. These people, many of whom did identify themselves with Bulent Ersoy in their childhood and adolescence—particularly because she was the only transgendered person in the media—now feel cold toward her not only because of her homophobic and heterosexist comments and her apathy towards the problems of transgendered people but also because of her ultranationalism. In fact, Esmeray has said, "Bulent Ersoy is as transsexual as Michael Jackson is black" (Ogunc 2008). Thus, while Ersoy has rejected transgenderism and her transgender identity, she has in turn been rejected by the transgender community. While one may argue that this rejection was caused by the identity Ersoy chose to perform, it also serves the construction of this identity.

Bulent Ersoy, as a transgendered individual, has managed to survive and thrive in contemporary Turkish society thanks to the power she obtained as a "heterosexual" man, and only to the extent that she rejected her transgendered identity and opportunity to resist the dominant hegemony. The more she reproduced the dominant discourses, including the homophobic and transphobic ones, the more social acceptance she enjoyed. When she dared to deviate from the norm, she would be reminded of the bargain not only by the state but also by the people. This is how Ersoy's personal history has become the story of a Muslim, nationalist, upper-class woman and seems bound to remain so.

RUSTEM ERTUG ALTINAY is a graduate student in the philosophy department of Bogazici University.

NOTES

1. Dink was a Turkish Armenian journalist and columnist who worked for Turkish-Armenian reconciliation and human and minority rights in Turkey. Being critical of both Turkey's denial of the Armenian genocide, and of the Armenian diaspora's campaign for its international recognition, Dink was prosecuted three times for "denigrating Turkishness" and received numerous death threats before his assassination by an ultranationalist.

2. Here, I borrow the terms "tactic" and "strategy" from Michel de Certeau (1984).

3. Previous political regimes had equally made use of popular singers as showpieces. At the time of Ataturk, it was Safiye Ayla, a young girl who grew up in a state orphanage. In the newly established republic of Turkey, Ayla was not only a beautiful voice but also a showpiece of the Kemalist revolution. Having grown up in a state orphanage, she was considered a daughter of the republic, someone who could represent the new woman with her education and professional success and also with her secular body. For Ayla as a leading female figure in the "Turkish Republican Enlightenment," see Ergun 1997. For other biographies of Ayla, see Seckin 1998 and Gungor 2006.

4. This is especially important in comparison with an incident that took place under the regime of Kenan Evren. In *Girgiriye*, a well-known Turkish comedy about the Roma community in Turkey made in the year in which Ersoy's public performances were banned, one of the characters appears on the stage of a nightclub in drag and is immediately taken to police headquarters. As a member of the Roma community, he exists in a space of abjection and enjoys the "tolerance" of the state, personified in the police chief. But this tolerance is not absolute; it is negotiated. Petty crimes can be forgiven as mischief perpetrated by these childish adults, especially because the crimes are of an apolitical nature. But when a male member of the Roma community appears on stage in drag, the situation is more serious, as transgendered people are less tolerable than the Roma. Therefore, the character has to promise the police chief that he would not do anything else that would be against "the moral order of the society," in order not to lose the tolerance he enjoys and be punished as Ersoy was.

5. *Biz Ayrilamayiz*, in 1988, and *Istiyorum*, in 1999, with their star-studded casts, helped Ersoy in her comeback; the former also launched the career of Gulben Ergen, who became one of Turkey's most popular stars.

6. A similar example of transgendered women legitimizing their existence with reference to the past—and using the examples of gay and bisexual men as well as transgendered individuals—can be found in the narratives of the transgendered people interviewed by Berghan (2007) and Kandiyoti (2002).

7. In Berghan 2007; Ogunc 2007; and Selek 2007, as well as numerous press releases by queer activists, transgendered individuals, virtually all of whom are sex workers, tell how it is not possible for them to find employment in any other sector, especially the public sector.

WORKS CITED

Alpman, Zazim. 2006.

Bax, Daniel. 2008 "Pop Diva Speaks Out Against Turkish Militarism: War Criticism in TV Casting Show." In *quantara.de*. Trans. Aingeal Flanagan. http://www.qantara.de/webcom/show_article.php/_c-478/_nr-738/i.html

Beauvoir, Simone de. 1974. *The Second Sex*. Trans. H. M. Parshley. New York: Vintage.

Berghan, Selin. 2007. *Lubunya: Transseksuel kimlik ve beden*. Istanbul: Metis.

Bornstein, Kate. 1994. "Gender Outlaw: On Men, Women, and the Rest of Us." New York: Routledge.

Buker, Secil. 2002. "The Film Does Not End with an Ecstatic Kiss." In *Fragments of Culture: The Everyday of Modern Turkey*, ed. Deniz Kandiyoti and Ayse Saktanber. New Brunswick: Rutgers University Press.

Cingoz, Yonca. 2007. "Bu isi yapmak ruhumda var." *Radikal*, 16 June.

de Certeau, Michel. 1984. *The Practice of Everyday Life*. Trans. Steven Rendall. Berkeley and Los Angeles: University of California Press.

DHA. 2008. "Batman Bulent Ersoy Caddesi." *Radikal*, March 3, http://www.radikal.com.tr/haber.php?haberno=249079

Dundar, Can. 2007. "Huysuz Virjin varolus mucadelesi veriyor." *Milliyet*, December 21, http://www.milliyet.com.tr/2007/12/21/pazar/yazdundar.html

Ercivan, Ali, et al. 2006. *Ne yanlis ne de yalniziz; Bir alan arastirmasi: Escinsel ve biseksuellerin sorunlari*. Istanbul: Lambdaistanbul.

Ergun, Perihan. 1997. *Cumhuriyet aydinlanmasinda oncu kadinlarimiz*. Istanbul: Tekin Yayinevi.

Gunersel, Tarik. 2007. "12 Eylul teroru hakkinda kamuoyuna duyuru," http://www.pen.org.tr/tr/node/595.

Gungor, Necati. 2006. *Safiye Ayla'nin Anilari*. Istanbul: Heyamola Yayinlari.

Isiguzel, Sebnem. 2000. "Hanfendiler ve travestiler." *Radikal*, http://www.geocities.com/gayankara/hanfendiler.htm.

Kandiyoti, Deniz. 2002. "Pink Card Blues: Trouble and Strife at the Crossroads of Gender." In *Fragments of Culture: The Everyday of Modern Turkey*, ed. Deniz Kandiyoti and Ayse Saktanber. New Brunswick: Rutgers University Press.

Ogunc, Pinar. August 04, 2007. "Michael Jackson ne kadar siyahsa Bulent Ersoy O kadar transseksuel." Radikal, http://www.radikal.com.tr/ek_haber.php?ek=cts&haberno=6867.
Seckin, Nalan. 1998. *Musalladan sohrete Safiye Ayla*. Ankara: Bilgi Yayinevi.
Selek, Pinar. 2007. *Maskeler, suvariler, gacilar*. 2nd ed. Istanbul: Istiklal Kitabevi.
Sirman, Nukhet. 2004. "Kinship, Politics, and Love: Honour in Post-colonial Contexts—the Case of Turkey." In *Violence in the Name of Honour: Theoretical and Political Challenges*, ed. Shahrazad Mojab and Nahla Abdo. Istanbul: Istanbul Bilgi University Press.
Stokes, Martin. 1989. "Music, Fate and State: Turkey's Arabesk Debate." *Middle East Report* 160:27–30.
———. 1992. "Islam, the Turkish State, and Arabesk." *Popular Music* 11(2):213–227.
Tanis, Tolga. August 28, 2005. "Lirik Bir olaydir Bulent Ersoy." Hurriyet, http://webarsiv.hurriyet.com.tr/2005/08/28/693536.asp.
Tulgar, Ahmet. 2004. "Musikiden ozur diliyorum" Milliyet, June 1, http://www.milliyet.com.tr/2004/06/01/pazar/axpaz01.html.

NOT FOOD OR LOVE

PATRICIA CARLIN

The time of spiders arrived:
that seemed pure play of light,
ideas borne on light.

Light said, Now watch this:

★ ★ ★

Murray said, "It has a / life.
Body. We can take

The hot dog vendor closed down his stand
learned how to process

—death in the air," he said gently /
death but haven't known how to make the material surface.

★ ★ ★

. . . others. I sat
darting alertness

convinced / she was saying something
of stable meaning

minutes passed
familiar and elusive at the same time

★ ★ ★

Sleep might have been a structure
to protect the eyes

only repeating / some TV voice.
body a dreaming mound

minutes later that I was surrounded by noise / and commotion
instructing us through a bullhorn. In that silence I . . .

horns, the / first of what would become . . .

★ ★ ★

To reverse,
to reverse, the girl to pedal backwards /

through tracers and smoky arcs.
The bands of color : life

Night brings crowds
pushing up the incline,
bending low to push against the incline

★ ★ ★

over. Got out of the car.
See,
overpass all the time

now and then a car
actually crosses the overpass

★ ★ ★

snows   the air turned clear and still

already back inside,
looking through glass.

still today.

bills, forms and coupons were scattered across the table.
"Want dinner so early?" she said in a sexy whisper.
"Sure to keep it in the back of our minds."

PATRICIA CARLIN is the author of the poetry collection *Quantum Jitters,* forthcoming in 2009 (Marsh Hawk Press). Previous books include another the poetry collection, Original Green (2003), as well as *Shakespeare's Mortal Men*, a critical study of selected plays. Her poems have appeared in numerous journals and anthologies, including McSweeney's Internet Tendency, American Letters & Commentary, Verse, Boulevard, Pleiades, and BOMB. She co-edits the poetry journal *Barrow Street*, and she is an Associate Professor at New School University, where she teaches literature and poetry writing in the Writing Program.

TRANSGRESSIVE AND TRANSFORMATIVE GENDERED SEXUAL PRACTICES AND WHITE PRIVILEGES: THE CASE OF THE DYKE/TRANS BDSM COMMUNITIES

ROBIN BAUER

In this essay I explore the personal-political pleasures and limits of transgressing and transforming cultural/social/political categories of hierarchy through embodied, sexualized practices. To do so I analyze how dyke/trans BDSM practitioners privilege the practice of transgressing and transforming gender boundaries by neglecting or marginalizing the conscious engagement with racial transgressions and transformations.[1] In the essay I draw on my empirical study on dyke/trans-inclusive and queer BDSM communities.

EXPLORING AND TRANSGRESSING BOUNDARIES THROUGH BDSM PRACTICES

The frame for playfully engaging with and transgressing social hierarchies and norms, cultural taboos, and personal boundaries within BDSM is the construction of a social space (Schütz and Luckmann 1979, 48 f.) that is experienced as a *safe space* (Matt, Scout, Terry, United States, Tony, Germany), "playground" (Connie, Germany) or "field for experimentation" (Jonas, Europe).[2] What qualifies the space as safe for playing and experimenting is in part general BDSM standards and characteristics, such as negotiating and establishing consensuality; communicating, respecting, and pushing boundaries; dramatizing and thus making visible and debatable power relations and stereotypes; emphasizing emotional and physical intensity in sexuality; and translating sexual fantasies into reality, most notably through role play.

Yet the pushing of individual and sociocultural boundaries and the quest for intense bodily and psychological experiences also situates BDSM practices in a complex and sometimes paradoxical matrix of danger and safety: the risky nature of some BDSM practices necessitated the implementation of safety measures and ethics in the community in the first place.[3] A frame of safety and consensuality ensured by certain commonly accepted standards of behavior simultaneously is exactly what enables some individuals to explore BDSM practices, while for others it takes off the edge or thrill by making things too safe and sterile when it is exactly the inherent risks or dangers that make this path worthwhile or sexy. The white bisexual femme Anya (Europe) considers BDSM an emotionally dangerous path in that one can never foresee what feelings certain acts might trigger, but like many other BDSM practitioners, she values transgression of one's own limits as a chance to grow. Indeed, for some of my interview partners the main incentive to practice BDSM is to explore and get to know one's own boundaries or push/transgress them, or both, within a framework of negotiated consent.

Another great motivation for queers and trans people to engage in BDSM is that in contrast to everyday life, in BDSM spaces one can consciously choose and negotiate roles and identities for play. Therefore, the participants may agree upon the gender, race, age, class, or status one chooses for a scene in a consensual manner, and in this sense BDSM has the potential to become the playground Connie refers to.

Additionally, the dyke+ community excludes cis men, straight BDSM practitioners and vanilla people who might have prejudices against grown-ups who love to play in this way or might not be able to cope with queer sexualities.[4] As the white pansexual genderqueer femme Neila (Germany) points out, it creates a space that is perceived as devoid of *predefined* power relations in regard to gender and sexuality, if not in regard to other social power structures such as race or class. Therefore, most people who move in (and sometimes out) of the dyke+ BDSM communities share the view that "SM provides a safe space for people to fuck with their gender and also for their gender identity to be respected" and that gender is "not at all based on biology, because there are lots of people who don't identify as boys in their everyday life, but within SM context they'll be boys" (Matt), which sets this community apart from the gay male and straight BDSM communities as well as the vanilla dyke/lesbian communities (Hale 2003).[5] Gender-based play often incorporates sexual preference and age as well, as is evident through the popularity of "fag play" and "Daddy/boy."

A lot of role plays explicitly or implicitly make references to class and some to race, most notably "Master/slave." Yet as white queer transgendered stone butch Terry (United States) puts it,

I am less comfortable engaging with race and class; perhaps because I have privilege in those areas and been very politicized around that; antiracist is one of my core activist identities. Those things feel very loaded for me. But I think it's more than that; I have experienced anti-Semitism, and I would not play with that, I could not do it, and it's not hot for me. Similarly, I would not play with fat oppression or disability, and I have experienced those things on the bottom, both because they are too loaded for me, and because I don't find them hot. Age, gender, and sexuality are really hot for me.... Other hierarchies are not, for the most part.

Since his statement seems to summarize a tendency within the dyke+ BDSM community, I will trace my interviewees' comments on sex/gender, sexuality, age, class, and race in relation to their individual BDSM practices and on the community level, to discuss why this might be the case.

TRANSGRESSIVE AND TRANSFORMATIVE BDSM ACTS

A few BDSM queers regard transgression of social values and personal boundaries in itself as a political goal; for example, the white queer genderqueer Femmeboy (United States) states that "anything that limits me feels repressive and is against my political stance." Others are trying to establish criteria for which transgressions are evaluated as positive and which boundaries should not be violated or question the value of transgression per se. As the white queer femme Teresa (United States) put it, "I think that trying to be transgressive is kind of reactionary, because it stops being about what feels best to you and following your pleasure. And it becomes about reacting to the Victorian morals." Teresa is critical of what can be seen as a heritage of the feminist sex wars in which some SM dykes equated the rebellion against sexual morals as progressive on its face. By contrast, for the queer transwoman of color Leslie (Europe), "being into SM it's so much more exciting and so much more sexually arousing because it's actually sort of a forbidden fruit you're touching." So at least for some it is exactly the breaking of social taboos that generates lust.

For the queers I interviewed, the main reason to practice BDSM is that it is sexually arousing. Yet the majority also experienced it as a tool for personal growth and healing (see Barker 2007; Easton 2007) and as possessing political potential in that it enabled them to question cultural assumptions about power in general and sex and gender specifically. When trying to assess these kinds of trans-queer-feminist and antioppressive potential as well as limits of certain BDSM practices within certain contexts, I find it helpful to distinguish between acts in which *transgressing* individuals or sociocultural boundaries, or both, generate (or prevent) a lustful experience in terms of violating a taboo, and *transformative* acts that additionally create new meanings that might hold promising utopian or political potential or both, beyond the private or semipublic BDSM setting. In the case of the dyke+ BDSM communities, gender-based play has created new subcultural skills around sex/gender (sometimes as they interrelate with age, sexuality, and class) that are partially transferable to the everyday lives of the interviewees (see Bauer 2007b) and thus may be viewed as transformative, while no such skills have been developed when it comes to race.

THE DYKE+ BDSM COMMUNITIES IN WESTERN EUROPE AND THE UNITED STATES

Since BDSM practices are marginalized within heteronormative societies, where non-BDSM, genitally focused sexuality between two (monogamous, opposite-sex, able-bodied, same-race, same-generation) partners (imagined as egalitarian, in a private setting) remains the norm, BDSM practitioners face issues similar to those of other sexual minorities (see Weiss, 2006; Wright, 2006). The individuals experience their own version of a coming-out process (Kamel 1995; Chaline 2007) and may enter one of the real-life or online BDSM communities, which offer a variety of educational and social events that enable novices to gather information and learn how to engage in BDSM in a safe or risk-aware, ethically sound way. In the United States and Western Europe, real-life BDSM communities are organized around sexual preference and are rather segregated.[6] While the gay male and straight communities are quite large, with various venues at their disposal, the dyke+ BDSM community is so small that it hardly exists on local levels; only in a few metropolitan areas specific "women/trans only" organizations or play parties exist.[7] Instead it manifests itself transnationally at annual or biannual gatherings such as the Women at Amsterdam Leather Pride as well as through individual friendships and play partner networks.

The overall BDSM community in the United States and Western

Europe as it exists today had its roots within gay male biker clubs mostly composed of World War II veterans whose experiences in the war and whose homosexuality prevented them from going "back home"; instead, they stayed in the Bay Area of San Francisco and fashioned themselves as outcasts in all-male friendship networks (Thompson 1991; Sisson 2007). This so-called Old Guard based much of their social interactions on the discipline, hierarchy, and homosocial/sexual camaraderie they were familiar with from the military. They were a small, secretive community, and novices were introduced to BDSM practices through personal mentors and had to undergo certain initiations. Safety was further ensured through social control. A larger, mixed BDSM scene emerged after the "sexual revolution" in the 1970s, but quickly split up into a straight and a gay male segment.

The few dykes interested in BDSM had no community of their own until the mid-1980s, when SAMOIS in San Francisco and the Lesbian Sex Mafia in New York City were founded as women-only groups (Califia 1982). Before, BDSM dykes in the United States usually "found shelter" in the gay male leather community and therefore elements of that sexual culture entered into the emerging women's BDSM community.

Today the style of the Old Guard has mostly been replaced by a community that is open to anyone interested in joining and that educates its members through manuals, workshops, and other means and forms broad national and transnational alliances to fight for social acceptance and public recognition. For example, the community works toward the removal of BDSM as a psychopathology from the *IC-D10* and the *DSM-IV* (Reiersøl and Skeid, 2006). Some dyke, trans, and queer BDSM practitioners organize within the mixed BDSM community, while most prefer the dyke+ BDSM community (or, for trans and queer practitioners, the gay male and emerging queer community, respectively).

My sample was mainly recruited from the dyke+ BDSM communities in the United States and Western Europe. What had started out as the women's BDSM scene usually includes, at this point, self-defined dykes/lesbians; bi/pansexual and queer women; butches; femmes; and other genderqueers, who do not necessarily consider themselves women; the whole FtM spectrum; as well as transwomen (but not MtF transvestites or cross-dressers).[8] I therefore refer to it as the dyke+ BDSM community, to do justice to both the historical background and the identities of the individual members.

This variety of genders and gender expressions is further complimented by identities created and assumed for play. A number of members of this community, such as genderqueers, have assumed gender identities that transgress the binary gender system. While genderqueers do not identify full time as either men or women, they do not conceive of themselves as in the middle of the spectrum or as androgynous either. Their gender is rather fluid (shifting) and multiple at the same time, which means that their positioning within a variety of genders depends on the context. For example, a person might express a femme side in an encounter with a butch and express a fag partial identity with a gay transguy the next day.

While my research is qualitative and therefore not designed to be representative, I would tentatively question the stereotype of BDSM people being overwhelmingly highly educated and of middle- to upper-class upbringing, in adult life situations, or a combination of these, at least in the case of the dyke and trans population, since my sample is rather diverse in this regard. However, some interviewees put forth the idea that high-quality BDSM is only for those whom they perceive to be highly educated, "intelligent" or "classy" individuals, thus endorsing potentially excluding class-based criteria for membership in the community. Others point out the exclusionary dynamics of parts of the organized BDSM community caused by the expectation of being able to pay for expensive outfits, toys, and entrance fees for play parties.

While my interview partners have found ways to practice BDSM that do not require ample resources, the question of economic resources nonetheless restricts the access of poor people and queers of color (QOC) as well, as the white, queer transguy Matt suggests: "Most of the play parties I've been to have been really white and also play parties can be really expensive. And I think there's a big issue in terms of class....And also I think the race thing is partly class stuff and it's partly because most of the play parties that I've been to have been organized by white people."

METHODS AND SAMPLE

I regard my interviewees and myself as positioned within complex social power structures, which influence—though not determine—how we perceive ourselves, our practices, and our surroundings. Thus, the discourses my interviewees generate in describing their practices and experiences as well as my own analyses represent embodied, *situated* knowledges

(Haraway 1991b). To enable the critically engaged reader to assess the investments these situated knowledges carry with them and to make myself accountable for the kinds of knowledges I produce, I position myself and my interviewees (as they have labeled themselves) in regard to structural power relations. I consider these strategic-political positionings, not essentialist categories or identities.

On all levels, my academic work (research questions, field access, manner of conducting interviews, analysis, presenting results, and so on) is informed by my positioning as a white German, queer, polyamorous, BDSM top, and transfag with a working-class and activist background.[9] Because of certain inclusions, exclusions, and my own biography of transition, I am also situated between certain BDSM communities, with roots in the dyke+ scene and faced with only limited acceptance in the gay male scene. On the basis of my notion of queer politics I have a vested interest in generating valid knowledges about BDSM practices and communities from a queer perspective.

Therefore, I conducted fifty qualitative semistructured, in-person interviews with self-identified dykes, trans people, and queers from the United States and Western Europe who practice BDSM, addressing them as experts on the topic. For this reason, I chose not to document their individual biographies as a whole, but to hone the focus in regard to their status as representatives of certain BDSM practices and communities. In one set of questions, I asked interviewees to position themselves in terms of gender identity and sexual preferences and practices and discussed their personal experiences with BDSM in depth vis-à-vis such issues as power, healing, politics, spirituality, social marginalization, intimate relationships, and gender. Another set of questions addressed standards and norms in the BDSM communities they were familiar with and their own positioning within these.

Since I searched for interviewees mostly through personal contacts and community vehicles such as mailing lists, my personal-political background, outlined above, both facilitated and restricted my ability to reach certain groups of people; BDSM queers who don't have access to the Internet or are not in touch with the organized BDSM communities for whatever reason are underrepresented in my research. Although I received sufficient responses from white people with a working-class background or limited economic resources, and my sample includes people between twenty and sixty years of age, people of color are underrepresented, which might have to do with the fact that I'm white myself and did not mention discussing race and class as a focus of my study when searching for interview partners. Even setting aside my failure at the time to adequately address how my own whiteness might inform the sampling of my research project, the low participation of QOC might be "representative" of the mixed-race dyke+ BDSM community, as it is predominantly white.

The BDSM community has developed a culture of open discussion about sexual fantasies and practices and created communication skills that are much more sophisticated than those of sexual "majorities." Furthermore, interviewees have repeatedly pointed out that they were willing to talk frankly about their experiences with me as the researcher because of my having been a well-known member of the community. It was thus possible to discuss the issues at hand in a mostly "uncensored" way. Interviews were between one and four hours long, taped, transcribed word by word, slightly edited to correct grammar, and authorized by the interview partners. The interviews were analyzed within the framework of the coding paradigm from grounded theory (Strauss and Corbin, 1990). From the wealth of my data, I generated a number of categories through coding procedures, some of which I present in this essay. Given the highly articulate and reflective discursive culture of the community at hand, in vivo codes were preferred, also in order to give this underresearched and often misrepresented community its own voice (for an overview of the research on BDSM in general, see Weinberg 2006; note that there are no empirical studies of the dyke+ subgroup so far, with the exception of Duncan 1996).

THE DYKE+ BDSM COMMUNITIES AS PLAYGROUND FOR EXPLORING GENDER

The BDSM space provides its members with the possibility for self-exploration, especially for *exploring gender*, including its intersections with sexual identity, age, and class. The venue for exploring gender is often role-play, because many people find that—especially in a DS (dominance/submission) context—role-play benefits from the specificity of the assumed roles, especially when it comes to fleshing out the gender, age, and class background of the characters. White dyke Mistress Mean Mommy (United States) compares exploring different personas to reading a book such as James Joyce's *Portrait of the Artist as a Young Man*:

I can't understand what it's like to be a fifteen-year-old Irish boy in an all-boy's boarding school. But I can read the book and have a sense of what it's like. So if you wanna go out and buy a schoolboy's uniform and wear it and have somebody be the schoolmaster and I get to play it, now I have a sense of what it's like, even as me in my body as a woman. I'll never be a fifteen-year-old boy. I get to experience what I think a fifteen-year-old boy would be like. And that might be freeing in some way. Maybe it will give me a different perspective, maybe I'll suddenly understand something I never understood about young boys.

Self-exploration in role-play thus provides the players with certain *insights* about themselves and about how gender and other categories of social distinction take on different meanings and functions from the perspective of someone whose positioning is different within society from what it is for themselves (at least how they would experience a different position). This allows them to experience the *situatedness* of perspectives, and in contrast to reading a book, sexual role-play is an *embodied* experience. This embodied way of *understanding* an identity or a power dynamic is a common and valued theme among BDSM queers and points to the emphasis they place on looking at gender and how it intersects with age, class, and sexuality from different perspectives as a means of acknowledging and respecting difference, both within themselves and interpersonally. Mistress Mean Mommy sees a liberating potential in understanding how it might feel to be a fifteen-year-old boy. What starts out as play-acting may become enacting partial identities and this may enable to feel connections across differences.

TRANSFORMATIVE SUBCULTURAL SKILLS

Exploring gender concepts and identities in this way has the transformative effect of creating (new) *subcultural skills*, which—as interviewees suggest—are partly transferred to the everyday and political life of queer BDSM practitioners. I will briefly discuss three of these subcultural skills that my interviewees have repeatedly referred to and described, and which seem to be significant in the process of queering gender: *renaming/reassigning, recognition,* and *integration* (for a more detailed discussion, see Bauer 2007b).

Because of the importance of fantasy in BDSM role-play, interviewees insist on the fact that "it's really happening in the head." However, it is also central to BDSM practices to work with and manipulate the body. These seemingly contradictory characteristics of BDSM provide a starting point for people who are exploring and expanding gender concepts to rename or recode body parts and sexual practices according to the meaning they have for the participants involved as opposed to heteronormative (outsider) perspectives, while simultaneously reassigning their bodies with gendered meanings that differ from those of biological or medical assignments.

I combine the terms "renaming" and "reassigning" to point out that the process entails a simultaneously discursive and material understanding of bodies and sexual practices as "material-semiotic generative nodes" (Haraway, 1991a, 208). Haraway calls upon feminist theorists not to regard the body—and by extension, sex—as a passive entity for social inscriptions (including gender). The body is neither simply speaking its own truth, nor passively waiting to be decoded. Instead, Haraway imagines the body as an entity akin to the figure of the Native American trickster, a changeling with an obscene sense of humor, trying to manipulate his powers for his own (sometimes sexual) benefits, but oftentimes stumbling over his own feet. Thus the analysis of bodies cannot be reduced to (semiotic) discourse, but has to incorporate the material agency of bodies, which sets boundaries to our (re)defining of (sexed and gendered) bodies. The boundaries of bodies are understood as material-semiotic generative nodes, materialized through social interactions, but boundaries may also redraw themselves; boundaries are like tricksters, with a life of their own.

The story of the white trans-identified genderqueer butch dyke Scout, who had to undergo surgery in his youth because of an intersex condition, about his relationship with his transgender butch Sir is an example of a material-semiotic renaming/reassigment: "So, being a boy he was trying to teach me how to have a boy cunt and reassign my body in a way that I could survive in it." In their 24/7 relationship they consciously worked on inventing new language for their bodies and reassigning "female" body parts with trans masculine and genderqueer meanings as in the term "boy cunt," which combines masculine and female elements to create a new concept of a sexed/gendered body.[10]

Another common example of renaming/reassigning is the use of the term "dick" (instead of "dildo") to refer to a phallus/penis that is not permanently attached to the body. In both cases, language is used to capture a material experience that shifts bodily boundaries. Butches, FtMs, and their partners experience "dildos" as "real" parts of their bodies, with a dynamic of their own, stressing the trickster character of the sexed/gendered body that evolves through sexual practices.

Related to the subcultural skill of renaming/reassigning is *recognition*. The white queer transgender butch Tony recalls a situation "where I played at the bottom as a boy, and my partner undressed me and put me in front of a mirror. And for the first time, actually, I really consciously saw in my naked body an absolutely boyish or masculine body. And after that I had this experience of 'what biology tells us is simply complete bullshit' [laughs]. I see what I want to see and my partners can also see what they want to see." In this case the act of recognition refers to a certain insight that takes place during a transformative scene and assigns a heteronormatively female–coded body as boyish or masculine, but not as something that is actively sought; it happens rather spontaneously. Although it happened within the context of a series of BDSM encounters with a trusted partner, it is nevertheless not something that was or even could be planned ahead and thus once more demonstrates the trickster character of the sexed/gendered body. Tony suddenly *sees* "themself" gendered differently from before.

"Seeing" is a term that is commonly used by my interviewees, when referring to seeing oneself, but even more so for seeing others: recognizing somebody else's partial, play, or all-encompassing gender identity from the outside, stressing the importance of being recognized as what or who you are. Since Tony interestingly stands in front of a mirror, s/he is able to recognize themself, so to speak, from an outside perspective. Seeing in this sense as a subcultural skill is an embodied way of situated knowledge production by partial selves (Haraway, 1991b, 190). It is an active vision, reinventing and reconstructing sex and gender through hegemonic as well as semiotic-material queer knowledges and practices.

Exploring gendered selves in BDSM can ultimately lead to developing a trans or genderqueer identity in everyday life. Indeed, this seems to be a quite common experience. While for some this may result in a relatively stable FtM identity, for others the process of exploring gender is not easily put to an end (however temporary that end may be): "Roleplay to me is a lot about different aspects of my gender expression and I actually feel it's through those practices that my gender has coalesced. I've been able to kind of get on terms with parts of me that I may have rejected or have been splintered off. I feel role-play's been one of the most integrating things I've done." As in this quote, for the white queer genderqueer Firesong (United States) and others, who describe their gender identity as composed of different parts, personas, or nuances, the goal cannot be to attain a singular identity, but to *integrate* the various aspects into their identity.[11] BDSM space offers them possibilities to do that through playing with gender or expressing partial identities in gender-based play.

Experimenting and playing with different partial gender identities as a way of experiencing difference within the self may serve to disrupt of the usual normalizing process of excluding the "other" in the process of identification and open up a queer way of subverting the constant reproduction of exclusionary (heteronormative and other) dynamics and knowledge claims: "The knowing self is partial in all its guises, never finished, whole, simply there and original; it is always constructed and stitched together imperfectly, and *therefore* able to join with another, to see together without claiming to be another" (Haraway 1991b, 193) Interviewees use BDSM role-play to construct and stitch together imperfect gendered selves; they seek knowledge and understanding about gender through "partial connection" (193) and seeing without claiming to be another, as in the case of Mistress Mean Mommy when experiencing the perspective of a fifteen-year-old boy from her embodiment as a woman.

Firesong points out consequences of this way of dealing with intrapersonal diversity for interpersonal diversity: "As I recognize different roles in myself, that's an experience of diversity. So if that's something that people are exploring individually, then in the community that would probably be reflected as a common acceptance of valuing diverse expression." What interviewees describe as respecting, validating, valuing, and celebrating diversity in gender expressions on a community level is therefore a result of the transformative acts the BDSM space enables within a specific, gender-segregated context. Experiencing one's partial identities in an embodied way in a playful and sexual context fosters understanding and acceptance of a variety of gender identities within the dyke+ BDSM community as well as outside it.

Yet transformative acts or identities are not hot for everyone, nor are they experienced as equally sexy referring to other categories of social distinction such as class or race. Oftentimes overemphasizing stereotypes or transgressing cultural taboos around age, class, and especially race in a way that reinscribes rather than questions dominant images generates lust within a BDSM context. Sometimes transgressing one's own class or economic or educational status is incorporated into play. Interestingly, these transgressions are usually directed "downward" from middle- to working-class or "upward" to upper-class, but hardly ever is the goal to embody a middle-class character, which, on the contrary, has repeatedly been labeled as "unsexy" by interviewees. Working-class people are depicted as "more real," "more macho," or "more violent"; attributes that rely on class-based stereotyping and seem to reproduce them instead of transforming them.

Age play, which is often combined with gender play, is pretty popular, and the transgressions of cultural taboos around incest in embodying Daddy/boy and Daddy/girl relations seem to generate lustful experiences. For some, age play also becomes transformative in creating new patterns of queer kinship (see Bauer 2007a). But interviewees have also stated that there is a certain age line of the imagined child they cannot cross (BJ, United States; Wolf, Germany), thus implying that there are limits to pleasure through transgression as well. Within the dyke+ BDSM community, this holds especially true for race.

UN/LIMITED LUST: TRANSGRESSING RACE AS SOCIOCULTURAL TABOO

Some BDSM queers perceive breaking social taboos in BDSM play as erotically charged. But breaking taboos may also generate discomfort, for example, when contradicting one's political convictions (Nico, Germany; Terry) or when evoking feelings of shame or "doing something wrong" (Woltersdorff 2007). There are also psychological limits to translating the breaking of social taboos that may be hot in fantasy into actual BDSM play. While BDSM queers acknowledge some cultural taboos they won't break, they generally try not to judge others who might wish to do so, for example, when it comes to playing with Nazi scenarios. Rather, anything that is consensually negotiated between the partners (and in the case of Nazi play kept in the privacy of their homes) is commonly deemed acceptable independently of societal or subcultural morals and norms. The white queer high femme Zoe (United States) even regards BDSM as an appropriate means to help one "embrace all your monsters" and thus be able to let go of fears generated by social norms, which she connects to her Buddhist practice.

Yet play that somehow creates racial hierarchies or one's one whiteness more visible seems to present a discomforting taboo for white queers to deal with and thus has to be considered a hard limit when it comes to breaking social taboos and a serious challenge to the overall stance of being nonjudgmental of others' practices. Even talking about racializations in BDSM proved to be "too touchy" for some interview partners;

the majority was not able to consciously reflect on how race played into their BDSM practices at all; they felt "it did not matter."

Generally, I identified two dynamics in my interviews that can account for the fact that consciously playing with race does not seem to take place within the dyke+ BDSM community: the invisibility of one's own whiteness and the discomfort in dealing with racial hierarchy or interracial situations/imagery by white queers. There even seems to be a tendency among BDSM queers to deemphasize and thus depoliticize race by deracing historically raced institutions such as slavery, colonialism, or even contemporary racialized stereotypes: the white gay transman Jonas observes that the historical racialization of slavery is not referred to within the BDSM context; no racial slurs are used to enhance the mind space of the bottom as slave during role-play.[12] German interviewees often do not associate slavery with colonialism or with blackness in the German context. Interestingly, one interviewee interpreted playing a "gang boss" only as a class issue, even though the term is part of a highly racialized discourse in contemporary media.

The relevance of race and, by extension, nationality often becomes visible for whites in a critical or conflicting (interracial or international) situation. E.g. such conflicts may occur when Germans are asked to speak German in a scene with someone from another country, feeling they are being fetishized as German with a Nazi-connotation, which may make them uncomfortable.

In some cases the invisibility of one's own racial status as a white person may be partly attributed to varying degrees of role-play: some people do not invent a different persona, such as when playing as a slave, but express their partial identity as a slave. Thus, the question of skin color does not come up for them when entering the slave head space. Yet it remains a white privilege not to concern oneself with one's racial status and history when playing as a slave. The fact that many female-bodied individuals nevertheless consciously choose and negotiate to play as male or fags, thus putting gender and sexuality center stage while ignoring the relevance of race, may be explained partly through the gender segregation of the space, which opens up possibilities for queers who have experienced sexism to experiment with gender in the absence of "real life" men and "real life" sexism. Yet since it is a mixed-race space that is dominated by members of the privileged race, this seems to rather foreclose a playful approach in this regard. Most white interview partners had only played with other whites so far and some stated they would feel uncomfortable topping a black woman because of racial hierarchies or expressing other forms of "white guilt"; even witnessing a black person on the bottom in a play space was disconcerting to white queers.

Thus while they are able to see sex/gender, age, and class as performative and transformable, the same does not seem to hold true for race, which among other problematic effects limits the possibilities of exploration in BDSM for QOC, since they are predominantly read as racialized by white queers, whose own whiteness in turn remains largely *invisible* and thus seems the be the requisite for opening up the space for exploring other categories of difference, such as gender/sex, sexuality, age, and to a lesser degree class. Interviewees overwhelmingly did not think that race was of any relevance to their BDSM practices or that it was constructed in play if their race in their role resembled their real-life race. The only way they were able to think about race at all was in terms of (real-life as opposed to staged) interracial encounters in BDSM. The white, bisexual woman Franka (Germany), for example, stated that if she were to negotiate topping a QOC she would inquire which terms or actions might trigger connections to real-life racism for her bottom in order to avoid them during the session.

While I am far from suggesting that transgressing "racial taboos" within a community dominated by white queers would in itself be a politically progressive act, the problematic dynamic remains that gender and sexuality (and to a lesser extent age and class) are highly visible and consciously negotiated in dyke+ BDSM spaces, while racialization of the white majority remains invisible and unexplored and functions as a nontransgressable and probably also nontransformable cultural taboo when it comes to interracial imaginary.[13]

CONCLUSION

The possibility of playing with, experiencing, transgressing, and transforming the stereotypes and dynamics associated with categories of social hierarchy in a pleasurable way seems to depend on the fact that in daily life the members of the dyke+ BDSM communities do not have straight (and, for the most part, male) privileges. The fact that most members of this community have racial privileges seems to prevent them from experimenting with and transforming race and race relations in a similar fashion.

The diversity of queer genders in the dyke+ BDSM scene has been fostered by a combination of certain BDSM characteristics and the exclusion of privileged genders (specifically straight and gay cis men), thus creating a social space that is perceived as a safe playground to explore genders. Gender exploration leads to awareness and certain insights, especially an embodied understanding of nonheteronormative gender identities. It creates an expansion of gender concepts and identities that enables the emergence of specific subcultural skills, which I have called "renaming/reassigning," "recognition," and "integration."

These practices translate to valuing gender diversity on a community level and are partly transferred into everyday life, especially in terms of identities; Femmeboy describes her fag play with her trans lover thus: "Some people would say we were not really [being fags] because 'you're not a fag and he's not a bio boy,' or whatever, but I really felt that I was exploring that fag part of myself. So it's not just a fantasy, it's a real part of me. You know, I feel it. So there's a bridge, there's a bridge." While fag play enables Femmeboy to express a real fag part of herself also in everyday life, a transferal to other communities and mainstream society, remains limited because of heteronormative, sexist, and other hierarchical social structures, as her comment on how outsiders perceive them reveals.

It is not simply the gender segregation of the dyke+ BDSM space that makes it such an interesting venue for working out gender identities; BDSM in general encourages a playful, sexually charged, embodied engagement with power, social roles, and cultural stereotypes. Furthermore, BDSM combines elements of power exchange and role-play that stress the performative character of gender and sexual identities with elements that stress the material limits of the body (sensation play and bondage), thus providing BDSM queers with a potential starting point for experiencing and discussing their bodies and sexual acts as material-semiotic entities.[14] As a consequence, within the community the sexed and gendered body is generally perceived as more performative than in mainstream culture, its boundaries not necessarily restricted by its own skin (for example, when "dildos" become "dicks"), but the limits to its semiotic reinvention are also acknowledged (such as through witnessing previously identified non-op FtMs starting to transition).[15]

In summary, analysis of my data seems to suggest that within the dyke+ BDSM communities, transformative acts occur mainly in terms of gender, sexuality, and age, while class-based play seems to be purely transgressive for the most part, and consciously race-based play seems to present too strong a taboo within a mostly white community to be employed for either transgressive or transformative practices. Rather, the invisibility of whiteness seems to be a prerequisite for transgressions in other realms. However, this conclusion is tentative, since it might partly result from a bias in my original research design, which focused much more on questions of gender and sexuality than on questions of age, class, race, and other categories of social hierarchy and might therefore not be sufficient to adequately analyze the complex issue at hand. Future research will be needed to further analyze the trans-queer-feminist potential and limits of embodied transgressions and transformations of categories of social hierarchy through BDSM practices.

ROBIN BAUER is a lecturer in gender and science studies and queer studies at the University of Hamburg and University of Göttingen. He is currently working on his PhD on queer BDSM practices and communities in sociology. He has published numerous articles on BDSM, transgenderism, polyamory, and gender and science studies curricula, seeking to combine his activism with his academic work. E-mail Robin Bauer at Robin.Bauer@gmx.de.

NOTES

1. "BDSM" is an acronym increasingly used to replace the former "SM," which overemphasizes the pain aspect of BDSM practices and is associated with pathology. BDSM, in contrast, encompasses a broader range of practices (bondage, discipline, dominance/submission [the exchange of power, or DS] and sadomasochism [inflicting or receiving intense sensations]) and is a nonpathological self-definition originating within the BDSM community.

2. Names shown in parentheses are interviewees, interviewed by the author. Names have been changed to ensure anonymity. Places are not specified further than United States, Germany, and Europe (Europe stands for European countries other than Germany, since the community is too small to ensure anonymity otherwise). I would like to thank my interview partners for providing me with their expertise and support.

3. Currently two major approaches are common within the community: SSC (safe, sane, and consensual) and RACK (risk aware consensual kink); the latter representing a critique of the former as being too normative in terms of what practices are acceptable. For a more thorough discussion, see Stein 2002; Switch 2001 (for community discourse) and Downing 2007 (for a scholarly analysis of the exclusionary effects of community discourse on safety).

4. "Cis" refers to people whose gender identity matches the sex they were

assigned at birth. "Vanilla" is used within the BDSM community to refer to non-BDSM sexual activities.

5. Even though there are MtF transvestites and transsexuals in the straight scene, according to the perspective of the interviewees they are either fetishized or confronted with other misogynist, sexist, and transphobic attitudes, as the use of the term "forced feminization" demonstrates.

6. This essay focuses on real-life communities as opposed to the fast-growing online communities, in which some people practice BDSM solely as cybersex. The research participants in my sample all mainly practice BDSM in real-life encounters. Since the dyke+ BDSM community is so small that it is a transnational entity, the Internet is used for networking and organizing.

7. I use the term "straight" to refer to the mixed-gender BDSM community that does not further position itself, but is predominantly composed of heterosexuals and is heteronormative to various degrees. Play parties are events at which BDSM practitioners meet to socialize and practice BDSM in a semi-public setting. Entrance is usually restricted to BDSM people, sometimes of a certain sex or gender (gay male– or women/trans–only events), enforced through door policies such as dress codes. BDSM people of color have also organized venues that enable them to exclusively or predominantly connect with other people of color interested in BDSM. For a description of play parties within the straight BDSM community, see Moser 1998.

8. The term "bisexual" has been replaced in certain communities by "pansexual," to acknowledge that there are more than two genders and to designate people who are attracted not only to men and women, but to a variety of genders, or have a choice of partners that is independent of sex/gender.

—"Butch" has historically been a self-definition for dykes or queer women with a masculine gender expression who predominantly were sexually involved with femmes (dykes or queer women with a feminine gender expression). Butch and femme are concepts that are constantly evolving and increasingly defined independently of each other. Some butches identify as women; some identify as transgendered. Some femmes identify as lesbians or dykes; some identify as queer or transsensual, if they are attracted to transgendered butches or transmen. The butch-femme couple with its overtly sexual dynamic was an early visible expression of lesbian/dyke desire.

—"Genderqueer" in this sense is used as an umbrella term for all gender identities that defy the heteronormative, bipolar assumption that there are only two genders, based on two distinguishable biological sexes.

—"FtM" stands for "female-to-male" and is used as an umbrella term for all those who were assigned female at birth, but do not identify as women, including transgender butches and transsexual men.

9. Polyamory is a nonmonogamous practice of engaging in multiple relationships, either within a model of primary/secondary or multiple primary partners networks.

—A "transfag" is a gay FtM. Most transfags view both biological men and other FtMs as potential partners.

10. The expression "24/7," twenty-four hours a day, seven days a week, indicates that the partners interact in their chosen roles constantly (Dancer, Kleinplatz, and Moser 2006).

11. Interviewees (Firesong and Femmeboy) use the term "integration" themselves, and I have found it an appropriate in vivo code (Strauss and Corbin 1990) for the phenomenon that others describe as well. It bears some resemblance to the Jungian term "integration," in terms of embracing the hidden parts; however, the partial gender identities that are integrated into my interviewees' personalities are not necessarily derived from the Jungian shadow.

12. If white BDSM practitioners avoid further explicit racial references within Master/slave plays, the intent behind it might, of course, be antiracist in terms of not wanting to be disrespectful of the raced real-life history of slavery by trying to disassociate it from that history. This explanation is not satisfactory though, since the logical conclusion would be to use different concepts and terms in the first place, which is exactly what some interviewees have chosen to do, as they refrain from using the word "slave."

13. Even though it is not visible in the white dyke+ BDSM community, race play does take place. At this point it seems that predominantly BDSM people of color or with a Jewish background (and their white partners) consciously engage with it and critically discuss it, such as in the context of the concept of cultural trauma. (Hernández 2004).

14. Hart (1998) therefore distinguishes between the body as performative or socially mediated and the flesh as "real" or "authentic" and suggests that masochists seek the authentic experience of the flesh through BDSM practices.

15. Which is not to say that post-op trans people do not *also* semiotically reinvent their bodies, but to stress that they do not do so *exclusively*.

16. There is not enough research about people of color–only BDSM venues, yet to conclude whether a race-segregated space could possibly enable its members to explore race in a similar way as gender is being explored in women-only spaces. Quotes from interviewees in Berlinger's (2006) study on black leather at least seem to suggest that race play in various forms is more common than apparent to the white eye and is experienced by some people of color as liberating in a similar fashion as is gender play in my sample.

WORKS CITED

Barker, Meg, Camelia Gupta, and Alessandra Iantaffi. 2007. "The Power of Play: The Potentials and Pitfalls in Healing Narratives of BDSM." In *Safe, Sane, and Consensual: Contemporary Perspectives on Sadomasochism*, ed. Darren Langdridge and Meg Barker. Houndmills/New York: Palgrave.

Bauer, Robin. 2007a. "'Daddy liebt seinen Jungen': Begehrenswerte Männlichkeiten in Daddy/Boy-Rollenspielen queerer BDSM Kontexte." In *Unbeschreiblich Männlich: Heteronormativitätskritische Perspektiven,* ed. Robin Bauer, Josch Hoenes, and Volker Woltersdorff. Hamburg: Männerschwarmskript.

———. 2007b. "Playgrounds and New Territories: The Potential of BDSM Practices to Queer Genders." In *Safe, Sane, and Consensual: Contemporary Perspectives on Sadomasochism*, ed. Darren Langdridge and Meg Barker. Houndmills/New York: Palgrave.

Berlinger, Cain. 2006. *Black Men in Leather*. Tempe, AZ: Third Millennium.

Califia, Pat. 1982. "A Personal View of the History of the Lesbian S/M Community and Movement in San Francisco." In *Coming to Power: Writings and Graphics on Lesbian S/M*, ed. SAMOIS. Los Angeles: Alyson.

Chaline, Eric. 2007. "On Becoming a Gay SMer: A Sexual Scripting Perspective." In *Safe, Sane, and Consensual: Contemporary Perspectives on Sadomasochism*, ed. Darren Langdridge and Meg Barker. Houndmills/New York: Palgrave.

Dancer, Peter L., Peggy J. Kleinplatz, and Charles A. Moser. 2006. "24/7 SM Slavery." In *Sadomasochism: Powerful Pleasures*, ed. P. J. Kleinplatz and C. Moser. Binghampton, NY: Harrington Park Press.

Downing, Lisa. 2007. "Beyond Safety: Erotic Asphyxiation and the Limits of SM Discourse." In *Safe, Sane, and Consensual: Contemporary Perspectives on Sadomasochism*, ed. Darren Langdridge and Meg Barker. Houndmills/New York: Palgrave.

Duncan, Patricia L. 1996. "Identity, Power, and Difference: Negotiating Conflict in an S/M Dyke Community." In *Queer Studies. A Lesbian, Gay, Bisexual and Transgender Anthology*, ed. B. Beemyn and M. Eliason. New York: New York University Press.

Easton, Dossie. 2007. "Shadowplay: S/M Journeys to Our Selves." In *Safe, Sane, and Consensual: Contemporary Perspectives on Sadomasochism*, ed. Darren Langdridge and Meg Barker. Houndmills/New York: Palgrave.

Hale, C. Jakob. 2003. "Leatherdyke Boys and Their Daddies: How to Have Sex Without Women or Men." In *Queer Studies. An Interdisciplinary Reader* ed. Robert J. Corber and Stephen Valocchi Malder. Oxford: Blackwell

Haraway, Donna. 1991a. "The Biopolitics of Postmodern Bodies: Constitutions of Self in Immune System Discourse." In *Simians, Cyborgs, and Women: The Reinvention of Nature*. New York: Routledge.

———. 1991b. "Situated Knowledges: The Science Question in Feminism and the Privilege of Partial Perspective." In *Simians, Cyborgs, and Women: The Reinvention of Nature*. New York: Routledge.

Hart, Lynda. 1998. *Between the Body and the Flesh: Performing Sadomasochism*. New York: Columbia University Press.

Hernández, Daisy. 2004. "Playing with Race." *ColorLines* 27. http://www.colorlines.com/printerfriendly.php?ID=46.

Kamel, G. W. Levi. 1995. "The Leather Career: On Becoming a Sadomasochist." In *S&M. Studies in Dominance and Submission*, ed. T. S. Weinberg. Amherst, MA: Prometheus Books.

Moser, Charles. 1998. "S/M (Sadomasochistic) Interactions in Semi-Public Settings." *Journal of Homosexuality* 36(2):19–29.

Reiersøl, Odd, and Svein Skeid. 2006. "The ICD Diagnoses of Fetishism and Sadomasochism." In *Sadomasochism. Powerful Pleasures*, ed. P. J. Kleinplatz and C. Moser. Binghampton, NY: Harrington Park Press.

Schütz, Alfred, and Thomas Luckmann. 1979. *Strukturen der Lebenswelt* Bd. 1. Frankfurt: Suhrkamp.

Sisson, Kathy. 2007. "The Cultural Formation of S/M: History and Analysis." In *Safe, Sane, and Consensual: Contemporary Perspectives on Sadomasochism*, ed. Darren Langdridge and Meg Barker. Houndmills/New York: Palgrave.

Stein, Slave David. 2002. *"Safe, Sane, Consensual": The Making of a Shibboleth.* http://www.lthredge.com/ds/ssc.pdf.

Strauss, Anselm L., and Juliet Corbin. 1990. *Basics of Qualitative Research: Grounded Theory Procedures and Techniques.* Newbury Park, CA: Sage.

Switch, Gary. 2001. *The Origin of RACK/ RACK vs. SSC.* http://www.albanypowerexchange.com/BDSMinfo/rack_vs_ssc.htm.

Thompson, Mark, ed. 1991. *Leatherfolk: Radical Sex, People, Politics, and Practice.* Los Angeles: Alyson.

Weinberg, Thomas S. 2006. "Sadomasochism and the Social Sciences: A Review of the Sociological and Social Psychological Literature." In *Sadomasochism: Powerful Pleasures*, ed. P. J. Kleinplatz and C. Moser. Binghampton, NY: Harrington Park Press.

Weiss, Margot D. 2006. "Mainstreaming Kink: The Politics of BDSM Representation in U.S. Popular Media." In *Sadomasochism: Powerful Pleasures*, ed. P. J. Kleinplatz C. Moser. Binghampton, NY: Harrington Park Press.

Woltersdorff, Volker. 2007. "Meine Dämonen füttern: Paradoxe Bearbeitungen von Geschlechtertabus in der sadomasochistischen Subkultur." In *Geschlecht als Tabu: Orte, Dynamiken, und Funktionen der De/Thematisierung von Geschlecht*, ed. U. Frietsch et al., Bielefeld, Germany. transcript.

Wright, Susan. 2006. "Discrimination of SM-Identified Individuals." In *Sadomasochism: Powerful Pleasures*, ed. P. J. Kleinplatz and C. Moser. Binghampton, NY: Harrington Park Press.

TRANSLATING WOMEN AND GENDER: THE EXPERIENCE OF TRANSLATING *THE ENCYCLOPEDIA OF WOMEN AND ISLAMIC CULTURES* INTO ARABIC

HALA KAMAL

Translation is not merely an act of transferring information, but a process of knowledge production. Thus, the idea of translating the *Encyclopedia of Women and Islamic Cultures (EWIC)* is an extension of *EWIC* itself, being a project conscious of the importance of knowledge production in the field of gender and women's studies and Islamic cultures.[1] Suad Joseph, the general editor of *EWIC*, expresses in her introduction the editorial board's awareness of the significance and consequences of producing encyclopedic knowledge about women and Islamic cultures. *EWIC* was originally published in English with the aim of presenting state-of-the-art research in gender and women's studies and Islamic cultures to an English-speaking readership. Moreover, the authors taking part in the production of *EWIC* are a group of specialized researchers in this area, who, though coming from various cultural backgrounds and disciplines, share an interest in women's studies and specialize in different parts of the world dominated by Islamic cultures. The project attempts to define and present examples of specialized and crucial studies in this field, with the prospect of producing knowledge and encouraging novel and continuous research.

The *Encyclopedia of Women and Islamic Cultures (EWIC)* is an ongoing seven-volume interdisciplinary and cross-cultural project. Joseph, professor of anthropology at the University of California, Davis, worked with an advisory board of scholars and academics specialized in women's studies and Islamic societies, as well as a group of associate editors, in addition to the contributors. The associate editors were each responsible for a specific region: Afsaneh Najmabadi (Turkey, Iran, India, Bangladesh, Pakistan, Afghanistan, Central Asia as far as the borders of Mongolia, and the Muslim republics of the former Soviet Union), Julie Peteet and Seteney Shami (the Arab countries in the Gulf, Eastern Mediterranean, and North

Africa, as well as Israel, Andalusian Spain, and Europe under the Ottoman Empire), Jacqueline Siapno (China, Mongolia, the Philippines, Indonesia, Malaysia, Brunei, Burma, Thailand, Vietnam, Singapore, Cambodia, Hong Kong, Taiwan, the Asian Pacific and Australia), and Jane I. Smith (Western Europe, sub-Saharan Africa, and the Americas). Volume 1 alone includes forty-six thematic entries and twenty-two disciplinary entries, created by specialists—who, with very few exceptions, are women academics affiliated with American and British universities (Joseph 2003, xxi–xlix).

THE TRANSLATION OF *EWIC* INTO ARABIC

The idea of translating this encyclopedia into other languages, starting with Arabic, highlights several points. First, it reveals the interest held by the editorial board and the publishing house in the wide dissemination of this work, beyond the boundaries of an English-speaking readership, to the extent of providing a free online Arabic edition. Even given the worldwide lack of equality in access to the Internet, the initiative of providing *EWIC* for free to Arabic-speaking researchers and scholars is in itself a step that can only be appreciated and valued by those living in the Arab world who experience or recognize the inability of most academic institutions to provide such a resource via their institutions. The requirements of annual subscription fees and Internet connection costs exceed the capacities of many (if not most) researchers and academics in the Arab world. We hope that the online edition is a step preceding a low-cost print edition of *EWIC* in Arabic.

Second, beginning with Arabic in the project of translating the encyclopedia grows out of an awareness of Arab researchers' need for access to this work, in view of the fact that English, in the Arab world, is a language known by only a small number of researchers, and perfected by an even smaller minority, as the majority's educational backgrounds are Arabic based. Therefore, an Arabic version of *EWIC* is, for many (if not most) readers, their only means of access to state-of-the-art studies and research in the fields of women's and Islamic cultures. This gains more value as we consider the great importance of getting acquainted with the research methodologies and paradigms as well as the sources introduced and listed in this encyclopedia.

Third, the choice by the *EWIC* editorial board of the Women and Memory Forum (WMF) as the group to supervise the translation is a continuation of the *EWIC* vision regarding the production of knowledge about women and Islamic cultures.² For us at WMF, the project of translating *EWIC* (to create the volume I call *EWIC Arabic*) coincides with our efforts to produce and disseminate knowledge in Arabic to both specialized researchers and the general public, concerning women, history, and culture, in terms of personal experiences, empirical expertise, and theoretical knowledge. This translation thus extends the aims of *EWIC* itself, as it expands its accessibility to a larger number of specialized researchers and scholars living in the Arab world, possibly leading to an activation of research in cultural and women's studies in Arabic, through introducing the methodologies, paradigms, and sources presented in *EWIC*, and hence spurring further epistemological interaction, through processes of continuity or contestation as well as other forms of intellectual and academic interaction.

In what follows, I begin by presenting some theoretical concerns related to translation, then discuss the problematics of translating an encyclopedic work of the size and with the content of *EWIC*. I then give examples of the main issues that surfaced during translation process. In the context of encyclopedic knowledge production, I will look at the translation process and outcome theoretically, in the light of translation studies, in an attempt to tackle some of the problematics of translating *EWIC*, in terms of transferring and hence producing encyclopedic knowledge about women and Islamic cultures in Arabic.

THEORETICAL CONCERNS AND TRANSLATION STRATEGIES

Accurate translation of a specialized text requires the translator to have extensive specialized knowledge. This can prove difficult when translation in general continues to be governed more by professionalism than by specialization. Lawrence Venuti discusses the idea of "simpatico translation," by which he refers to an affinity between author and translator: "The translator should not merely get along with the author, not merely find him [or her] likeable; there should also be an identity between them" (1995, 275, 273). Immanuel Wallerstein, in his article on the problems of translating concepts in the social sciences, moves beyond "affinity" and requires specialization:

> The translator must be someone not merely skilled in translation as a generalized technique but familiar with the literature of the

subfield over a long period of time, and preferably someone with a direct interest in the material under discussion in the text. This ideal will never be realized until we move towards the creation of a body of translators specialized in the social sciences and trained in both translation techniques and social science. (1981, 89)

Wallerstein further explains the "appalling" results of translation in the social sciences caused by the lack of specialization. The same applies to the translation into Arabic of texts in gender and women's studies.

It was a challenge to identify translators with knowledge and interest in cultural and women's studies. Instead of our preparing a list of well-known professional translators, a twofold procedure was carried out: we compiled one list of specialized researchers in cultural studies and women's studies who are proficient in both English and Arabic and another list of professional translators with experience and an interest in translating texts on women, history, and culture. Then the matching process between articles and translators began.

Translation theory points out the general misconception of translation is, as Susan Bassnett describes, "as a secondary activity, as a 'mechanical' rather than a 'creative' process" (1998, 2). Bassnett further explains the "hegemonic distinctions between writing and translating" that lead to a general condition in which the translators become "invisible beings whose literary skills are obliterated" (2006, 173). At the same time, in a conversation between Andrew Chesterman (a theorist) and Emma Wagner (a professional), they point out that the result of a translation project is supposed to not reveal the translator: "If readers suspect at any point that they are reading a translation, then there must be something wrong with it"; it is either a bad translation or a translation of a translated text (2002, 29). In this sense, translation theory refers to the translator's implied "invisibility," as traditional translation valorizes the transparency of the translated text, in which the translator remains invisible, while the author retains prominence. According to this trend, the more the text seems to be original, and the less it betrays the translator's presence, the higher it is ranked. Again Venuti explains "the illusion of transparency":

> The illusion of transparency is an effect of fluent discourse, of the translator's effort to insure easy readability by adhering to current usage, maintaining continuous syntax, fixing a precise meaning.

> What is so remarkable here is that this illusory effect conceals the numerous conditions under which the translation is made, starting with the translator's crucial intervention in the foreign text. The more fluent the translation, the invisible the translator, and presumably the more visible the writer or the meaning of the foreign text. (1995, 1–2)

Looking at the translator's invisibility through a feminist lens, invisibility becomes unacceptable, since feminism, in theory and practice, is concerned with restoring women from a history of marginalization, silencing, and obscurity. It is therefore self-evident that in the translation of *EWIC*, and any translation carried out by a feminist, there would be a consciousness of the dynamics leading to the subordination of the translator; and to accommodate agency, there would even be a strategic acknowledgment of the role of the translator, as well as his or her being given space for overt self-expression.

In addition to the critique of invisibility, there are other factors to consider: the past few decades have witnessed further serious revision and critique, as deconstruction and postmodernism gave rise to the idea of translation as rewriting, translation as representation, and translation as interpretation. Stephen Davis Ross, for instance, underscores the role of the translator in his or her involvement in selection and judgment during the translation process, and results that reflect representation rather than synonymity and equivalence (1981,14-18). Moreover, selection and representation suggest the prevalence of interpretation, which is by definition subjective and ideological (Tymoczko 1999, 24), and it is in this sense both a skill and an art (Straight 1991, 48). Being the translation editor of *EWIC Arabic*, I therefore consciously and intentionally included a "Note on Translation" to offer an explanation of the process that governed the selection of equivalents in the translation of gender-related terminology.

Taking into consideration the nature of the translated text, it becomes clear that the translation of *EWIC* is not merely an effort to transfer the text of this encyclopedia from the English language into the Arabic, but also an attempt to highlight dimensions related to the linguistic and cultural contexts in the transference of knowledge and the concomitant process of the production of knowledge in Arabic. In her introduction to *EWIC*, Suad Joseph refers to the characteristic of encyclopedias, seeing these compilations as representing "a particular and peculiar form of knowledge" and noting their tendency "to stabilize concepts." She adds that such "presumptions of encyclopedic knowledge production were problematic" to the editors of *EWIC*, who "wanted to destabilize concepts, complicate ideas, document the 'fuzziness' of reality" (2003, xxiv). The translation itself follows a similar position, reflected in the strategies emerging from *EWIC Arabic*.

Given these theoretical concerns, and in an attempt to foreground the translation process as well as to avoid the stabilization of concepts in Arabic, and because there has been a team of translators working on *EWIC Arabic*, two major translation strategies were adopted in the resulting translation. First, *EWIC Arabic* intentionally seeks to destabilize concepts through maintaining a sense of variety in the translation of certain terms and concepts—a feature that was consciously kept present throughout the revision and editing processes as long as it provided a degree of flexibility that would prevent stabilizing concepts, while at the same time producing a translation that reflects the philosophy governing the original text. Yet sometimes terms and words had to be unified on the basis of the role of *EWIC Arabic* in knowledge production and the formulation of Arabic terms of expression for this knowledge.

The other general strategy underlying the translation has to do with shattering the "illusion of transparency" by means of relying on several translators (to create a stylistic variety mirroring the differences created in *EWIC* by virtue of its large body of contributors). Moreover, as mentioned above, the translation process was further highlighted through the inclusion of the note on translation at the beginning of *EWIC Arabic*, so as to give due credit to the translation process and involve the readers in the translation decisions. And finally, a glossary was added at the end, not with the intention of stabilizing terms, but as a means of presenting the outcome of the translators' efforts in finding and coining "equivalent" terms to those in the original text. It is, to my knowledge, the first such English-Arabic glossary of gender-related terms prepared in the epistemological framework of cultural studies and women's studies.

PROBLEMATICS OF TRANSLATING *EWIC*

As writing is in itself a "translation" of thought and culture, and involves its transference from the realm of intellectual awareness and cultural experience to the world of letters and words, so too the process of translation is in itself a "rewriting" that involves transferring written thought and culture into another culture-bound language. Therefore, translation theories refer to several modes of translation, including free, literal, and explanatory translations. There are, furthermore, two main methods of translation, which Tymoczko applies to the postcolonial context:

> In translation studies a distinction is often made between "bringing the text to the audience" and "bringing the audience to the text." The same type of distinction can be projected with respect to postcolonial writing: some texts make more severe demands on the audience, requiring the audience to conform to the beliefs, customs, language and literary formalism of the source culture, while other works conform more to the dominant audience's cultural, linguistic and literary expectations. (1999, 29–30)

In both cases, translation theory goes hand in hand with reception theory, in terms of sensitivity to the readers' cultural, social, political, and other backgrounds. Thus, the translator's starting point is the "source text," which is subjected to linguistic analysis hand in hand with sensitivity to its cultural nuances, followed by its transference to another language—a process requiring a re-creation of a linguistic and cultural text, necessitating a great extent of linguistic competence together with knowledge and creativity, while at the same time restricted by limitations that guarantee production of a translation that is as close as possible to the original text in style, form, and content. Translation is founded on both guidelines and vision, combining knowledge, craft and art.

EWIC Arabic is not merely a project that can be studied from the perspective of translation studies alone, but involves gender and women's studies as well as cultural studies. It is a translation project insofar as it expresses linguistic sensitivity and reveals an awareness of the major trends in translation theory that generate its translation strategies. However, the choices made in this process are closely linked to a deep feminist consciousness of the gender power relations governing women's lives and Islamic cultures, as expressed in life and through language. And finally, the translation of *EWIC* emerges as a cultural project—a work inflected by and reflecting the powers of representation, interpretation, and knowledge production. I will now give examples of the problematics of translating *EWIC* into Arabic, manifesting the intersection of language, feminism, and power politics in producing knowledge about women.

The Title

I consider first the translation of the title, *Encyclopedia of Women and Islamic Cultures*, and particularly the word "women."[3] "Women" appears in the English title in the plural form, yet the fact that it is translated into the plural form in Arabic is not a matter of literal translation. When applying the common translation of "women" from English into Arabic, the use of the singular form in Arabic might be required, as a standard feature of the language, in which the singular is often used in reference to a general group. For example, "International Women's Day," "Women's Rights" and "Arab Women" would be translated into the Arabic equivalents of "Yawm al-Mar'a al-'lam," "Huq q al-Mar'a," and "Al-Mar'a al-'Arabiyya," respectively. The same applies to other concepts and formulas taken from the English, and consequently the title of the encyclopedia should logically be translated using the singular form in Arabic. Yet an understanding of the distinction between the concepts of "woman" and "women" in feminist theory, taking into account the emphasis on cultural diversity and plurality among women instead of dealing with "women" as a monolithic term and a singular entity, implies an understanding of cultural nuances and theoretical backgrounds, which cross the boundaries of word and text, almost forcing the translator into using the plural form in Arabic, with all the epistemological meanings and implications connecting the text to feminist discourse and feminist theory. This example reveals the importance of recognizing the significance of specific words during translation and shows that the translation of many words is not a mechanical process but requires a good deal of reflection, consideration, and selection.

Thus, the use of the word "women" in the title of *EWIC Arabic* is not a matter of literal translation of the English word, but is a linguistic and cultural translation and is in itself a contribution to the production of knowledge in Arabic through a stress on the significance of differentiating between "woman" and "women" in reference to a plural concept. Similarly, "women's studies" as the name of a discipline dealing with the theories and praxis of studies about women based on feminist theory, is translated here as the plural "al-Dir s t al-Nis 'iyya," instead of the phrase more commonly used in Arabic, in the singular form, "Dir s t al-Mar'a." This choice, again, derives from the singular form's implications that perpetuate an understanding of women within a monolithic formula instead of suggesting the variety of women's experiences and the multiplicity of women's identities.

Translating "Gender"

Standard English–Arabic dictionaries (such as *Al-Mughni al-Kabir* [1998] and *Al-Awwal* [n.d.b.]) limit the translation of "gender" to *al-jins*, which is the equivalent of "sex" in reference to the biological categories of male/female, or "gender" in the linguistic sense of masculine/feminine forms. The Academy of the Arabic Language (n.d.a.), regarded as the highest authority in translation and coinage of new terminology in Arabic, translates "gender" as *al-jins* and *al-naw'*. "Gender" translated as *al-jins* is further explained as referring to the state of an individual in terms of male and female; whereas *al-naw'* is defined as "a term which has become common recently instead of sex in cultural anthropology. It is used to distinguish between males and females, and it combines both biological and cultural characteristics as being the foundations or factors determining the social status of the male and female, as well as the role each of them plays in the society under study." Yet in practice, the translation of the term "gender" into Arabic carries more variety, in itself as much as in its derivative forms. The development of the term in women's studies and Western feminism, with all its sociocultural implications, was reflected in its translation into Arabic with the increase in its usage in Arabic writings and translations since the 1990s.

An early common translation of the word "gender" was an explanatory one—*al-naw' al-ijtim'*, meaning "social gender," soon simplified as *al-naw'* in the fields of development and social sciences—and became widely used after extensive translation of developmental documents and material under the auspices of international development organizations. In the context of cultural studies, another explanatory translation appeared as "the sociocultural construction of the sexes" and was used by prominent feminist scholars, such as Hoda Elsadda, in their writings in Arabic. By contrast, with the growing understanding of its meanings and implications, making the term self-explanatory, the journal *Alif* proposes *al-jun sa* as a translation of "gender" ("Editorial" 1999). *Al-jun sa* was created in an attempt to move beyond the search for an equivalent meaning of "gender" and into the process of coining the term *al-jun sa* by deriving it from the Arabic root (*j n s*), a parallel with the terms *al-thuk ra* (masculinity) and *al-'un tha* (femininity). The new term was seen as being open to further development. However, *al-jun sa* has not received general acceptance since its introduction in *Alif*.[4] Meanwhile, we notice that the word *al-jender* (gender) is being increasingly used, now found frequently in Arabic writings and enjoying derivational flexibility through the application of Arabic grammatical rules to the root (*j n d r*).

Consequently, it was inevitable during the production of *EWIC Arabic* that the issue of translating "gender" would arise. Looking back at the history of the translation of the term into Arabic it becomes evident that the word *al-naw'* does not carry the cultural connotations or the feminist dimensions that are essential to the term. I also claim that because of the extent and constantly repeated usage of this translation in development literature and some sociological writings, the word *al-naw'* carries developmental connotations when used, for instance, in literary or political contexts. However, for a person such as myself, coming from a background of literary studies, the term *al-naw'* initially denotes "genre" rather than "gender." I therefore consider it too limited and not an appropriate equivalent to the notion of "gender." Concerning the explanatory phrase "the socio-cultural construction of the sexes," it is obvious to me that it stresses the limitations prevalent in *al-naw,'* which required an explanatory translation when using the term "gender" in contexts other than a developmental one, and particularly in the field of cultural studies.

Now, with the widespread use of the concept of gender in Arabic, and the fact that it has become self-explanatory to the majority of specialized readers, I find it logical to use the word "gender" transliterated in Arabic, because of its cultural and epistemological connotations and implications, particularly when used within a feminist discourse. *Al-jender* is therefore used in *EWIC Arabic* as a translation of the same word in English, not as an easy way out, but based on a recognition of the specificity of the term—its history, meanings, connotations, and implications. The word "gender" is among the most problematic terms in Arabic translation—a complexity intensified by the fact that it is often understood in the Arabic sociocultural context as a foreign concept; and since it implies the empowerment of women, it is looked upon with skepticism, if not rejected altogether. Thus the Arabic translation of the word "gender" mainly appears in feminist and development contexts, and the Arabic equivalent is not yet well-defined. Arabic seems still to be in the process of experimentation with the translation of "gender"; so as part of this experimentation, and with the hope of reaching a comfortable equivalent of the word in Arabic, I, as the translation editor, was given the right, by WMF, to take the responsibility of, and for, selecting the translation of "gender" in *EWIC Arabic*. Again, whenever the issue was raised with the translators, they provided their own suggestions, but accepted my final decision as translation editor. It is a choice for which I consider myself fully responsible.

This decision was encouraged by the fact that Arabic has always assimilated and appropriated words from other languages (for example the word *al-firdaws* comes from "paradise") and there are modern examples of foreign words being easily Arabicized (for example: *d moqr tiya* and *l ber liya*) without sensitivity and even being subjected to Arabic morphological and syntactical rules. However, the word *al-jender* does not appear here in its derivational forms because they have not been yet widely used in Arabic; the aim in *EWIC Arabic* is to suggest its use rather than insist on its derivatives. It is through the articles appearing in *EWIC Arabic* that an attempt is made to promote the use of the word *al-jender* as an Arabic translation of the English word (and notion of) "gender," instead of equivalent and explanatory translations, which have been still used here in the sentences and contexts using "gender" in its derivative forms.

Explanatory Translation

Unlike the term "gender," which does not seem to require explanation in specialized writings, we faced a term for which we could not but use an explanatory translation. Seham Abdel-Salam and Aida Seif el-Dawla, in two of the articles they were translating, faced the term "queer" in relation to specific sexual individual and group identities. Although the word "queer" (*kw r*) has started appearing in Arabic on certain Web sites, it remains unknown to the vast majority of the public; hence the demand for an explanatory translation of the concept, which had not developed with its sexual and cultural connotations up to the 1990s.

The word "queer" appears in volume 1 of *EWIC* in two entries: Nadine Naber's "North America: Early Twentieth Century to Present" and Frédéric Lagrange's "Sexualities and Queer Studies," translated by Aida Seif el-Dawla and Seham Abdel-Salam, respectively. Aida and Seham involved me in the problem facing them in the translation of this term, for which there does not yet exist in Arabic an accurate equivalent that is reflective of its gender and political dimensions.⁵ So far, when not using a transliteration of "queer," the word is usually mistranslated in terms of either the judgmental notion of "deviance" (*shudhudh*) or through the misguided oversimplification in "gays and lesbians" (*mithliyyun wa mithliyyat*). Aida, Seham, and I worked on a translation of "queer"; during our discussions and our endeavors to come up with the closest possible translation, Aida suggested the use of the phrase *al-hawiy t al-jinsiya al-l namatiya*, more or less equivalent to "atypical sexual identities."⁶

The significance of this formulation, at this stage of translation, lies in translating the term into a value-free explanatory equivalent; and the focus was therefore placed on a sexual identity and its reference particularly to a specific atypical identity. As we put forward this explanatory translation of "queer," we are well aware of its shortcoming in highlighting a gender identity ("gender" being already a problematic term in its translation into Arabic). Nevertheless, with the current absence of an equivalent of "queer" in Arabic, we hope that perhaps with an increasing interest in tackling and writing about this issue in Arabic in the years to come, translation alternatives will appear, either turning the word "queer" into a familiar term in Arabic, or using shorter derivative forms (such as *al-l namatiya*" and so on).

Addition

One example of conscious addition can be found in the translation of nouns from English into Arabic. In English, nouns as such are not marked as masculine or feminine—unlike proper names and pronouns. Hence the noun "researcher" in English is not restricted to a particular gender but is applied to both the feminine and masculine. The predominant translation of "researcher" into Arabic is *b hith*, which is limited, and excludes the feminine, dismissing the possibility of the English noun's reference to *b hitha*. This could not be ignored in an encyclopedia based on feminist theories and feeding into women's studies. Therefore, such nouns appear in *EWIC Arabic* in phrases that include the nouns in a conjunction of the feminine and masculine forms (for example, *al-b hith wal-b hitha* or *al-mutarjima wal-mutarjim*), following the grammatical rules of Arabic, except of course in cases where a noun clearly refers to the masculine or feminine through concrete qualifiers (proper nouns or pronouns).

The issue acquires more complexity in the case of the plural form, as according to Arabic grammar, the noun in masculine plural form can include both men and women. We chose not to abide by the rule, at the same time not to break it; hence the translation of, for instance, "researchers" as "*al-b hith n wal-b hith t.*" Here, the addition in Arabic of the noun in feminine form expresses an ideological stance, stressing equality between men and women and reflecting *EWIC*'s feminist discourse. Apart from the linguistic accuracy in translation, the repetition of Arabic phrases, which include both feminine and masculine forms, is an attempt on our part to establish the use of conjunction, moving toward a linguistic balance that reflects a feminist position in form and content.

CONCLUSION

If the act of translation refers, indirectly, to the existing imbalance in access to and production of knowledge, then the process of translating *EWIC* is a form of resistance to this inequality and an attempt at spreading specialized knowledge by presenting the methodologies, paradigms, and sources related to women's studies and Islamic cultures, with the aim of encouraging interaction and propagating further research in Arabic. Translation is also a process of knowledge production in Arabic, particularly since it involves the work of a group of researchers and scholars specialized in Islamic cultures intersecting with Arabic culture/s.

In this sense, I view translation as a political act that seeks to spread knowledge and prevent the monopolization of access to and production of knowledge. Moreover, providing researchers and scholars in the Arab region with access to *EWIC* allows for more balance in making the methodologies, paradigms, and sources used by Western-based scholars available to Arab-based researchers and scholars, who can thus combine their own experiences, methodologies, and sources with those presented in *EWIC*. And finally, the role of translation carried out by the Women and Memory Forum in Egypt goes hand in hand with our political role in resisting epistemological hegemony and empowering Arab women. This is achieved here through translation, which creates a discourse in its own right, and through the production of knowledge in Arabic on the basis of feminist consciousness.

HALA KAMAL is an assistant professor at Cairo University and is coordinator of the Translation Project at the Women and Memory Forum.

NOTES

1. *EWIC* includes six volumes: vol. 1, *Methodologies, Paradigms and Sources* (2003; translated into Arabic); vol. 2, *Family, Law and Politics* (2005); vol. 3, *Family, Body, Sexuality, and Health* (2006); vol. 4, *Economics, Education, Mobility, and Space*; vol. 5, *Practices, Interpretations, and Representations*; and vol. 6, *Supplement and Index* (vols. 4–6 forthcoming).

See http://sjoseph.ucdavis.edu/ewic/. The translation is available in a free online edition, at http://sjoseph.ucdavis.edu/ewic/volume1.htm.

2. The Women and Memory Forum (WMF) is an Egyptian research center, registered as a nonprofit nongovernmental organization, concerned with the study of women in Egyptian and Arab history. The founding members are a group of Egyptian women academics, who seek to combine research with activism. The main WMF projects include the Archive of Voices (women's biography project); Memory Papers (published studies); Storytelling (re/writing fairytales from a feminist perspective); Translation Project; and working toward the establishment of a specialized library and documentation center. The Translation Project currently involves the production of seven readers in Arabic on gender and feminism. For more information on the Women and Memory Forum, see http://www.womenandmemory.org.

3. I am focusing my discussion here on the translation of the word "women." The translation process problematizes the term "women" versus "woman," while it accepts and retains the original usage of the phrase "women *and* Islamic cultures." In her elaborate introduction to vol. 1 of *EWIC*, Suad Joseph mentions that the initial title of this project was *Encyclopedia of Women in the Muslim World*. Although she does not explain the reasoning behind the change of title, Women and Islamic Cultures proves more inclusive, as it involves women in relation to Islamic cultures in different parts of the world (including non-Muslim countries). http://www.arabicacademy.org.eg/FrontEnd/SearchResult.aspx?key=gender.

4. In her article "Translating Gender," Samia Mehrez (2007) explores the derivational process of *al-Jun sa* and promotes its usage in Arabic as a replacement to all other alternatives.

5. In his comprehensive recent study of Arab sexual identity politics, Joseph Massad (2007) refers to the Arab versions and translations of identities such as gays, lesbians, and transvestites. However, he does not tackle the "queer" identity, nor does he address the forms of existence (or absence) of its cultural equivalent in the Arab world or the Arabic language.

6. *Al-hawiy t al-jinsiya al-l namatiya* is a phrase combined of three words: *al-hawiy t*, which means "identities"; *al-jinsiya*, which can be roughly translated as "sexual;" and *al- l namatiya*, which means "atypical." It is worth noting that *al-jinsiya* is derived from the Arabic word *jins*, which carries old and new meanings, including "sex," "biological sex," "national origin," and "type" or "kind," which are in turn derived originally from the Greek *genos*—the origin of the English "gender." For more on the cultural history of the word *jins* and its derivatives in Arabic, see, for example, Massad 2007, 171–72.

WORKS CITED

Bassnett, Susan. 1988. New York: Routledge.

———. 2006. "Writing and Translating." In *The Translator as Writer,* ed. Susan Bassnett and Peter Bush. New York: Continuum.

Chesterman, Andrew, and Emma Wagner. 2002. *Can Translation Help Translators? A Dialogue Between the Ivory Tower and the Wordface.* Manchester, U.K.: St. Jerome's.

"Editorial." 1999. "Gender and Knowledge: Contribution of Gender Perspectives to Intellectual Formations." Special issue, *Alif: Journal of Comparative Poetics* (American University in Cairo) 19:6–7.

"Gender." 1998. *Al-Mughni Al-Kabir: A Dictionary of Contemporary English (English-Arabic).* Beirut, Librarie du Liban.

"Gender." n.d.a. Academy of the Arabic Language. http://www.arabicacademy.org.eg/FrontEnd/search.aspx.

"Gender." n.d.b. *Al-Awwal English-Arabic Dictionary.* http://www.al-awwal.com/formpost4.asp.

Joseph, Saud. 2003. Introduction to *Encyclopedia of Women and Islamic Cultures.* Vol. 1, *Methodologies, Paradigms, and Sources.* Boston: Brill. Available online at http://sjoseph.ucdavis.edu/ewic/volume1.htm.

Joseph, Suad, et al., eds. 2003. *Encyclopedia of Women and Islamic Cultures.* Vol. 1, *Methodologies, Paradigms, and Sources.* Boston: Brill. Available online at http://sjoseph.ucdavis.edu/ewic/volume1.htm.

Massad, Joseph A. 2007. *Desiring Arabs.* Chicago: University of Chicago Press.

Mehrez, Samia. "Translating Gender." *Journal of Middle East Women's Studies* 3(1):106–27.

Ross, Stephen, Davis. 1981. "Translation and Similarity." In *Translation Spectrum: Essays in Theory and Practice,* ed. Marilyn Gaddis Rose. Albany: State University of New York Press.

Straight, H. Stephen. 1981. "Knowledge, Purpose, and Intuition: Three Dimensions in the Evaluation of Translation." In *Translation Spectrum: Essays in Theory and Practice,* ed. Marilyn Gaddis Rose. Albany: State University of New York Press.

Tymoczko, Maria. 1999. "Post-colonial Writing and Literary Translation." In *Postcolonial Translation: Theory and Practice,* ed. Susan Bassnett and Harish Trivedi. New York: Routledge,.

Venuti, Lawrence. 1995. *The Translator's Invisibility: A History of Translation.* New York: Routledge.

Wallerstein, Immanuel. 1981. "Concepts in the Social Sciences: Problems of Translation." In *Translation Spectrum: Essays in Theory and Practice,* ed. Marilyn Gaddis Rose. Albany: State University of New York Press.

TRANS GENITAL BLUEPRINT

JOHN NEFF

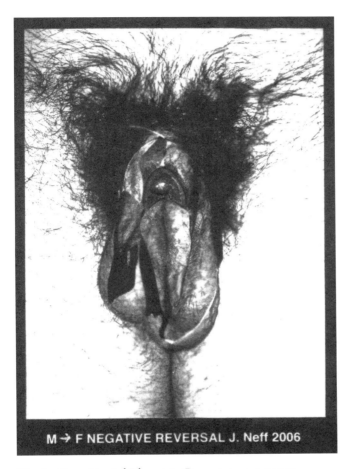

Fig. 1. *Trans Genital Blueprint.* Cyanotype on paper. 8 1/2 x 11 inches. Image courtesy of Western Exhibitions

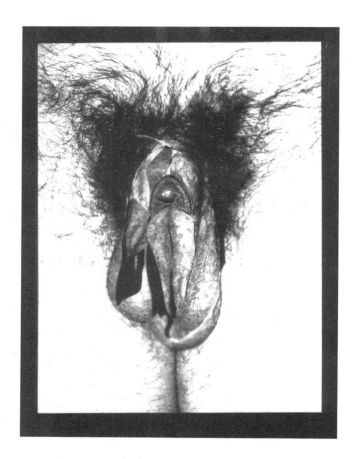

Fig. 2. *Trans Genital Blueprint* (Etching). Cyanotype on paper. 8 1/2 x 11 inches. Image courtesy of Western Exhibitions

This work is from Neff's *Trans Genital Blueprints* series, a collection of unique cyanotypes (literally blueprints). All of the prints were exposed using the same negative, a photographic transparency of Neff's male genitals that was cut and reassembled to depict a schematic vagina.

JOHN NEFF produces works of art, organizes gallery exhibitions and practices short-form critical writing. He lives and works in Chicago.

TRANSPARENT

SUSAN DAVID BERNSTEIN

I'll begin with an incident when my child was seven years old. Nora and her father, Daniel, take a bike ride with Hannah, also seven, and her father, Roger. They have matching "alley cats," third wheels with seats and handlebars that attach just behind the seats of their fathers' bikes. This way, they can pedal when they like and get some sense of what balancing on a bike is all about, yet they're always being pulled along by the master biker up front—an interactive metaphor for modern parenting.

When they take a water break, Nora mentions that she wants to have a "sex change." Hannah asks, "Daddy, what's a sex change?" at which point Roger, who occasionally works as an EMT, launches into a rather long-winded and detailed explanation, much more than we imagine Nora could possibly know.

As Daniel tells me about this sex change exchange, I cringe at what Hannah's parents probably think—what responsible parent would tell a six-year-old about gender reassignment, transsexuality, and the like? Well, I would, although not with graphic accounts, but simply to open up the possibilities of gender; after all, it's a commonplace to encourage children to try on all sorts of identities. But I quickly learned that many adults prefer the disciplining of gender in children rather than the threat of experimentation.

When Nora was around four or five years old, I read her a book published in the 1970s, called *What Is a Boy? What Is a Girl?* by Stephanie Waxman. Photographs of children are coupled with text that runs like this: "What is a boy? Some people say a boy is someone with short hair. But Mimi has short hair. And she's a girl." All the usual suspects in gender-profiling parade across the pages with a child of the opposite sex pictured to upset the typecasting. The finale, Nora's favorite bit, sports in a row of pages four photographs: a girl, a boy, a man, and a woman, all fully and frontally nude, with the females pictured on a beach with plenty of ocean in the background, conjuring up Botticelli's *Birth of Venus*. The text here nails the thesis down: "Then what *is* a girl? A girl is someone with a vulva and a vagina. Every girl has a vulva and a vagina." And for the adult version: "If you are a girl, you will grow up to be a woman. Every woman has a vulva and a vagina."

Because I admired the book's eloquently simple boldness, I had given a copy to a friend's daughter. This friend laughed at the certitude, the essentialism, of this argument: "Judith Butler wouldn't agree with that!" Butler's *Gender Trouble* and *Undoing Gender* make mincemeat out of the notion of an unchanging gender identity fixed at birth by the "nature" of someone's genitals. I think it was probably in the spirit of gently troubling gender that I said to Nora, when reading the pages about the sex paraphernalia of "every man" or "every woman," that once in a while boys grow up and decide to be women, and the other way too. Had I known someone who'd gone through gender reassignment, I might have offered an illustrative story. So I left the matter as a rather abstract aside, but apparently in Nora's variously asserted plans for the future, the idea stuck.

I soon learned that it's not possible to "gently" undo gender, because adult tolerance for transchildren is low. A friend who teaches a women's studies undergraduate course on gender and sexuality asked me to describe to her class some of Nora's gender-bending episodes. One student responded by asking if I had enlisted psychiatric counseling for Nora's "disorder." Another wondered why I would "allow" my child to assume a transgendered identity at the age of seven. In that classroom discussion, I had been careful not to use the lexicon of the new gender politics while exploring Nora's mixed-gender expressions precisely because I understood such experimenting with "sex change," as Nora put it, as a crucial aspect of childhood play, something miles away from adult life-altering decisions. Yet the reactions from many people, including those in a university women's studies course, were more accusatory than laudatory. Did my playful parenting around gender open up floodgates of trouble that might dog Nora into puberty? I am lured by the fantasy of a mapped line between the social and the biological. And while I want to believe that it's nurture rather than nature that largely explains how we turn into people, this theory entails an overwhelming responsibility that comes with the power of parenting. At the same time, my encouragement of Nora's sex and gender play at age two, four, or six is only a leavening agent of the massive cultural forces of gender and sexual normativity that surround any child from birth—and now, increasingly, before that.

It was sometime in her seventh year when Nora began to ask for a short haircut. I discouraged this, saying that she would be mistaken for a boy, just to test her resolve (and, I suppose, my own ambivalence), which passed with flying colors. A week after she turned seven, Nora got her wish. Her blonde curls were clipped off by my own hairdresser. Sally gave us a few magazines on hairstyles to flip through because she wanted a picture of what kind of haircut we had in mind. Nora chose plain, boxy, bland haircuts, all worn by boys. I picked out a few with modish lines, spiky and interesting, all worn by girls or women. We couldn't agree, and Sally acted as mediator, remarking, "Well, at least this gives me some ideas." She seemed versed in this sort of diplomacy. I found it distressing to watch those golden locks, although they were mousy brown from the shampooing, fall to the floor, and so midway through that haircut, I decided to leave for twenty minutes. It was one of those pivotal parenthood moments when I realized I couldn't control my child's appearance or competently manipulate her desires anymore. I suppose I could have refused to take her for the haircut. I could have come up with subterfuges and tried scare tactics, or just flat out not taken her. But I wanted Nora to be able to exercise the freedom to experiment with how she put herself together for the world. When I returned, Sally had put some mousse in Nora's cropped hair. She looked adorable—"baby dyke," one friend called her new look.

I took this remark to mean Nora had a hip hairdo, yet I began to discover the ways in which people overlay gender style with assumptions about sexuality. Does gender at seven have much of anything to say about sexual identity at seventeen? Is Nora by virtue of her hair and dress now on the fast track of the lesbian continuum or is her penchant for a boy-look the signs of budding transgenderhood? I'm shocked by my visceral response of worry that my child might have to weather the blistering challenges of being differently sexed and gendered. Yet I expect these hurdles shrink compared with a generation ago when there were no LBGTQA groups or gay-straight alliances, now standard items on many American high school club menus. As for the baby dyke 'do, Nora wasn't into hair goos and gunk, and eventually that boxy, bland boy's style she'd selected and I'd rejected framed her face on a daily basis.

This haircut opened up the sluice valves of gender confusion, and Nora handled it like a trooper. As a baby and toddler, she was frequently taken for a boy because Daniel and I didn't mark her gender through colors, styles, and patterns with dolls or flowers. I quickly learned that masculinity is the default gender; when in doubt, people assume "boy." I never corrected strangers who would engage a toddling Nora at airports or in stores as a "little guy" or "young man" because what did it matter? But when they caught on, by overhearing "Nora," we were showered with profuse apologies and absurd attempts at recovery: "Oh, of course—with that smile" or "with those eyelashes," as if boys come preloaded without grins and standard facial parts.

A month after the haircut, we were checking into a hotel in Atlanta, and while we sorted out reservation details at the front desk, Nora was entertaining an employee with some choice conversation. I wasn't really paying attention until it was time to find our room, and then I heard the reception clerk saying, "You're such a smart little guy! Hey, buddy, what grade are you in?" Nora answered, "Second." Wanting to get settled in our room, I said, "Come on, Nora." The woman had the good sense to allow the name to unsettle her assumption, but not without registering her amazement, "You're a girl! Get out of here, really??"

Nora reported that she liked fooling people about her gender, and that's why she didn't correct them. But she didn't always appreciate the crooked stares that were pitched her way in public restrooms. She told me, "They give me these looks like, 'You're so cute—too bad you can't read the sign on the door.'" At school older girls who didn't know her told her she didn't belong in the girls' room. Once Nora came home from school absolutely delighted with herself. An unfamiliar woman had encountered Nora in the girls' room and said, with a smile, "I think this is the girls' room!" and Nora, echoing the woman's intonation, quipped, "I think I'm a girl!"

As is evident from these anecdotes, the haircut at seven matched Nora's wardrobe preferences. She didn't like dresses, regarded shades of pink and floral patterns as a vampire would garlic, and began asking to wear swimming trunks like boys rather than suits like girls. Daniel explained about "mores" in our society that decree that women's breasts should be covered up in public places, to which Nora replied, "I don't have breasts yet. When I do, I'll wear a suit." We're suckers for logic, but still, I desisted. "You'll be teased by all the kids at the pool who know you."

Nora's sartorial desires spread to ties, vests, Oxford shirts, and sport coats. Even nearing age eleven, when many other girls are sprouting breast buds, Nora continued to prefer to go topless in the summer heat. During her twelfth summer, we were at a picnic where boys were running about on the lawn wearing only shorts. Nora, at this point fully aware of the stares and discomfort from girls her own age at her penchant for toplessness, turned to the assembled group of parents and asked, "Would anyone be offended if I took my shirt off?"

"No, go right ahead," said one of the parents, with a smile, as Nora whipped off her shirt and trotted toward the kids under the sprinkler across the grass. No one seemed to skip a beat with this remarkable request. I figured this low-key response had more to do with the fact that the other children were younger boys, but of course I don't really know what these parents thought. I was proud of Nora's moxie to pursue her style of herself. At the same time, I noticed and paused, wondering where this seeming self-confidence against the tide of how girls her age are expected to dress or undress will take her. I marvel at some kind of interior psychological upholstery I certainly didn't possess as a child or an adolescent. But wouldn't it be easier somehow if she were more a sheep in a flock of girls than a gender renegade?

The most surprising discoveries I've stumbled upon in this transparent adventure are the divergences among adults on issues of gender fashioning. I hadn't sensed anything aberrant or alarming in Nora's exploratory trying out—sometimes merely through talking—different gender identities. But the reactions of other parents around me gave me pause—was I too haphazard, too naive, about all this? By not enforcing clearly the norms of gender around her body, was I stage-crafting scenes of transitioning and eventual social disasters? Some people have applauded the kind of permission we've given Nora around gender. But stray comments here and there, such as the remarks of the students in the women's studies course, make manifest that some see Nora's parents as doing her a disservice by not encouraging her to package herself generally around more clear-cut models of young femininity.

I've learned to appreciate a cautious conservatism among children who cling to consistency and sameness as their bodies and minds whirl rapidly toward full sized. But I hadn't quite expected that most adults are, at the end of the day, like most children. Is my parenting that powerful? Did Daniel and I nudge her into this sex change fascination by not dressing her regularly in girl style, by introducing the idea that sometimes people do switch from "f" to "m," or experiment with gender borders? I have heard so many nearly identical accounts of feminist parenting at home overshadowed by a culture of he-men and she-women where children are bombarded continually with images of well-defined binary genders of blue and pink, trucks and dolls.

And then I wonder what this gender conflation experimenting must feel like for Nora out in the world. Besides the endless incidents of public restroom harassment, the passing assumptions of strangers who talk to Nora as "buddy" or "he" or "him," the accumulation of particular incidents, must take some toll on how she sees herself. Or do all these experiences contribute to a remarkable stamina and resourcefulness? Once when we were on holiday with some friends in England whose two daughters hadn't seen Nora in a year or two, these children didn't want to undress in front of her because she looked like a boy. Although they knew that the Nora from before was a girl, they were caught in a dilemma given the evidence before their eyes. We parents had to insist again and again on our child's gender. What could this feel like to her?

As Nora headed toward her twelfth birthday, she reflected that she'd like to be a boy and a man until she wants to have children, then after she's given birth a few times, she would decide whether to continue as a woman or switch back to a man. "It's a man's world," she became fond of saying. And although this realization somehow grated on me, it's of a piece with a feminist or gender-ranting susceptibility that Nora has exhibited for some years now, a sensitivity my unhousewifely suburban mother seemed to imply. Some children appear to be alive to the disabilities of their gender assignment. Nora struggled to see both sides, even more so as puberty loomed on the horizon.

Seven years after Nora's watershed haircut, she remade her gender in what seemed a definitive act. I remember the date, the shopping, and what she said. About to enter a large high school with some trepidation, Nora declared to me, "I want to change how I look. I'm going to grow my hair and get some new clothes." That summer before ninth grade, she traded her baggy cargo shorts for tight jeans and her oversized T-shirts for tank tops, and she grew her hair out, much like someone reverting to the shade underneath the dye. But the way Nora approached her yet newer look made this, too, seem an experiment in gender shaping. That fall, some of her older friends on her sports team took her to the mall to shop for a dress for Homecoming. Nora came back with a tarty, slinky slip of a dress, red, with glitter splattered about the front. Before the dance, her teammates fixed her hair and applied some makeup. Once again, Nora seemed to be dressing up, in costume, even with Halloween around the corner. To me, she was in drag, but then I reflected, "Ah, she's transitioning again." I had mixed feelings still, lamenting the loss of my boy-girl, and steeling myself for battles over too much eyeliner and tight, revealing outfits, and a general uneasiness about an ultralipstick femininity seemingly around the corner.

But that skimpy dress came off along with the cosmetics and femmy hair style, as Nora settled into an in-between mode. She grew her hair below her shoulders, but showed no interest in self-grooming. Often without bothering with a brush, she tied her hair back so that it wouldn't get in her way when she worked out. Athletic, sporty clothes became her new wardrobe, not miles away from the earlier boy-look, but no longer does anyone readily mistake her gender. And while she's alive to the social merits of having a boyfriend, the culture of dating in any direction doesn't seem to interest her. Her high school identity is clearly that of an athlete-scholar.

I have read that we live in a postethnic, postracial, even postnational age of globalization where we're no longer pinned irrevocably to the fixed contours of an identity politics. The "post" is supposed to imply a productive instability and flexibility, and even some kind of choice where everyone has a range of options—perhaps one parent is an Egyptian Muslim, the other is Italian Catholic, and so the offspring of this person decides to go with the former identity, at least for a while. Although I'm a bit wary of the concept of "choice" here, maybe my transparent story is about a culture transitioning into a postgender era. Clearly Nora has resisted in different ways the imperative to check either "F" or "M" on the forms, so to speak. A late-Victorian poet and novelist, Amy Levy, who may have been a lesbian, smoked cigarettes and styled herself masculine in a sketch of herself in her room at Newnham College. Levy longed for a future culture in which women would no longer be categorized as either wife or spinster. Thus she concluded her poem, "A Ballad of Religion and Marriage," written shortly before her suicide in 1889:

> Grant, in a million years at most
> Folk shall be neither pairs nor odd—
>   Alas! we sha'n't be there to boast
> "Marriage has gone the way of God!"(2006, 235)

Let's hope that the either/or straitjacket of gender and sexuality is waning in productive ways now, long before Levy's ironic "in a million years at most." At least, the possibilities seem manifold compared with what I saw and knew in my own firmly gendered childhood. My mother schooled me into the conventions of femininity of the 1950s and 1960s with all the accouterments—hairstyles with ribbons, curls, barrettes; organdy and lace pinafores and patent-leather shoes; toy cosmetics of candy lipsticks and shadows; ballet and modern dance lessons; and the grand finale, for my teen years, a terrifying course at charm school. But I think my mother was uncertain too, although she did not have any formal discourse such as feminism to convey this. The messages came through underground in ways that made me especially uneasy about the package of domesticated femininity because I had no language to articulate my confusion. Today's multiplication of options, though inevitably a challenge, definitely bespeaks a better chance for adult postgender happiness. Whether mine is a transparent story remains to be seen.

SUSAN DAVID BERNSTEIN teaches at the University of Wisconsin–Madison. She has published on gender and confessional modes in contemporary feminist theory and in the Victorian novel. She is currently working on a study of women writers and activists in the Reading Room of the British Museum, from George Eliot to Virginia Woolf, and on a memoir titled *Unlikely Loves*.

WORK CITED
Levy, Amy. 2006. "A Ballad of Religion and Marriage." In *The Romance of a Shop*, ed. Susan David Bernstein. Peterborough, Ontario: Broadview.

COMPULSORY GENDER AND TRANSGENDER EXISTENCE: ADRIENNE RICH'S QUEER POSSIBILITY

C. L. COLE AND SHANNON L. C. CATE

> *If women are the earliest sources of emotional caring and physical nurture for both female and male children, it would seem logical, from a feminist perspective at least, to pose the following questions: whether the search for love and tenderness in both sexes does not originally lead toward women; why in fact women should ever redirect that search; why species survival, the means of impregnation, and emotional/erotic relationships should ever have become so rigidly identified with each other and why such violent strictures should be found necessary to enforce women's total emotional, erotic loyalty and subservience to men.*
>
> Adrienne Rich,
"Compulsory Heterosexuality and Lesbian Existence"

Adrienne Rich's "Compulsory Heterosexuality and Lesbian Existence," originally published in 1980 in *Signs* and reprinted in numerous publications, immediately unsettled feminist thinking. That the article eventually faded from more recent feminist and queer studies debates has been explained as a result of supposed breaks: between essentialists and post-structuralists, second-wave and next-wave feminists, feminist and queer studies (Hesford 2005, 239). Yet the current interest in Rich's work—especially this particular article—over the past five years seems to suggest a renewed appreciation from a variety of feminisms for the kind of work that Rich was doing in her canonical piece.[1]

We were delighted to receive an invitation to revisit "Compulsory Heterosexuality" in this *WSQ* issue on "trans." Although trans issues are not specifically addressed by Rich, we draw our inspiration from the theme of this issue, to read transgender issues back into the piece's theoretical core.

"Compulsory Heterosexuality and Lesbian Existence" was devoted to denaturalizing heterosexuality. Rich's attention to the many ways heterosexuality was forced upon women began the job of teasing apart how heterosexuality might be understood as a patriarchal tool of control over women and the ways women—even feminists—reproduced it. At the time, this was a challenging idea for many feminists, and Rich knew it. She compiles irrefutable evidence of heterosexuality's coerced nature: "The female wage scale, the enforcement of middle-class women's 'leisure,' the glamorization of so-called sexual liberation, the withholding of education from women, the imagery of 'high art' and popular culture, the mystification of the 'personal' sphere" (223). But she also admits that "to acknowledge that for women, heterosexuality may not be a 'preference' at all, but something that has had to be imposed, managed, organized, propagandized, and maintained by force is an immense step to take if you consider yourself to be freely and 'innately' heterosexual" (216).

Denaturalizing something masked by power as organic, normal, the sign of mature sexuality, and the basic human social unit, was something Rich realized would unsettle many of her readers. Yet these self-identified heterosexual feminists were the very people Rich hoped to bring into solidarity with lesbian interests. The history of next-wave feminist and queer studies shows us that, for the most part, theorists heeded her call, following so much in the path of her critique that those in these and related fields today can take her then-radical claims as baseline assumptions in their work.

Leaping then, from these baseline assumptions, we can take Rich's logic into the realm of trans theory and politics.

In her denaturalizing of heterosexuality, Rich asked readers to reconsider it as a form of what she termed "male-identification." Coupling male-identification with the abandonment of "female-identified values," Rich seems at first blush to be grounding her argument in a simplistic, biologically based belief in the category "woman." Yet given her project and the conceptual logic of the piece, an idea of static, binary gender doesn't make sense. How can we resolve this seeming contradiction within her argument? We contend that when Rich asks heterosexual women to question the natural inevitability of their "choice," in fact, she suggests the contingency of heterosexuality's basic foundation: the male/female binary sex system.

Rather than positing some kind of simplistic battle of the sexes, Rich uses the idea of male-identification as a way to explain and think about women's (including feminist's and lesbian's) investments in the institution of heterosexuality. Male-identification, as she imagines it, is a political and social practice that reproduces heteronormativity and erases lesbian existence.

She uses the terms "lesbian continuum" and "lesbian existence" to avoid the heteronormative, historical, and clinical associations with the term "lesbian." As she puts it:

> Lesbian existence suggests both the fact of the historical presence of lesbians and our continuing creation of the meaning of that existence. I mean the term lesbian continuum to include a range—through each women's life and throughout history—of women-identified experience; not simply that a woman has had or consciously desired genital sexual experience with another woman. If we expand it to embrace many more forms of primary intensity between and among women, including the sharing of a rich inner life, the bonding against male tyranny, the giving and receiving of practical support . . . we begin to grasp the breadths of female history and psychology which have lain out of reach as a consequence of limited, mostly clinical definitions of "lesbianism." (217)

In spite of the blind alley Rich stumbles down in her notes about "heterosexual role-playing" on the part of some lesbians (Gertrude Stein and Alice B. Toklas are her examples),[2] it is not hard to hear a call to resist normative gender in passages like this one:

> The lie keeps numberless women psychologically trapped, trying to fit mind, spirit and sexuality into a prescribed script because they cannot look beyond the parameters of the acceptable....The lesbian trapped in the "closet," the woman imprisoned in prescriptive ideas of the "normal" share the pain of blocked options, broken connections, lost access to self-definition freely and powerfully assumed. (221)

In "Compulsory Heterosexuality and Lesbian Existence" Rich develops a strategy for generating a deeply felt self-understanding of woman as an identity or subject position in a context defined by systemic patriarchal violence and domination. And she calls this strategy the lesbian continuum. But her argument is not aimed at simply gaining visibility for lesbians, at least not in any uncritical or predictable way. For Rich, the lesbian continuum is a strategic mechanism for generating politically viable identities and alliances. It is a way of shifting investments, a reorientation that attempts to demystify and recognize women's complex lived experience. Thus, her call for female-identification, is, to use Victoria Hesford's (2005) characterization, not intended to be a description, but a prescription. It is a standpoint, a mechanism for interrupting hetero-patriarchy, in Rich's terms, male-identification.

Where Rich would have heterosexual feminists in the 1980s strategically claim a place on the "lesbian continuum," today, we might use her logic and her calls to challenge prescriptive sexuality to imagine a transgender continuum on which so-called male-born men and female-born women can find themselves building political connections with those whose gender is more obviously outside society's narrow frame of the "normal," ultimately challenging heteronormative and homonormative investments in binary genders altogether.

FROM GLBT TO A TRANSGENDER CONTINUUM

One form this solidarity might take is to look beyond the alphabet soup approach of queer politics as a matter of adding "T" to "GLB" and reorganizing queer politics around expanding the reach of a transgender continuum.

We might take Rich's logic of untangling prescriptive, patriarchy-constructed sex/gender from emotional and erotic desire and into more liberating territory. If, as Judith Butler (1988) claims, "within the terms of culture it is not possible to know sex as distinct from gender," then neither does it really make sense to claim political or even erotic identities based on the idea of acultural, essential sex (as in "lesbian" or "gay" when those terms mean "women-attracted-to-women" or "men-attracted-to-men"). This fallacy becomes evident when self-identified lesbians or gay men are asked nervously by same-sex heterosexual friends if they find such friends attractive. The fact is, more often than not, supposed lesbians or gay men are in fact attracted to specific genders within the broad, clinical category of "female" or "male," and those genders require much more description than the all-but-meaningless labels "woman" or "man."

The need to endlessly add letters to the GLB soup is evidence of the breakdown of essentialist, gender-binary logic. Rich's idea of a continuum based on identities claimed through political goals, strategies, and work is a much more useful way to imagine queer identities and political action today. The afterthought "T" at the end of "GLB" could be, thus, usefully moved to the front and center of a political movement for freedom from both the gendered and eroticized restrictions of binary sex. For example, women of all kinds ("female-born," "lesbian," "heterosexual," "transsexual," "transgender," and so on) might take a place strategically on a transgender continuum for the purposes of challenging the prescriptive patriarchal sex binary that not only posits two and only two static sexes, but also enforces heteronormativity and rewards it by refusing to recognize all other genders and all other sexual attachments or family formations.

Paisley Currah, Richard M. Juang, and Shannon Price Minter (2006) begin this kind of work in their introduction to their volume, *Transgender Rights*. Currah, Juang, and Minter offer several possibilities for trans identification and political solidarity, from transsexuals to butch lesbians. But they also caution that "ultimately, the effectiveness with which the transgender movement addresses the diversity of its constituents will depend less on finding a satisfactory vocabulary and more on how actual strategies for social change are implemented." Critically, they go on to point out that "the same is true for creating effective connections with people who do *not* see themselves as transgender. Put simply, the movement's effectiveness will depend heavily on who benefits from its successes" (xv).

When identities now most often considered to be based in the realm of the sexual (gay, lesbian, and so forth) are reconsidered in light of their *gender* deviance (however "gender-conforming" an individual might seem to be), many more people become eligible to benefit from increased freedoms of gender expression and identity.

WHEN IS AN L ALSO A T?

In her essay "Transgender History, Homonormativity, and Disciplinarity," Susan Stryker (2008) points to the problem of the GLBT construction as one that ultimately preserves homonormative power within queer movements not only by marginalizing trans-identified people, but also by using the "T" "as a containment mechanism for gender trouble of various sorts that works in tandem with assimilative gender-normative tendencies within the sexual identities" (148). The assumption behind a GLBT label is that each of these categories is distinct from the other, that only one might be occupied at a time, when the lived reality of many is identification with more than one of them at the same time, or different configurations of one or more of them over the course of an individual's life, or both. Stryker describes trans identity as intersecting with sexual orientation rather than falling somewhere along a hetero-homo continuum, putting the "T" on an entirely different plane from the "G," "L," and "B." A transsexual woman might also be a lesbian, Stryker suggests by way of an example, just as a gay man might also be black.

Yet the idea that transgenderism and same-sex sexual orientation have some more natural affinity to each other than say, class and gender or race and sexuality, persists in much literature on the subject. And some gays or lesbians are assumed, in some kind of commonsense way, to be more or less transgendered than others. Often, for example, the butch lesbian is imagined as a kind of bridge figure between a trans and a lesbian identity.

But if we were to shift to thinking in terms of putting the G's, L's and B's (not to mention antipatriarchal heterosexuals) on a Rich-inspired, politically activated transgender continuum, the butch is joined by a less obvious, but, as it turns out, quite likely, suspect, namely, the femme.

If all sex, gender, and desire are the result of performed acts, there is no need to assume that a femme lesbian is any more "natural" a woman than a butch one simply because her publicly performed gender appears at first glance to fall more or less within the narrow patriarchal prescription for women.

Under compulsory heterosexuality, in fact, a lesbian who performs woman in a way that patriarchy possessively regards as properly and rightfully its "own" challenges hetero-patriarchy. The work of being a woman, when done for the satisfaction of herself and other women, becomes not just what Rich calls "both the breaking of a taboo and the rejection of a compulsory way of life…[and] also a direct or indirect attack on male right of access to women" but also a giving of the rights and privileges demanded by the patriarchy *of* women *to* women.

A femme lesbian refuses to respond to the prescriptions of the culture on women's performance by trying to impossibly imagine a performance of woman that falls outside culture or outside patriarchy (which for the time being and, as far as we can imagine, the time to come, *is* culture). A femme, instead, takes up the performance of woman with both pleasure and irony, seeing it for what it is, and choosing to wear it or not, according to her own desires, including her desire to please other women.

Whether or not her performance also pleases heterosexual men is beside the point. She may be reperformed and packaged in pornography to satisfy heterosexual male desire, but this is an effect of living within the dominant gender order. No woman escapes commodification of her sexuality within heteropatriarchy, even if it is a reactionary form of commodification, such as stereotyping the butch as a "man-hating feminazi." Trying to interrogate the origin of gendered desire is futile. Nonetheless, "putting on" femme, like putting on drag, is a performance that, as Judith Butler has famously pointed out, calls attention back to itself *as* performance and thus can call all gender into question.

A femme may be more cognizant of her challenge to compulsory gender binarism than a heterosexual woman who wears the same shade of lipstick. But, by sharing that lipstick, perhaps it is the femme, even more so than the butch, who is the best bridge across which political alliances can form as more people begin to recognize themselves and their interests as falling upon a transgender continuum. About heterosexuality, Rich concluded: "Within the institution exist, of course, qualitative differences of experience; but the absence of choice remains the great unacknowledged reality, and in the absence of choice, women still remain dependent upon the chance or luck of particular relationships and will have no collective power to determine the meaning and place of sexuality in their lives" (223). The challenge in Rich's words is that women living in heterosexual relationships recognize that whether they are individually happy or not, the question of choosing heterosexual identity is really moot within patriarchy. Similarly, gender-conforming people may find themselves quite comfortable and even successful in the gender they perform, but political consciousness should cause them to recognize the limits and constraints of this performance. Thus might the most gender-normative individual be brought within a strategic political spectrum of agitators for transgender rights and freedom.

THE TRANSGENDER CONTINUUM/THE TRANSGENDER RIGHTS IMAGINARY

In a context defined by an increasingly visible and vibrant transgender movement and, relatedly, regular legal and medical challenges to the sex binary, Paisley Currah (2003) conceived "The Transgender Rights Imaginary." In "The Transgender Rights Imaginary" Currah asks how we might reconcile two seemingly contradictory trajectories: "How should we negotiate the tensions between an identity politics movement of gender-variant people that seeks primarily to amend the definitions of the binary sex classification scheme, and the larger goal of dis-establishing sex as a meaningful legal category, a category that remains in place as a means of distributing rights and resources equally?" (705).

Indeed, Currah's question recalls the different kinds of work performed by Rich's continuum and suggests the sort of political activism that the transgender continuum might ideally inspire. Just as Rich denaturalized heterosexuality *and* foregrounded its violences and its real effects, it is crucial that the transgender continuum foreground the violences of sexual binaries. Identifying inconsistencies in paradigmatic binary sexing; drawing attention to the diversity of lived, gendered experience; and capitalizing on gender performativity are mechanisms for denaturalizing sex. At the same time, they point to the remarkable resiliency of sexual regulation, the ongoing policing of bodies and the very real violence it entails, and the absolute need to address those injustices. While the trajectories may not be the same, they are only seemingly distinct and contradictory: we need to remain open to the possibilities that each holds for the other.

C.L. COLE is professor of gender and women's studies and media studies at the University of Illinois at Urbana-Champaign, where she also serves as the director of Media Studies.

SHANNON L.C. CATE received her PhD in American literature from George Washington University and currently teaches courses on gender, race, and sexuality at the University of Illinois at Urbana-Champaign.

NOTES

1. For example, "Compulsory Heterosexuality" served as the thematic focus for *Journal of Women's History* in 2003 and for *Sexualities*' (2008) recently published series of articles.

2. Even in the case of her comments on Stein and Toklas, it is possible to argue that it wasn't these women themselves (and their gender expressions) Rich objected to, but their seeming *acceptance* by the patriarchy, which she believes results from what it mistakenly recognizes as an imitation of itself. She does not go into enough detail in her short footnote to be accused of believing that Stein and Toklas were intentionally, in fact, mimicking patriarchy.

WORKS CITED

Butler, Judith. 1988. "Performative Acts and Gender Constitution: An Essay in Phenomenology and Feminist Theory." *Theatre Journal* 49(1):519–31.

Currah, Paisley. 2003. "The Transgender Rights Imaginary." *Georgetown Journal of Gender and the Law* 4:705–20.

Currah, Paisley, Richard M. Juang, and Shannon Price Minter, eds. 2006. *Transgender Rights*. Minneapolis: University of Minnesota Press.

Hesford, Victoria. 2005. "Feminism and Its Ghosts: The Spectre of the Feminist-as-Lesbian." *Feminist Theory* 6(3):227–50.

Stryker, Susan. 2008. "Transgender History, Homonormativity, and Disciplinarity." *Radical History Review* 100:145–57.

Rich, Adrienne. 1993. "Compulsory Heterosexuality and Lesbian Existence." In *Adrienne Rich's Poetry and Prose*, ed. Barbara Charlesworth Gelpi and Albert Gelpi. New York: W. W. Norton.

TRANSPEDAGOGIES: A ROUNDTABLE DIALOGUE

VIC MUÑOZ AND EDNIE KAEH GARRISON (MODERATORS)
Anne Enke, Darcy A. Freedman, Ednie Kaeh Garrison, Jeni Hart, Diana L. Jones, Ambrose Kirby, Jamie Lester, Vic Muñoz, Mia Nakamura, Clark A. Pomerleau, Sarah E. VanHooser (Participants)

AT THE KITCHEN TABLE (AGAIN)

The eleven participants in this roundtable submitted their work for consideration to the editors of this issue of *WSQ*. Rather than include just one essay from authors, the editors wondered how it would work to include a group of authors who had proposed to tackle trans-focused pedagogical issues within women's studies. The editors invited us to moderate this "textual conversation" with the understanding that one of our mandates was to imagine practical ways to produce this more experimental form. To make space for the multiplications and unexpected convergences to pop out of this dialogue, we adopted the term "transpedagogies" as a coalitional concept that includes transsexual, transgender, and gender/queer pedagogical perspectives. While it is imperfect, we are excited by the outcome, as the results reflect a community effort to create a dialogical space that invites further participation.

From our first readings of research-based abstracts, we identified a series of themes through which to frame ideas for how this varied group of participants might be placed in conversation with each other. The themes that emerged were named thus: Feminist Trans-Masculinities/Femininities; TransCrossings: Cultures and Histories; Transgendering Male Privilege: Transguys in Feminist and Women's Studies; Transdisciplinary Work in the Academy; Making the Body In/Visible in the Classroom; and Transforming Women's Studies. With these themes as a jumping-off point, all the authors and coauthors wrote individual statements grounded in their teaching, scholarship, experiences, and theoretical affiliations. Subsequently, the authors and coauthors provided written shorter responses to two of the statements. And, finally, the authors and coauthors responded briefly to the responses written about their own statements. We compiled everyone's writing and sent the completed piece to all the participants. We then received feedback in the form of questions and suggestions as well as editorial corrections. We took all these and integrated them into the piece.

Our guiding theme has been to engage in a conversation that would spark a wider, more diverse and expansive one among scholars, activists, and educators. We hoped to explore the experiences of transgender, transsexual, and gender/queer students and faculty within specific learning environments, such as women's colleges and doctoral programs, as well as the experiences of those teaching and working with variously trans and queer faculty and students.

Because of space limitations, the published Transpedagogies Roundtable does not include all the original statements and responses, but the complete piece, including all works cited by the participants, is available online at http://www.feministpress.org/wsq/.

DESTABILIZING GENDER IDENTITY
Mia Nakamura

Western transgender discourse presupposes that everyone has gender identity. As a Japanese, I argue that the concept of gender identity needs to be reconfigured to accommodate our gendered reality and that this will provide a vantage point from which to see where transgender studies intersects with interests of feminist as well as liberal-minded students.

The concept of gender identity was introduced in the mid-twentieth century, and it naturally stemmed from the ideology of that time. Having examined the contemporary theoretical assumptions that informed the concept initially and looked critically at how it has proliferated in transgender discourse, I have come to believe that gender identity has been nourished indisputably by Western principles of the autonomy of the self (M. Nakamura 2006). In fact, the Japanese did not have a word for identity before the Westernized term was introduced, because there was no indigenous concept of "identity" in the Western sense. Even though the Japanese now use the word identity as a foreign loan word (and Japanese transsexuals claim that they have "gender identity disorder"), Japanese people are in general apt to conceive of themselves according to their positionality relative to others as well as depending on the situation. Here, one's identity is understood not so much as who one is but as how one relates to the world.

Interestingly enough, this Japanese search for one's positionality links with Western postmodern perspectives on identity. For instance, Anthony Giddens discusses that identity of the self is "not just given, as a result of the continuities of the individual's action-system, but something that has to be routinely created and sustained in the reflexive activities of the individual" (1991, 52). Gender identity is, then, a dialogical process of defining one's positionality: a constant interpretation of the self as well as a continually revised political statement of how one situates oneself in the social world.

"Gender-creative," meaning being creative about one's gendered life, is the term I coined several years ago through my studies of transgender individuals in Japan (M. Nakamura 2005). Transgenders, whether those who choose the neither-man-nor-woman status or those who follow traditional gender roles, must find their own mode of gender living, creating their own gender-being in which they feel self-fulfilled. And it is here, I believe, that feminism and transgenderism have the same concern. Judith Butler defined gender as "the discursive/cultural means by which 'sexed nature' or 'a natural sex' is produced and established as 'prediscursive,' prior to culture, a politically neutral surface on which culture acts" (1990, 7). But gender at the individual level is, in fact, less something "prediscursive" than what one, more or less consciously, engenders out of one's psychological, social, and political needs. What we have to defend is the right to keep creating gender categories for one's own sake.

It is an important task of women studies and transgender studies to discuss effective strategies for achieving this goal. This will make the collaboration of the two fields more productive and bring about a new possibility of our gendered beings.

Enke Responds to Nakamura

Nakamura's discussion reminds us that the concept of "gender identity" is culturally specific, rooted in Western constructs of both "gender" and "identity." These constructs did not and do not translate smoothly into Japanese cultural contexts. At the same time, Western postmodern perspectives might understand self situationally and in relation to others.

I find in this, and in Nakamura's use of the term "gender-creative," good reminders that the concept of gender identity fails to translate well into most cultural contexts in the West as well (not only in various countries, but also across race, class, ethnicity, region, location, age, ability, religious background, legal status, and so on). The need to "keep creating gender categories" indicates the failure of a binary gender system and individual autonomy and also the failure of the concept of gender identity to adequately describe anyone's social situatedness, desire, and experience. If we are gendered, gender might be a verb and a process—something that we do and that happens to us, ensuring that "our gendered beings" are never stable but gain salience and meaning in relation to other cultural processes such as racialization, class distinction, nationalism, and globalization.

Women's studies, with its often transnational field of vision, and transgender studies, with its intense interrogation of what gender is, are *together* ideally poised to newly theorize gender and also to develop new ways of addressing subjects that do not require attachment to gendered status. Activism is needed too: as so many have pointed out, the distribution of material and social resources is intimately linked to gender legibility and consistency within a highly culturally specific set of expectations.

Muñoz Responds to Nakamura

Wesley Thomas (1997) and Clive Aspin (2005) explore similar concepts as the ones that Nakamura explores here. Thomas was the first to undertake an empirical study on the diversity of gender roles within Diné culture from a Navajo perspective. Aspin explores sexual and gender diversity among the M ori from a M ori perspective. As does Nakamura, Thomas and Aspin find that Western concepts of gender erase diversity. It's interesting that when Thomas defines "Transgenderism" within his writing (1997,164) he references Western sources exclusively. Aspin links a renewal of the use of the M ori term, *Takat pui*, among M ori LGBT people as a form of decolonization and M ori cultural pride.

This leads me to think, as does Nakamura, that Western concepts of "identity" are untranslatable at best and hegemonic at worst. Nakamura's term "gender-creative" has commonalities with diverse gender identities documented by Thomas and Aspin that expand Western definitions. All articulate the need for cultural self-determination in relation to gender and sexuality. They illustrate how gender is relational, not just individualistic. It is in this relational understanding of gender—of how we co-construct each other through what we do and who we are within our own cultural histories—that trans-cultural understandings of trans-decolonial pedagogies can begin. I very much look forward to continuing this dialogue.

WHAT IS TRANS? TOOLS FOR AN OPEN DIALOGUE
Ambrose Kirby

Clearly defined concepts help provide participants in a discussion with common ground and can break down barriers to communication. Exploring "transpedagogies," then, requires some basic definitions in order to produce strategies for transforming the (women's studies) classroom, feminism, and society at large. In the present dialogue, for example, "trans scholar" variously includes anyone from transsexual and transgender people in the academy to those who "cross" disciplinary boundaries and potentially many others in between. As a general term, "trans" may create openings for multiple identities and interdisciplinary approaches to transformative and antioppressive pedagogy within supposedly discrete academic spaces/disciplines (such as women's studies). However, because it is a general term with many specific meanings, invoking "trans" may just as often limit or erase actual lived realities, precarious identities, and complex pedagogical strategies from those spaces.

"Trans" is most often used to signify in between, beyond, crossing, or a combination of these. In particular, the use of "trans" in the term "transgender" gestures toward the space between, beyond, and on the other side of a male/female binary. Transgender people resist, reject or simply don't fit into this binary and so may occupy a third or fluid space instead. Further, "trans" is also used to simultaneously represent the limits or extremes of a term and the space between a set of terms. This is particularly true of academic theorizations about transsexual people. In many cases, transsexual men and women are transphobically depicted as neither male nor female (in-between male and female) or as representing the limits of either male/masculinity (in the case of MtFs) or female/femininity (in the case of FtMs). The idea that transsexual people cross, are in-between, mark the limits of, or transcend a male/female binary, in many cases, is contrary to the assertions and lived reality of transsexual people. Indeed, the assertion that "trans" is always/only between, beyond, or crossing is made possible by denying the claims to authentic maleness made by some transsexual men and to authentic femaleness made by many transsexual women.

Acknowledging complex readings and erasures of "trans" allows us to critically examine the meaning of the term for both women's studies and feminism. The white supremacist; Eurocentric; and dominant sexuality-, ability-, and class-based deployment of the term "woman" within feminism has been solidly critiqued by many feminists variously located within structures of race, sexuality, ability, class, gender, sex, nation, and age. Nevertheless, this "woman," as the unified subject of feminism, continues to ground dominant feminist conceptions of "difference"—of who belongs and who doesn't. Accordingly, whether transsexual women and men and transgender folks belong to feminism is somehow up for debate. Within a feminism grounded by "woman," our bodies are transphobically received as suspect or as "other" and the claims to essential maleness or femaleness of many transsexual men and women are seen as potentially sexist. By articulating "trans" as simply between, beyond, or crossing, "trans scholars" risk reproducing a feminism grounded by dominance—one where "others" must strip down to "woman" to get through the door.

GENDER-INCLUSIVE FEMINIST PRAXIS IN CONTESTED SPACES
Clark Pomerleau

Women's studies (WS) developed my knowledge of feminism and of trans going beyond "woman" or "man." But WS remains contested space. A recent explosion among masters students exemplifies transpedagogy's importance to WS's subjects and praxis. Trans-identified students found their transphobia-education posters tossed while anti-male sisterhood posters they found exclusionary decorated the TA office. A student called the trans posters "aggressive" and "offensive;" denied anyone there was transphobic; and asserted, "Well, it is *women's* studies after all!" Cisgendered women and trans-masculine students engaged with feminist cultural criticism became one faction. The trans-hostile cisgendered women's faction questioned feminist loyalty based on gender identity and commitment to theories they did not understand as advancing feminist practice.

The conflict represents persistent exclusionary woman-identification and a rift over how to meld theory and practice. WS can capitalize on students' activist focus and guide students toward theoretically sophisticated thinking that still addresses material conditions through transpedagogy that tackles who can be feminist, what feminism covers, and coalition politics. Experiential models, such as that in "Cisgender Privilege" (n.d.; a takeoff on McIntosh 1990) introduce structural inequality. Koyama's (2001) eminently readable "*Transfeminist Manifesto*" incorporates trans to extend feminist issues: defining "woman" without biologizing, male- and non-trans privilege, body image, violence against women, reproductive health options. Genealogies of gender construction span Beauvoir and Firestone to criticisms of a universal "woman" by U.S. women of color and non-Western scholars (Mohanty 1988) to explicitly multigender models such as Butler's analysis of what counts as a person and a coherent gender (2004 58, 67–70, 74). Advocating self-determination beyond binary gender furthers women's interests by validating multiple ways for bodies to live and further exposing how narrow gender ideals oppress everyone. Butler pairs with transnational firsthand accounts such as in Lamas (2004) to answer the question, "To what extent does the body *come into being* in and through the mark(s) of gender?" (Butler 1990, 8). *The Transgender Studies Reader* directly addresses the relationships among trans, feminism, and queer theories as well as intersecting with masculinities, race, and nationality. Several transguys introduce variation and non-normativity in masculinities to address male privilege and continue the lesson that gender does not operate in isolation but is always inflected by other factors. Noble (2006) proposes gender incoherence to create antiracist feminist masculinity. In an interview, Essi addresses differences among masculinities with his experience transitioning from being read as a black woman to seen as a black man (Hinchcliffe 2006).

Impediments to change include not only the ways that gender stereotypes get perpetuated in feminism but also limited interest in adopting trans-inclusive sources as part of addressing emotional discord that repeatedly threatens feminist groups. When I advised that WS students would continue to be split unless there was curricular inclusion, a professor on the committee that was formed to address the poster incident balked. But numerous trans writers engage feminist issues. Including their work shifts parameters by moving away from binary gender to a model that can address cisgendered women's stake in anti-trans gender discrimination and how to create a multifront campaign for justice and equality.

Kirby Responds to Pomerleau

The feminist claim that gender is *always and only constructed* seems as likely to be true as the claim that gender is *always and only an essential fact* of our birth (bodies). Nevertheless, social construction theories act as dominant feminist frameworks for resisting and overcoming the oppression of women. Accordingly, women's liberation involves the destruction/transcendence of a (male-female) sex/gender binary that establishes essential differences between men and women.

Transgender and queer movements have also embraced social construction theories as they create spaces for disrupting normative gender expressions and for legitimizing a third or fluid location between/beyond the sex/gender binary. Attempts to align transgender politics/studies with women's studies and feminism have been based on a common understanding of the centrality of an identity politics rooted in social constructionist theories of gender. But the differences between fighting the sex/gender binary from a location within it and fighting it from a marginalized position supposedly on the outside of it often go unexamined.

Moreover, the project of destroying/transcending the sex/gender binary precludes transsexual men and women *being men and women*. Henry Rubin's (1998) essay "Reading Like a (Transsexual) Man" and Max Wolf Valerio's (2002) essay "Now That You're a White Man…" unapologetically embrace manhood/masculinity as a viable location from which to live or to fight gender (and sex) oppression, or both. Viviane Namaste's (2000) book *Invisible Lives* exposes the everyday violence perpetuated by the academic and institutional erasure of viable transsexual and transgender identities. The challenges that transsexual and transgender lives/politics pose to feminism may be divisive—perhaps a useful opening for dialogue.

EXPERIENCES IN A TRANS-DISCIPLINARY SOCIAL SCIENCE DOCTORAL PROGRAM
Darcy Freedman, Diana Jones, and Sarah VanHooser

Transdisciplinary (Stokols 2006) efforts in the academy facilitate the possibility of having programs, departments, teaching styles, and research that are situated in between the rigid structures of traditional academic disciplines and, as a result, have the potential to transform the process of knowledge creation and transmission. Our experiences as doctoral students in a transdisciplinary social science program shed light on the overarching and powerful norms guiding understandings of space and place within the academy, as well as the consequences—both positive and negative—of violating these norms.

Traditional disciplines possess institutionalized markers of authority and create hierarchies ordered by a belief that those with greater mastery of a disciplinary canon are legitimate "experts," while those with less experience are appropriately stationed lower in the hierarchy. In contrast, our transdisciplinary doctoral program rejects the notion of a canon and, like many women's and gender studies programs, purposely challenges hierarchical divides related to institutional positionality. While residing in a transdisciplinary academic program is at times considered avant-garde, our ambiguous identity is frequently unintelligible. Our identities require continuous explanation and negotiation, and despite these efforts we are often referred to as representatives of "that whatever you call it" program, even among those who have had repeated interaction with our department and program, currently in its seventh year.

Our program contests the boundaries between researchers and participants and espouses the participatory action research paradigm of knowledge creation, a method and value shared by many feminist scholars. Participatory action research questions the position of researchers as experts, instead conceptualizing researchers as collaborators, facilitators, and popular educators. This approach to research attempts to destabilize the boundaries between university and community, teacher and learner, knower and known. Although these boundaries are constructed, their social meaning is "real," and crossing them as if they were real is often the first step in their deconstruction. Transgression, however, is risky in a context that values single ownership and timely production of knowledge.

The labor-intensive practice of transdisciplinary scholarship requires learning other languages, traditions, and practices, with the hope that these experiences can integrate with and transform conventional ways of knowing and doing. This terrain is often fluid and uncertain, and a great deal of opportunity, freedom, and creativity exists for the transdisciplinary scholar practitioner. To the extent that each is willing and able to build relationships and explore opportunities across campus or within the community, productive, interesting, and useful collaborations have emerged. The border crossing inherent in transdisciplinary work provides opportunities for deconstruction and innovation that from other vantage points are sometimes difficult to achieve. It is long past time to explode the arbitrary categorical restraints of discipline. Transdisciplinary scholarship offers fertile ground for the development of theories, methods, and pedagogy aimed at the academy's penultimate goals of knowledge creation and transmission.

Garrison Responds to Freedman, Jones, and VanHooser

Freedman, Jones, and VanHooser's position that transdisciplinary scholarship provides "fertile ground" to "explode the arbitrary categorical restraints of discipline" resonates strongly. As an interdisciplinary American studies and women's studies scholar, I've felt the pressure of being nowhere and everywhere—often being treated as a nonlocatable oddity. Too social scientific for the humanities; too humanities for the social sciences. As women's studies advocates debate the "disciplining" of the field, the categorical restraints of discipline bear on arguments that sexuality is best studied by those in queer studies, and the lives and experiences of people of color in ethnic studies, and that everything that doesn't have to do with "women" but with the United States belongs to American studies. Not only are the queers of color erased from view (again) everywhere, but "women" are re-essentialized, "sex" is reduced to a binary, and those of us who cross between and exist within these interdisciplinary spaces are made to disappear as boundaries rigidify. What happens to the capacity to create knowledge—new, unexpected, transformative—when the "inter" and the "trans" are contained within the already established categories of discipline? And how does a student/scholar who resides within the space of the "inter" and the "trans" respond to the compulsion toward the disciplinary? What's the fear of moving across, beyond, or between disciplines about? What's at stake in insisting that nations remain distinct, that genders remain confined within the binary, that disciplines remain pure of permutation? Why do we desire such narrow frames of reference?

Enke Responds to Freedman, Jones, and VanHooser

I received my MA from an interdisciplinary (and somewhat Marxist) cultural studies program (Comparative Studies in Discourse and Society), and then left to complete my PhD in a history department. Legitimacy and legibility in the academic job market were (ignobly) among my motivations. I believed that being legible might require proof of being disciplined in a conventional discipline, and the clearest proof was in the form of a degree from a department with a name that didn't confuse people. Interdisciplinarity seems prized by resource-granting institutions, but credentialing systems are largely based on disciplinary frameworks. Border crossing is frequently policed, as disciplines demand convincing papers of those who would intermingle with them. Translation is needed between conventional disciplines and transdisciplinary scholarship; but translation—communication—requires enough legibility to inspire open collaboration and a willingness to be changed.

Can we analogize transdisciplinarity and transgendering? Disciplinary regimes seek to regulate bodies, minds, practices. Substituting "transgender practice" for "transdisciplinary scholarship": in what ways might transgendering require "learning other languages, traditions, or practices, with the hope that these experiences can integrate with and transform conventional ways of knowing and doing"? Can transgendering subjects "explode the arbitrary categorical restraints" of discipline/gender? Feminist, queer, and trans theory are good at deconstructing gender, but how can we go further and develop a usable language that allows us to talk about and practice as subjects from an anti-gender-disciplinary perspective? What kinds of legibility and legitimacy do we need in order to collaborate within and across disciplinary regimes and to experience our trans-ness as opportunity, freedom, and creativity?

TRANSGENDER STUDENTS IN A WOMEN'S COLLEGE: CHALLENGES TO THE REPRODUCTION OF GENDER ESSENTIALISM
Jeni Hart and Jamie Lester

What is the responsibility of a women's college that admits female students who later express gender in ways that are not normatively female? A small number of higher education institutions across the country are considered women's colleges—they admit exclusively the female sex. These institutions can be microcosms for gender essentialism in society; women's colleges represent and reproduce notions of gender essentialism by conflating sex with gender. Many within these college communities (faculty, staff, students, alumnae) want the college's image to be shaped by students who both have female genitalia and perform femininity. Transgender persons are seen as violating strict notions of gender essentialism; they rebut the gender dichotomy by performing and identifying in ways contradictory to their sex (and often seeking surgical alterations, thus becoming transsexual [Kessler and McKenna 1997]). This performance is often a blending of genders (Devor 1989; Ekins and King 1997) as they willfully violate social rules of dress, communication styles, and emotions by adopting and performing the gender that is different from their sex (Harley et al. 2002).

In an all-women's campus environment, these *violations* present challenges for transgender individuals, as well as for the academic community. For example, transgender students question the use of and participation in gender-specific facilities (K. Nakamura 1998). Bathrooms, athletics, the Greek system, dormitories, scholarships, and locker rooms are often separated on the basis of societal constructions of gender and are only available for women in an all women's college. Transgender individuals who have transitioned to male do not have proper facilities, except in some rare cases. Second, institutional bureaucracies rely on means of name determination, such as identification cards that offer access to libraries and other college facilities, and certain assumptions about gender are made through determination of the names. The process of presenting oneself with a male name in an all-women's college contradicts the very notion of serving a single sex. These concerns are further exacerbated by evidence that transgender students perceive a significant lack of resources from colleges to support them (McKinney 2005).

More important, transgender students challenge the very existence and mission of all-women's colleges. In an examination of one all-women's college, we found that despite some efforts by members of the campus community (primarily students, but also some faculty and staff), the organizational culture, practices, and discourses still essentialized gender and maintained the essence of a women's college where the female sex defined gender. It appears that there is a substantial amount of resistance that directly influences the transgender student population. This resistance splinters the campus community and reinforces the power of the dominant discourse about gender, as narrated by the administration.

We contend that the existence of transgender students in an all-women's college represents and highlights the issues that arise when our institutions (educational and beyond) rely on notions of gender essentialism. The very existence of a group of individuals who do not conform to gender-essentialized categories questions underlying assumptions of a structure that seeks to separate and categorize individuals based on sex. Furthermore, the case of transgender students at this women's college reveals implications for the individual as well as for structures when gender essentialism becomes requisite for access and participation in those structures.

Nakamura Responds to Hart and Lester

When women's colleges were built, there was a firm cultural belief about gender dichotomy and gender roles. But times have changed and it is now evident that the belief is not necessarily substantiated. If not open to male students, then women's colleges must seek other raisons d'être. In fact, there are many positive reasons for women's colleges contributing to society without adhering to gender essentialism. For instance, women's colleges give their students a valuable opportunity to rethink their own women's identity by situating themselves in a women-only community, in which heteronormative gender roles are not taken for granted. They need to find their own roles and identity based on something other than societally given gender. This will make them aware of how to see themselves and how to be seen by others, which greatly helps build their independent-minded communication skills.

Women's colleges with a good gender studies program incorporating transgender issues will encourage students to find their own gender-wise being, not simply following the societal norm but positively created by their own needs. The graduates from the program would have potential to change suffocating and uneconomical patriarchal organizations, creating a new type of productive social framework. It is important to redefine the meaning of a "women's college." This does not mean completely denying the traditional values of women colleges, however. A queer approach to bringing about an epistemological change in the meaning of the term may be beneficial (Butler 1993).

TRAPPED IN THE WRONG CLASSROOM: MAKING DECOLONIAL TRANS-CULTURAL SPACES IN WOMEN'S STUDIES
Vic Muñoz

Before Wells College "went co-ed" there were students who were men in our classrooms. One young man, William Liberi (1984–2007) was courageous in claiming both feminist space in women's studies and transgender space in psychology. Teaching the course Psychology of Women with Will as a student was the first time I taught that class in a co-ed environment. Will transgendered women's studies because his body confused the concept of the classroom as "women's space" at a women's college. I needed to make room so that we would not be trapped in the wrong classroom.

If feminist pedagogies emerge from and with women's studies, then how do transpedagogies emerge from and with transgender studies? What have been the problems and limits of feminist pedagogies within women studies? Can we expect these same limitations within transgender studies?

As a faculty member who identifies as genderqueer and of color, it's important to and for me to consider these questions within cultural, political, and historical contexts. The classroom I occupy is very far from where I was born (Puerto Rico/Borinquen). Yet my own diaspora takes place within the diaspora of the Cayuga Indian Nation. I am always made aware that we are occupying Cayuga territory. The land claim by the Cayuga Indian Nation against New York State for violation of treaty rights has been a long-term struggle. Over these years a sustained resistance to the Cayuga's land claim has emerged locally among vocal and politically powerful non-Native people living on this land for generations. Driving along Route 90, one of our most traveled roads and one designated a "Scenic Byway," you will see signs that state, "No Sovereign Nation, No Reservation!" I write this to underline that issues of self-determination where I teach are very much alive in the daily lives of displaced peoples here, namely, the Cayuga.

In my teaching I feel it is necessary to interrogate gender and colonialism. I ask myself: How can I make transpedagogical approaches intersect with feminist and decolonial approaches within my classroom? This question arises from a sense of needing to teach in ways that acknowledge our geographic location as well as our political and historical locations so as to make space for self-determination of gender and culture. To not make connections between transgender, feminist, and decolonial studies feels like being trapped in the wrong classroom.

To expose gender as transitional within a changing cultural, political, geographic, and historical matrix creates feelings of confusion that dislodge fixed notions of identity, whether these be racial, ethnic, economic, or sexual. Gender is an essentializing binary that, when exposed as a changeable construct, simultaneously reveals the false security of every other identity. To transgender the curriculum, then, is to decolonize gender. To decolonize the curriculum is to understand that we learn on occupied territories with histories of catastrophic displacements. To teach within the conflicts of transition, for me, is the liberatory power and the potential for self-determination of transgender pedagogies.

TEACHER-STUDENT-LEARNING-STUDENT-TEACHER; OR, WHY BODIES MATTER IN THE CLASSROOM
Ednie Garrison

Will Liberi (1984–2007) taught me profoundly what's at stake in teaching from/about trans realities. I met Will in 2003 on my first day of classes at Wells College. Over the summer I'd worried about teaching Intro to

Women's Studies at a women's college because I'd never taught in a single-sex environment. I've always started Intro with a two-week period of "seduction" when I convince the men that they are invested in understanding gender, despite their anxieties about "women's" studies. Perplexed, I walked into class the first day planning to announce the dilemma and see what students had to say.

But there was Will. I had no idea that a male-identified person would be there. The registrar could have used Will's chosen name, but did not. My roster contained only female names. That moment of shock affected how I taught the whole course, and it has affected my teaching ever since. It also affected the students, in part because Will willfully embraced the work of teaching hir classmates (and teachers). I've always admired hir insistence that people accept hir for who ze was. Ze was clear to everyone—"I'm Will, I'm transgendered, I'm male." Ze didn't want to have to argue for hir right to be who ze was in the room, or at Wells College.

Years before, I'd adopted pedagogical materials from transgender scholars, activists, and performance artists to trouble the idea that gender was a simple biological phenomenon. Kate Bornstein's (1993) film, *Adventures in the Gender Trade*, has been especially important because it helps disrupt students' expectations. Bornstein's a wonderfully accessible pedagogue. Additionally, I assign a short story by Lois Gould (1972) called "X: A Fabulous Child's Story," in which a couple are asked to raise a child whose biological sex remains unknown. Experts want to learn whether a child raised with balanced gender experiences—rather than single-sex-stereotyped roles, behaviors, and adornments dictated by genitalia—will be psychologically healthy.

Female students often insist that they were raised like X, while men mostly deny any similarity, but overwhelmingly, students feel certain that we are all Xs nowadays, despite referring to each other in gendered terms, and completely empathizing with the anxieties of the other children's parents about X's mental health. However, students in this class took their analysis to a place it had never gone before. They criticized the author for failing to imagine genderlessness—a child neither male nor female, but something else. While Bornstein's film helped facilitate this critique, Will made a difference in the class's engagement with the story. Hir presence and work helped them feel a personal stake in producing transgender critique of a positive feminist story.

I learned from Will and hir classmates how important it is to understand the historical relevance of the sex/gender system concept and to problematize its essentially biological assumptions so that transgender experience can make more sense as a hope-filled countercritique of normative gender. Such troubling is perfectly congruent with a vision of women's studies as a site of transformation and critical thinking.

CONCLUSION: SPARKING THE DIALECTICS

Audre Lorde once stated, "Difference must be not merely tolerated, but seen as a fund of necessary polarities between which our creativity can spark like a dialectic" (1984, 111). The creativity sparked by feminist knowledge production has affected the ways people experience the relations of power that shape our encounters with each other locally, globally, intimately, intra- and inter-personally, socially, and across cultures. It is time for practitioners in women's studies to engage these complex ideas about the politics of difference and "the fund of necessary polarities" more concretely.

It seems to us that the dialectics offered by the participants in this transpedagogy roundtable dialogue provide many valuable pedagogical, material, and practical possibilities for such work. The central questions and themes raised here suggest many of these possibilities. Yet they also signal some crucial challenges that continue to block the ability of educational, activist, and scholarly women's studies communities to confront and grow from and through transformative and transformed knowledges.

Out of this roundtable dialogue have emerged necessary and urgent questions. Ambrose Kirby sent us questions in relation to our writing about our experiences with our student Will Liberi. We believe that these questions are important for *all* of us to consider: What impact do *our* bodies have when we step into the classroom, the teacher's lounge, faculty meetings, the dean's office? In writing about trans issues, where and how do *we* locate ourselves? How are *we* read? How are *we* viewed by trans students? How do we engage with the privileged spaces we occupy as trans and nontrans educators as a way to build alliances that are liberatory rather than oppressive to one another? We need to continue to explore how we take all these questions into our feminist classrooms.

The "sparks" generated by contested knowledges and lived experiences between *and* within gender, race, class, ethnicity, ability, age, and sexuality provide new ways of seeing ourselves and imagining the possible. Driven toward what Paulo Freire named *conscientização* (conscientization), we hope the dialogue initiated here will move beyond these pages as a shared commitment to expounding on and envisioning the possibilities of trans in women's studies. For, to return to the importance of acting in the world in the process of self-determination, "there is no transformation without action" (Freire 2003, 87) and there is no action without, first, asking the questions that enable imagining the possible.

ANNE ENKE is a historian of sexuality and social movements and teaches LGBT studies, gender and women's studies, and history at the University of Wisconsin–Madison. She is currently working on gender and generation within and outside the academy.

DARCY A. FREEDMAN is a graduate of the Community Research and Action Program at Vanderbilt University and is currently an assistant professor at the University of South Carolina, College of Social Work. She is a "trans" scholar with an intellectual history in the disciplines of zoology, public health, community psychology, community development, and women's and gender studies. She is interested in the ways that transdisciplinary work offers an immanent critique of traditional disciplinary boundaries as well as the use of cross-disciplinary scholarship as a strategy of resistance.

EDNIE KAEH GARRISON is an independent scholar and an adjunct online instructor of women's studies for Washington State University. She is working on a book titled *Rhizomatic Divergences: Queer Studies, Women of Color Feminism, Women's Studies and Ruptures in U.S. Feminist Consciousness*. Her piece, "Sitting in the Waiting Room of Adult and Family Services at SE 122nd in Portland, Oregon, with My Sister and My Mother Two Hours Before I Return to School" appeared in Anzaldúa and Keating's *This Bridge We Call Home* (2002). She is committed to balancing formal academic writing with more creative modes of communication.

JENI HART is an assistant professor in the Department of Educational Leadership and Policy Analysis at the University of Missouri. She has chapters on faculty activism forthcoming in *Establishing a Family-Friendly Campus-Best Practices* and *New Horizons for Leadership Development of Faculty and Administrators in Higher Education*. Her agenda centers on gender issues, the faculty, and organizational transformation within academe.

DIANA L. JONES is a doctoral candidate in the Community, Research and Action program at Vanderbilt University. She earned a BA in psychology from Adrian College, an MA in sociology from Emory University, and a Master of Theological Studies from the Candler School of Theology at Emory University. Her dissertation is on the mediating and moderating roles of spirituality in congregation-based community organizing.

AMBROSE KIRBY lives in Montreal. He is active in antioppression organizing at Le Frigo Vert, a collectively run anticapitalist food cooperative and community resource center.

JAMIE LESTER is an assistant professor of higher education at George Mason University. She received a PhD and MEd in higher education, respectively, from the University of Southern California and a dual BA in English and women's studies from the University of Michigan. Lester has three forthcoming books on gendered perspectives in community colleges, family friendly policies in higher education, and ways to restructure higher education to promote collaboration.

VIC MUÑOZ is professor of psychology at Wells College and visiting fellow in the Feminist, Gender, and Sexualities Studies Program at Cornell University. Vic is completing a book, based on empirical, qualitative data collected over a period of years, called "Orienting Gender, Disorienting Sex."

MIA NAKAMURA is a part-time lecturer at several universities in Tokyo. Publications include books and numerous academic and educational essays on sexual health, gender, sexuality, and cultural representations. Mia is transgendered and had studied musicology and sexology in the United States.

CLARK A. POMERLEAU teaches women's/gender/sexuality history at the University of North Texas, has taught women's studies, and has advised feminist trans students. Pomerleau has researched the significance of gender-role stereotypes in post–World War II U.S. society and social justice movements, and second wave feminisms and conscious development feminist masculinities.

SARAH E. VANHOOSER is a doctoral student in Community Research and Action at Vanderbilt University. Her dissertation research is with an intentional community in Nashville that is committed to facilitating recovery and healing in the lives of women who have survived addiction and abuse.

WORKS CITED

Aspin, Clive. 2005. "The Place of Takat pui Identity within M ori Society: Reinterpreting M ori Sexuality within a Contemporary Context." Paper presented at the "Competing Diversities: Traditional Sexualities and Modern Western Sexual Identity Constructions" conference, Mexico City. www.tpt.org.nz/downloads/takatapuiidentity.doc.

Bornstein, Kate, Susan Marenco (director), and Jay Mason (codirector). 1993. *Adventures in the Gender Trade*. Video cassette. New York: Filmmaker's Library.

Butler, Judith. 1990. *Gender Trouble: Feminism and the Subversion of Identity*. New York: Routledge.

———. 1993. *Bodies That Matter: On the Discursive Limits of "Sex."* New York: Routledge.

———. 2004. *Undoing Gender*. New York: Routledge.

"Cisgender Privilege." n.d. http://www.t-vox.org/index.php?title=Cisgender_Privilege (last modified June 28, 2007).

Devor, Holly. 1989. *Gender Blending: Confronting the Limits of Duality*. Bloomington: Indiana University Press.

Ekins, Richard, and Dave King. 1997. "Blending Genders: Contributions to the Emerging Field of Transgender Studies." *International Journal of Transgenderism 1*. http://www.symposion.com/ijt.ijtc0101.htm (accessed March 1, 2007).

Freire, Paulo. 2003. *Pedagogy of the Oppressed*. New York: Continuum International. (Orig. pub. 1970.)

Giddens, Anthony. 1991. *Modernity and Self-Identity: Self and Society in the Late Modern Age*. Stanford: Stanford University Press.

Gould, Lois. 1972. "X: A Fabulous Child's Story." *Ms. Magazine*. http://www.nomajesty.net/embryomystic/writing/babyx.html.

Harley, Debra A., Theresa M. Nowak, Linda J. Gassaway, and Todd A. Savage. 2002. "Lesbian, Gay, Bisexual, and Transgender College Students with Disabilities: A Look at Multiple Cultural Minorities." *Psychology in the Schools* 39(5):525–38.

Hinchcliffe, Ellen Marie. 2006. "I Will Always Be Your Daughter. I Will Always Be Your Son." Interview with Juma Blythe Essie. *Clamor* 38(Fall), http://clamor-magazine.org/issues/38/gender.php.

Kessler, Suzanne, and Wendy McKenna. 1997. "Who Put the "Trans" in Transgender? Gender Theory and Everyday Life." *International Journal of Transgenderism*, http://www.symposion.com/ijt/gilbert/kessler.htm (accessed March 1, 2007).

Koyama, Emi. 2001. *The Transfeminist Manifesto*. http://eminism.org/readings/pdf-rdg/tfmanifesto.pdf. Reprinted in *Catching A Wave: Reclaiming Feminism for the 21st Century*, ed. Rory Dicker and Alison Piepmeier. Boston: Northeastern University Press, 2003.

Lamas, Juan-Alejandro. 2004. "GenderFusion." In *From the Inside Out: Radical Gender Transformation, FTM and Beyond*, ed. Morty Diamond. San Francisco: Manic D Press.

Lorde, Audre. 1984. "The Master's Tools Will Never Dismantle the Master's House." *Sister Outsider: Essays and Speeches*. New York: Crossing Press.

McIntosh, Peggy. 1990. "White Privilege: Unpacking the Invisible Knapsack." Excerpted from "White Privilege and Male Privilege: A Personal Account of Coming to See Correspondences Through Work in Women's Studies." Working paper 189 (1988). Excerpted and reprinted in *Independent School* (Winter). 31–36.

McKinney, Jeffery S. 2005. "On the Margins: A Study of Experiences of Transgender College Students." *Journal of Gay and Lesbian Issues in Education* 3(1): 63–75.

Mohanty, Chandra Talpade. 1988. "Under Western Eyes: Feminist Scholarship and Colonial Discourses." *Feminist Review* 30(Autumn):61–88.

Nakamura, Karen. 1998. "Transitioning on Campus: A Case Studies Approach." In *Working with Lesbian, Gay, Bisexual, and Transgender College Students: A Handbook for Faculty and Administrators*, ed. Ronni L. Sanlo. Westport, CT: Greenwood Press.

Nakamura, Mia. 2005. *Kokoro ni Seibetsu wa Aru no ka? Sei douitsusei shogai no Yoriyoi Rikai to Kea no Tame ni (Is There Sex Difference in Your Mind? For Better Understanding and Care of Gender Identity Disorder)*. Tokyo: Iryo bunka sha.

———. 2006. "Atarashii Gender Identity Riron no Kochiku ni Mukete: Seibutsu-/I-gaku to Gender-gaku no Kadai (Creating a New Gender Identity Theory: Challenges for Biology/Medicine and Gender Studies). *Gender and Sexuality* (The *Journal of the Center for Gender Studies, International Christian University*) 2:3–23.

Namaste, Viviane K. 2000. *Invisible Lives: The Erasure of Transsexual and Transgendered People*. Chicago: University of Chicago Press.

Noble, Jean Bobby. 2006. *Sons of the Movement: FtMs Risking Incoherence on a Post-Queer Cultural Landscape*. Toronto: Women's Press.

Rubin, Henry. 1998. "Reading Like a (Transsexual) Man." In *Men Doing Feminism*, ed. Tom Digby. New York: Routledge.

Stokols, Daniel. 2006. "Toward a Science of Transdisciplinary Action Research." *American Journal of Community Psychology* 38:63–77.

Thomas, Wesley. 1997. "Navajo Cultural Constructions of Gender and Sexuality." In *Two-Spirit People: Native American Gender Identity, Sexuality, and Spirituality*, ed. by Sue-Ellen Jacobs, Wesley Thomas, and Sabine Lang. Urbana: University of Illinois Press.

Valerio, Max Wolf. 2002. "'Now That You're a White Man': Changing Sex in a

Postmodern World—Being, Becoming, and Borders." In *This Bridge Called My Home: Radical Visions for Transformation*, ed. Gloria Anzaldúa and Annalouise Keating. New York: Routledge. "Cisgender Privilege" http://www.t-vox.org/index/php?title=Cisgender_Privilege

DONNA J. HARAWAY'S *WHEN SPECIES MEET*, VOLUME 3 OF POSTHUMANITIES, EDITED BY CARY WOLFE, MINNEAPOLIS: UNIVERSITY OF MINNESOTA PRESS, 2008

MANUELA ROSSINI

Meet a true alpha bitch and her human and nonhuman companions. Messmates at table and partners in play, they run fast along the high-speed train of biotechnological evolution, they bite hard at rampant global capitalism, and they risk alien encounters likely to cause pain and indigestion when face to face with incommensurable differences and asymmetrical power. The complexities and contradictions of living and dying in the age of technoscience are not easy to stomach, but that is no excuse for not chewing at them as responsively, politely, and gracefully as possible. Call it a commitment to queer cosmopolitics, an ethics of cross-species flourishing, or sf (science fiction) other-worlding in order to nourish a viable future for animals and human critters alike.

In *When Species Meet*, Donna Haraway shares various ways of doings so, lessons she learned herself about eight years ago, when her hand shook the paw of Cayenne, an individual of the Australian Shepherd breed. The insights and Web sites; the informative, evocative and provocative, personal-political, sad, and humorous stories; and the variety of species herded into the covers of this book are the consequences of that touch. Through touching, living creatures inherit each other's histories in the flesh and in logic. True to her heritage as the daughter of a sportswriter, Haraway writes about the game of co-constitutive entanglement across machinic, animal, and human species. When species meet, they do not come together as fixed units. Rather, all participants are *becoming with* each other in "a subject- and object-shaping dance of encounters" (4).

Part 1 (making up half of the book), "We Have Never Been Human," contains a strong antidose against "human expectionalism," the virus that severs the ties between humankind and all other kinds on the basis of some features unique to the former. Instead, Haraway invites us to see the human as just another knot in the worldwide web of interspecies dependencies, as always already *in*-formed by organic and technological nonhumans. The term she proposes for all these old, new, and yet-to-(be) come "mixed breeds" is "companion species," offered as an alternative category also to the cyborg and other figures currently subsumed under the label "posthuman" or, rather, as a new point of orientation from which to look at (and look *back* at—*respectere*, "to hold in regard") animals and as a different way of theorizing relationality and co-presence with significant others of all types in twentieth-century naturecultures.

Foregrounding processes of optic-haptic relating and adding "encounter value" to the Marxian values of use and exchange in relations of labor and capital, a companion-species approach starts from the premise that "all mortal beings...live in and through the use of one another's bodies" (79) and are hence reciprocally means and ends to each other. In other words, instrumentality should be thought outside the dualistic taxonomies of master/slave, powerful/powerless, free/unfree, active/passive—even though it cannot be denied that pain and suffering is distributed extremely unevenly between human and nonhuman animals. Living within the same instrumental economy, Haraway continues, in her carefully written chapter on experimental lab practices, human beings should learn how to share that suffering in nonmimetic ways, namely, not by taking the place of the animal victim but by understanding what the animal is going through in order to get this unequal relationship and power structure right—emotionally, intellectually, ethically, and operationally.

Part 2, "Notes of a Sportswriter's Daughter," tells the most intimate and touching accounts in the book of what can happen in specific contact zones where different species share the same working conditions. The love letters and e-mails assembled here speak of the love and friendship between a father and a daughter and between a woman and a dog beyond the framework of the Oedipal family romance, anthropocentrism, or anthropomorphism. They speak of the love of team sports (baseball, agility) whereby the partners transform themselves as they are engaged in it and are provoked into unexpected emotions and behavior that complicate preconceived understandings of domestication, pleasure, authority, and much else. And, not least of all, they speak of the love of writing to script fuller lives. Moreover, the encounters and practices describe how a body is always under (de)construction and reconstruction, never alone but always *becoming-with* other bodies, that is, constituted in relating. When her father, Frank , died on September 29, 2005, the knots to the living bodies with whom he had related flesh to flesh became undone, but by writing about him, his daughter, Donna, found a responsive way of re-membering him.

Part 3, "Tangled Species," takes a dive into the ocean to introduce us to more "wild" critters there and to cast a different eye on the world—metaphorically and literally, by not only "compounding eyes" but also compounding the human "I," turning s/he into a companion-species "we": to provide material for the *Crittercam* TV show, humans attach cameras on marine animals and thereby mingle living and nonliving agents into a multispecies hermeneutics. When following Chicken Little around the globe, our eyes are opened to the shocking realities of illegal trafficking in animals and the massive exploitation not only of avian but also human workers in the poultry industry while we are also being presented with a paradigmatic example of a chicken-human encounter that promises the future well-being of both species. And yet, as the intertwined narratives about "educating" feral cats and community college students in Sonoma County, California, make us see, becoming-with-companions in technoculture is full of contingencies, neither easy to play "fair" for the human beings nor simply good or bad for the animals in the game.

Perhaps bit(e)s of the food for thought and action of *When Species Meet* won't go down well with some animal rights activists or some ecofeminists. Significantly, I think, Haraway ends the book with the story of how when she came to Santa Cruz in 1980 for a job interview she got in touch with a community whose members have nourished her "worldliness" ever since, raising her cosmopolitical consciousness through meetings in which people responded to seriously different truth claims in respectful, albeit noncompromising, ways. Coming to the same table from different standpoints and breaking bread together ("companion" is from the Latin *cum panis*) often means conflict but it also offers opportunities for alliances across diverse gulfs to work toward a more liveable and just world in companionship with other human and nonhuman bodies. Nothing less than getting on together is at stake.

MANUELA ROSSINI holds a PhD in English from the University of Basel and is currently working as a project manager for the Transdisciplinarity Network (td-net) of the Swiss Academies of Arts and Sciences. She also codirects the Riga-based international cultural initiative e-text+textiles. She is working on a book titled *Science/Fiction: Imagineering the Future of the Human*. Rossini is on the editorial board of the Critical Posthumanisms series (Rodopi) and coedits the *Experimental Practices: Technoscience, Art, Literature, Philosophy* series (Rodopi).

SALLY HINES'S *TRANSFORMING GENDER: TRANSGENDER PRACTICES OF IDENTITY, INTIMACY, AND CARE*, BRISTOL, U.K.: POLICY PRESS, 2007

JULIA HORNCASTLE

Well balanced and refreshingly sensible, *Transforming Gender* is a critical and insightful book. It aims to "contribute to the development of a sociology of transgender" (6) and avoids privileging unitary perspectives on trans- issues. To emphasize the diffuse everyday realities of trans- subjectivity, Sally Hines casts empirical research findings alongside recent social and cultural trans- theories to explore how broad understandings of trans- phenomena can be further developed. Hines's further aim is to privilege a sharper focus on issues such as intimacy, identity, parenting, partnership, friendship, and citizenship.

Transforming Gender discusses a range of gender identities and experiences that Hines locates under the umbrella term "transgender." This term is used throughout the book to broadly signify "practices and identities such as transvestism, transsexuality, intersex, gender queer, female and male drag, cross-dressing and some butch/femme practices" (1).

The empirical material is U.K. focused, although a range of contemporary Western perspectives (for example, Butler, Feinberg, Halberstam, Foucault, Grosz, Walby, Bourdieu) informs the theoretical basis of the book. Non-U.K. and non-Western perspectives would, as Hines notes, produce different findings. These are not explored, and the book is very clearly defined in terms of Hines's own exclusive research, although she does gesture toward some perspectives of identity and community that are non-Western, non-nuclear, and postcolonial (191).

Transforming Gender is not writerly in style. It is, however, lucid and evaluative, covering the quotidian, and the contentious, issues of (U.K.) lived trans- experiences with well-informed and nuanced understandings of politics and power relations around (for example) the "right"/"wrong" body, passing, medical discourse, sexuality, and increasing interest (public and academic) in trans- phenomena.

Transforming Gender informs us of the necessity to keep in sight the everyday realities of transgender life as they complicate, in myriad ways, subjective experience and power relations. It also tackles the "location" of different theories, some of which have, in Hines's view, given unsatisfactory accounts of trans- phenomena. This necessary critique begins in Chapter 1, where Hines provides a succinctly argued overview of some social/cultural/discursive analyses. Medical discourse, ethnomethodology, lesbian and gay studies, radical feminism, and pluralist feminism are critiqued for producing restricted or biased theories of trans- phenomena.

Hines also provides grist for the theoretical mill through her provocations to queer and poststructural theories that "lack attention to subjectivity, [which] is problematic for a social theorising of transgender" (5). Hines claims that queer sociology is well suited to the task of bridging the gaps between social, cultural, and poststructuralist theories of identity, which have through their paradigmatic intractabilities insufficiently analyzed the diversity of trans- people's experiences (8). Certainly, Hines adds to the conversations about the efficacy of queer, feminist, gay and lesbian, sociological, or cultural theories to render wide-ranging and relevant accounts of trans- phenomena, especially in relation to subjective experience.

However, Hines's analysis of disparate theories (beyond which queer sociology is employed as the remedy for ungrounded or nonmaterialist perspectives) is contentious. Hines's theoretical analysis could be further extended precisely because it is the foundation from which her empirical studies are framed and on which much of the book rests.

As it has become commonplace to read of "the developing field of interdisciplinary transgender studies" (5) I found myself wanting to know more about Hines's assertion that the "intersections of transgender studies and queer studies offer a theoretical space in which to conceptualise a queer sociological approach to transgender" (185). Queer sociology—which is also developing—goes largely unquestioned.

One minor drawback of *Transforming Gender* is its rather dry style: it tends to read as a condensed doctoral thesis. As a book reader, one too easily feels the "legacy" of an overly careful explanation of methodology and argument structure. Although Hines directs the reader to a discussion of methodology in the appendix, one is still very aware of the methodology's place within the main text. Nevertheless, if the reader does not mind the book's formulaic and repetitive structure (indeed students may benefit from it) the work will be seen as a valuable addition to contemporary academic trans- discourse.

Of particular note in *Transforming Gender* is Hines's vigorous questioning of how theory and experience inform our knowledges of trans- practices and experiences. The book as a whole does have a tenacious grasp on the question of how we can better understand and theorize the diversity and complexity of gendered ways of living in the world. Hines's precise articulations of historicity and context alongside the desire to illustrate "real" details of life-specificity are thorough and concise. Throughout, she offers even-handed evaluations of varied and differing trans- perspectives and personal commentaries.

Transforming Gender champions the diversity of trans- phenomena and also champions queer sociology as a means to accurately read that diversity "beyond current limitations" (185). The extent to which Hines's readership will agree with the latter premise adds a contentious (and thus enjoyable) aspect to the book.

Transforming Gender is tightly argued and thus an ideal resource for students and teachers who are new to trans- theory or looking to review their current perspectives. Such readers will appreciate Hines's foregrounding of the place of theory making and the successes and limitations of theory in relation to "real" people's lives.

JULIA HORNCASTLE earned her PhD in women's studies, specializing in queer/gender theory, from Murdoch University, Western Australia. She currently teaches gender studies in the School of Media Communication and Culture.

SUSANNAH B. MINTZ'S *UNRULY BODIES: LIFE WRITING BY WOMEN WITH DISABILITIES*, CHAPEL HILL: UNIVERSITY OF NORTH CAROLINA PRESS, 2007

ANANYA MUKHERJEA

Susannah B. Mintz's *Unruly Bodies* provides a much needed discussion of disabled women's understandings of their own lives, bodies, and identities and of the meanings that their disabilities have and produce in the world—for others who are disabled and for the "able bodied." As Mintz explains, this book links disability theory with feminist autobiography studies in discussing the illness and disability narratives of eight American women. In his classic work *Stigma*, sociologist Erving Goffman managed to link the experiences of people with highly visible disabilities (extreme facial disfigurements, missing limbs) with those of people with much more subtle physical anomalies, without diminishing the lives or knowledge of either group. He did so by focusing away from relative physical ability or disability and examining, instead, the concept of social identity and how, in his words, social identity can sometimes be "spoiled" by the body's failure (refusal?) to conform to the categories and roles that others may expect of it. The disabled body, then, is not so much a determinant of individual value as its presentation, performance, and interpretation are media through which to understand what a society values and how individuals navigate such knowledge.

Similarly, Mintz adapts Arthur W. Frank's ideas that *bodies* give disability stories their meaning (123) and that the life writing of disabled women are life stories told *through* the body (9). Mintz writes, "The autobiographers studied in *Unruly Bodies* are compelling precisely because they write their bodies—their gendered, disabled bodies—as textually produced but also phenomenologically alive" (4). Trinh T. Minh-ha, in *Woman, Native, Other*, exhorted women of color to resist the seemingly rational, masculinist impartiality of academic discourse by "writing their bodies," speaking from their own subjectivities, experiences, and practical knowledge as influenced by their physical bodies and the categories and political positions through which those bodies pass. Mintz offers a discussion of the writing of disabled women who do the same. As with Trinh's work and women of color, the pertinence of this subject and book, while certainly significant for English language studies and for disability studies, reaches beyond to gender studies, to women's history, to sociology, and to sexuality studies.

While Mintz's book has much to offer as it studies a spectrum of life writing by contemporary disabled women, it is particularly noteworthy for highlighting the sexual and emotional lives of these writers, aspects of their lives that have been left out of much work in disability studies. Queer disability studies has been one exception to this oversight, but Mintz makes a real contribution by refusing (as do the writers she discusses) to redeem the disabled by presenting them as particularly brave, creative, or wise. Rather, it is in narrating her everyday life that Mintz disavows any need for redemption or constant comparison to the lives of the "normal" or "able bodied." It is in such mundane reportage that the author is able to "set right" mistakes or misunderstandings from the past; in the case of Denise Sherer Jacobson's story of parenting her infant son, "*The Question of David* becomes the arena in which Jacobson can transform submissive . . . behavior into scenes of . . . resolute expression" (148).

In discussing Nancy Mairs's detailed, matter-of-fact writing about her life with multiple sclerosis (MS), her experiences as the mother of adolescents, or her erotic relationship with her husband, Mintz writes,

> Mairs's own phenomenology demands reckoning with a degenerative condition whose specific effects . . . force a continual renegotiation of the nature of selfhood. . . . To counteract the essentializing maneuvers of patriarchal discourse, Mairs presents a self both indeterminate and adamantly embodied, capable of becoming unhinged from cultural categories but also defined by the realities of MS. Asking that her readers acknowledge both the ordinariness and radical difference of her "crippled" female self, Mairs exposes the boundaries apparently inherent in [oppositional categories]." (26)

Mintz's focus on life writing as phenomenology and her insistence that the careful reader work hard to strike a balance between seeing "the ordinariness and radical difference" of the experiences of these authors is crucial. Because of this, I can imagine using this book in advanced undergraduate or graduate courses introducing students to phenomenology, microsociology, and studies of the body as well as in courses in the fields mentioned earlier in this review. For those teaching or studying queer or sexuality studies, Chapter 3, discussing the writing of Connie Panzarino and Eli Claire, is particularly useful in thinking about the continuum that links bodies rendered "abnormal" through physical disability and those designated so through socially delegitimized desire or gender identity. Mintz writes, for example, that just as Adrienne Rich argues about compulsory heterosexuality, Robert McRuer writes that able-bodiedness deceptively seems to be natural and, thus, a nonidentity (95).

The topic of this book is exceedingly important, and I found the collection of what I prefer to call life writers (memoir writers) that Mintz presents to be compelling. Moreover, her analyses are, on the whole, subtle and convincing and intersect with a wide variety of other inquiries and disciplines. Her language is sometimes too full of disciplinarily self-reflexive jargon to be easily accessible or persuasive for the interdisciplinary reader, and Mintz and only partially explains her references at times. That, however, did not prevent me from learning a great deal from her work or from making me want to find and read the memoirs of the authors she discusses. *Unruly Bodies* makes a much-needed contribution to that intersection of disability theory and feminist autobiography studies for which Mintz intends it.

ANANYA MUKHERJEA is assistant professor of women's studies and sociology at the College of Staten Island, City University of New York (CUNY). She serves on the board of the Center for Lesbian and Gay Studies at CUNY.

WORKS CITED

Goffman, Erving. 1963. *Stigma: Notes on the Management of Spoiled Social Identity*. New York: Simon and Schuster.

Trinh, Minh-ha T. 1989. *Woman, Native, Other*. Bloomington: Indiana University Press.

SUSAN STRYKER AND STEPHEN WHITTLE'S *THE TRANSGENDER STUDIES READER*, NEW YORK: ROUTLEDGE, 2006.

BRICE SMITH

In the foreword to *The Transgender Studies Reader*, coeditor Stephen Whittle never uses the word "transgender," opting instead for "trans." He even refers to the field as "trans studies" rather than "transgender studies." Whittle's preference for "trans" suggests that "transgender" is already dated and anticipates an evolution in transgender studies, as reflected in this issue of *WSQ*, published just two years after *The Transgender Studies Reader* appeared. Perhaps no word better characterizes the field of transgender studies than "evolution." As trans theory and identities move over, across, and beyond, transgender studies, as the discursive site for such movements—as exemplified by *The Transgender Studies Reader*—is evolving at an alarming rate. With *The Transgender Studies Reader*, coeditors Susan Stryker and Stephen Whittle successfully encapsulate the evolutionary discourse of what (in the past decade) has been labeled "transgender studies." What makes *The Transgender Studies Reader* invaluable to the field is the ability of its contributors to show how we have arrived at this moment, how individuals and ideas responded to and built upon one another. To illustrate this point, the evolving dialogues around agency and binary sex/gender ideology can be traced through various selections.

Stryker and Whittle begin the collection with the section "Sex, Gender, and Science" because the medical-scientific establishment initiated the discussion on what Stryker calls the "transgender phenomena." The relationship between those within the medical-scientific establishment and transgender individuals is a long one fraught with tension, particularly in regard to agency. However, this tension has been dialogically generative. For example, later selections in *The Transgender Studies Reader* (including those by transgender authors) repeatedly reference the works and theories of Harry Benjamin, Harold Garfinkel, and Robert Stoller, all of whom have selections included. Joanne Meyerowitz's and Henry Rubin's contributions both attest to Benjamin's prominence in the administration of treatment. Benjamin's criteria for who was a "true transsexual" (and thus treatable) appeared in his book *The Transsexual Phenomenon*, and Sandy Stone illustrates the frustrations and feelings of deception harbored by those administering treatment when they realized that patients seeking treatment obtained and used the same information. Garfinkel and Stoller are referenced in selections by Meyerowitz, Jacob Hale, and Dean Spade in conjunction with their treatment of a patient named Agnes, who successfully presented herself at the UCLA Gender Identity Clinic as "intersexed" and was able to obtain sex reassignment. Garfinkel's "Passing and the Managed Achievement of Sex Status in an 'Intersexed' Person" in the volume describes his theories of gender as an interactive process as exemplified by Agnes, who later disclosed (after undergoing sex reassignment surgery) that she was not intersexed but rather had been taking feminizing hormones. For Garfinkel, this revelation further confirmed his theories. Stoller, by contrast, became an outspoken critic of what he considered patient deception and manipulation. He generated another dialogue with his popularization of the sex/gender distinction.

In "Selection from *Biological Substrates of Sexual Behavior*" Stoller articulates the sex/gender distinction, a problematic concept found at the center of feminist debates around transgender exclusion made legendary by Janice Raymond. Raymond's *The Transsexual Empire: The Making of the She-Male* is the book most referenced in *The Transgender Studies Reader*. Stryker and Whittle chose the chapter "Sappho by Surgery: The Transsexually Constructed Lesbian-Feminist," in which Raymond argues that biology defines gender and that MtFs' undesired penetration of women's spaces is tantamount to rape. In their introduction to Raymond's contribution, Stryker and Whittle claim that it is "the chapter that has caused the most offense among transgender people," and understandably so. Selections that engage with this work include those by Stephen Whittle, Kate Bornstein, Jay Prosser, Emi Koyama, Carol Riddell's "Divided Sisterhood: A Critical Review of Janice Raymond's *The Transsexual Empire*," and Sandy Stone's "The *Empire* Strikes Back: A Posttranssexual Manifesto." Raymond personally attacked Stone in *The Transsexual Empire* for infiltrating the women-only organization Olivia Records and then causing divisiveness among feminists (Aaron Devor and Nicholas Matte briefly discuss the Olivia controversy in their selection, as does Riddell). However, Stone takes the high ground, providing a nuanced critique of feminist notions of womanhood (like Raymond's) through a poststructuralist analysis of gender. As a reader for trans*gender* studies, many authors in the volume engage in a discussion of the binary sex/gender ideology, and not just in terms of feminism. The texts chosen by Stryker and Whittle make it possible to trace the evolution in thinking about this problematic binary across nearly a century, from sexologist Magnus Hirschfeld in 1910 to transgender scholars Whittle and Stryker in 2006 (see Whittle's foreword and Stryker's "(De)Subjugated Knowledges: An Introduction to Transgender Studies"). Other contributors are Dean Spade, David Valentine, Jordy Jones, Henry Rubin, Jason Cromwell, and T. Benjamin Singer.

As both a prefix and an adjective, "trans" goes over, across, and beyond, making the possibilities seem endless for trans(gender) studies. However, to advance or progress requires some point of departure. For trans(gender) studies to evolve, we must have a solid understanding of where it all began. *The Transgender Studies Reader* is indispensable for its ability to encapsulate the century of dialog that has become what appears to be a decade-old phenomenon.

BRICE SMITH is an associate lecturer in comparative ethnic studies and is a history PhD student (modern studies concentration) at the University of Wisconsin–Milwaukee. Zir dissertation is titled "'Yours in Liberation': The Life and Works of Lou Sullivan."

LISA JEAN MOORE'S *SPERM COUNTS: OVERCOME BY MAN'S MOST PRECIOUS FLUID*, NEW YORK: NEW YORK UNIVERSITY PRESS, 2007

ELROI J. WINDSOR

In *Sperm Counts*, Lisa Jean Moore explores how Western culture has made sense of sperm, examining the abundant oppositional constructions of "man's most precious fluid" as creator/destroyer, hero/villain, erotic/toxic, and powerful/disempowering. Using varied sources for information, Moore argues that cultural meanings of sperm reveal important information about men, masculinity, and related social issues.

Moore bases her analysis on fifteen years of research. She relays information obtained through working on the board of a sperm bank and from interviews with sex workers. She also analyzes the content of forensics and criminal texts, children's facts-of-life books, pornographic film and the industry's news review, crime drama television shows, and DNA sleuth sites. This impressive collection of information illustrates sperm's social manifestations within family, law, science, media, and commercial sex arenas. In this investigation, Moore links cultural understandings of sperm to more complicated notions of manhood and masculinity. Throughout the book, she is reflexive in her role as a researcher and peppers her account with interesting personal stories. She employs a straightforward writing style that makes the book accessible to both academic and popular audiences.

Moore begins her study of sperm by contextualizing it historically, tracing its evolution as a cellular identity able to be studied. She reviews the Western origin of sperm in religious and scientific discourse and relays how these accounts mirrored notions of masculinity. She describes how sperm-competition theories situated men as wholly responsible for sexual reproduction. She then examines how anthropomorphic and heroic depictions of sperm in children's facts-of-life books carefully instill normative values in children. The book includes vivid illustrations that exemplify how these story lines indoctrinate stereotypical gender in children's socialization.

The most fascinating chapter in *Sperm Counts* is Moore's examination of sperm in the adult entertainment industry. Moore juxtaposes the glorification of sperm in pornography with the intense management of semen in prostitution. She interrogates the significance of the revered "money shot" in pornography and posits compelling explanations for the idolization of ejaculation. She considers how heterosexual men incorporate this cinematic feature into their erotic repertoires, arguing that the glamorization of ejaculation is a marketable feature that responds to cultural depictions of semen as dangerous, disgusting, and taboo and that men are assuaged through depictions of women who cherish it. Moore analyzes another, contrasting aspect of commercial sex by reviewing the ways sex workers treat semen as hazardous yet also employ creative strategies to avoid compromising their customers' masculinity in the process. She then shifts her analysis to a different economic aspect of semen—the sperm-banking industry. Here, Moore argues that sperm banks reify hegemonic masculinity by imbuing disembodied sperm with desirable characteristics. She discusses how the selling of "technosemen" (107) to single-mothers-by-choice has inspired fatherhood rights groups to reassert men's roles in the reproductive process—a contemporary response to a masculinity in crisis.

The final analysis examines traces of semen identified through DNA-testing technology. With sophisticated theoretical grounding, Moore demonstrates the ways sperm and the men who leak it are constructed negatively. She contrasts fictional representations of sperm on crime television dramas with real-life DNA sleuthing sites. She convincingly argues that the clinical authority of DNA testing laboratories functions to individualize and rank sperm, subjecting the male body to increased surveillance. Matching sperm to criminal or "bad" men serves to subordinate the masculinities of sexually dysfunctional men. Moore concludes that "sperm is at the same time more interesting, complicated, and specialized, and yet more accessible, programmable, deployable, and predictable than ever before" (147). Finally, she imagines future problems and possibilities with advances in sperm technology and how these might affect masculinity.

While the book is comprehensive in many ways, including Moore's in-depth analyses of sperm within numerous cultural forms, some questions remain unanswered. Moore acknowledges that her account does not examine "what sperm means to men" (162). She presents a wealth of evidence, but directly engaging the men who produce sperm would have enriched the project. For example, when sperm donors are rejected, do they feel emasculated? How might sperm buyers interpret banking catalogs, and how do they prioritize the characteristics listed? For men who struggle with fertility, what techniques do they use to enhance their sperm and how do they appreciate these processes? How do infertile men redefine manhood? In pornography, is semen stratified wherein actors are rewarded for longer, denser, and more powerful ejaculations? Do men who partner with men view sperm differently from men who partner with women? How do race, class, age, and other social markers affect associations between semen and masculinity? Additionally, how do transgender men and women position semen within their constructions of gendered embodiment? Certainly, Moore could produce another compelling account that addresses these issues—possibly even as a companion book to *Sperm Counts*—to complement her analysis. Incorporating men's perspectives and lived experiences within another feminist study would offer a more well-rounded understanding of masculinity and gendered embodiment.

Overall, *Sperm Counts* is an important work that expands gender studies both theoretically and empirically. Moore's research supports concepts generated in masculinities studies and contributes to social understandings of the sexual body. This book engages readers with enlightening perspectives on a previously undertheorized aspect of the male body.

ELROI J. WINDSOR is a doctoral student in the Department of Sociology at Georgia State University. Windsor's current research focuses on the disparate regulation of surgical body modification for transgender and cisgender consumers.

DAVID VALENTINE'S *IMAGINING TRANSGENDER: AN ETHNOGRAPHY OF CATEGORY*, DURHAM: DUKE UNIVERSITY PRESS, 2007

NOMVUYO NOLUTSHUNGU

After decades of writing, activism, and community building, what does the category "transgender" mean? In *Imagining Transgender*, David Valentine questions what is left out, what remains, and on what foundation the category rests. Using mapping, participant observation, and interviewing to discern the meanings of transgender at its apex in the late 1990s, his book continues the work of transgender history, research (and its critique), and activism. He turns the lens of inquiry on the creation of these fields, asking, in effect, What *is* transgender?

The book's connections between and disruptions of gender, identity, sexuality, and class send the reader spinning as Valentine consciously forces a confrontation between knowing oneself and external legibility. His descriptions of outreach to populations framed as "transgender" in circumstances where there are few who identify transgender, or of the struggle in identifying people as transgender, poke fun at the paradoxes of identity categories while clarifying the risks (in terms of care, recognition, and access to institutional power) of falling out of those categories.

The passage, in the fall of 2007, of the Employee Non-Discrimination Act (ENDA) and the debates around it brought the high politics of "LGBT" ownership and the politics of categorization into clear view. Currently stalled in the Senate, ENDA spent the better part of the year dividing sexual from gendered (paring down ENDA) and reinstitutionalizing and cementing what transgender means in the American political landscape in much of the same ways Valentine critiques. The book is divided into three sections, which represent transgender as descriptive and historical, as a political and identity marker, and as a scientific and political category, respectively. Valentine spends the first third of the book beginning with the rise of "transgender" and subsequent attempts to historicize it. He charts a space for the "imagination" of transgender, starting with Virginia Prince's articulation of the term, followed by the appropriation of "transgender" as a "community" term (a sense he returns to in the second section of the book) in the 1990s. He parallels this history with that of gay activism, which used emerging psychiatric divisions to distinguish sexuality from gender performance. Perhaps Valentine's most damning critique of the "transgender" category is that it rests on foundations of normative gender privileges for mainstream (white, middle class) gays and lesbians.

In the second third of the book Valentine details his travels between support group meetings, street outreach, and social spaces as a researcher, activist, outreach worker, and volunteer. In each of the events and spaces he attends (and participates in), "transgender" has a variety of meanings. Some reject the term because of their eroticism around gender transformation. Others reject it in favor of "gay." Still others prefer more specific terms such as "fem queen" or employ transgender as one constellation of identities. Alternately, the hospital support group Valentine attends, described at the opening of his book, understands him (as a nontransgender-identified person) as one of them (at least initially) because they are all "gay."

Valentine also demonstrates how inclusion in the category "transgender" correlates with exposure to "mainstream" institutions and power. His parallel of Cherry, twenty years old, African American, transgender identified, and involved in social service support groups, and Mona, twenty two years old, African American, identifying as gay, woman, and "butch queen up in drags" and uninvolved in social service networks, is one of a series of instances in which Valentine shows both the institutional power and the limitations of "transgender."

In the final section, Valentine shows that the specificity of human experience makes academic narratives that determine who or what is transgender futile and dangerous, because, similar to the practice whereby outreach workers name ball participants or sex workers "transgender," such narratives ignore that people "know what [they are]." Not only do simultaneous attempts by transgender activists to operationalize this category perpetuate violence against excluded subjects (by flattening difference), but in their appeal to the state they ignore broader structural and, indeed, state-based violence.

Sharpest when addressing the question of what meanings surround transgender, and what is necessary for a responsible politics of recognition, Valentine's poststructuralist account of "transgender" is nonetheless hopeful. Although the book requires careful attention to language, it rewards the diligent reader with a sharp if unsettling sense of what transgender politics can mean and emphasizes the ongoing need for both a recognition of violence and a political call to action as well as a "critical" and open approach to identity and community building. Given the speed of field and policy development in transgender studies and activism, it would be nice to see a more contemporary revision of Valentine's perspective (his fieldwork is now more than ten years old). The book should be mandatory reading for both policy makers and academics in gender and sexuality studies and for those working in contemporary politics moregenerally.

NOMVUYO NOLUTSHUNGU is a graduate student at the City University of New York Graduate Center, pursuing a PhD in political science. She currently works at the Center for Lesbian and Gay Studies at the Graduate Center and at the Ralph Bunche Institute for International Studies.

HEATHER LOVE'S *FEELING BACKWARD: LOSS AND THE POLITICS OF QUEER HISTORY*, CAMBRIDGE: HARVARD UNIVERSITY PRESS, 2007

WAN-CHUAN KAO

Heather Love's work is haunted by figures from the past, both real and fictive, who have refused to behave themselves as redeemable (queer) subjects for (queer) critics. Reacting against "the need to turn the difficulties of gay, lesbian, and transgender history to good political use in the present" (104), Love contends that the faith in the power of Foucauldian reverse discourse, best exemplified in the ideology of gay pride that transforms sexual shame into social affirmation, has resulted in a critical blind spot. Armed with this insight, Love thus participates in the recent (re)turn to temporalities in queer studies that reexamines conceptions of time in queer historiography and that seeks to envision a queer future. Annamarie Jagose, for instance, wonders about "the ease with which we reify queer temporality" (2007, 186). Too many critics, Love points out, have promised "to rescue the past when in fact they dream of being rescued themselves" (33). Resisting the idealization of cross-historical intimacies, Love postulates a queer critical practice rooted in a "backward future" (147) that both insists on a rigorous embrace of the past and orients itself towards the future. Love not only turns backward, but also cleaves to the negative affects from the past that seem especially "bad" for political agency. Because contemporary queer subjects continue to experience shame and stigma, what is needed is not necessarily an affirmative genealogy but "a politics forged in the image of exile, of refusal, even of failure" (71).

Focusing on the late nineteenth and early twentieth centuries, Love analyzes authors whose works fall under the rubric of "backward modernism" (7): Walter Pater, Willa Cather, Radclyffe Hall, and Sylvia Townsend Warner. Against the emergence of modern homosexual identity, these artists have clung to the past and turned their back on any attempted rescue from the "future." Of particular interest is the chapter on Hall's 1928 novel *The Well of Loneliness*, a work that has continued to vex critics who seek to incorporate it into a progressive teleology. The novel's protagonist, Stephen Gordon, named and raised by her father as a boy, is "mannish" in every physical and psychic way except her genitalia. Exiled from her family's class privileges, Stephen leads a life marked by failures, stigma, and loneliness. Love, while acknowledging the critical tradition of the novel from hostility in the 1970s to cautious embrace post-2000, resists an unproblematic labeling of Stephen as a transgender ancestor. To do so would constitute another act of historical/self rescue, and Stephen is "beyond the reach of such redemptive narratives" (119). Love attends, instead, to Stephen's loneliness as "a social experience insistently internalized and corporeal" (108). The question, for Love, is not whether Stephen is a pretransition-FtM, but whether Stephen's existential negativity can be confronted, not redeemed.

Despite the "politics" in the subtitle, Love's book remains a work of literary criticism and not a political manifesto in the usual sense. The objects of her study are first and foremost aesthetic artifacts. At one point, Love cites Herbert Marcuse, who reads the mythic figures Orpheus and Narcissus as symbols of pleasure and death associated with art, and who sees "the difficulty in translating these figures out of art and into politics" (68). The tenuous divide between art and politics extends to the nebulous fissure between academia and activism. Elsewhere, Love has noted that "perhaps the most insidious aspect of academic life is the constant pressure to be interesting" (2004, 258). But maybe the real pressure for academics stems from their complicated relationship with "real" politics. What Love offers in *Feeling Backward* is an examination of the uneasy histories of queer activism and queer studies, which have not always moved in parallel or complementary courses. Harking back to the early days of activism, she observes that "while queer studies borrowed from the general approach of queer activism at the time, it did not always fully embrace the 'forcibly bittersweet' tone of the movement" (157). And it is this "bittersweet" tone, Love cogently argues, that has always been a persistent part of modern queer lives.

But much as she foregrounds the foundational role of negative affects in queer activism, Love steps back from fully bestowing blessing on any "backward"-oriented politics galvanized by negativity. Responding to Judith Halberstam's proposed archive of negative political feelings, Love insists that "while feeling bad *can* result in acting out, being fucked up can also make even the apparently simple act of 'fucking shit up' seem out of reach" (161). Love's own turn to negativity is rooted in Raymond Williams's concept of "structures of feeling"—one that organizes social experiences as sets of thoughts and feelings—that are more diagnostic than prognostic in connecting affect to subjectivity. Of course, Love's readings are themselves acts of reclamation if not identification. And insofar as writing and teaching are political acts, Love's volume provides an invaluable intervention in queer studies. The challenge is to see how "far" this historiographic practice of backward feeling may be taken up by other critics and extended to the more distant, "premodern" past.

WAN-CHUAN KAO is a doctoral candidate in English at the City University of New York Graduate Center. His dissertation, "Whiteness in Play: Color and Limits of Normativity in the Late Middle Ages," examines the imbrications of the trope of whiteness with the normalization of sexual, religious, and protonational and racialist discourses in various late medieval English texts.

WORKS CITED

Jagose, Annamarie, et al. 2007. "Theorizing Queer Temporalities: A Roundtable Discussion." *GLQ* 13(2–3):177–95.

Love, Heather. 2004. "'Oh, the Fun We'll Have': Remembering the Prospects for Sexuality Studies." *GLQ* 10(2):258-261.

EXPECTING BODIES: THE PREGNANT MAN AND TRANSGENDER EXCLUSION FROM THE EMPLOYMENT NON-DISCRIMINATION ACT

PAISLEY CURRAH

In April 2008, news about an Oregon man's impending parenthood spawned a media tsunami across the United States and even internationally. "Man Is Six Months Pregnant," reported CBS news. "The Pregnant Man Speaks Out," announced *People* magazine as it hyped the first published show-all pictures. "Pregnant Man Is Feeling Swell," punned the *New York Post*. ABC news highlighted his television debut in its story "'It's My Right to Have Kid,' Pregnant Man Tells Oprah." "She's Pregnant, but She's a Man," headlined the *Sydney Morning Herald*. "Pregnant, yes—but not a man," huffed an editorialist in the *International Herald Tribune*.

The riveting "pregnant man" lead drew readers and viewers further into the story. It was usually in the second paragraph that audiences were provided with an explanation. The pregnant man was Thomas Beatie, a transgender man who had had "top" surgery and been on hormone therapy but had stopped taking testosterone in anticipation of getting pregnant. A quick and unscientific survey of the blogosphere indicates that the news was met with disbelief, curiosity, revulsion, annoyance, indifference, and, less often, celebration. Some bloggers felt that "she" was still a woman; others thought transitioning should mean Beatie had forfeited his right to give birth; still others (usually women) expressed annoyance at all the attention the first "pregnant man" was getting. A small proportion seemed to have no problem getting their mind around the idea.

The story originally came to light at the end of March, when Beatie published a first-person account in the *Advocate*, a *Time*–like weekly magazine marketed to the U.S. gay community. In that essay, Beatie describes the travails he and his wife went through as they tried to find medical professionals who would work with them. Some refused to treat Beatie because of their religious beliefs; one physician told Beatie he would have to shave his beard; a third consulted with his hospital's ethics board and then turned him away (Beatie 2008).

For trans people in the United States, much of Beatie's narrative resonated with their own experience. While it is rare, but not unheard of in trans communities, for people who have transitioned to give birth, his larger story of discrimination in the health care industry is depressingly familiar. T. Benjamin Singer has studied the inability of many medical professionals to provide appropriate care to people whose bodies somehow exceed conventional expectations. He examines the "terror" engendered by the unknown through a frame he labels the "transgender sublime," which he describes as the "conceptual limit to a service-provider's ability to recognize the legibility and meanings of trans identities and bodies" (2006, 616). The "common sense" of gender says that birth sex, gender identity, and the secondary sex characteristics that later develop will all be in alignment.

But the histories, spatial arrangements, and physical terrains of trans people's bodies can confound conventional expectations. Some bodies are modified through hormones, various types of gender reassignment surgeries, or both, to produce bodies culturally commensurate with gender identities. In those cases, the perceived incongruence comes only from knowing the *history* of that individual's body. Other bodies, however, have unexpected configurations in their particular *geographies*—for example, breasts with penises for some, male chests with vaginas in others—that produce a dissonance. (This dissonance, to be clear, belongs not to the trans body but to those gazers who have conventional gender expectations.) The more easily read and specific physical terrains of bodies, such as the presence or absence of facial hair, baldness, or patterns of musculature, can add a third layer of potential contradiction. (Ironically, these configurations of geography and terrain often are determined by one's lack of access to medical care. Medicaid and almost all private insurance plans specifically exclude hormones and gender reassignment surgeries for trans people. From personal choice or because of the great expense, the vast majority of transgender men and most transgender women forego genital surgery (Pooja and Arkles 2007). Hormones, whether attained through prescriptions or bought on the street, are cheaper.)

The stupefied resistance to bodies that confound gender expectations isn't limited to ob-gyn offices or maternity wards. The presence of someone whose gender identity or gender expression is not traditionally associated with the sex assigned to them at birth can bring people to very brink of cognition, and beyond it, in any setting customarily segregated by gender: bathrooms and locker rooms, homeless shelters, and correctional facilities, among others.

Judging (unscientifically, again) from informal conversations I've had with acquaintances, that a man can get pregnant may be the central, and for many the only, fact that most people in the United States now know about transgender issues. But among trans people, Beatie's story was of interest primarily because it generated so much scrutiny in the mainstream media. What really roiled trans communities in 2007–8 was the decision by Representative Barney Frank and House Speaker Nancy Pelosi to exclude transgender people from the federal Employment Non-Discrimination Act (ENDA). While so many people now know that a man can get pregnant, relatively few people outside queer communities are aware of the ENDA debacle, even though it is of much greater significance to the lives of transgender people.

ENDA, a bill that has been floating around Congress since the 1970s in some form or another, would prohibit workplace discrimination on the basis of sexual orientation. After decades of lobbying, in 2003 transgender rights advocates and their allies thought they had succeeded in persuading key gay rights advocacy players in Washington, including the Human Rights Campaign, to support only "transgender-inclusive" legislation (National Center 2003; Minter 2006). As with nondiscrimination bills at the state and municipal levels, the bill's statutory language would have defined gender identity as "gender-related identity, appearance, or mannerisms or other gender-related characteristics of an individual, with or without regard to the individual's designated sex at birth." That language would work to protect transgender people (Employment Non-Discrimination Act of 2007).

An alert reader might ask, Aren't transgender people already protected in federal law through the ban on "sex" discrimination in Title VII of the Federal Civil Rights Act of 1964? In earlier decades, advocates certainly had hoped that federal courts would view discrimination against transgender people as a type of sex discrimination. But that did not happen. In a 1984 decision, for example, a federal appellate court ruled against a transsexual woman who had lost her job as an airline pilot after transitioning, with the court deciding that she had not made a viable claim of sex discrimination. According to the decision:

After the surgery, hormones, appearance changes, and a new Illinois birth certificate, it may be that society...considers Ulane to be female. But even if one believes that a woman can be so easily created from what remains of a man, that does not decide the case.... If Eastern [Airlines] did discriminate against Ulane, it was not because she is female, but because Ulane is a transsexual—a biological male who takes female hormones, cross-dresses, and has surgically altered parts of her body to make it appear to be female. (*Ulane v. Eastern Airlines* 1984)

In recent years, courts in a few jurisdictions have begun find that "sex" discrimination encompasses bias against individuals whose gender identity doesn't conform to cultural expectations based on their birth sex (Schroer v. Billington 2008). But most courts still do not. That's why transgender rights advocates turned to federal and state legislatures for redress (Currah and Minter 2004).

The beginning of 2007 brought in the first Democratic majority in the House of Representatives since 1993. That meant ENDA had a real opportunity to pass in the House and possibly in the Senate. For Representative Frank, an out gay representative and the chief sponsor of ENDA, a realistic chance of passing meant that transgender people, generously included when the bill was pie in the sky, would now have to be cut from the bill before it was introduced. Over the vociferous objections of a united coalition of three hundred gay, lesbian, bisexual, and transgender groups (but not including the coffer-rich Human Rights Campaign), Frank and House Democratic leadership cut "gender identity" from the bill.

Representative Frank's opposition to including transgender people evokes the "transgender sublime" response to unexpected bodies showing up in gender-segregated spaces. But in the case of the ENDA debate, it's not the very rare situation of people with beards in maternity wards that incites terror, it's a different body part appearing unexpectedly in another type of gender-segregated space. "Transgendered people want a law that mandates a person with a penis be allowed to shower with women. They can't get that in ENDA," Frank told the *Advocate* in 1999 (Dahir 1999). Like some of Beatie's detractors, Frank appears to subscribe to a system of naturalized gender logics in which a transgender woman who retains her penis is not really a woman.

Throughout the years, Frank has remained remarkably loyal to that position. For example, even when he toyed with the idea of including gender identity, he insisted on adding statutory language that would prevent a transgender woman who had been barred from a women's shared shower or dressing facilities from making an actionable discrimination claim (and vice versa for transgender men). But by 2007, even that exemption didn't meet his objections, and gender identity was entirely cut out.

As a result, we now have two Employment Non-Discrimination Acts. HR 3685, referred to as the "bad ENDA" in GLBT rights circles, includes only sexual orientation and is being pushed by Frank and House Democratic leadership. The "good ENDA," HR 2015, also includes gender identity. The "bad ENDA" passed the House by a vote of 235 to 184 and its correlate in the Senate stands a good chance of being passed there. The "good ENDA" languishes in the House. But since President George W. Bush has promised to veto any version of ENDA that reaches his desk, GLBT advocates in D.C. say the battle to pass the good ENDA is far from over. There will be other opportunities to convince House leadership to push for a transgender-inclusive bill.

It's not just in gender-segregated physical locations like locker rooms or maternity wards where the sex binary is policed. State processes of sex classification also rely on the idea that the body must cohere in predictable ways with gender identity. For example, in 2005–6, advocates attempted to get New York City to amend its rules for sex classification on birth certificates. They argued that requiring transgender people to have genital surgery before changing their sex on their birth certificate was unfair and did not reflect current state of transgender health care (Currah and Moore 2009). The public response to the proposal is summed up by this comment: "How might it be possible for someone with male genitals to now be listed as being female? Is everyone expected to be blind? I can understand if one had a sex change but simply dressing in the clothing of the opposite sex does not qualify a person of that sex" (New York City Board of Health and Mental Hygiene 2006). The effort failed. In New York City, to have the "M" on their birth certificate replaced with an "F," transgender women must prove they have had a vaginoplasty; to have an "M" on the birth certificate, transgender men must prove they have had a phalloplasty, although less than 3 percent of trans men have had one, according to one study (Newfield, Hart, Dibble, and Kohler 2006).

In the past three decades, feminist theory and activism has had great success in dislodging the notion that gender is the same as sex. Many of the social imperatives that used to be explained through the biologistic prism of sex difference are now framed as gender norms. For example, even conservatives have accepted the gradual expansion of sex discrimination laws to include discrimination based on gender stereotyping. As Justice Antonin Scalia points out, "The word 'gender' has acquired the new and useful connotation of cultural or attitudinal characteristics (as opposed to physical characteristics) distinctive to the sexes" (J.E.B. v. Alabama 1994).

Despite the inroads made in divorcing sex from gender *norms* and gender *expression*, however, we haven't yet succeeded in disentangling gender identity from sex. In much of the legislation, case law, and administrative rules that discipline the identities of transgender people, it's still the sexed characteristics of bodies that matter. And notions of sex are still governed by logics demanding coherence. Bodies that disrupt those expectations aren't always welcome.

For a biography of PAISLEY CURRAH, please see the guest editors' introduction to this issue.

WORKS CITED

Beatie, Thomas. 2008. "Labor of Love." *Advocate*, March 26, 2008. http://www.advocate.com/exclusive_detail_ektid52947.asp.

Currah, Paisley, and Shannon Minter. 2004. "Unprincipled Exclusions: The Struggle for Legislative and Judicial Protections for Transgendered People." In *Regulating Sex: The Politics of Intimacy and Identity*, ed. Elizabeth Bernstein and Laurie Schnaffer. New York: Routledge.

Currah, Paisley, and Lisa Jean Moore. 2008. "'We Won't Know Who You Are': Contesting Sex Designations on New York City Birth Certificates." *Hypatia: Journal of Feminist Philosophy* 24(3).

Dahir, Mubarak. 1999. "Whose Movement Is It?" *Advocate*, May 26, 50–55.

Employment Non-Discrimination Act of 2007. 2007. U.S. Congress. House. HR 2015 and HR 3685. 110th Cong., 1st session.

Gehi, Pooja S., and Gabriel Arkles. 2007. "Unraveling Injustice: Race and Class Impact of Medicaid Exclusions of Transition-Related Health Care for Transgender People." *Sexuality Research and Social Policy: Journal of NSRC* 4(4):7–35.

J.E.B. v. Alabama Ex Rel. T.B. 1994. 511 U.S. 127 (1994).

Minter, Shannon Price. 2006. "Do Transsexuals Dream of Gay Rights? Getting Real About Transgender Inclusion." In *Transgender Rights*, ed. Paisley Currah, Richard M. Juang, and Shannon Price Minter. Minneapolis: University of Minnesota Press.

National Center for Transgender Equality and the Transgender Law and Policy Institute. 2003. "Transgender Leaders Laud Unified Voice of GLBT Community in Federal Legislative Efforts." News release, June 17. http://www.transgenderlaw.org/release.htm.

Newfield, Emily, Stacey Hart, Suzanne Dibble, and Lori Kohler. 2006. "Female-to-Male Transgender Quality of Life." *Quality of Life Research*, 15(9): 1447-57.

New York City Board of Health and Mental Hygiene. 2006. "Resolution Comments-NYC Birth Certificate for Transgender People."

Schroer v. Billington, N.05-1090(JR), 2008 U.S. Dist. 2008 U.S. LEXIS 71358, (D.D.C. September 19, 2008).

Singer, T. Benjamin. 2006. "From the Medical Gaze to *Sublime Mutations*: The Ethics of (Re)Viewing Non-normative Body Images." In *The Transgender Studies Reader*, ed. Susan Stryker and Stephen Whittle. New York: Routledge.

Ulane v. Eastern Airlines, Inc. 1984. 742 F.2d 1081 (7th Cir. 1984).

Women & Performance:
a journal of feminist theory

Women & Performance is the only peer-reviewed academic journal dedicated to the conjuncture of feminist theory and performance studies. Established in 1983, the journal continues to affirm its commitment to feminist writing, and to extend and reformulate notions of performance and performativity so as to advance, challenge and reinvent critical debates on gender and sexuality.

The journal features scholarly essays on performance, dance, film, new media, and the performance of everyday life from interdisciplinary feminist perspectives. We encourage dialogue between varied fields of performance scholarship (performance studies; theater, dance, and music history and criticism; ethnography; cinema and cultural studies; queer and post-colonial theory), and explore critiques of race, ethnicity, class, sexuality, technology, and nation.

Submit a Paper

The editorial collective invites submissions of scholarly essays on performance, visual and sound art, theater, dance, ritual, political manifestations, film, new media, and the performance of everyday life from interdisciplinary feminist perspectives. We also welcome performative texts, suggestions for themed issues and recommendations on books and performances for review.

Manuscripts can be submitted electronically to Jeanne Vaccaro, Managing Editor: **jeanne@womenandperformance.org**

For more information visit:
www.informaworld.com/rwap

*F*EMSPEC

an interdisciplinary journal committed to challenging gender through speculative art, fiction, poetry, and criticism

Recently and Forthcoming in *FEMSPEC*

TINA ANDRES, Growing Thick Skin (Memoir)
K. A. LAITY, Eating the Dream (Fiction)
LOUISE MOORE, Joan of Arc, Circe, Cassandra, The Annunciation Angel (Poems)
SYLVIA KELSO, "Failing That, Invent": Writing a Feminist Utopia in the 21st Century(Criticism)
MARY GINWAY, "Interview with Argentine Author Liliana Bodoc"
MIKHAYLA HARRELL, Two Pieces (Sculpture)
DIANE DIPRIMA, Creation Story: Northern California, Show Me Your Other Body (Poems)
REVIEWS by Ritch Calvin, Ardys Delu, Gerardo Cummings, Phillipa Kafka,
Lani Ravin, Janice Bogstad and Li Weinbaum

Advisory Board

Suzy McKee Charnas
Florence Howe
Joanna Russ
Pamela Sargent

Contributing Editors

Paula Gunn Allen
Marleen S. Barr
Samuel R. Delany
Gloria Orenstein
Darko Suvin

Submissions* and Subscriptions to:

FEMSPEC
c/o Batya Weinbaum, editor
1610 Rydalmount Road
Cleveland Heights, OH 44118

Subscribe online at
www.femspec.org/subscriptions.html

Individuals $40 (2 issues).
Institutions $95 (2 issues)
[International subscribers, please add $10]

*To ensure anonymous peer review, please send two copies
with no contact information, cover letter with contact information, and disk.

FRONTIERS
A JOURNAL OF WOMEN STUDIES

An Interdisciplinary and Multicultural Feminist Journal

Peer-reviewed scholarship written in highly accessible language

Creative works in the written and visual arts

Personal essays

NEW—*"Feminist Currents"*
An interactive discussion of thought-provoking questions
(To view the current question visit www.asu.edu/clas/history/frontiers/fem.html)

Does your library subscribe to Project Muse? If so, you may have access to the electronic version of *Frontiers*. Consult your library for more details. Back issues of *Frontiers* are also available on JSTOR.

University of Nebraska Press
P.O. Box 84555 • Lincoln, Nebraska 68501-4555
800.755.1105 or 402.472.8536 • www.nebraskapress.unl.edu

Women's Review of Books

If you don't know **Women's Review of Books**, you've been missing a lot—great reviewing from Alicia Ostriker, Tricia Rose, Karin Aguilar-San Juan, Lisa Jervis and a host of other smart, provocative writers and scholars, to say nothing of poems, author interviews, cartoons, and photographs.

You'll find articles in **Women's Review of Books** about books and ideas you won't hear about in mainstream newspapers and magazines, which tend to give short shrift to critical writing by and about women. **Women's Review of Books** is a genuine alternative.

So, join the conversation! A year of **Women's Review of Books**—six great issues—costs $37. That's about the price of a movie date (with popcorn).

Join the conversation today!

You can now subscribe quickly and easily online—go to:
www.oldcitypublishing.com and click on
Women's Review of Books subscriptions

CONTEMPORARY WOMEN'S WRITING

Edited by
Mary Eagleton and Susan Stanford Friedman

- Prestigious international editorial team

- Submissions relating to all literary forms and from a wide variety of theoretical and interdisciplinary perspectives welcomed

- Offers rapid publication

Contemporary Women's Writing critically assesses writing by women authors who have published approximately from 1970 to the present. The journal aims to reflect retrospectively on developments throughout the period, to survey the variety of contemporary work, and to anticipate the new and provocative in women's writing.

Visit www.cww.oxfordjournals.org to:

- View tables of contents
- Access articles (if your library subscribes)
- Read author guidelines
- Recommend the journal to your library
- Sign up for table of contents email alerts
- And more!

Celebrate Women!

Jude Narita's plays about Asian and Asian American women
illuminate the universal humanity of us all

"Potent eloquence…unforgettable in its emotional directness.."
NYTheatre.com

"Narita's performance is lustrous, shining, radiant, and precious."
The Georgia Straight, Vancouver

"Burns clean through your consciousness, leaving you breathless and astonished."
Berkeley Voice

"Powerful…Profoundly moving… emotional tours de force."
Los Angeles Times

With laughter and the memory of sorrow, Narita's women are breaking stereotypes, creating true identity, surviving war and internment, cherishing family, and holding on to their dreams for the future.

To book a performance or for more information please go to www.judenarita.com

TRANSFORMATIONS
THE JOURNAL OF INCLUSIVE SCHOLARSHIP AND PEDAGOGY

Transformations: The Journal of Inclusive Scholarship and Pedagogy is a peer-reviewed journal published semi-annually by New Jersey City University. It is an interdisciplinary forum for pedagogical scholarship exploring intersections of identities, power, and social justice. The journal features a range of approaches—from theoretical articles to creative and experimental accounts of pedagogical innovations—by teachers and scholars across all areas of education.

Please see our website at www.njcu.edu/assoc/transformations for submissions guidelines and information on future issues. Send mail to: TRANSFORMATIONS, New Jersey City University, Hepburn Hall, Room 309, 2039 Kennedy Boulevard, Jersey City, NJ 07305.

SUBSCRIPTIONS

Rates

INDIVIDUAL:	One year - $20	Two year - $35
INSTITUTION:	One year - $50	Two year - $85

International subscribers should add $10 per subscription for surface mail and $20 per subscription for air mail.

Name

Address

City   *State*   *Zip*

Telephone

Email

Make check or money order payable to: New Jersey City University
Mail this form to: TRANSFORMATIONS, New Jersey City University, Hepburn Hall, Room 309, 2039 Kennedy Boulevard, Jersey City, NJ 07305.

TRANSFORMATIONS *is published semi-annually
by New Jersey City University*

Indiana University Press/*Journals*

Bridges
A Jewish Feminist Journal

EDITED BY CLARE KINBERG

A showcase for the creative work of Jewish feminists

Bridges is a showcase for the creative work of Jewish feminists. Each issue includes articles, commentary, discussions of politics and culture, scholarly essays, fiction and poetry, visual art, graphics, photography, and archival materials, including oral histories, interviews, diaries, and letters.

PUBLISHED SEMIANNUALLY
eISSN 1558-9552 | pISSN 1046-8358

800-842-6796/812-855-8817 | http://inscribe.iupress.org
Available in electronic, combined electronic & print, and print formats

 INDIANA UNIVERSITY PRESS
INDIANA UNIVERSITY

601 North Morton Street, Bloomington, Indiana 47404-3797 USA

Indiana University Press/*Journals*

Meridians
feminism, race, transnationalism

Makes scholarship by and about women of color central to contemporary definitions of feminism

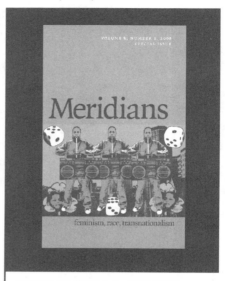

EDITED BY PAULA J. GIDDINGS

PUBLISHED SEMIANNUALLY
eISSN 1547-8424
pISSN 1536-6936

800-842-6796/812-855-8817
http://inscribe.iupress.org
Available in electronic,
combined electronic & print,
and print formats

Meridians provides a forum for the finest scholarship and creative work by and about women of color in U.S. and international contexts. The journal recognizes that feminism, race, transnationalism, and women of color are contested terms and engages in a dialogue across ethnic and national boundaries, as well as across traditional disciplinary boundaries in the academy.

INDIANA UNIVERSITY PRESS
INDIANA UNIVERSITY

601 North Morton Street, Bloomington, Indiana 47404-3797 USA

Indiana University Press/*Journals*

Nashim

A Journal of Jewish Women's Studies & Gender Issues

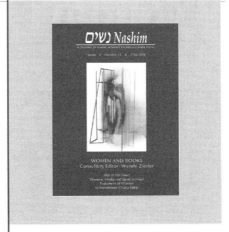

Aims to create communication channels within the Jewish gender studies community

EDITED BY RENÉE LEVINE MELAMMED

Nashim provides an international, interdisciplinary academic forum in Jewish women's and gender studies. Each issue is theme-oriented, produced in consultation with a distinguished feminist scholar, and includes articles on literature, text studies, anthropology, archeology, theology, contemporary thought, sociology, the arts, and more.

PUBLISHED SEMIANNUALLY
eISSN 1565-5288 | pISSN 0793-8934

800-842-6796/812-855-8817 | http://inscribe.iupress.org
Available in electronic, combined electronic & print, and print formats

 **INDIANA UNIVERSITY PRESS**
INDIANA UNIVERSITY
601 North Morton Street, Bloomington, Indiana 47404-3797 USA

Women's Writing

www.tandf.co.uk/journals/rwow

EDITOR: Marie Mulvey-Roberts, *University of the West of England, UK*
CONSULTANT EDITOR: Janet Todd, *University of Aberdeen, UK*
ASSOCIATE EDITOR (UK): Caroline Franklin, *University of Wales, UK*
ASSOCIATE EDITOR (North America): Lisa Vargo,
University of Saskatchewan, Canada
REVIEWS EDITOR: Jennie Batchelor, *University of Kent, UK*

Women's Writing is an international journal focusing on women's writing up to the end of the long nineteenth century. The editors welcome theoretical and historical perspectives, and contributions that are concerned with gender, culture, race and class. The aim of the journal is to open up a forum for dialogue, discussion and debate about the work of women writers, and hopes to reflect the diversity of scholarship that can be brought to bear on this area of study.

SUBSCRIPTION RATES

Volume 16, 2009
(3 issues per year)

Print ISSN: 0969-9082

Online ISSN: 1747-5848

Institutional rate
(print and online)
US$499; £313; €398

Institutional rate
(online only)
US$474; £297; €378

Personal rate
(print only)
US$79; £50; €63

For further information, please contact Customer Services at either of the addresses below:
T&F Informa UK Ltd, Sheepen Place, Colchester, Essex, CO3 3LP, UK
Tel: 020 7017 5544 Fax: 020 7017 5198 Email:tf.enquiries@tfinforma.com Website:www.tandf.co.uk/journals
Taylor & Francis Inc, 325 Chestnut Street, 8th Floor, Philadelphia, PA 19106, USA
Tel: +1 800 354 1420 (toll-free calls from within the US)
or +1 215 625 8900 (calls from overseas) Fax: +1 215 625 2940
Email:customerservice@taylorandfrancis.com

"How did Christianity become a religion of finitude and guilt rather than one of promise and celebration? Brock and Parker ran with the evidence, showing us the importance of art, ritual, devotional practices, and liturgical space for early Christians. This tangible past transformed their research and led them to see that paradise in this world lies at the heart of Christianity."

—**DIANE APOSTOLOS-CAPPADONA**, author of *Dictionary of Christian Art*

For more information and a gallery of images, visit
WWW.SAVINGPARADISE.NET.

Available at bookstores everywhere and from www.beacon.org
Visit www.beaconbroadside.com, the blog of Beacon Press

The Feminist Press at the City University of New York is a nonprofit literary and educational institution dedicated to publishing work by and about women. Our existence is grounded in the knowledge that women's writing has often been absent or underrepresented on bookstore and library shelves and in educational curricula—and that such absences contribute, in turn, to the exclusion of women from the literary canon, from the historical record, and from the public discourse.

The Feminist Press was founded in 1970. In its early decades, The Feminist Press launched the contemporary rediscovery of "lost" American women writers, and went on to diversify its list by publishing significant works by American women writers of color. More recently, the Press's publishing program has focused on international women writers, who remain far less likely to be translated than male writers, and on nonfiction works that explore issues affecting the lives of women around the world.

Founded in an activist spirit, The Feminist Press is currently undertaking initiatives that will bring its books and educational resources to underserved populations, including community colleges, public high schools and middle schools, literacy and ESL programs, and prison education programs. As we move forward into the twenty-first century, we continue to expand our work to respond to women's silences wherever they are found.

For information about events and for a complete catalog of the Press's 300 books, please refer to our web site: www.feministpress.org.